KAUA'I

KEVIN WHITTON

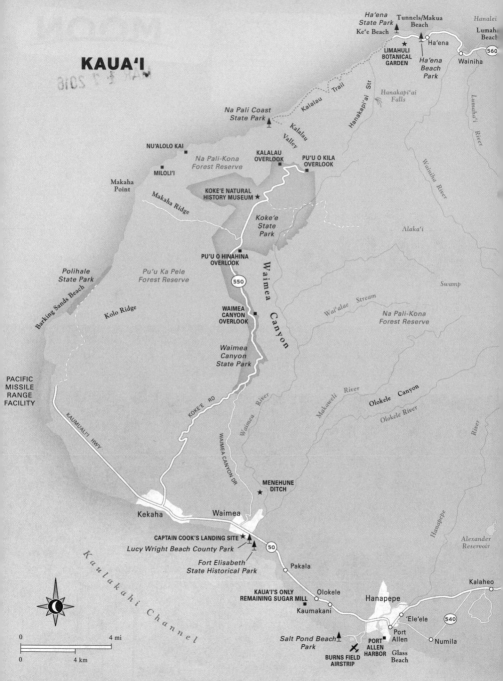

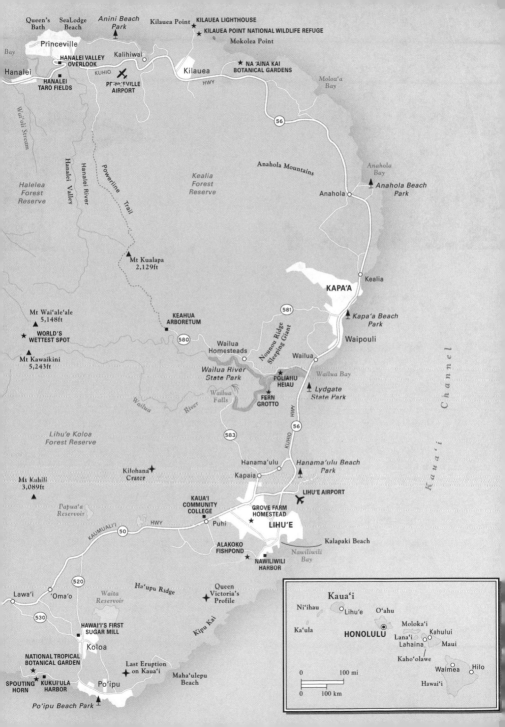

Contents

Kaua'i

The oldest of the Hawaiian Islands, Kaua'i is a verdant retreat where natural wonders and quiet towns peacefully coexist. Its laid-back old-Hawai'i charm makes it the perfect getaway. No one is in a hurry, and relaxing at the beach or trekking through the mountains is all the entertainment you need.

It's easy to see how the famed "Garden Isle" earned its nickname. Approximately 90 percent of the island is uninhabited, with Mount Wai'ale'ale (the wettest place on earth) and its towering ridges reaching from the center of the island out toward the sea in all directions. Sculpted by erosion, the beautiful and vast Waimea Canyon and Na Pali Coast offer majestic lookouts and hiking trails that weave from ridgelines to canyon floors. Kaua'i's waterfalls and wide rivers flow to the ocean, telling the story of the island's rain-cloaked natural history.

This gorgeous island offers civilized pleasures as well. Internationally renowned chefs showcase their one-of-a-kind Hawai'i Regional Cuisine. Kapa'a town's eclectic shops, full of locally crafted jewelry and art, draw shoppers, and couples find renewal at the luxury resorts.

Clockwise from top left: wild rooster; Spouting Horn; plumeria; banana tree; Kilauea Lighthouse; Anini Beach.

But without question, the beaches are the island's main draw. Sunbathers find secluded nooks of fine white sand to soak up rays, surfers revel in the world-class waves along the north and south shores, and snorkelers rejoice in the vibrant underwater world along the island's reefs. Kauaʻi is a gorgeous testament to the natural and cultural beauty of Hawaiʻi. It's *aloha* at its best.

Clockwise from top left: Hanalei Bay; monk seal resting on the sand at Tunnels Beach; rainbow; Opaekaʻa Falls.

Planning Your Trip

Where to Go

Lihu'e and the East Side

The east side, also known as the Coconut Coast, stretches from Lihu'e to Anahola. The area offers historical sites, river kayaking, waterfalls, and beautiful coastlines. **Lihu'e,** home to Kaua'i's largest airport, is the hub of commerce and government for the island. **Wailua** is home to the famous **Wailua Falls** and **Wailua River** cultural sites. The biggest draw is **Kapa'a,** a colorful town known for its whimsical cafés and eateries, as well as its eclectic shops with locally made goods. Inland behind Kapa'a are miles of great hiking trails with amazing views.

Princeville and the North Shore

The north shore is a true tropical paradise with vibrant green cliffs and streaming, ribbon-like waterfalls backing some of the island's most

spectacular white-sand beaches. The area is known for surfing and snorkeling. Upscale **Princeville,** perched on a bluff high above the ocean, features luxury accommodations, vacation rentals, and a residential community. Down in **Hanalei Valley** is quaint **Hanalei** town with charming shops and great restaurants. At the end of the road is the **Na Pali Coast,** where miles of strenuous hiking trails lead adventurers to secluded beaches, waterfalls, and valleys.

Po'ipu and the South Shore

Po'ipu is home to endless sunshine and the bulk of the island's accommodations. The region has white-sand beaches that offer snorkeling, swimming, surfing, and golfing. **Po'ipu Beach** and the **Maha'ulepu Beaches** provide an exquisite setup for the perfect beach day. On the west

the rugged south shore

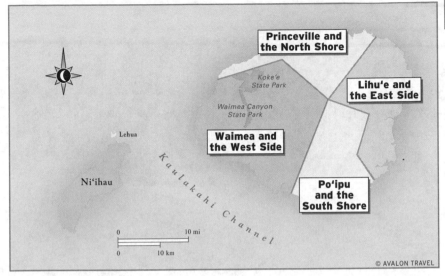

Koke'e
State Park

Waimea Canyon
State Park

**Princeville and
the North Shore**

**Lihu'e and
the East Side**

**Waimea and
the West Side**

**Po'ipu
and the
South Shore**

Lehua

Ni'ihau

Kaulakahi Channel

0   10 mi

0   10 km

© AVALON TRAVEL

end of Po'ipu are some must-see sights, including **Spouting Horn** and the **National Tropical Botanical Garden.** Inland from Po'ipu is historic and local town **Koloa,** with eateries and shopping.

Waimea and the West Side

The wild and remote west side is known for its deep canyons, pristine forests, seemingly endless white-sand coastline, empty beaches, and historic towns. **Hanapepe** is home to almost 20 art galleries and popular **Art Night in Hanapepe.** Most **Na Pali Coast** tours depart from **Port Allen.** Some of the island's most spectacular viewpoints and trails are found at **Waimea Canyon** and in **Koke'e State Park.** And at the end of the road is one of the island's most beautiful and secluded beaches, **Polihale State Park.**

Know Before You Go

High and Low Season

Kaua'i's **high tourist season** begins a few weeks before Christmas and lasts until late April. It slows down a bit until June and then is quite busy until August. If you are visiting during the busy season, it's imperative to make **car and hotel reservations** in advance. It's not unheard of for rental car companies to be completely sold out during the high season.

Visiting Kaua'i in the **off-season,** from September to December and late April to June, is recommended. The island will be less crowded, and prices for cars, airline tickets, and hotels will generally be a little lower.

Weather

Kaua'i is beautiful any time of the year. The weather is consistent, with rain coming and going, especially on the north shore. At any time, there's a good chance Po'ipu or the west side is sunny. Although winter is the official **rainy season,** most showers pass quickly. Sometimes all it takes is a drive to the other side of the island to find sunshine.

Na Pali Coast

Best Times for Recreation

Experienced surfers will find world-class waves on the north shore during the winter months of **October to March.** The south shore breaks best from **May through September.**

On the flip side, if you prefer a **calm ocean** for swimming and snorkeling, you'll definitely prefer a trip to the north shore during the summer or the south shore in winter, when the waves are generally flat in those regions.

Kayaking the Na Pali Coast is strictly a seasonal, **summertime** activity. Visitors who hope to see humpback whales must make sure they visit during **whale season,** from **December through May.**

Winter weather also determines the safety and comfort level of Kaua'i's **hiking trails.** Wet weather means muddy, slippery, crumbling, and dangerous trails along the Na Pali Coast and up in the Alaka'i Swamp. Flash flooding also occurs in the rivers along the Na Pali Coast and up in Waimea Canyon, which can unexpectedly swell and recede within hours, affecting hikers.

The Best of Kaua'i

The majority of visitors to Kaua'i spend one to two weeks on the island. For newcomers, an itinerary that circles the island with a new home base every few days affords the most time in each region. Packing and unpacking a few times will far outweigh wasted time spent driving all over the island on a daily basis or getting stuck in traffic.

Return visitors usually make a base in one locale for the duration of their stay with the flexibility to bounce around the island to suit their vacationing needs, whether that be sun, surf, sights, dining, or shopping.

North Shore
DAY 1
After securing your rental car at the airport in **Lihu'e**, get on the highway and start heading north. If you need to pick up groceries or toiletries, stop at Safeway or Foodland in Waipouli. Continue north on Kuhio Highway, picking up lunch in **Kapa'a** if you're hungry. Take your time driving. Even though you're excited, you'll notice

right away that the pace of life on Kaua'i is slower than what you're probably used to. Head to your accommodation in **Princeville** or **Hanalei**, check in, and relax. If you forgot anything, there is a Foodland grocery store in Princeville. Once you're settled, head to the beach at **Hanalei Bay** and get in the water. After all, that's probably what you came for. **Black Pot Beach Park** is a great zone to get acquainted with Hanalei. Take a long walk up the coast and soak in the scenery. For sunset, head up to the **St. Regis** in Princeville and have a beverage and pupu overlooking Hanalei Bay at the St. Regis Bar for the sunset champagne ritual. Pinch yourself—the view is that good.

DAY 2
Start your day early and drive out to **Ke'e Beach** at the end of the road. Hike the beginning of the **Kalalau Trail** two miles in to **Hanakapi'ai Beach.** If you're up for it, another half mile back into the valley will bring you to **Hanakapi'ai**

Limahuli Botanical Garden

Hanalei Bay

Hanalei Valley

Falls. Back at Keʻe Beach, jump in the natural pool along the shore for a swim. Snorkeling is great here too. If you're not into hiking, just head out to Keʻe for a beautiful morning at the beach. Pack a lunch and enjoy a picnic. On the way back to Hanalei, stop at **Limahuli Botanical Garden** and the wet and dry caves along the road. After a hard day outdoors, treat yourself to an exquisite meal at **Bar Acuda Tapas and Wine** or **The Dolphin Hanalei.**

DAY 3
Golfers should get on the green in Princeville. For those not golfing, head to **Kilauea.** Stop at **Kauai Juice Company** for a cold-pressed fresh juice, and then continue on to the **Kilauea Point National Wildlife Refuge and Lighthouse.** If you're into birds, this is the spot to be on the north shore to check out the seabirds soaring overhead and nesting on the cliffs. Head down to **Anini Beach,** a great place to snorkel in the shallow waters or stroll along the beautiful beach. There is a main beach park area, or you can venture north and pull over on the side of the road and find your own nook of beach, which skirts along

the cliff and Princeville up above. Head back to Hanalei town for lunch. While you're in town, stroll around and shop. Pick up some local art or a ukulele. After that, kayak or stand-up paddle the **Hanalei River** or surf the main break out in the bay. Beginners can surf near shore at **Black Pot Beach Park.** For dinner, take it easy and have some great Mexican food at **Federico's** in Princeville.

WITH MORE TIME
Avid hikers should hike the **Na Pali Coast** along the infamous 11-mile **Kalalau Trail.** If you have your permits for overnight camping, take your time along the 11-mile hike and camp once along the way, at the end of the trail at Kalalau Beach, and once again on your way back to civilization.

East Side
DAY 4
Jump on the highway heading south and make your way to the east side. There are ample accommodations from Kapaʻa to Kalapaki Bay in **Lihuʻe.** Stash your stuff at the hotel and head to the **Wailua River,** where tour companies

lead kayaking tours. After the tour, drive up to **Opaeka'a Falls** for a great view. Head back to Kapa'a town, park the car, and stroll around. Go treasure hunting in the eclectic shops, full of locally crafted jewelry, art, clothing, and home wares. Grab dinner at **Olympic Cafe** or **Kintaro.** If you'd like to experience a *lu'au*, try the riverside *lu'au* at **Smith's Tropical Paradise.**

DAY 5

Check out one of the cafés or breakfast nooks in Kapa'a town, then spend the morning exploring the history of the island at the **Kaua'i Museum** or at **Kilohana Plantation.** Afterward, it's back to the beach. **Lydgate Beach Park** has great snorkeling in protected pools and a huge wooden playground for the kids. Bodysurfers should head to **Kealia Beach.** If you like to bicycle, there's a great path along the coast in Kapa'a and plenty of outfitters to rent a bike. For beginner surfers and stand-up paddlers, head to **Kalapaki Beach** and take a lesson from **Kaua'i Beach Boys.** For dinner, eat at **Duke's Kauai** at Kalapaki Beach.

South Shore
DAY 6

From the east side, jump on Kuhio Highway heading south. Make sure to stock up at Safeway or Foodland in Waipouli on any supplies or food you'll need for the rest of your trip. Make a beeline to your accommodation, which is most likely in **Po'ipu.** Get settled and then get to the beach, especially if it has been cloudy or rainy up north or out east. Adventurers should try the more secluded beaches at **Maha'ulepu.** Families, snorkelers, and surfers will prefer **Po'ipu Beach Park.** Have lunch at **Brennecke's Beach Broiler** or pack a picnic lunch and enjoy your day in the sun and surf. Stop at **Keoki's Paradise** for dinner and drinks.

DAY 7

Take a morning walk along the beach, then head over to the **National Tropical Botanical Garden** for a tour of Allerton and McBride Gardens. Afterward, stop by **Spouting Horn.** Head back to the hotel for a massage, and then over to **Lawa'i Beach** to watch the sunset. Have

stunning view into Waimea Canyon

SUNSETS

One of the best places to catch the sunset is at **Polihale State Park** (page 156) on the west side, where you'll see the sunset with Ni'ihau island in the distance. The **Beach House Restaurant** (page 121) in Po'ipu is a romantic restaurant and great place to watch the sunset.

WATERFALLS AND NATURAL POOLS

Enjoying a natural swimming pool under a waterfall may perhaps be the ultimate romantic experience. Waterfalls with swimmable pools include **Secret Falls** (page 43) on the Wailua River, the pools on the **Swimming Pool Trail** (page 48), and, for adventurous couples, **Hanakapi'ai Falls** (page 97).

EATS

Oasis (page 63) on the east side, **Bar Acuda** (page 111) on the north side, and **Keoki's Paradise** (page 138) in Po'ipu are great places for a romantic dinner.

CRUISES

Sunset and snorkel cruises are a romantic and classic Kaua'i experience. Contact one of the many boat tour companies leaving from the west side, which offer multiple cruises with combinations

a romantic sunset in Po'ipu

of snorkeling, sunset sails, and dinners. A company with romantic options is **Blue Dolphin Charters** (page 131). It offers a two-hour South Side Sunset Sail in the Po'ipu area. Food, cocktails, and romantic sunsets are enjoyed on this tour, along with whale-watching during whale-watching season.

dinner at **Beach House Restaurant,** which overlooks the water.

DAY 8

Golfers—it's another day on the green in Po'ipu. Lucky you. For non-golfers, spend the morning **ziplining,** riding **ATVs** on private land, or taking a guided nature **hiking tour** or **horseback ride** to a secluded beach. Finish the day at **The Shops at Kukui'ula,** where you can shop and have a wonderful dinner at Merriman's Fish House, Merriman's Gourmet Pizza & Burgers, Josselin's Tapas Bar & Grill, or Eating House 1849.

West Side

DAY 9

Accommodations are limited on the west side, so you'll most likely be making day trips to the west side from your south shore accommodation. Wake up early, grab some breakfast and snacks from **Living Foods Market and Cafe** in Po'ipu at The Shops at Kukui'ula, and head to **Waimea Canyon.** After taking in the view at the lookout, continue on to other lookouts in **Koke'e State Park** or try one of the many trails in the area. After a day in the mountains, head back to Waimea town or Hanapepe or both. **Waimea** town has a few historic sites and restaurants, and **Hanapepe** is known for its thriving art scene and many galleries. Food choices are limited, and some prefer to eat back in **Po'ipu.**

DAY 10

No visitor should leave without exploring the **Na Pali Coast.** Most tours depart from **Port Allen,** and there are all types of tours depending on the season and conditions. You can sail, snorkel, fish, whale-watch, ride on a small speedboat, and explore the coast off the "forbidden island" of **Ni'ihau.** Most of the tours are all-day affairs.

If you're not into boats, drive out to the end of the road, to **Polihale State Park,** where white-sand beaches meet with the verdant, vertical Na Pali Coast cliffs.

WITH MORE TIME

For backpackers and hikers, **Koke'e State Park** has a network of trails and camping opportunities. Stay awhile and hike out to **Alaka'i Swamp,** an ecosystem found nowhere else in the state. Sunset lovers should consider camping on the beach at **Polihale** to really take in the sunset. Facilities are limited to toilets and cold showers.

Best Beaches

POLIHALE STATE PARK (PAGE 156)

The west side's Polihale State Park stretches for miles with a blanket of fine white sand terminating at the tall **sacred cliffs** of the Na Pali Coast. Every visitor should experience at least one vibrant **sunset** over forbidden **Ni'ihau.**

PO'IPU BEACH PARK (PAGE 125)

Home to a long strip of fluffy white sand, Po'ipu Beach is great for **surfing**—both for beginners and experienced surfers—snorkeling, and safe **swimming.** Restrooms, showers, and a grassy park add to the convenience of the easily accessible location.

MAHA'ULEPU BEACHES (PAGE 123)

For a short journey into an **undeveloped** part of the south side, take the bumpy dirt road out to the Maha'ulepu Beaches for often-secluded beach time. You'll have your choice of **Gillin's Beach** and **Kawailoa Bay,** or take a cliff-side hike.

LARSEN'S BEACH (PAGE 78)

Larsen's is a **secluded spot** with a very long strip of white sand. When conditions allow, the rocky area to the right offers **great snorkeling.**

SECRET BEACH (PAGE 78)

Expansive Secret Beach isn't exactly a secret, but it offers plenty of space to find a spot all to yourself. You never know what you may find here—a **waterfall** midway down the beach, swimmable **tide pools** at the end, a peaceful ocean, or giant surf.

SEALODGE BEACH (PAGE 80)

Nestled below **Princeville's cliffs,** SeaLodge Beach is a small cove of paradise accessible via a roughly **15-minute hike.** Shade-giving trees back the small crescent strip of sand; the water offers good swimming and great **snorkeling** when conditions allow.

HANALEI BAY (PAGE 82)

The long, crescent moon-shaped beach offers fine white sand to stroll on, **calm waters** for swimming, and popular **surf breaks** for all levels.

HA'ENA BEACH PARK (PAGE 84)

Nestled up to a backdrop of lush green mountains near the **end of the road** on the north shore, this beach has full amenities including a lifeguard, and it's great for **beachcombing** and **watching surfers.**

Po'ipu Beach Park

Ha'ena Beach Park

Best Outdoor Adventures

Hiking

NOUNOU MOUNTAIN TRAILS (PAGE 46)

Three intersecting trails weave along the **Sleeping Giant,** otherwise known as Nounou Mountain. The **East Trail,** the **West Trail,** and the **Kuamo'o-Nounou Trail** all offer sweeping views and secluded places to enjoy peaceful time on the east side's interior.

NORTH SHORE BEACH WALKS

One of the most peaceful and rejuvenating things to do on Kaua'i is simply take a long beach walk. Make the short hike down to **Secret Beach** (page 78) and then take a stroll to the very end, where you'll encounter a small waterfall and views of the Kilauea Lighthouse. Take a peaceful stroll along **Hanalei Bay** (page 82) and its two miles of white sand backed by lush mountains, or enjoy a walk along the mile-long **Lumahai Beach** (page 83) with a refreshing river to swim in.

KUILAU TRAIL (PAGE 47)

This trail offers some of the most beautiful mountain views, including an amazing view of **Mount Wai'ale'ale** and sweeping vistas from Kapa'a to Lihu'e. A two- to three-hour hike, this is a moderately strenuous trail with wonderful rewards.

ILIAU NATURE LOOP AND KUKUI TRAIL (PAGE 160)

The family-friendly Iliau Nature Loop in **Waimea Canyon State Park** wanders through native forest during the 20-minute walk. Experienced hikers can connect to the Kukui Trail, which will take you down to the **Waimea River** in the canyon, which is roughly four hours round-trip.

PIHEA TRAIL AND ALAKA'I SWAMP TRAIL (PAGE 163)

Known as otherworldly, these trails take you through dwarf forests, vine-covered trees, and the world's highest swamp. Amazing views to

These beaches offer unforgettable snorkeling. Find the best conditions along the south shore from October to April, and on the north shore from May to September.

KE'E BEACH (PAGE 87)

At the end of the road on the north shore is a semi-protected pool with great snorkeling, as well as an outside snorkeling area in the open ocean where the truly spectacular snorkeling exists. Beginners will enjoy the pool while only very experienced water people should explore the outer area, and only when the waves are small.

TUNNELS/MAKUA BEACH (PAGE 87)

Possibly the most renowned snorkeling spot on the island when conditions permit, snorkelers will see marine life not far from shore while experienced snorkelers will see amazing creatures out by the ledge that drops off into the deep ocean.

ANINI BEACH (PAGE 86)

The calm and shallow water makes Anini a great family-friendly beach for snorkeling.

LYDGATE BEACH PARK (PAGE 40)

This is one of the most popular snorkeling locales on the island, with two protected pools. It's perfect for snorkelers of all ages and levels.

PO'IPU BEACH PARK (PAGE 128)

Out on the south shore, this beach offers a lively underwater world on both the east and west ends of the beach.

PK'S (PAGE 128)

Across from the south shore's Prince Kuhio Park, the reef beyond this tiny strip of beach offers a much-frequented underwater spot for fish grazing on the seaweed growing on the rocks.

snorkeling at Tunnels/Makua Beach

LAWA'I BEACH (PAGE 128)

This rather small beach is a popular south side snorkel spot. There's usually something to see close to shore, as the rocks and seaweed attract fish.

SALT POND BEACH PARK (PAGE 157)

This beach park with full amenities is the best bet for snorkeling on the west side, with calm and protected water.

NA PALI COAST (PAGE 88)

You'll find the island's most spectacular snorkeling along the Na Pali Coast, reachable only through a boat tour. Take a snorkel cruise to see jaw-dropping underwater terrain and an array of sea life from dolphins to sea turtles.

the north shore can be seen at the **Kilohana Overlook.**

KALALAU TRAIL (PAGE 96)

The Kalalau Trail is a strenuous, 11-mile hike—one way—with unmatched views of the **Na Pali Coast** and switchbacks, mud, hills, and stream crossings. You'll pass **Hanakapi'ai Beach** and end on the secluded **Kalalau Beach,** a true escape.

HANAKAPI'AI BEACH AND HANAKAPI'AI FALLS (PAGE 97)

Beginning at **Ke'e Beach,** the first section of the Kalalau Trail, which is roughly four hours round-trip, features beautiful views of the **Na Pali Coast** and ends with a dip in the cool freshwater pool at Hanakapi'ai Falls.

SWIMMING POOL TRAIL (PAGE 48)

Scenes of *Jurassic Park* were filmed at the start of this trail, which offers views of **Mount Wai'ale'ale** and a reward of a cool natural swimming pool to dip in after cutting through a tunnel below ground.

Water Sports

KAYAKING THE NA PALI COAST (PAGE 92)

Arms of steel are necessary for the intense, 16-mile sea kayak journey along the Na Pali Coast. **Outfitters Kauai** offers the tour from mid-May to mid-September on Tuesdays and Thursdays.

WATERSKIING AND WAKEBOARDING ON THE WAILUA RIVER (PAGE 44)

To mix water with adventure, try waterskiing, wakeboarding, kneeboarding, or a hydrofoil ride on the Wailua River. The only company to offer these kinds of boarding activities is **Kaua'i Water Ski and Surf Co.**

SURFING AT PO'IPU BEACH (PAGE 129)

For experienced surfers, the island is your oyster. For novice surfers, Po'ipu Beach is the place to take lessons. For lessons with a true surf pioneer,

Ke'e Beach

Anini Beach

Lumahai Beach

the world-famous Kalalau Trail

try **Surf Lessons by Margo Oberg** for group, semiprivate, or private sessions.

Wildlife-Watching

WHALE-WATCHING IN PO'IPU (PAGE 131)

Whale season runs from November through April. While on Kaua'i in whale season, simply keep your eye on the ocean when you're on the beach, surfing, or even in a car. There's a good chance you'll see whales. For whale-watching boat tours December through April, contact **Captain Andy's Sailing Adventures.** Another option is **Blue Dolphin Charters,** which offers whale-watching tours December through March.

BIRDING IN KILAUEA AND KOKE'E STATE PARK (PAGES 99 AND 164)

Stop by the **Kilauea Point National Wildlife Refuge** to see huge frigate birds, dressy red-footed boobies, swift tropic birds, and the endangered Hawaiian nene goose. For birding in Koke'e, try the 3.5-mile **Alaka'i Swamp Trail,** the **Kaluapuhi Trail,** or the 3.7-mile **Pihea Trail.** For a shorter birding trail, take a stroll on the slightly over a mile **Halemanu-Koke'e Trail.**

Adventure Sports

ATV IN KOLOA (PAGE 130)

For some good, dirty fun, drive an ATV with **Kaua'i ATV.** Guided ATV tours take adventurous drivers on a waterfall, cane road, or private tour.

ZIPLINING AND TUBING IN LIHU'E (PAGE 50)

Outfitters Kauai offers various zipline adventures on the east side. **Kaua'i Backcountry Adventures** offers zipline and tubing on 17,000 acres of old sugar plantation land.

SKYDIVING ON THE WEST SIDE (PAGE 165)

Get a bird's-eye view of Kaua'i. For skydiving excursions, **Skydive Kauai** will spread your wings at 4,500 feet.

Best Cultural and Historical Sites

HO'OPULAPULA HARAGUCHI RICE MILL (PAGE 75)

In Hanalei, stop for a pre-booked tour at the Ho'opulapula Haraguchi Rice Mill, the last remaining rice mill in Hawai'i. The mill is within a **national wildlife refuge,** and the tour offers a view into the island's agricultural and cultural history, views of endangered **native water birds,** and information about the cultivation and uses of taro.

WAILUA RIVER SACRED SITES (PAGE 32)

The banks of the Wailua River were once the hub for Hawaiian *ali'i* (royalty), and along the river are many cultural sites. At the **Holoholoku Heiau,** it's believed that human sacrifice may have taken place, the **Pohako Ho'o Hanau** is where the *ali'i* were born, the **Poliahu Heiau** features a rock structure that shows a very large *heiau* (sacred place), and at the **Kamokila Hawaiian Village** you can wander through a replica of a traditional Hawaiian village.

PRINCE KUHIO PARK AND HO'AI HEIAU (PAGE 121)

In Po'ipu, Prince Kuhio Park's Ho'ai Heiau is a **monument** to the beloved prince who worked for the welfare of his people.

FORT ELISABETH STATE HISTORICAL PARK (PAGE 150)

Originally built and used by Hawaiians as a *heiau,* this park in Waimea dates from 1817. Its shape resembles an eight-pointed star.

KAUA'I MUSEUM (PAGE 28)

In Lihu'e, you'll find the best background information about the island at the Kaua'i Museum. There are several permanent and temporary exhibits and a gift shop with great books.

KILOHANA PLANTATION (PAGE 31)

The sprawling Kilohana Plantation is home to a perfectly **preserved mansion** built by a sugar plantation owner in the 1930s. You can browse the home and its many original pieces of decor, explore the beautiful grounds, and enjoy a historical train ride.

KILAUEA LIGHTHOUSE (PAGE 71)

Stop for both educational and photo opportunities at the Kilauea Lighthouse and the **Kilauea Point National Wildlife Refuge.** For decades the lighthouse served as a beacon to ships.

LIMAHULI BOTANICAL GARDEN (PAGE 76)

Check out the preserved **wetland taro terraces** and native plants at Limahuli Botanical Garden. A self-guided tour weaves through the verdant grounds.

HO'OPI'I FALLS (PAGE 47)

The peaceful hike to Ho'opi'i Falls is a stroll down a hill under a high tree canopy along the river that leads to two small falls.

WAIPO'O FALLS (PAGE 161)

On the west side, a roughly three-hour, strenuous hike to the 800-foot Waipo'o Falls, with beautiful views along the way, ends with a swim in a cool pool.

SECRET FALLS ON THE WAILUA RIVER (PAGE 43)

Secret Falls, also known as Uluwehi Falls, has a swimmable pool and is accessible via a beautiful kayaking excursion on the Wailua River and a short hike. Most visitors opt to do this trip with a guided kayak tour, but you can also rent a kayak and paddle to the trailhead on your own.

SECRET BEACH TIDE POOLS AND WATERFALL (PAGE 93)

The hike to the Secret Beach tide pools and water-fall is reserved for the spring and summer only, when the waves are flat. The ocean-side cliff walk leads to a small waterfall and several swim-mable tide pools.

HANAKAPI'AI FALLS (PAGE 97)

For a strenuous hike with a reward of a beau-tiful waterfall cascading down a high cliff into a large swimming pool, make the trek to Hanakapi'ai Falls. The four mile hike leads first to Hanakapi'ai Beach and then to the falls over generally rough terrain, but it's a rewarding experience.

Wailua Falls

WAILUA FALLS (PAGE 32)

For gazing at waterfalls from a drive-up parking lot, Wailua Falls is an easily accessible option. You'll have a good view from the lookout point down to the falls and into the pool.

OPAEKA'A FALLS (PAGE 32)

On the east side, you can view Opaeka'a Falls right from the parking lot. This is a convenient stop after looking at the sacred cultural sites along the Wailua River, such as the Poliahu Heiau across from the falls.

Lihu'e and the East Side

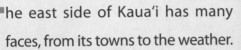

The east side of Kaua'i has many faces, from its towns to the weather.

Sometimes the sun is blazing and waves roll up on the fine, white sand at Kealia Beach, where surfers dot the lineup, or snorkelers gaze at marine life at Lydgate Beach Park. Some days can be windy and overcast, the ocean choppy and rough, a better day for cruising Kapa'a's cafes and shops. The beauty of this area is that most days are perfect to explore the rivers by kayak or stand-up paddle—unless it's pouring down rain, of course.

As you fly into Lihu'e Airport and get your first look at the east side, you'll realize just how small the island's biggest town is. Lihu'e—a plantation town until 1996 when the sugar mill shut down—is busy, practical, and central. Its neighbor, Kapa'a, is vibrant and colorful with a natural, laid-back vibe. Kapa'a is also known for an eclectic mix of craft shops, clothing boutiques, and galleries featuring local artists, as well as restaurants, cafés, and walk-up eateries where organic, fresh, and local food is almost always on the menu.

The stretch from Wailua Golf Course to Kapa'a's Kealia Beach is known as the Coconut Coast for the plethora of coconut trees a plantation entrepreneur planted along the highway and the coast. The palms still stand tall today, their slender trunks and delicate fronds moving gracefully in the trade winds.

The Wailua River is one of the main attractions on the Coconut Coast. The name Wailua, which means "two waters," celebrates the beautiful ocean and bay along with the freshwater river, where *ali'i* (Hawaiian royalty) gathered for sacred ceremonies, leaving archaeological relics to tell the story. Many *heiau* (sacred rock structures) were built in the area, and their sparse remains still can be seen along the banks of the river. The road leading along the Wailua River was called the King's Highway, and only those invited were allowed to approach the royal settlement. Today, this wide river is a beautiful place for anyone to explore by kayak.

Wherever you find yourself in this region, dramatic mountains and clear ocean water frame your view, and nature is in the eye everywhere you look.

ORIENTATION

Kaua'i's east side stretches from Lihu'e, where you'll find the airport and car rental services, a national brand shopping mall, the government center, and the Kaua'i Museum,

Previous: Lydgate Beach Park; kayaking the Wailua River. Above: Kaua'i style in Lihu'e.

Look for ★ to find recommended
sights, activities, dining, and lodging.

Highlights

★ **Kaua'i Museum:** Learn about the history and culture of Kaua'i to enhance your island experience (page 28).

★ **Kilohana Plantation:** Take a trip back in time while exploring an expansive and elegant estate. Ride the sugar train, sample locally produced craft rum, and enjoy a meal at the upscale restaurant (page 31).

★ **Wailua Falls:** Gaze at the iconic 80-foot waterfall, easily accessed by car (page 32).

★ **Lydgate Beach Park:** Bring your snorkeling gear and enjoy viewing reef fish in the calm, protected pools. Picnic tables, pavilions, and two amazing playgrounds make for an ideal day at the beach (page 38).

★ **Donkey Beach:** One of the more remote beaches in the area, this long and uncrowded stretch of white sand is perfect for sunbathing and beachcombing (page 39).

★ **Surfing at Kalapaki Beach:** The calm, crescent-moon-shaped bay is ideal for swimming, longboarding, and stand-up paddling. Watch surfers catch waves, or take a surf lesson and catch your own (page 41).

★ **Kayaking the Wailua River:** A waterfall, lush jungle, and calm waters make kayaking on the wide and smooth Wailua River a must-do adventure (page 43).

★ **Nounou Mountain East Trail:** This

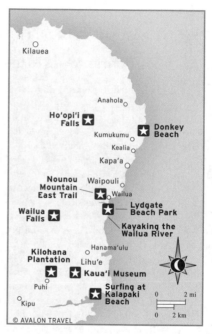

strenuous yet rewarding hiking trail offers solitude and spectacular coastal views from Mount Wai'ale'ale (page 46).

★ **Ho'opi'i Falls:** A gorgeous nature walk takes you through a tunnel of trees to these two waterfalls (page 47).

Lihu'e and the East Side

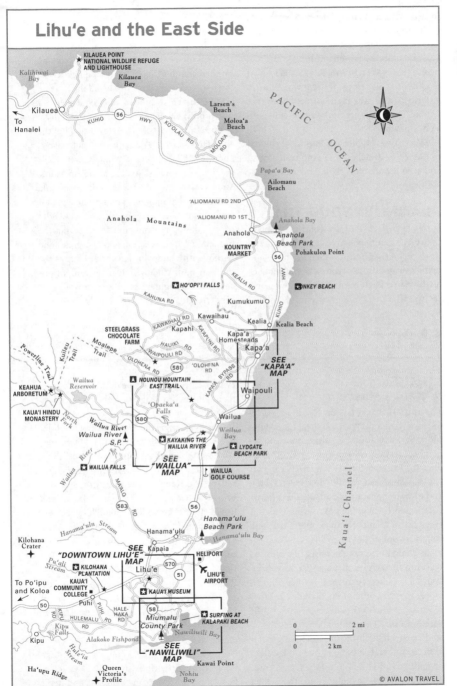

© AVALON TRAVEL

to **Anahola,** a sleepy residential community with a few beaches and a small outdoor market. In Lihu'e, the resort area is west of the airport, near the famous **Kalapaki Beach,** which fronts **Nawiliwili Bay,** Kaua'i's port of call for cruise ships. Sister towns **Wailua** and **Kapa'a** are the main attractions for the region. The towns are funky and quaint with a natural vibe.

Everything is right along **Kuhio Highway,** or Route 56—beaches, shopping, restaurants, and accommodations flank both sides of the highway in Wailua, Waipouli, and Kapa'a.

PLANNING YOUR TIME

For most visitors, the only time they spend in Lihu'e is when they arrive at the airport and stock up on supplies, and then when they return to drop off their rental car and get back on the plane. There are a few attractions worth seeing, like the Kaua'i Museum, Kilohana Plantation, and lunch at Duke's Kauai on Kalapaki Beach, and most can be seen in just a few hours while you're passing through on the way to another region. For those staying on the Coconut Coast, it's just a quick trip to town, if you can manage to avoid the traffic.

The towns, activities, and sights farther north on the Coconut Coast warrant at least a day, if not two, of your stay. Kaua'i is the only Hawaiian Island with navigable rivers, and the Wailua River is a gem, with waterfalls and tropical forests. You can stand-up paddle and kayak or hike the trails on the riverbank. This area also makes a great home base for day trips to the north, south, and west sides of the island. The only drawback is that the beaches on the east side are often overcast and windy with choppy ocean conditions, as the predominant trade winds blow straight onshore. On a brighter note, Kapa'a town is very bike friendly.

Sights

LIHU'E
★ Kaua'i Museum

The **Kaua'i Museum** (4428 Rice St., 808/245-6931, www.kauaimuseum.org, 10am-5pm Mon.-Sat., $10 adults, $8 *kama'aina* and seniors 65 and up, $6 students 13-17, $2 children 6-12, under 5 free) is a must-see. This two-building complex is in downtown Lihu'e, and although it's a good place to visit anytime, exploring it at the start of your trip provides history, culture, and context that will enhance your entire stay. The island art exhibits change on a regular basis; however, the museum focuses on displaying ethnic heritage such as koa furniture, feather lei, and more. Permanent exhibits include the *Story of Kaua'i,* which takes up two floors in the Rice Building. The exhibit constructs the island's past, highlighting the geological aspects of the island and settlement by the Hawaiian people. Island chiefs, Captain Cook, traders, and whalers are highlighted. The exhibit even features a life-size camp house to walk through, shedding light on the many different people who came to the island.

The William Hyde Rice Building was built in 1960 to house the museum, and the Albert Spencer Wilcox Building was built in 1924. Although small on the scale of national museums, the Kaua'i Museum exudes a strong presence with arches, a cement front, and broad steps. The building has a lava rock exterior, sloped roof, barrel-vaulted ceilings, original antique light fixtures, and a mezzanine with a balcony overlooking the first floor. The building is on the National Historic Register. The museum shop sells books, cards, Hawaiian prints, a magnificent selection of Hawaiian craft items, and a fine selection of detailed U.S. geological survey maps of the entire island.

In the Juliet Rice Wichman Heritage Gallery, exquisite finds are on display such as beautiful and rare N'ihau shell lei and items

The Best Day on the East Side

To experience the best of the best on the east side, begin early and be ready for a busy day. Because Kaua'i's most spectacular beaches are found on other parts of the island, a day on the east side should be spent with activities rather than lounging on the sand. Begin in Kapa'a and work your way toward Lihu'e because some of the Kapa'a and Wailua sights are best in the morning. If you begin your day early with breakfast around 8am, you should be finished and ready for dinner around 7:30pm.

- Welcome the day with breakfast at **Kountry Kitchen** or **Art Café Hemingway** in Kapa'a. If you prefer a lighter meal on the go, stop by **Kauai Juice Company** for a cold-pressed, organic juice concoction.

- Next, kayak the **Wailua River** or walk along the river to **Ho'opi'i Falls.** If you choose the hike, just head up the road, but if you'd rather paddle up the Wailua River, make sure to book a reservation in advance. Check with your outfitter to see if they provide lunch; you can grab lunch in Kapa'a afterward if they don't. If you're looking to skip strenuous activity for a day, take the drive up to **Wailua Falls** for a quick-stop photo op.

- After your morning nature experience, head back to Kapa'a for lunch at **Mermaids Cafe** or **Olympic Cafe.**

- After lunch, head south to **Lydgate Beach Park.** Cool off and snorkel in the calm pools. Spend some time viewing the underwater world and relaxing in the sun. Don't forget your snorkel equipment.

- Head over to Lihu'e for a visit to the **Kilohana Plantation.** Browse the shops and plantation grounds, or take a ride on the historical train.

- For dinner there are two great options in Lihu'e. For a spectacular dinner featuring local cuisine, try **Gaylord's.** To enjoy a classic Hawaiian restaurant in a semi-formal atmosphere, have a meal on the water at **Duke's.**

that belonged to Kaua'i *ali'i* and monarchs. In the Oriental Art Gallery exhibit, housewares from Asia are on display as are Asian china, sculptures, and art that had been in homes on the island. There are also temporary exhibits. These include exhibits on the Kekaha train robbery, various art and textiles exhibits, and an aviation history of Kaua'i.

It's a good idea to dedicate at least a couple of hours for a thorough visit. The entrance fee is valid for several days and includes docent tours, so ask for a pass if you'd like to return. Free family admission is offered the first Saturday of every month.

Alakoko Fishpond

The Alakoko (Rippling Blood) Fishpond is commonly known as Menehune Fishpond. Overlooking the Hule'ia River and the Ha'upu ridge on the far side, the pond tells the story

of Hawaiian history and myths. This fishpond has been used to raise mullet and other commercial fish. But unlike most other fishponds, which are built along the edge of the ocean, this pond was constructed along the riverbank and is said to have been built by the *menehune* (mystical "little people") in just one night.

Legend says that these little people built the rock wall surrounding this pond for a royal prince and princess and made only one demand: that no one watch while they were working. It's said that throughout the night the *menehune* passed the stones needed from hand to hand in a 25-mile-long line. Meanwhile, the prince and princess grew curious and watched from nearby. The *menehune* saw them and turned the royal pair into two pillars of stone that you can see on the mountain overlooking the pond. The small workers stopped their work and left holes in the wall.

Downtown Lihu'e

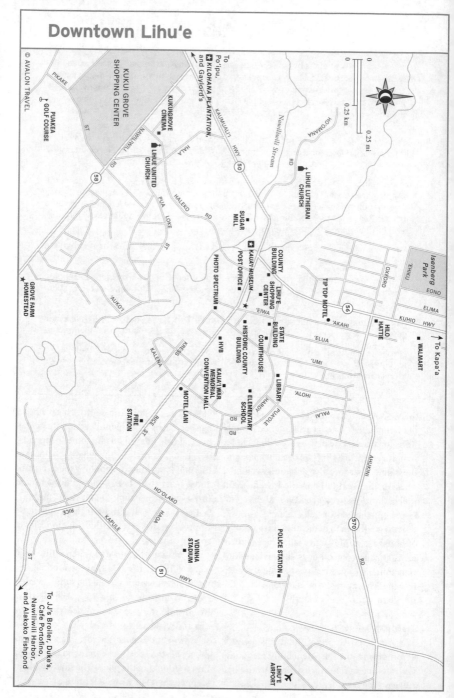

© AVALON TRAVEL

PIKAKE

PUAKEA
GOLF COURSE

KUKUI GROVE
SHOPPING CENTER

KUKUIGROVE
CINEMA

LIHUE UNITED
CHURCH

To
Po'ipu,
KILOHANA PLANTATION,
and Gaylord's

KAUMUALI'I HWY

Nawiliwili Stream

50

HO'OMANA

RD

LIHUE LUTHERAN
CHURCH

SUGAR
MILL

HALEKO RD

PHOTO SPECTRUM

POST OFFICE

KAUAI MUSEUM

COUNTY
BUILDING

LIHUE
SHOPPING
CENTER

'EIWA

STATE
BUILDING

COURTHOUSE

HISTORIC COUNTY
BUILDING

HVB

KAUA'I WAR
MEMORIAL
CONVENTION HALL

MOTEL LANI

'ELUA

'UMI

HARDY

'ALOHI

PLA'OLE

PALAI

LIBRARY

ELEMENTARY
SCHOOL

TIP TOP MOTEL

'EHIKU

Isenberg
Park

OXFORD

EONO

ELIMA

56

'AKAHI

KUHIO HWY

HILO

HATTIE

WALMART

To Kapa'a

AHUKINI

POLICE STATION

570

RD

GROVE FARM
HOMESTEAD

'AUKOI

KALENA

RICE ST

KRESS

FIRE
STATION

HO'OLAKO

HAOA

RICE

KAPULE

ST

51

HWY

VIDINHA
STADIUM

To JJ's Broiler, Duke's,
Café Portofino,
Nawiliwili Harbor,
and Alakoko Fishpond

LIHUE
AIRPORT

0   0.25 km

0   0.25 mi

NAWILIWILI RD

58

HALA

PUA LOKE ST

RD

To Kapa'a

To get here, follow Hulemalu Road until you see the overlook. It's a beautiful sight.

Grove Farm Homestead

The **Grove Farm Homestead** (4050 Nawiliwili Rd., 808/245-3202, www.grovefarm.net, tours Mon., Wed., and Thurs. 10am and 1pm, $20 donation for adults, $10 for children 5-12) is a former sugar plantation that was started in 1864 by George Wilcox, the son of Congregational missionary teachers who worked for the original owner of the bordering land. Wilcox bought 500 acres for $12,000 through a lease-to-purchase arrangement. The property had been chopped out of a large grove of kukui trees—hence the name Grove Farm. Bringing water down from the mountains, Wilcox operated one of the most profitable sugar plantations in Hawai'i. He purchased more land as the years went by, and now the property encompasses 22,000 acres (one of the five largest landholdings on the island).

The homestead was a working plantation until the mid-1930s when Wilcox died. His nieces went on to care for the property, and in 1971 Mabel Wilcox created a nonprofit organization to preserve Grove Farm Homestead as a historical living farm. Reservations for tours are preferred, but the staff will most likely accommodate unexpected visitors. They ask that visitors call at least 24 hours in advance to book a tour. Reservations are also accepted by mail up to three months in advance by writing to Grove Farm Homestead (P.O. Box 1631, Lihu'e, HI 96766). Exact directions will be given on the phone. Wear comfortable shoes that can be slipped off because, as in most homes in Hawai'i, shoes are not worn indoors here. Tours are sometimes canceled on rainy days.

★ Kilohana Plantation

For an elegant trip back in time, visit the **Kilohana Plantation** (3-2087 Kaumuali'i Hwy., 808/245-5608, www.kilohanakauai.com, shops open 9:30am-9:30pm Mon.-Sat., 9:30am-5pm Sun., free), a sprawling estate with manicured lawns, fruit, flowers, a train, and the former mansion of Gaylord Wilcox. At the time that Gaylord Wilcox moved the business offices of Grove Farm from the homestead site, he had the 16,000-square-foot Kilohana plantation house built in 1936. After decades of family use, the building was renovated in 1986 and turned into shops that sell arts and crafts. Exploring the antique mansion's rooms, still decorated with original furnishings, jewelry, and other elegant artifacts, serves as a tangible experience of history.

Kilohana Plantation has several restaurants, as well as Lu'au Kilohana every Tuesday and Thursday evening. A horse-drawn carriage operates 11am-6pm daily. Just show up and stand in line near the front entrance to take a ride. The 20-minute carriage ride is $12 for adults and $6 for children; call 808/246-9529 for reservations.

The **Kauai Plantation Railway** (www.kauaiplantationrailway.com) is a popular attraction on the plantation. Complete with a whistle, the 1939 Whitcomb diesel engine, named Ike, pulls mahogany coaches modeled after King Kamehameha's personal car. The Signature Train Tour is 40 minutes and tours 105 acres. You'll see orchards, vegetable gardens, tropical flowers, forest, and animal pastures with donkeys, goats, cattle, ducks, geese, and wild pigs. It costs $19 adults, $14 children 3-12, infants are free. The tours run daily at 10am, 11am, noon, 1pm, and 2pm. Check in 30 minutes before departure. There also are packages that include the train tour and nature walk and lunch, as well as a train tour and *lu'au*.

WAILUA
Fern Grotto

The Wailua River's Fern Grotto, a natural rock amphitheater where a dense forest of ferns hangs from the grotto, is a popular place to visit. An upriver tour run by **Smith's Kauai** (Kuamo'o Rd., 808/821-6895, www.smithskauai.com, boats depart 9:30am, 11am, 2pm, and 3:30pm daily, $20 adults, $10 children 3-12) is the way to access it. A two-mile,

90-minute round-trip river journey takes you to the grotto. On the trip you'll also be treated to a hula dance and Hawaiian music.

It's a pretty sight, but some say the grotto isn't as romantic as it used to be. This is due to Hurricane 'Iniki taking a toll on the overlying canopy and ferns in 1992 and a lack of water seepage from the close of the sugar plantation. Although it has regrown, it isn't quite as wonderful as it once was. In an effort to reestablish the ambience, improvements have been made to bring back the irrigation to the ferns. Many couples come here to get married.

Kamokila Hawaiian Village

For a cultural experience, explore **Kamokila Hawaiian Village** (Kuamo'o Rd. along the Wailua River, 808/823-0559, www.villagekauai.com, 9am-5pm daily, $5 adults, $3 children 5-12). Kamokila means stronghold, and is Kaua'i's only re-created Hawaiian village. It was built on the site of an ancient royal village, the first of seven ancient villages in this valley. Resting on four acres, the location was once home to the last reigning king of Kaua'i, King Kaumuali'i. Village sites include the canoe house, the *Outbreak* movie set, a birth house, taro patches, a wood-carving house, the village lagoon, petroglyphs, medicinal plants, and a lot more.

Several huts have been reconstructed with traditional methods. In the courtyard traditional Hawaiian games are featured, such as spear throwing and Hawaiian bowling. Kamokila was resurrected to give visitors a glimpse of what island life was like for ancient Hawaiians. It opened in 1981 and was almost destroyed by Hurricane 'Iwa in 1982, only to be damaged again in 1992 by Hurricane 'Iniki. The village also offers outrigger canoe rides, hiking and swimming, access to Secret Falls, weddings, and a *lu'au*. When fruit is in season, visitors are welcome to help themselves to it.

★ Wailua Falls

One of Kaua'i's most beautiful and easy-to-view waterfalls is the 80-foot Wailua Falls, which was featured on the opening credits of the television show *Fantasy Island*. Legend says the Hawaiian *ali'i* would dive off the falls to prove their physical prowess, and commoners were not allowed to participate. Surrounded by wide-open pasture, it's a beautiful drive up Ma'alo Road to get to the falls. It's about four miles to the end of the road, so you can't miss it. The falls can be viewed from a lookout spot where there is a parking lot, which is a perfect place for a photo op. There is usually a line of onlookers here and hat makers selling their woven palm hats. The lookout spot is the only place to view the falls unless you take one of the two trails down to the falls, but both are slippery and can be dangerous.

Smith's Tropical Paradise

Smith's Tropical Paradise (5971 Kuhio Hwy., 808/821-6895, www.smithskauai.com, 8:30am-4:30pm daily, $6 adults, $3 children 3-12) is a 30-acre botanical and cultural garden along the Wailua River. On the property many plants are labeled, including an array of fruit, and common topical foliage as well as other plants that are rare and hard to find. There are two main buildings here; one is home to a *lu'au* and the other is a lagoon theater used for music shows. A path over one mile long leads you around the property. There is also a Japanese garden.

Opaeka'a Falls

Two miles up Kuamo'o Road are the 150-foot majestic Opaeka'a Falls. The scenic lookout is on the right after the first mile marker and has a large parking lot and restrooms. The beautiful falls are easy to see and make for a good photo opportunity. Along Kuamo'o Road on the way to the falls, look out for sacred *heiau*, such as the Poliahu Heiau.

Kuamo'o Heiau

Along the Wailua River off Route 580 are seven **sacred** *heiau* from the pre-contact period that are easily accessible. At the river mouth are several ancient petroglyphs that can be seen at low tide—if they're not covered by sand or sediment. The first *heiau* is

Wailua

© AVALON TRAVEL

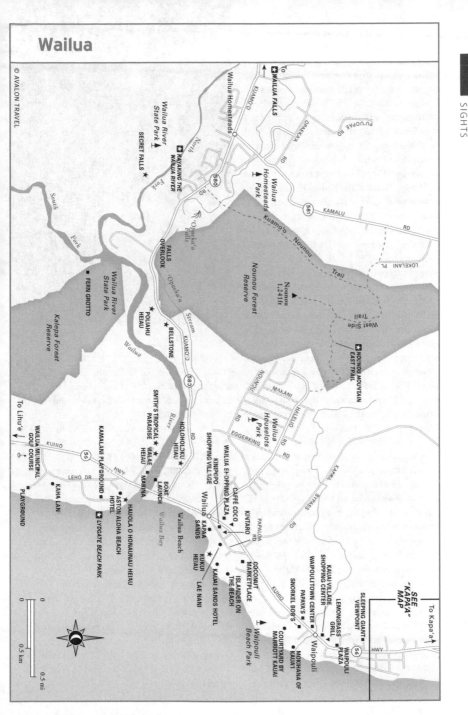

called **Hauola O Honaunau** and was where *kapu* (rule) breakers came to make up for their indiscretions by having a priest redeem them. It's located on the south side of the river mouth. Near the marina entrance is **Malae Heiau,** which is said by some to have been constructed by the *menehune*. It's on the road into Smith's Tropical Paradise and is believed to be the biggest *heiau* on Kaua'i. There isn't much to see here; it's the cultural significance that counts. On the outcrop of land at the end of Wailua Beach is the **Kukui Heiau.** There is only a tiny part of the structure left, but it once measured 230 by 70 feet. It's not worth the walk over, but knowing of it enhances the sacredness of the area. Traditionally it was used as a makeshift lighthouse, a fire beacon to lead canoes to shore. It's located on what is now property belonging to a condominium.

Holoholoku Heiau is up Kuamo'o Road right after the state park boat-launch area along the river on your left. Some say this place was used for human sacrifice, and some say for animal sacrifice. There is a big flat stone near the front of the area that was the altar. Very close is **Pohako Ho'o Hanau,** the royal birthstones where the royal women came to give birth. The mother rested her back on one of the two stones and placed her feet on the other while giving birth.

Along the river and just before Opaeka'a Falls is **Poliahu Heiau.** This was once a very sacred site and is said to have been built by the *menehune* and used by King Kaumuali'i, Kaua'i's last king. Although its exact function is not known and the structures inside are long gone, the size of it leads archaeologists to believe that it was a *luakini heiau* (human sacrifice). A rock wall in the shape of a rectangle is all that's left, which is more than most other *heiau*. Please don't walk on the wall. There is a great lookout here over the Wailua River and a good photo opportunity. Farther up the road, turn down a dirt road after the first mile marker, head to the end of the road, and walk down the path past the guardrail till you see a few large stones.

Wailua Falls

One is known as the **Bellstone.** When it is struck a certain way, the stone produces a metallic sound, which historically announced the birth of a royal child.

KAPA'A
Kaua'i Hindu Monastery

A very intriguing place to visit is the **Kaua'i Hindu Monastery** (Kaholalele St., 888/735-1619, www.himalayanacademy.com, 9am-noon daily). Located up the Wailua River, the monastery is built completely from hand-carved stones from India. Each stone takes seven years to carve and there are 4,000 of them. Free, guided tours are offered once a week, but it is open for visitation daily. The holidays vary with the Hindu calendar. Wear long pants and shirts that cover the shoulders; no miniskirts for women or going shirtless for men. On-site are the Kadaval Hindu Temple, Ganesha Shrine, and Bangalore Gallery. Call for specific guided tour dates and to reserve a parking space.

Kapa'a

To Kilauea,
Kealia Beach,
and ✈ DONKEY BEACH

MAILIHUNA RD

■ KAPA'A SCHOOL

LOOKOUT ■

56

■ MAHELONA HOSPITAL

KAUA'I PRODUCTS FAIR ■

Kapa'a Beach Park

SWIMMING POOL

KAUAI INTERNATIONAL HOSTEL

● KAUA'I BEACHHOUSE
● HOTEL CORAL REEF
LIBRARY

581

Kapa'a

○ MERMAIDS CAFE

ABC STORE ■

To Kaua'i Hindu Monastery

NANI MOON MEADERY ■

KAPA'A SHOPPING CENTER ■

Kaua'i Channel

0   0.5 mi
0   0.5 km

SLEEPING GIANT VIEWPOINT ●

SEE "WAILUA" MAP

To Waipouli Beach and Wailua River

○ Waipouli

© AVALON TRAVEL

At Kipuni Place is the **Sleeping Giant Viewpoint** pull-off. From this angle you can see the mountain, and with some imagination you can see why they call it Sleeping Giant. You can see the vague outline of legs and an incline going up to a chest and head. Wonderful trails go up both the front and the back of this hill, bringing you up to a picnic spot on the chest; from there a narrow trail leads over the throat to the chin and forehead. Note that these hikes are composed of narrow trails along a ridgeline with vertical cliffs on both sides. They are very dangerous.

Honey Wine-Tasting at Nani Moon Meadery

Nani Moon Meadery (Yasuda Center, 4-939 D Kuhio Hwy., 808/823-0486, www.nani-moonmead.com, noon-5pm Tues.-Sat.) offers an opportunity to enjoy the tastes of the islands at the state's only producer of honey wine. Made with local ingredients, the tasty honey wine is produced, bottled, and sold on-site at the tasting room. Try the Cacao Moon mead, made with macadamia nut blossom honey and Kaua'i cacao.

Steelgrass Chocolate Farm

Steelgrass Chocolate Farm (5730 Olohena Rd., 808/821-1857, www.steelgrass.org, 9am-noon Mon., Wed., and Fri., $60 adults, children under 12 free) offers a tour called Chocolate from Branch to Bar. The eight-acre farm specializes in vanilla, bamboo, and cacao, the chocolate tree. The tour reveals everything about growing and harvesting cacao fruit and turning it into chocolate. Smelling and tasting is part of the three-hour tour, where you explore the gardens and the orchard and enjoy an 11-course chocolate tasting. Exploring a chocolate farm in Hawai'i is an experience unique from what the rest of the United States has to offer, as Hawai'i is the only state with an environment hospitable to cacao.

Nounou, the Sleeping Giant

Legend says that a long time ago, a giant lived in Kawaihau behind Kapa'a town. He was very friendly and helped the people of the area. He had a hard time staying awake for more than a hundred years at a time, and when he would sleep, he would use a small hill as a pillow. The people called him Kanaka Nunui Moe, the sleeping giant. After a chief requested that the people bring rocks and trees from Koke'e and Waimea to build a *heiau* for him, the giant helped, bringing all the material down. To show appreciation, the people provided the giant with a wonderful meal of poi, pig, and fish. He filled his belly and was so full he lay down to rest for the last time.

Kaua'i's Own Mokihana Flower

While on Kaua'i, you will most likely see and hear the word *mokihana* often. Although it's commonly referred to as a flower, it's actually a light green berry. Deemed the island's official lei-making material, the mokihana berry is strung like beads and usually intertwined with the maile plant. The berries emanate the faint scent of anise. Found in wet forests of high elevations around 1,200-4,000 feet, the mokihana is found only on Kaua'i and is also the island's official flower.

Beaches

The shoreline on the east side is dotted with numerous white-sand beaches, and every nook has a different look and feel. Sunbathe or surf in Lihu'e, snorkel and barbecue in Wailua, or bodysurf or enjoy a beachside bike ride in Kapa'a. They're all tropical gems; however, a few are some of the more popular and crowded beaches in Kaua'i. If you're staying in Lihu'e and don't want to go far, they will more than satisfy, but the pervasive trade winds can whip up choppy ocean conditions, blowing sand and thick cloud cover at a moment's notice. Conversely, if you happen to be on the east side when the trade winds are light or from a northerly direction, the east-side beaches change face into some of the most dynamic, inviting, and easily accessible beaches on the island.

LIHU'E
Niumalu Beach Park

Just west of the Nawiliwili Small Boat Harbor, Niumalu is a county park resting along the bank of the Hule'ia River, where scenes from *Raiders of the Lost Ark* were filmed. Popular with locals, it has pavilions, showers, and toilets. The beach park is used mostly for launching kayaks to explore the river, for barbecues, and for family functions. If you're in the area and looking for a quick picnic stop this will do, but other beaches are much nicer. To get here, turn off Nawiliwili Road onto Niumalu Road. Follow it to the end.

Kalapaki Beach

Although Kalapaki Beach fronts the Kaua'i Marriott Resort, the beach is open to the public. The sand is white, but down by the stream it's a little darker from dirt and sediment. Because it's so popular and fronts the hotel, it lacks the feeling of seclusion that many Kaua'i beaches offer. The nice thing about Kalapaki Beach is that the waves break pretty far out, so they've usually turned into gentle surges of water before they get to shore. The nearshore waters are great for swimming, and occasionally snorkeling. Farther out on a shallow reef in the bay, stand-up paddlers, longboarders, and bodyboarders take advantage of the gentle, yet perfectly shaped waves. The popular eatery Duke's fronts the beach here, and is another reason why it's a well-known spot.

Kalapaki Beach fronts **Nawiliwili Bay.** To get here, take Rice Street down toward the ocean and stick to your right as it becomes Route 51. Access is via the hotel on your left if you park in the visitors' area. Or, if you keep going, on the north end of Nawiliwili Park before the Anchor Cove Shopping Center there's a small parking lot. Look for the narrow footbridge going over Nawiliwili Stream to the hotel property and the beach.

Ninini Beach

Located to the harbor side of Ninini Point and the lighthouse, Ninini Beach is a narrow, sandy beach fronting the low cliff. It's calm

Nawiliwili Bay

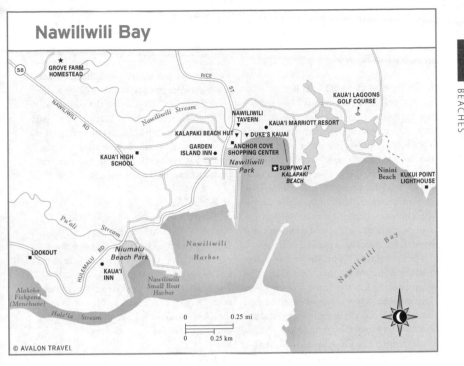

© AVALON TRAVEL

most of the year, but during large surf or windy days the beach can be a little rougher. This is a small and less-visited beach that is very good for sunbathing and a secluded beach day. Snorkeling can be good on the left side by the rocks, but it's dangerous. To get here, take Pali Kai Road past the Marriott, walk along the edge of the Kaua'i Lagoons Golf Club, and keep to your right until you see the steep trail to the beach below. If you take the fork on your left you'll find its sister beach, also known as Ninini, which is another less-visited area for sunbathing and swimming.

Hanama'ulu Beach

Hanama'ulu is another beach that is popular with locals. People utilize the picnic tables, showers, toilets, pavilion, and camping ground for weekend getaways. The facilities are a bit rundown, but there is a small playground. It's not a top choice to spend a beach day, but considering it's just north of

the airport, it will suffice for a lunch break or a place to recoup while figuring out your next stop. Follow Hehi Road off Route 51 to the beach park.

WAILUA
Wailua Beach

Wailua Beach stretches from the mouth of the Wailua River to the first rocky point heading north. On this point are the nearly nonexistent remains of a sacred *heiau,* one of many in the area. Surfers sometimes catch waves breaking along a shallow reef offshore, but the blustery trade winds, choppy ocean conditions, and strong currents tend to keep beachgoers away. However, when the ocean and wind are calm, it is a local favorite for a beach stroll and sunbathing. The river mouth adds an element of action, but when the river is flowing heavily it's an extremely unsafe place to hang out in the water. It's not one of Kaua'i's most spectacular beaches, but it's centrally located in an area that was important to Hawaiians in the past. Petroglyphs can be seen carved into rocks at the mouth of the river when the tide is very low. You can pull up roadside off Route 56.

★ Lydgate Beach Park

On the south side of the Wailua River and behind the Aston Hotel lies Lydgate Beach Park, where two protected pools are the highlight of the beach. The pools are protected by lava rock barriers that create perfect places to swim and snorkel, regardless of surf conditions. It's safe for young children and anyone else who prefers to relax in the water worry-free. There is a lifeguard here, as well as sheltered picnic tables, grills, and restrooms and showers, but camping is not allowed.

The **Kamalani Playground** is any child's dream. Located on the mountain side of the beach parking lot, the castle-like, wooden playground has towers, bridges, slides, swings, balancing beams, climbing features, and interactive areas such as a huge xylophone, which means it's easy to entertain children for a long time. A large pavilion on-site is perfect for lunch or a birthday party. To get to the beach park and playground, turn off Route 56 onto Leho Drive and then onto Nalu Road. You will find several parking lots along the beach. The pools and playground are located at the northern end of the beach.

A newly created section of the beach park has a number of bike paths and walkways as well as more restrooms, picnic benches, and another children's playground. To get to the second section, drive down the paved road at the northern end of the Wailua Municipal Golf Course until it branches toward the sea. Turn onto Leho Drive; there are two access roads that head to the ocean. You can find parking along the way to the beach.

KAPA'A
Waipouli Beach

Just north of Wailua Beach is Waipouli Beach. Although it's not ideal for swimming because of strong currents and a sharp reef, its paved trail is a great place for a long ocean-side jog. The beach is narrow and stretches good distance in front of a number of hotels, such as the Kaua'i Sands Hotel, Islander on the Beach, Lae Nani, and Kapa'a Sands Resort.

Waipouli Beach Park (Baby Beach)

While on Kaua'i, you'll probably hear the name Fuji Beach or Baby Beach. Both refer to Waipouli Beach Park, lying north of Waipouli

Lydgate Beach Park

Beach. Perfect for children and a popular spot for local families, it's a wonderful location to spend the day in the water. A long, natural stone breakwater protects a large part of the ocean, and unless the waves are huge, this spot is great for swimming. Turn onto Pahihi or Makana Street and Moanakai Road runs parallel to the ocean. Although it's known as a great spot for children, always check out the ocean conditions first.

Kapa'a Beach Park

A little north of Baby Beach is another local favorite, Kapa'a Beach Park. The white-sand beach scattered with rocks runs north from Waikaea for almost a mile between mile markers 8 and 9, until it ends near a community swimming pool and the Kapa'a library. Various roads lead to the beach from the highway and all are obvious; there is nothing obstructing the view from highway to coast. The beach park is 15 acres, with a pavilion, picnic tables, showers, toilets, and grills at the southern end. Several patches of sand break up the somewhat rocky beach, and swimming is doable if the waves are mellow. It's a nice place for a meal or a bike ride along the coast, but otherwise it's best to move on to a sandier beach for swimming.

Kealia Beach

Shortly after Kapa'a Beach Park is Kealia Beach, a popular spot for locals and visitors alike. The half-mile-long beach has restrooms, lifeguards, and pavilions with picnic tables. The east end of the beach is usually the emptiest and is often covered with debris from the mouth of the Kapa'a Stream. Parking usually isn't a problem here as numerous parking spots back the beach. This is a popular place with locals for surfing, bodysurfing, and bodyboarding, and is good for swimming when the waves are small. This is definitely one of the more crowded beaches on Kaua'i, but it makes for an easy swim while in the area. The shorebreak often pounds the shore, so it's best to stay on the beach if you're not a strong swimmer and the waves are up. The beach begins about a half mile before mile marker 10.

★ Donkey Beach

A short distance down the road from Kealia Beach is Donkey Beach. This is a beautiful, remote white-sand beach where the swimming is less than ideal but the atmosphere is wonderful. It is a hidden treasure thanks to the 10-minute walk down to the beach. Swimming can be rough, but it's a peaceful

Kealia Beach

zone to relax and sunbathe thanks to the ample space and the good chance you'll be alone. The ocean here is choppy with strong currents on a regular basis and has no lifeguards. The occasional monk seal is spotted here; if you see one, stay a good distance away. This is a beach known to be a favorite for those who like nude sunbathing, but most likely you'll find the beach empty or see a few people enjoying it with their suits on.

To get here, turn right about a half mile past mile marker 11 at the brown sign with hikers on it. Parking is up top near the restrooms, and the easily noticeable trailhead is on the east end of the parking lot.

ANAHOLA TO KILAUEA
Anahola Beach Park

Like many of Kaua'i's beach parks, Anahola Beach Park has an open area for picnic tables, grills, showers, restrooms, and various camping spots if you have a county permit. This is a popular camping spot for locals, who like to set up elaborate camps for the weekend, so it's generally not a secluded spot, but visitors are welcome to enjoy it. The swimming is safe in the protected cove on the eastern end of the beach as well as in the river. Toward the north end the currents are usually stronger

and the waves are bigger. If you plan to camp, don't leave your possessions unattended for too long; the area is known for occasional incidents of theft. The ironwood trees provide natural shade and a break from the sun. To get here, take either Aliomanu Road or Anahola Road from Route 56.

On the north side of the stream is **Aliomanu Beach.** Homes and vacation rentals border this less-visited beach. It's long with white sand, and there are some rocky spots in the water, but it can be a nice place to stroll and, most likely, be alone. The northern end of the beach is nicer. To get here, turn right onto the second Aliomanu Road, just a bit after mile marker 15, and keep to your right to access the eastern beach, or take the first left and then right to access the northern beach.

Papa'a Bay

Papa'a Bay is another beautiful white-sand beach that is rarely visited by visitors or locals. It's great for a stroll or sunbathing, but not for swimming. To get here, turn right onto the second Aliomanu Road, just a bit after mile marker 15. Take the first left and then a right, then follow the trail on the left. Park up here and walk about five or ten minutes down through some bushes and over large rocks.

Water Sports

SNORKELING AND DIVING

The east side of Kaua'i has one spectacular snorkeling spot—Lydgate Beach Park—and several other reefs worth exploring. More often than not, however, the trade winds and choppy ocean conditions will have you traveling elsewhere to snorkel. Remember, if you're a water lover, it's a great idea to keep a complete snorkel set in the car no matter where you go on Kaua'i. That way you're always prepared to jump in the water if the conditions are right. On the east side it's easy to make a quick stop and pick up any last-minute beach

gear because the shops and beaches are in very close proximity.

Wailua
LYDGATE BEACH PARK

Lydgate Beach Park is your best bet for snorkeling on the east side, with two protected ocean pools that offer an easy and relaxing place to snorkel and swim. There are plenty of fish to see, and they rarely fail to present an explosion of vibrant tropical colors underwater. The ponds are almost always swimmable and calm, unless the surf is abnormally huge. Don't forget your underwater camera. Keep in mind that there are normally quite a few other snorkelers and general beachgoers sharing the sights.

OUTFITTERS AND RENTALS

At **Boss Frog's Dive & Surf** (4-746 Kuhio Hwy., 808/823-0220, www.bossfrog.com, 8am-5pm daily), divers and snorkelers can find everything they need to explore Kaua'i's underwater world. Snorkel rentals include basic to full professional snorkel sets. The average snorkel set that will get you through an enjoyable session rents for $6 per day or $42 per week for two sets. You can also purchase your own snorkel set. The shop offers all other beach needs, such as board rentals and other beach gear. The service is friendly and the workers are happy to guide you to the best spots.

Another tried-and-true place for snorkel rentals is **Snorkel Bob's** (4-734 Kuhio Hwy., 808/823-9433, www.snorkelbob.com, 8am-5pm daily). They offer complete sets, including a mask, snorkel, and net gear bag with grade A surgical-quality silicone for ultimate comfort and water seal. The adult package goes for $35 per week or $22 per week for children. The budget crunch package offers a basic mask, snorkel and fins, and dive bag for $9 per week. A unique rental package is what they call The 4 Eyes RX Ensemble, to compensate for nearsightedness while snorkeling. This includes a mask with a prescription lens for $44 per week for adults and $32 for kids. They also offer rentals for single snorkels ($7-12/week), various fins ($8-12/week), wetsuits ($20/week), snorkel vests, life jackets, and flotation belts ($20/week), and boogie boards ($26/week). A fish identity card is a fun thing to pick up so you can tell friends later on what you saw.

Seasport Divers (4-976 Kuhio Hwy., 808/823-9222, www.seasportdivers.com, 9am-5pm daily) has been in business since 1987 and is locally owned and operated. The Kapa'a location only rents gear and takes reservations for tours. They offer complete snorkel gear sets for *kama'aina* rates of $6 per day or $19 per week and visitor rates of $8 per day or $25 per week. Seasport Divers offers the Ni'ihau, or Forbidden Island, dive, where you explore the waters around Ni'ihau and Lehua Island. Thanks to the lack of visitors and fishing on the island, Ni'ihau's waters are alive and thriving. There are wall dives, lava formations, and caves to explore. Dives off a boat are offered from $200 for just snorkeling or $335 for 2-3-tank dives for certified divers.

Kapaa Beach Shop (4-1592 Kuhio Hwy., 808/212-8615, www.kapaabeachshop.com, 8am-6pm Sun.-Fri.), a small, family-run store, rents snorkel sets for $6 per day and $15 per week, flotation vests for $6 per day and $12 per week, and 3mm short wetsuits for $7 per day.

SURFING AND STAND-UP PADDLING

Surfing on the east side is usually at two main surf breaks: Kalapaki Beach and Kealia Beach. If you want to try surfing on the Coconut Coast and are a beginner, it's a good idea to get a surf lesson at Kalapaki Beach rather than renting a board and going for it alone. Experienced surfers will have fun at these breaks but should be comfortable in crowded waves with some currents. If you're not traveling with your own board, there are several surf shops that offer rentals; rentals are also available on the sand at Kalapaki Beach. Stand-up paddling is best done at Kalapaki Beach, where you can surf the wave or paddle the sheltered bay.

Lihu'e

★ **KALAPAKI BEACH**

A great place for beginner surfers, stand-up paddling, and bodyboarding, Kalapaki Beach is a local favorite. Right out in front of Duke's restaurant is a small and mellow right- and left-breaking wave over a shallow reef. The rights are longer and gentler. The lefts tend to be steeper and shorter, and end on a very shallow reef. Mornings usually provide the best conditions. From Rice Street, turn into the small dirt parking lot by the river. You'll see signs for Duke's Kauai parking.

OUTFITTERS

For surfing lessons at popular Kalapaki Beach, try **Kauai Beach Boys** (3610 Rice St., 808/246-6333, http://kauaibeachboys.com), which offers 90-minute classes at the beach with no more than four people in a class. Classes begin with about 30 minutes on land with the instructor giving tips and sharing information, and the rest of the class is in the water. Classes include boards, rash guards to protect against sun and rash, and booties for foot protection. Lessons are daily at 10am, noon, and 2pm and are $75 per person. Stand-up paddle lessons are also 90-minute lessons for $75 per person, but they are offered daily at 9am, 1pm, and 3pm. They also offer 45-minute canoe rides for $39 per person and a one-hour sailing trip for $39 per person.

To explore a river on a surfboard, try the stand-up paddle tour offered by **Outfitters Kauai** (2827A Po'ipu Rd., 808/742-9667, www.outfitterskauai.com). The tour starts with a paddle up the calm Hule'ia River and includes a hike to waterfalls, and even some water zipline action. The two-mile paddle lasts about a half day. The tour is $126 for adults and $96 for children 12-14. It is offered Monday, Wednesday, Friday, and Saturday and departs at 7:45am.

Kapa'a
KEALIA BEACH

Kealia Beach is very popular, and is generally crowded with locals hanging out on the beach, surfing, bodyboarding, and bodysurfing. The waves break outside and then re-form and break on shore, offering a pounding shore-break. The conditions are usually choppy and windy with strong ocean currents, but when the trade winds are light, it can be a great wave. Best suited for intermediate to experienced surfers, the crowds can make catching a wave a bit tough. You can't miss Kealia in full view from Route 56, near mile marker 10 at the northern end of Kapa'a. The parking lot stretches the length of the beach, and you can even pull up in the sand, right to the shore, on the north end of the beach. Just make sure to drive on the hard-packed path.

OUTFITTERS

Tamba Surf Company (4-1543 Kuhio Hwy., 808/823-6942, www.tambasurfcompany.com, 9am-5pm Mon.-Sat., 10am-3pm Sun.) is the premier east-side surf shop for surfboards, gear, and rentals. It's the locals' choice for good reason. They offer all different kinds of shortboards, even a few fun shapes and mini-tankers, as well as soft-top longboards

Calm conditions make Kalapaki a favorite spot for stand-up paddling.

and stand-up paddleboards. Surfboard rentals are $25 for 24 hours, $40 for two days, $55 for three days, and every day after that is an additional $10 per day. Stand-up paddleboards rent for $40 for 24 hours and $20 per day for each day thereafter. Racks for your vehicle are provided if you need them.

Kapaa Beach Shop (4-1592 Kuhio Hwy., 808/212-8615, www.kapaabeachshop.com, 8am-6pm Sun.-Fri.) rents all kinds of beach gear. They have beach chairs and umbrellas for $5 per day, bodyboards for $7 per day, and eight-foot soft-top surfboards for $20 per day.

KAYAKING

Kayaking is an extremely popular activity on east-side rivers, especially the wide and gentle Wailua River. Kayakers will find exciting river adventures, beautiful scenery, and calm water. While you can launch into the ocean, the pervasive trade winds and choppy ocean conditions make river kayaking the obvious choice.

Lihu'e
OUTFITTERS
Outfitters Kauai (2827A Po'ipu Rd., 808/742-9667, www.outfitterskauai.com) offers a half-day adventure on the gentle Hule'ia River. Kayak two miles downwind taking in the sights of the surrounding national wildlife refuge, hike through lush jungle to a secluded waterfall, and relax on the way back aboard a motorized canoe. The tour is $120 for adults and $100 for children 3-14. The tour departs at 8:45am. They also rent kayaks at their Hule'ia and Wailua River locations.

Kapa'a
★ **WAILUA RIVER**
The Wailua River is Kaua'i's most popular spot for kayaking. Up the river you'll find **Fern Grotto,** a natural amphitheater where ferns hang in abundance; **Secret Falls** with its swimmable pool; and gorgeous views inland and along the banks. **Uluwehi Falls,** also known as Secret Falls, lies on the north side and is reachable after a paddle and a hike. It's about five miles round-trip and roughly

three hours without stopping to explore the river. The most common way to navigate the river is with a guided kayak tour. Only a few companies rent kayaks for independent paddling up the river. The Hollywood film *Outbreak* was filmed on the north side of the river.

OUTFITTERS
Ali'i Kayaks (174 Wailua Rd., 808/241-7700, www.aliikayaks.com, 7:30am-7:30pm Mon.-Sat., $40) offers a Wailua River kayak tour. A local guide shares Hawaiian history and legends during the adventure. The tour heads up the river's north fork and takes a short hike through the rainforest, ending at Secret Falls. Offered every day except for Sunday, check-in time is either 8:30am or 10:30am, and reservations are required. They provide kayak equipment, a dry bag, and walking sticks. The tour lasts approximately 4.5 hours and includes four miles of kayaking and 1.5 miles of moderate hiking.

Another reliable option is **Kayak Kaua'i** (5-5070 Kuhio Hwy., 808/826-9844, www.kayakkauai.com, 7am-8pm daily, $85 plus tax adults, $60 children under 12). They offer a five-hour guided paddle up the Wailua River and hike to Secret Falls. The tour is great for families and allows you to swim in the freshwater stream or pool of the falls. Offered daily except Sunday, this tour has a 12-person capacity. Check in is at 7:45am, 8:45am, 12:15pm, and 12:30pm. They provide kayaks with foot pedals and rudders, dry bags, life vests, juices and water, and a deli sandwich lunch with snacks and a vegetarian option.

Kayak Kaua'i is one of the few selected by the state to be an exclusive outfitter for lone kayaking up the Wailua River. They rent kayaks to those who wish to go unguided. The Wailua River rental package includes double kayaks with a permit, life preservers, car racks, paddles, back rests, a map, and bow line. Dry bags, coolers, and walking sticks can also be rented separately. Kayakers need to bring lunch and other necessary supplies on this trip. The kayaks are dispatched between

8:30am and 11:30am and can be returned after sunset or before 8am the next day to the Kapa'a shop. No singles are available, and the price is $27 per person.

Kayak Wailua (4564 Haleilio Rd., 808/822-3388, www.kayakwailua.com, Mon.-Sat., $48) offers guided tours about two miles up the Wailua River. They offer dry bags and coolers to bring your own refreshments and food. They even offer adult-sized triple kayaks for a family or group of friends. A trip up the river and a hike and swim usually lasts about 4.5 hours. Tours depart at 9am, 10am, noon, and 1pm.

Wailua Kayak Adventures (6575 Kuamo'o Rd., 808/822-5795, www.kauai-wailuakayak.com, Mon.-Sat.) offers four tours a day. The roughly 4.5-hour tour provides paddlers with a two-mile round-trip paddle and a hike to Secret Falls for a swim. They offer cruise ship shuttle services for $80 per van. Price is $47.87 with tax per person. They also rent kayaks: $25 single, $50 double per day.

A favorite with many is **Outfitters Kauai** (2827A Po'ipu Rd., 808/742-9667, www.outfitterskauai.com), which offers a guided Wailua River tour to Secret Falls. A lunch is included, and cold drinks are available throughout the day. Prices are $102 per adult and $82 for children 5-14. The company asks that participants are comfortable kayaking for 60-90 minutes and walking two miles of rugged trail.

One of the original kayak companies on the Wailua River, **Wailua Kayak and Canoe** (169 Wailua Rd., 808/821-1188, www.wailuakayakandcanoe.net) offers both four-hour guided kayak tours as well as five-hour kayak rentals (single $45, double $75). The four-hour waterfall guided tour includes a class I easy paddle and a short hike to Secret Falls for $49. The company does not provide lunch.

WATERSKIING, WAKEBOARDING, AND OTHER POWER SPORTS
Wailua

The only company to offer these kinds of boarding opportunities is **Kaua'i Water Ski and Surf Co.** (4-356 Kuhio Hwy., Kinipopo Shopping Village, 808/822-3574, www.kauaiwaterskiandsurf.com, 9am-5pm Mon.-Fri. and 9am-noon Sat.). For a unique experience on the gorgeous Wailua River, hop on some water skis for an experience you'll never forget. The company also offers wakeboarding on the river, kneeboarding, and hydrofoil,

waterskiing the Wailua River

where your board rises above the water while supported by a hydrofoil wing that remains under the water. The company offers the experience for beginners as well as experienced boarders who want to work on their technique while in Kaua'i. The boat fits five extra passengers, who can come along for free and watch while you board around the river. Rates are $90 for a half hour or $175 per hour, and reservations are required.

FISHING
Lihu'e

Departing from Lihu'e's Nawiliwili Harbor, **Kai Bear Sportfishing Charters** (808/652-4556, www.kaibear.imoutdoorshosting.com, reservations required) offers a variety of shared and exclusive private charters for a range of interests and budgets. Charters go out on one of their two boats, the 38-foot *Kai Bear* or the 42-foot *Grander*. The boats offer at least one custom-made Blue Water Rod and Penn International Gold two-speed reel. Four-hour charters range $130-945. Six-hour charters range $130-1,395. Eight-hour charters range $1,400-1,795, and for a to-be-determined price you keep all the fish, a unique offer considering the catch usually belongs to the captain. Bottled water and soft drinks are provided, and guests are allowed to bring their own food and alcoholic beverages, but no glass containers.

Lahela Sportfishing (Slip 109, Nawiliwili Small Boat Harbor, 808/635-4020, www.lahela-adventures.com, reservations required) leaves out of Nawiliwili Harbor and takes guests out on the 34-foot *Lahela*. The boat is the only fishing boat certified by the Kauai Coast Guard in operation on the island and takes up to 14 passengers. Private fishing charters range from $575 for four hours to $1,725 for 12 hours. Deluxe, shared charters are priced at $219 with spectators at half price. Economy shared charters require a minimum of four anglers at $135. Guests must be at least seven years old.

Kapa'a

C-Lure Charters (Nawiliwili Harbor, 808/822-5963, www.clurekauai.com) takes anglers out on the *Mele Kai,* a custom-built 41-foot Noosa cat equipped with Shimano tackle, depth sounders, and a GPS. It seats six people in the shade and has a fighting chair. Guests must bring their own food and alcoholic beverages, but C-Lure provides fishing tackle, bait, soft drinks, and water. They cannot take more than six people but can arrange for additional boats to caravan if you want to bring more people. Charters range from half-day to whole-day trips and custom charters. Prices range from $100 for non-fishing spectators to $1,050 for a full day with up to six anglers.

Going out with **Hawaiian Style Fishing** (1651 Hoomaha Pl., 808/635-7335, www.hawaiianstylefishing.com) means cruising on a 25-foot Radon. They offer sport and bottom fishing and say they're prepared for any fish. You're invited to bring along your lucky lure or pole and the captain will most likely give it a try. Four-hour shared charters run from $130 per person, while private charters are $600. Eight-hour private charters are $900.

Hiking and Biking

HIKING

Miles of trails weave through the east side's interior behind Wailua and Kapa'a. You can hike trails that wind through lush green forest, along rivers, to waterfalls, or out in the open sun. The air is thick with moisture and the smell of wild tropical fruit like guava and passion fruit, the views are abundant, and the scenery—both along the trail and up and down the coast—is breathtaking.

Wailua

Three trails comprise the Nounou Mountain Trails. They are all in the mountains above Wailua and zigzag over Nounou Ridge, the Sleeping Giant.

★ NOUNOU MOUNTAIN EAST TRAIL

Many feel the nearly two-mile-long (each way) east trail is the prettiest of the three, and it can easily take up most of the day if you take your time enjoying views and lunch. The trail, which climbs to 1,000 feet in elevation, is strenuous. The east side of the trail begins off Haleilio Road. The trailhead leads to a series of well-defined switchbacks. It continues with an incline through lush forest providing some shade. As you walk, look for flowers, guava, and passion fruit. Feel free to enjoy some. At the half-mile mark there is a fork; *be sure not to go to the left here.* It's dangerous, as are most side trails on this hike. At the 1.5-mile marker the west trail intersects, but stick to the east trail. Farther along at the main fork in the trail, take the left path, which leads to a picnic table, shelter, and bench. Take in the views because they're spectacular. At the table, you'll see a trail that goes south up to the giant's head and face. If you're a novice hiker, your hike should end here, at the table.

The remainder of the trail is for expert hikers only. The trail is narrow, steep, and dangerous. For the truly adventurous, the view is an amazing reward as is the satisfaction of the accomplishment. If you proceed, you'll walk along the spine of the mountain with sheer cliffs on each side. To get to the trailhead, drive 1.2 miles up Haleilio Road. Parking is by the 38th pole on the right, which has a sign indicating it is pole 38.

KUAMO'O-NOUNOU TRAIL

The Kuamo'o-Nounou Trail is about two miles one way and is tough, but suitable for a fit family. The trail begins with a wooden bridge over the Opaeka'a Stream. From here you veer left gradually at an incline. It takes about one hour each way and sees about an 800-foot elevation gain or loss depending on which way you're going. This trail is steeper than the east trail. The end of the trail intersects the west-side trail. About three-quarters of a mile from the trailhead is a shelter on a perch with great views of Kaua'i's highest point, Kawaikini, Wailua Homesteads, and views to the northwest. At the 1.8-mile point, it begins the decline to the west trail. You can usually see waterfalls if it's been raining. To get to the trailhead, head up Kuamo'o Road, after Opaeka'a Falls. There is a pasture on the near corner of Maile Street on the right side and a home on the far corner. You'll see the Nounou Trail sign.

NOUNOU MOUNTAIN WEST TRAIL

The Nounou Mountain West Trail is 1.5 miles long and one hour each way. A little shorter and less steep than the east trail, the west trail has more shade and meets up with the Kuamo'o-Nounou Trail after about a half mile in. The trail ascends faster than the others, making it quite a workout. Keep going and you'll meet up with the east trail and then have access to the incredibly dangerous trail to the summit and giant's head.

Kapa'a

★ HO'OPI'I FALLS

This low-impact hike is a forest walk along Kapa'a Stream that leads to two waterfalls. The 2.2-mile hike stays under the forest canopy. Look for *liliko'i* (passion fruit) on the ground. Along the trail are thimbleberry bushes that have bright red berries similar to raspberries. Give one a try. When you come down to the river, hang a right slightly up from the river and continue on the well-worn, narrow trail. You'll see multiple offshoot trails going down to the river. They're a bit steep, and the red dirt can be slippery. When you can hear the falls, take a side trail down to the top of the falls. Here you can sit and spend some time, eat, or just hang out near the falls and along the river. To get to the bottom of the falls, you'd have to continue downstream then head back up in the water. When you're done here, backtrack up the side trail and continue on.

Eventually you'll have to go down to the river and walk along the edge. Stay near the water's edge to stay off private land. Right before the second waterfall the trail goes over the river to the top of the falls; this is the end of the trail. Don't forget your camera on this hike, and make sure you have enough time to leisurely explore. If you want to really enjoy this hike, bring mosquito repellent.

To get to the trailhead, turn onto Kawaihau Road from Kuhio Highway. Head inland for about 12 minutes and then take a right onto Kapahi Road. Look for the yellow metal post on your left at the trailhead. Right past here is a dirt pull-off spot that fits about three cars. Please go very slow on this neighborhood road to show respect to the residents.

POWERLINE TRAIL

This 13-mile, strenuous hike will take you from the east side to the north shore over the course of the day. The trail is actually a rough road built for the installment of power transmission lines between Lihu'e and Hanalei, although some believe the trail was originally a connection between the two areas for early Hawaiians. If you choose to complete the whole thing, you'll need a pickup on the north shore, or you can take the bus back to the east side. For a shorter hike, just go as far as you like and turn around when you're ready.

Starting at the Kapa'a trailhead, you'll encounter a rather steep incline for a little while, and from there it's pretty level traveling with an eventual descent into Hanalei. Not too far from the beginning you'll see **Kapakaiki Falls** on your right, and soon after is **Kapakanui Falls.** These falls aren't close enough to access, but make a nice sight. While the scenery may be dense, lush, and green, the road itself is bare, dry, and hot. This means that although the surrounding foliage is thick, the trail itself provides no shade. Remember to bring plenty of water for this trail. Roughly halfway down you begin to see the ocean, and glorious views are offered along the way. Footing off the main road can be unstable, and the biggest thrills are found by sticking to the road. After completing the incline from the trailhead, you'll be treated to great views of **Mount Wai'ale'ale.**

On this trail you might encounter mountain bikers, dirt bikers, and hunters and their dogs in season. To get to the trailhead, head up Kuamo'o Road and pass the Wailua Reservoir till the pavement ends, then go about a mile to the Keahua Arboretum, where you should park. At the arboretum, cross the stream and walk up the steep road; you'll see a four-wheel-drive track heading uphill to your right. This is the start of the trail.

KUILAU AND MOALEPE TRAILS

The 4.5-mile Kuilau Trail begins about 200 yards before the entrance to the Keahua Arboretum and takes about 2-3 hours round-trip. There are a few parking spots at the trailhead marker on the right side of Kuamo'o Road. This somewhat mellow trail leads to a picnic area with tables and shelter after about a mile. Not long after this, the prize of this trail is the mountain views, which are some of the best you can find. Views to Mount Wai'ale'ale and the crater and down to Kilohana and Ha'upu Ridge are in view. From here, keep following the trail, circling around the hill until you come to a small wooden footbridge. Here, about two miles from where you began this nature stroll, the Kuilau Trail meets the Moalepe Trail. After crossing the bridge, the Kuilau Trail weaves through a tunnel of trees to an open flat spot and then turns east. The Moalepe Trail begins at the end of Olohena Road. This trail is popular with local horseback riders and offers awesome views before joining back with the Kuilau Trail almost three miles from Olohena Road.

SWIMMING POOL TRAIL

For a cool pool and Mount Wai'ale'ale views, take this hike, which is about five miles round-trip. This trail heads into the center of the island and leads to a stream-gauging station and dammed section of the river. The locked gate at the beginning of the trail is where scenes of the entrance gate were filmed for *Jurassic Park*. Walk around the gate and head up the inclined road for roughly 45 minutes till you make it to the gauging station and the dammed part of the river. Here, you are very close to the center of the island. This is a great place to just relax, meditate, or enjoy a picnic lunch. From here you can see the crater, and if it's been rainy, as the center of Kaua'i usually is, you may see many waterfalls cascading down the green cliffs.

From here it's about an hour and a half via either a walk through a tunnel in the hill that requires most people to hunch over or a trek over the hill to the falls and the refreshing pool at the bottom. A flashlight is a good idea for the tunnel. Soon after, you'll see the chilly and refreshing pool, and if you swim through it and stick to the right for just a few minutes you'll come to the falls, with another small and refreshing bubbling pool. Only go in if the water flow is calm—it's a highly enjoyable experience.

To get to the trailhead, head to the Keahua Arboretum off Kuamo'o Road and follow the gravel road running across the stream at the arboretum. Stick to the main road for about four miles. The road is marked as being for four-wheel-drives, but it is usually fine for two-wheel-drives unless it is very muddy. At the fork in the road keep to the left, then there's another fork with a gate. If the gate is open keep driving, and if it's closed park here and you'll just have to walk longer. The second gate is the *Jurassic Park* gate. Go around the gate and begin your adventure.

Movies Made in Kaua'i

Kaua'i's vast uninhabited land with its unique landscape has long been a favorite location for Hollywood filmmakers. Movies have been shot on the island for decades, and the trend doesn't appear to be waning. Next time you watch one of these well-known movies, see if you can recognize the Kaua'i locales.

- *Blue Hawaii*
- *Dragonfly*
- *Fantasy Island*
- *George of the Jungle*
- *Honeymoon in Vegas*
- *Hook*
- *Jurassic Park*
- *King Kong*
- *Lord of the Flies*
- *Mighty Joe Young*
- *Outbreak*
- *Pirates of the Caribbean: On Stranger Tides*
- *Raiders of the Lost Ark*
- *Six Days/Seven Nights*
- *Soul Surfer*
- *South Pacific*
- *Starsky & Hutch*
- *Tropic Thunder*
- *White Heat*

HIKING TOURS AND GEAR

For all the hiking gear you could need, stop by **Da Life** (3500 Rice St., on Kalapaki Beach, 808/246-6333, www.livedalife.com, 8am-8pm daily). The shop offers a thorough array of outdoor gear. Name brands fill the store, providing all the hiking gear you could need. Stop by for anything you might have forgotten, especially before any serious hikes.

For a private guided tour, contact **Kaua'i Hiking Adventures** (808/822-4453, www.kauaihikingadventures.com, full-day tours $285, half-day tours $185). The tours are suitable for all fitness and ability levels. Each tour is customized to the hiker's personal preference, ability, and weather conditions. The guide shares knowledge of Hawai'i's plants, history, and culture while hiking. Prices include you and up to three of your friends. The guide is a National Outdoor Leadership School Certified Outdoor Skills and Ethics Trainer and has explored Kaua'i extensively.

BIKING

Much of Kaua'i's narrow, winding roads can be unsafe for biking, but if you really enjoy cruising on two wheels, you're in luck because the east side is home to the 6.6-mile **Ke Ala Hele Makalae bike path.** The name translates to "the path that goes by the coast," and true to its name, the bike path stretches along part of the east coast while staying almost entirely level. Multiple beaches, swimming, and picnic spots are located along the path. The path begins at the Lihi Boat Landing to the south and winds north to Kealia Beach.

Lihu'e

Longtime bike doctor **Bicycle John** (2955 Aukele St., 808/245-7579, 10am-6pm Mon.-Fri., 10am-3pm Sat.) offers a thorough selection of road and mountain bikes to rent and own. Also available is a selection of other biking gear including bikes, helmets, lights, repair services, and more. Bicycle John himself is known to be a straight-to-the-point kind of guy, no bells (except for bikes) or whistles, but he knows what he's doing.

Kapa'a

At **Coconut Coasters Beach Bike Rentals** (4-1586 Kuhio Hwy., 808/822-7368, www.coconutcoasters.com, 9am-6pm Tues.-Sat., 9am-4pm Sun.-Mon.), you will find a variety of bikes: classic and three-speed cruisers ($22 half day, $25 full day, $95 weekly) for adults and children, tandem bikes ($36 half day, $45

the Ke Ala Hele Makalae bike path

full day, $190 weekly), mountain bikes ($25 half day, $30 full day, $120 weekly), trainers that attach to adult bikes for 6-9 year olds, and covered trailers for toddlers that connect to the back of the bike. The classic beach cruiser is slightly less expensive. Rates for kids' mountain bikes and cruisers vary. Reservations are required for rentals.

Kauai Cycle (934 Kuhio Hwy., 808/821-2115, www.kauaicycle.com, 9am-6pm Mon.-Fri., 9am-4pm Sat.) offers cruisers, road bikes, and mountain bikes for rent. It also provides maps, trail information, clothing, accessories, and guidebooks. Rentals include a helmet and a lock and start at $20 per day. Multiday rates are also available, as well as car racks. It also has a certified repair shop in case your own bike needs help.

Adventure Sports and Tours

LIHU'E
Zipline and Tubing

Kaua'i Backcountry Adventures (3-4131 Kuhio Hwy., 808/245-2506, www.kauaibackcountry.com) offers ziplining and tubing on 17,000 acres of old sugar plantation land. You have the choice of seven different courses for your zipline experience. Zipline sessions begin at 8am, 10am, noon, and 2pm daily for $99.

Tubing begins at 9am, 10am, 1pm, and 2pm daily for $102. The ride takes you down the plantation's old irrigation system. Float through open canals and several tunnels dug in the late 1800s.

Outfitters Kauai (2827A Po'ipu Rd., 808/742-9667, www.outfitterskauai.com, 7am-5pm daily) offers ziplining in the Kipu area on the southern border of Lihu'e. The Zipline Trek Nui Loa offers a 1,800-foot tandem zipline over the Ha'upu Mountains, valleys, waterfalls, and huge trees. Zip for about a quarter mile, enjoying over 90 seconds of airtime. This tour includes a picnic lunch and cold water. It costs $152 for adults and $132 for children 14 and under. Another zipline trek is the Kipu Zipline Safari, which includes kayaking two miles up a river, exploring swimming holes and waterfalls, enjoying views of features that appeared in the films *Jurassic Park* and *Raiders of the Lost Ark,* and ziplining through jungle terrain. This tour includes snacks, a picnic lunch, and cold drinks. It costs $182 for adults and $142 for children 14 and under.

ATV

Drive an all-terrain vehicle (ATV) with **Kipu Ranch Adventures** (Kipu Rd., 808/246-9288, www.kiputours.com, 6:30am-6pm daily). Guided ATV tours take adventurous drivers into 3,000 acres of Kaua'i's uninhabited interior. Driving yourself into otherwise inaccessible parts of the island offers awesome views, mud puddles to plow through, and exciting terrain in Kipu Ranch just outside of Lihu'e. The land is former plantation property turned working cattle ranch and offers adventure driving through its pastures and up to Kilohana Crater. Drivers must be 16 or older, but there are other vehicles available for younger guests. Long pants and shoes are a must. After getting muddy and dusty, drivers can cool off in a stream. Three different tours are offered and range $65-160 depending on guests' ages and the tour chosen.

Aloha Kaua'i Tours (1702 Haleukana St., 800/452-1113, www.alohakauaitours.com, 7am-7pm daily) offers a range of tours into the interior of the island. The rainforest hike is actually a combo of four-wheel-driving and hiking. The tour goes inland from Wailua into the heart of the island. After a bumpy ride, the tour walks from the gate where scenes from *Jurassic Park* were shot. Guests walk for about three miles to freshwater pools while learning about Hawaiian culture and history. The guides provide umbrellas, ponchos, and walking sticks as well as backpacks, snacks, and beverages. Groups are required to be a minimum of four and maximum of 12. Adults cost $80 and children 5-12 are $62.50. They also offer a Kaua'i back roads four-wheel-drive tour over the 22,000-acre Grove Farm Plantation, offering a scenic route of the interior. The half-day tour departs at 8am and 1pm from Kilohana Plantation. The tour covers 33 miles of mostly private roads from the top of 1,250-foot Kilohana Crater, along the rugged coastline of Maha'ulepu, and through a cane tunnel. Prices are $80 for adults and $62.50 for children under 12. Tours run seven days a week.

Helicopter Tours

Blue Hawaiian Helicopters (3651 Ahukini Rd., 808/245-5800 or 800/745-2583, www.bluehawaiian.com, 7am-5pm daily) offers a tour they call the Kaua'i ECO adventure. The company's new American Eurocopter ECO-Star offers more interior room to take you over the Hanapepe Valley, then on to Manawaiopuna, otherwise known as Jurassic Falls. Then it's on to the Olokele and Waimea Canyons, then over the Na Pali Coast, Bali Hai Cliffs, and Hanalei Bay. If weather permits, you get to explore the crater of Mount Wai'ale'ale by air for a finale. Regular price is $240 with special online prices.

Near the airport is **Jack Harter Helicopters** (4231 Ahukini Rd., 808/245-3774, www.helicopters-kauai.com, 8am-6pm daily), which offers two tours. The 60- to 65-minute tour hits all of Kaua'i's major scenic areas in their AStar and Hughes 500 helicopters. Price totals $269 including fuel surcharge. A longer tour of 90-95 minutes flies at slower speeds and explores deeper into Kaua'i's valleys and canyons. In this tour the helicopter takes more turns than in the other, providing more photo opportunities. The only tour on the island of this length, it takes place

only on the Astars. Regular price is $404 including fuel surcharge.

With **Safari Helicopters** (3225 Akahi St., 808/246-0136, www.safarihelicopters.com, 7:30am-5:30pm daily) you have the opportunity to tour a waterfall owned by the owner of Ni'ihau. The Deluxe Waterfall Safari is a 60-minute trip to Wai'ale'ale Crater, Waimea Canyon, and the Na Pali Coast. Regular price is $239 per person with special web fares. For the Kaua'i Refuge Eco Tour they offer a 90-minute trip over the same sites as the other tour as well as a stopover at the Kaua'i Botanical Refuge overlooking Olokele Canyon. The price is $304 per person with special web fares.

Sunshine Helicopters (Kahului Heliport #107, 866/501-7738, www.sunshinehelicopters.com, 6am-8pm daily, starts at $244) offers a tour called the Ultimate Kaua'i Adventure, which leaves out of Lihu'e before 8:30am. The tour flies over Waimea Canyon, Mount Wai'ale'ale and the nearby Alaka'i Swamp, and Wailua Falls. Views of the Na Pali Coast are also offered. The flight is about 45-55 minutes. There are discounted rates for booking online.

Island Helicopters (Ahukini Rd. across from the Lihu'e Airport helipads, 808/245-8588 or 800/829-5999, www.islandhelicopters.com, 7am-6pm daily) flies over the sought-after Manawaiopuna Falls, otherwise known as Jurassic Falls. The Kaua'i Grand Circle Tour provides views of Waimea Canyon, the Na Pali Coast, and the north shore. The tour lasts 50-60 minutes but doesn't include a landing at the falls. The regular rate is $297 per person with online discounted fares. The Jurassic Falls Tour lasts about 75-85 minutes and includes all views from the Grand Circle Tour as well as a stop at the 400-foot falls. The regular rate is $371 with online discounted fares.

Golf and Tennis

LIHU'E
Kaua'i Lagoons Golf Club

The Kaua'i Marriott Resort's new and improved **Kaua'i Lagoons Golf Club** (3351 Ho'olaule'a Way, 808/241-6000, www.marriottgolf.com) reopened in 2011 after being refurbished and renamed. This golf course has won many awards and was recently rated one of the top 50 golf resorts by *Golf World Magazine*'s Readers' Choice Award. In 2009 *Golfweek* rated it #5 for America's Best Courses You Can Play in Hawaii. The course, which sits atop a bluff over the ocean, can be experienced two ways. The Kiele Moana Nine features all new putting surfaces and bunkers, boasting the longest stretch of continuous ocean holes of any course in Hawai'i. These nine holes have been paired with the original front nine holes, the Kiele Mauka Nine, to create 18 holes of Jack Nicklaus-inspired golf. To accommodate golfers of all levels, the 18-hole course offers gold tees with a 7,120 yardage, blue with a 6,675 yardage, white with a 6,252 yardage, and red with a 5,377 yardage.

Eighteen-hole prices range $75-120 depending on the time of day, $75-175 for visitors. Nine-hole fees range $65-75 depending on time of day, and $95-100 for visitors. Guests at select hotels can receive discounted rates. Juniors pay $60 before 3pm for 18 holes and $20-35 for nine holes. Children under 15 years old play for free after 3pm when accompanied by a full-paying adult. One child is allowed to play for free per round for each full-paying adult. Also, free instruction is available for children under 15 when accompanied by an adult who is paying for a lesson at the same time with the same instructor. Proper golf attire is required for all ages at Kaua'i Lagoons Golf Club. Golfers must be at least six years old to play. Single rider golf is available, but you must contact the golf shop in advance for reservations and availability. Tee times can be made up to 30 days in advance.

Golf shoes are available, and rentals include a shared golf cart, two bottles of water, a cooler, and a warm-up bucket of range balls. The clubhouse at Kaua'i Lagoons has an upscale ambience on a lake, providing a convenient spot to enjoy a drink and recap your game while overlooking the lagoon.

Kaua'i Lagoons Golf Club also has **tennis courts.** It's free for hotel guests. The courts are open 7am-5pm daily. Call 808/241-6000 for reservations. Check in at the golf shop and they will give you a key for the courts.

Puakea Golf Course and Pro Shop

A favorite with local and visiting golfers, **Puakea Golf Course** (4150 Nuhou St., 808/245-8756, www.puakeagolf.com) ranked 14th in *Golf* magazine's Reader's Choice Awards in 2009. Just minutes from the Lihu'e Airport, the 18-hole course spans up, down, and around deep ravines. Beautiful Ha'upu Mountain views are in sight for three-quarters of the course, and ocean views are in sight for the rest of it. Shopping center "views" are also there, but the course is fun enough to keep your eyes off them. Golfers love that each hole is drastically different, inspiring a new challenge at each hole. Robin Nelson was the golf course architect, and golfers report repeated satisfaction with the course. The course begins on the easier side and increases in difficulty as you move along.

Green fees before 11am are $105, after 11am are $65, after 3pm are $45, and nine holes anytime are $45. Club rental fees before 11am are $40, after 11am are $25, and after 3pm are $15. The course is behind the Kukui Grove Shopping Center in Lihu'e. **The Pro Shop** (866/773-5554) offers a wide spectrum of golf accessories and clothing. After 18 holes, you can relax and enjoy a meal at The Grille. It serves up sandwiches, salads, pupu, and burgers.

Golf Gear

To meet all your golf needs, stop by the **Pro-Am Golf Shop** (4303 Rice St. #B9, 808/632-0609, 9am-5pm daily). It offers a variety of name-brand gear for a day on any of Kaua'i's courses.

WAILUA
Wailua Municipal Golf Course

Just a few miles north of the Lihu'e Airport, the **Wailua Municipal Golf Course** (3-5350 Kuhio Hwy., 808/241-6666, www.kauai.gov/golf) offers 18 holes, a golf shop, locker rooms with showers, a driving range, putting and chipping greens, and a practice bunker. For two players, tee times can be booked up to seven days in advance, while single golfers go out on a standby basis. The course offers blue tees at 6,991 yards, white tees at 6,585 yards, and red tees at 5,974 yards. The course hugs the ocean, and the ocean breeze enhances the experience. Visitor weekday price is $48, and weekends and holidays are $60. *Kama'aina* rates are $15 weekdays, and weekends and holidays are $20. Twilight prices are offered in the morning and afternoon for half the daily rate. Junior and senior rates are also offered. Motorized carts are $18. It's located directly across from the Kaua'i Correctional Facility.

Yoga and Spas

LIHU'E

Get pampered at the **Alexander Day Spa and Salon** (Kaua'i Marriott Resort, 3610 Rice St., Ste. 9A, 808/246-4918, www.alexanderspa.com, 8am-7pm) and you will truly get lost in a luxurious experience. Massages in the spa or beachside cabana range $70-175, and in your room they cost $150-200. Various modalities are offered, including couples, sports, deep tissue, Hawaiian *lomilomi,* aroma massage, and more. Body treatment combos of masks, scrubs, massage, and more range $70-185, and all involve island-themed scents and ingredients. Facials with delicious scents like green tea, ginger, and fruit range $70-180. For the ultimate luxurious experience, packages are offered with a combo of a facial, massage, mani-pedi, and more for $160-310. Full bridal services are offered.

KAPA'A

Get centered at **The Yoga House** (4-885 Kuhio Hwy., 808/823-9642, www.theyogahousekauai.com), which offers a wide array of classes and styles. In the Hot Power and Yoga Blast classes, yogis strengthen the body and relax the mind during a 75-minute heated session. During Hot Flow yoga, participants spend 75 minutes combining postures, breathing, and Vinyasa. Yin yoga addresses the health and suppleness of the joints, fascia, ligaments, and bones. Slow Flow Vinyasa encourages a balanced practice of challenging sun poses along with relaxing moon poses. Times and rates vary widely, so it's a good idea to call or visit the website. Drop-in rates are around $14.

The name says it all for **Kaua'i Yoga on the Beach** (808/635-6050, www.kauaiyogaonthebeach.com), where beach yoga is offered 6am-8:30am on various east-side beaches. Classes are $20 per person, and private lessons are offered for $50. Yoga mats are included. Bring a beach towel and water. Preregistration is necessary, which you can do via email or text.

Spa by the Sea at Waipouli Beach Resort (4-820 Kuhio Hwy., 808/823-1488, www.spabytheseakauai.com) has many options to indulge in. The experienced therapists offer a variety of massage techniques, from traditional Hawaiian *lomilomi* and hot stone to therapeutic deep tissue. Couples and beach massages are also available, and massages range $125-330. The spa uses the high-quality skin-care line Epicurean and offers organic skin-care treatments, including volcanic clay and custom facials ranging from $20 for an exfoliant to $1,140 for an anti-aging series.

It also offers Hawaiian sea salt body scrubs, volcanic wraps, and many more decadent choices. Ayurvedic, body, and foot treatments range $20-290.

Shopping

Lihu'e town serves the daily functional needs of island residents. Auto dealerships, a shopping mall, national brand stores, and industrial supplies are found here. You'll also find hiking and beach gear. Quaint, independent boutiques are found in Kapa'a. With shops lining the highway, you'll find clothing, arts and crafts, music, and furniture.

LIHU'E
Shopping Centers
KUKUI GROVE SHOPPING CENTER
In Lihu'e's largest shopping center, **Kukui Grove Shopping Center** (3-2600 Kaumual'i Hwy., 808/245-7784, www.kukuigrovecenter.com, Mon.-Thurs. 9:30am-7pm, Fri. 9:30am-9pm, Sat. 9:30am-7pm, Sun. 10am-6pm), you will find big-brand stores **Macy's** (808/245-7751) and **Ross** (808/245-3703), as well as **Kmart** (808/245-7742) and **Sports Authority** (808/245-2422). **Jeans Warehouse** (808/246-1086) offers low-priced clothing for trendy teens and young women. **Deja Vu Surf Hawaii** (808/245-2174) provides extensive surf gear and clothing, and for footwear stop into **Footlocker** (808/245-7595) or **Payless Shoe Source** (808/246-6860). If you're looking for electronics, there is a **Radio Shack** (808/245-7633). Several jewelry stores can be found here, along with a **GameStop** (808/245-9010) for the kids and a few salons.

KILOHANA PLANTATION
The historic plantation estate (3-2087 Kaumuali'i Hwy., 808/245-5608, www.kilohanakauai.com, 10:30am-9:30pm Mon.-Sat., 10:30am-3pm Sun.) has a selection of shops with art, knickknacks, handmade items, clothing, and other island-style products. The shops can be found on both levels of the house and include **Grande's Gems and Gallery,** offering jewelry with Tahitian black pearls, opals, tanzanite, and other unique items. At **Sea Reflections** you can find unique objects from the sea as well as Hawaiian shells. The **Artisans Room** on the lower level of the house is decorated with work from local artists. Originals, prints, and sculptures can all be found here. A fun shop is **The Country Store,** where distinctive gifts, collectibles, and local crafts like quilts and things made with local woods are found. A popular shop is **Clayworks at Kilohana,** a working ceramics gallery. Browse work by local artists or take a workshop and clay-making class yourself. **The Hawaiian Collection Room** has an array of intriguing island finds, like Ni'ihau shell lei, Hawaiian collectibles, and local jewelry and gifts.

WALMART
Walmart (3-3300 Kuhio Hwy., 808/246-1599, 6am-midnight daily) offers all the usual things but with an island twist. This is an affordable place for basic snorkeling, fishing, beach, and camping gear. There is a Hawai'i souvenir section with lei, chocolate-covered macadamia nuts, postcards, and koa wood bowls. Adult, baby, and children's clothing and accessories often have a Hawaiian theme and style. This store does not give out plastic bags, so bring your own or carry your items out.

COSTCO
For members, **Costco** (4300 Nuhou St., 808/241-4000, 10am-8:30pm Mon.-Fri.,

9:30am-6pm Sat., 10am-6pm Sun.) is a good place to stock up on food if you're going on a camping trip or staying in a vacation rental with your own kitchen. The card also enables you to fill up with some of the lowest-priced gas around. They usually have a basic stock of camping and beach gear too.

KAPA'A AND WAILUA

Galleries

Aloha Images (4504 Kukui St., 808/631-8026, www.alohaimages.com, 10am-6pm daily) prides itself on being a "candy store for art lovers" for 20 years. It's a good slogan as the shop is loaded with affordable local art. Hundreds of original works line the walls, along with giclees, prints, and other things for the home. Featured artists paint in the gallery daily.

Inside **Kela's Glass Gallery** (4-1354 Kuhio Hwy., 808/822-4527 or 888/255-3527, www.glass-art.com, 10am-7pm Mon.-Sat., 11:30am-4:30pm Sun.) is a dreamy, glistening underwater world of sculpted glass. With over 150 glass artists' work on display, Kaua'i's natural beauty is represented in jewelry to wear and decorative pieces. The staff is friendly and happy to help you find that perfect gift.

Earth and Sea Gallery (4504 Kukui

St., Ste. 3, 808/821-2831, 9:30am-9pm daily) is stocked with locally made products from over 30 artists. The boutique has something to offer for everyone, with shell jewelry, children's clothing and toys, artwork, bath and body products, and more. The staff is always friendly and outgoing, and the products are unique.

Clothing and Accessories

At **Island Hemp and Cotton** (4-1373 Kuhio Hwy., 808/821-0225, www.islandhemp.com, 9:30am-6:30pm Mon.-Sat., 10am-5pm Sun.) you will find a wide selection of clothing made from, you guessed it, hemp. The airy shop is in the center of downtown Kapa'a, and here you can find dresses, boxers, surf shorts, shoelaces, smoking pants, and even some really nice aloha shirts.

A lovely shopping stop is **Bamboo Works** (4-1388 Kuhio Hwy. #C-109, www.bambooworks.com, 808/821-8688, 10am-6pm Mon.-Sat., 11am-4pm Sun.), which offers women's clothing, accessories, and home decor made from bamboo with a down-to-earth elegance. The bamboo clothing is amazingly soft with a classy look. The owners also offer prefabricated buildings and other supplies made from the sustainable material.

Island Hemp and Cotton in Kapa'a

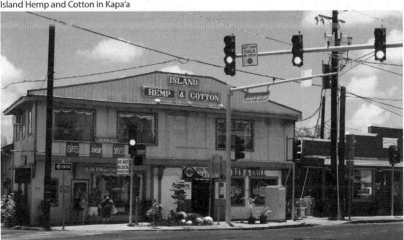

Women love the clothing at **The Root** (4-1435 Kuhio Hwy., Ste. 101, 808/823-1277, 9:30am-7pm Mon.-Sat., noon-5pm Sun.), where quality clothing is available in a combination of relaxed and classy. The skirts, dresses, and shirts are comfortable yet stylish and perfect for island wear or anywhere else.

Sweet Bikinis (4-871 Kuhio Hwy. #B, 808/821-0780, sweetbikinikauai.com, 10am-6pm daily) offers a selection of swimwear in a seemingly infinite array of colors and styles. Separates, tankinis, Brazilian-cut bottoms, and accessories like beach wraps and jewelry can also be found. They also have activewear swim attire. The staff is knowledgeable about which fabric holds up well for surfing and about sizing.

With all the hikes and beaches on the island, a stop at **Work It Out, Kaua'i's Active Clothing Store** (4-1312 Kuhio Hwy., 808/822-2292, 10am-6pm Mon.-Sat.) is necessary. The store is loaded with stylish apparel for hiking, biking, jogging, yoga, martial arts, and paddling. A running and walking group meets at the shop on Wednesdays at 6pm and runs the Ke Ala Hele Makalae bike path, a three- to seven-mile jaunt, before returning to the shop for refreshments. The staff is always happy to share input on Kaua'i activities.

Shopping Centers

Located on the ocean side of the highway, **Coconut Marketplace** (4-484 Kuhio Hwy., www.coconutmarketplace.com, 9am-9pm Mon.-Sat., 10am-6pm Sun.) is home to many shops and eateries. From high-end and locally made souvenirs to classy resort wear and amazing jewelry, you'll find it all here. Apparel can be found at **Crazy Shirts** (808/822-0100), which has an abundance of souvenir clothing; **By the Sea** (808/821-1979), which offers jewelry and resort clothing; and **Nakoa Surf Co** (808/822-6955), which has loads of surf-related stuff. Other highlights include **Island Rush/Mystical Dreams** (808/821-1054), offering fine gifts, souvenirs, clothing, and more; as well as **Elephant Walk Gift Gallery & Boutique** (808/822-2651), where you will find

unique art, home decor, jewelry, accessories, and clothing. The **Coconut Marketplace Farmers Open Market** takes place 9am-noon every Tuesday and is worth a look, with locally made gifts and locally grown food.

Surf Shops

Deja Vu Surf outlet (4-1419 Kuhio Hwy., 808/822-4401, www.dejavusurf.com, 9:30am-6pm daily) in Kapa'a has an extensive selection of surf gear: clothing, swimwear, boards for rent and sale, and everything else for catching waves or relaxing on the beach.

The locally owned and operated **Tamba Surf** (4-1543 Kuhio Hwy., 808/823-6942, www.tambasurfcompany.com) is a popular shop and brand with locals. They carry their own brand of clothing, as well as name-brand clothing, accessories, gear, and boards. Boards for rent and sale are also offered.

Gifts and Souvenirs

Densely stocked with souvenirs and beach gear, the **ABC Store** (4-831 Kuhio Hwy., 808/822-2115, www.abcstores.com, 8am-9:30pm daily) is a bit of a tourist trap, but it does have some last-minute necessities like sunscreen or bottled water. The store is loaded with all kinds of not-one-of-a-kind souvenirs, shirts, snacks, and general store basics. Drinks and alcoholic beverages are also for sale, along with underwater cameras, limited snorkel and beach accessories, and beach supplies.

Shell lovers must make a stop at the **Shell Factory** (4-901 Kuhio Hwy., 808/822-2354, www.shellskauai.com, 9am-5pm Mon.-Sat., 10am-5pm Sun.). The shop is adorned with beautiful tropical shells, although most are not from Hawai'i. Still, they are perfect, fully intact, and exhibit some of nature's most intricate work.

Jewelry

Imperial Jewelers (4-831 Kuhio Hwy., 808/822-0094, 10am-6pm Mon.-Sat.) sells Hawaiian handcrafted heirloom jewelry. Pendants, bracelets, rings, and earrings are available in the local style of carved 14-karat gold with a name in black if you like. The carvings come in an array of Hawaiian designs like whales, sea turtles, flowers, and more. A highlight is the plumeria lei flowers collection, where elegant small plumerias are connected in a permanent lei.

Jim Saylor Jewelers (4-1318 Kuhio Hwy., 808/822-3591, 9:30am-5:30pm Mon.-Sat.) sells unique pieces. The designer uses precious stones, black pearls, and diamonds in his unique settings and styles. He's been designing on Kaua'i for over two decades.

A very fun stop is **Kauai Crafters** (4-1176 Kuhio Hwy., 808/346-7700, www.kauaicrafters.com, 9am-6pm daily). The small shop is jam-packed full of local crafts with a strong shell theme. They sell *kahelelani* jewelry, koa and mammoth ivory fishhook necklaces, coconut faces, and a lot more.

Outdoor Markets

The **Kaua'i Products Fair** (4-1613 Kuhio Hwy., 808/246-0988, www.thekauaiproductsfair.com, 9am-5pm daily) is an outdoor market with a wide variety of souvenirs, clothing, and jewelry. Most items have an island theme and style, although many of the products aren't from Hawai'i. It's a great souvenir stop. Vegetables and fruits are also available.

A "no import" market, **Kealia Kountry Market** (4100-4199 Kealia Rd., 808/635-5091, 11am-4pm Sun.) brings local vendors together offering locally grown and made products. There is usually live music, and local crafts, produce, and ready-to-eat food are available. Locals come to shop and socialize.

On the way north out of Kapa'a is the **Anahola Marketplace** (4523 Ioane Rd., 9am-5pm Wed.-Sun.), another place for residents to sell fruit and veggies, locally made crafts, and other things. It's worth a stop to or from the north shore.

Supermarkets and Drugstores

For basic drugstore needs, stop at **Longs Drugs** (4-831 Kuhio Hwy. #500, 808/822-4915, www.cvs.com, 7am-9pm Mon.-Sat., 8am-8pm Sun.). The store has a pharmacy, body products, alcoholic beverages, limited stationery supplies, souvenirs, and limited camping gear, baby products, and housewares. It also has an electronics area to save you a trip to Lihu'e for a digital camera emergency.

In the same parking lot is **Safeway** (808/822-2464, 24 hours daily), with the usual supermarket products.

Health-Food Stores

In Kapa'a, **Hoku Natural Foods** (4585 Lehua St., 808/821-1500, www.hokufoods.com, 10am-6pm daily) has natural products and food. Natural and organic baby and body products, household cleaners, and food fill the spacious store. They also sell BPA-free water containers and other products.

Papaya's (4-831 Kuhio Hwy., 808/823-0190, www.papayasnaturalfoods.com, 8am-8pm Mon.-Sat., 10am-5pm Sun.) has long been the east side's staple health-food store (and where the hippies gather). They have a full selection of vitamins, body products, cleaning supplies, books, food, and more. If you're going to be around for a while, ask for their deli and frequent shopper card.

Wine and Spirits

The small **Kapa'a Liquor and Wine** (4-1397 Kuhio Hwy., 808/822-4151, 8am-5pm daily) has a good selection of beer in the old fridge behind the counter, but you have to read the handwritten lists on the front of the fridge and ask the worker to get it for you. Liquor lines the walls, and although they don't have an infinite stock, they'll probably have what you want.

Entertainment

LIHU'E

Cinema

Kukui Grove Cinema (4368 Kukui Grove St., 808/245-5055, www.kukuigrovecinema. com, $10) is the island's movie theater. It's in the Kukui Grove Shopping Center, and four screens show the latest blockbuster hits. Matinees are only $6.

Polynesian Dance, *Lu'au,* and Theater

Luau Kalamaku takes place at Kilohana Plantation (3-2087 Kaumuali'i Hwy., 808/245-5608, www.kilohanakauai.com) and entertains with hula, poi, food, music, and a full-scale theater experience. Luau Kalamaku is Kaua'i's only theatrical *lu'au.* Hula dancers, fire poi ball twirlers, traditional Polynesian fire knife dancers, and a vivid story line all combine for an exciting evening and view of Hawaiian culture. Your main course is cooked in the plantation's *imu,* an underground oven, and is unearthed while you are there. Then it's time for live Tahitian music, Hawaiian games, and hula dancing. The evening begins outside in the estate's garden for fun and games before entering the theater. A storyteller tells of the settling of the island by voyagers from Tahiti.

WAILUA

Lu'au and Theater

A riverside *lu'au* takes place at **Smith's Tropical Paradise** (5971 Kuhio Hwy., 808/821-6895, www.smithskauai.com, 5pm Mon.-Fri. Jun.-Aug., 5pm Mon. and Wed.-Fri. Feb.-May and Sept.-Oct., 4:45pm Mon., Wed., and Fri. Nov.-Jan., $88 adults, $30 children 7-13, $19 children 3-6). The garden *lu'au* dinner includes *kalua* pig cooked in an *imu,* teriyaki beef, mahimahi, chicken adobo, poi, and more. Hula is presented later on, and guests may go on stage to try out some moves. Tahitian drum dances and a Samoan fire knife dance are also treats.

Guests are welcomed with an *imu* ceremony, cocktails, and music, followed by the *lu'au* feast and ending with the rhythm of an aloha show. Those who choose to eat dinner elsewhere can purchase show-only tickets.

In the 1950s, the film *South Pacific* was filmed on Kaua'i, and paying homage to it is **South Pacific Dinner and Theater** (4331 Kaua'i Beach Dr. at the Kaua'i Beach Resort, 808/346-6500, www.southpacifickauai.com, 5:30pm Wed., $85 adults, $30 children 6-12, under 5 free, premier seating $105). Based on the original Broadway show, the production has been brought to Kaua'i by the Hawaii Association of Performing Arts and producer Alain Dussaud. The show tells the love story set on the island during World War II.

An all-you-can-eat buffet is included with the show with salad, pasta salad, teriyaki chicken, vegetables, desserts, coffee, and more. Tickets include the show, a buffet dinner, gratuity, and parking. A no-host cash bar is offered.

Food

Kaua'i's east side is home to many great restaurants and eateries. This is where you'll find the majority of the island's high-end and elegant restaurants, but there's also a great selection of hole-in-the-wall local eateries.

LIHU'E
American

Eat, drink, and be merry at the **Nawiliwili Tavern** (3488 Paena Loop, 808/245-1781, www.nawiliwilitavern.com, 2pm-1am daily, $5-10). The tavern is a very casual place to throw back a few drinks, watch some sports, and grab wireless Internet at Nawiliwili Bay.

A Lihu'e staple is ★ **JJ's Broiler** (3416 Rice St., 808/246-4422, www.jjsbroiler.com, 11am-11pm daily, $11-39) on Kalapaki Bay. It has a Chart House feel with sailboats hanging from the ceiling, and is a classic Lihu'e stop. Meats and local fish are offered on their extensive menu. The bi-level restaurant overlooks Kalapaki Bay, which enhances the experience. The bottom level is more casual, offering a full bar and a veranda. Upstairs is more formal and romantic. Their claim to fame is the Slavonic Steak, a thin, broiled tenderloin dipped in butter, wine, and garlic sauce. The portions are large, the food is good, and it rarely disappoints.

The tried-and-true **Kalapaki Beach Hut** (3474 Rice St., 808/246-6330, www.kalapakibeachhut.com, 7am-8pm daily, $6-10) serves up breakfast and lunch with burgers that have proved to be a local favorite and never a letdown. The restaurant offers views of the harbor, and for breakfast has the standard fare plus local dishes like *loco moco*. Lunch includes fish and chips and sandwiches along with buffalo, turkey, fish, veggie, and beef burgers. Also on the premises is **Kalapaki Shave Ice** (11am-6pm daily) serving shave ice, smoothies, and ice cream; and **Kalapaki Coconuts** (7am-8pm daily), serving fresh coconut water straight from the shell.

Sports fans should check out **Kalapaki Joe's** (3501 Rice St., 808/245-6266, www.kalapakijoes.com, 11am-10pm daily, opening at 7am Sat.-Sun. during football season). The sports bar's happy hour is 3pm-6pm daily, and they serve drinks and bar food.

Duke's Kauai at Kalapaki Beach

The Mighty Coconut

While on the Coconut Coast, make sure to try a fresh coconut. Available at several fruit stands in Kapa'a, the coconut water is a refreshing and very healthy drink. Although the name calls it a nut, it is a seed and fruit. Packed with electrolytes, coconut water is also full of fiber, protein, antioxidants, vitamins, and minerals. It's become a hot packaged commodity in recent years and now is stocked on supermarket shelves, but for many islanders there is nothing more satisfying and refreshing than a coconut straight from the tree. When you sample coconut water, make sure to ask the supplier if you can try the coconut meat. Lining the inside of the coconut, the fleshy white meat is also a tasty treat with a nutty flavor. The coconut meat in a young, green coconut is generally softer and more gelatinous than in an older one, which has thicker and firmer meat. Don't miss out on this Coconut Coast treat.

Hawai'i Regional

★ **Gaylord's** (3-2087 Kaumual'i Hwy., 808/245-9593, www.gaylordskauai.com, 11am-2:30pm and 5:30pm-9:30pm Mon.-Sat., 9am-2:30pm Sun. for brunch, $27-36) is a farm-to-table restaurant at the Kilohana Plantation. Using local ingredients, the classy restaurant features American comfort food and Asian-fusion cuisine options. They use produce grown in the fields at Kilohana, and their meat and fish come from Kaua'i ranchers and fishers. Some of the main dishes include potato-crusted mahimahi, sesame seed-seared ahi tuna, chipotle barbecued pork chop, and grilled rib eye steak. Lunch mains include salads, sandwiches, fish and chips, steak frites, and vegetarian quiches ranging $9-19, and they have a Sunday brunch buffet for $30 per person and $15 for children 5-12, including a Bloody Mary bar starting at 9am.

A classic eatery on Kaua'i, ★ **Duke's Kauai** (3610 Rice St., 808/246-9599, www.dukeskauai.com, 11am-11pm, $19-36) is a must-stop on the to-eat-at list in Hawai'i. Named after the legendary Hawaiian surfer Duke Kahanamoku, the restaurant is split into two levels, where railing-side seats with unobstructed ocean views are the best. The downstairs Barefoot Bar is steps from the sand and serves up sandwiches, burgers, fish tacos, Hawaiian plates, and more for $11-20. The dining room serves dinner daily and offers fresh fish and seafood, steaks and prime rib, and a salad bar. They have live music several nights a week.

On Kalapaki Beach is **Kukui's** (Kaua'i Marriott Resort, 808/246-5166, www.marriott.com, 7am-10:30am and 5pm-10pm Mon.-Sat., 7am-noon and 5pm-10pm Sun., $20-43), offering Pacific Rim food for breakfast and dinner. The poolside seating adds to the romantic and elegant experience. Sunday brunch is also offered. Reservations are recommended for dinner.

Italian

The open air and views over Kalapaki Bay from ★ **Cafe Portofino** (3481 Ho'olaule'a Way, 808/245-2121, www.cafeportofino.com, 5pm-9:30pm daily, $19-45) offer one of the most ideal backdrops, especially to enjoy excellent Italian food. The food is authentic and the wine selection is robust for Kaua'i standards. The owner is Italian, which reflects in the quality of the food. Seafood, pasta, veal, filet mignon, and other meat dishes are available, along with enough meat-free options for vegetarians. Homemade gelato and fruit sorbets are also served. This is romantic fine dining.

A local favorite, **Kaua'i Pasta** (4-939B Kuhio Hwy., 808/822-7447, www.kauaipasta.com, 11am-9pm daily, $12-33) is a family-owned, chef-driven Italian restaurant focusing on comfort food and upscale specials. Tasty appetizers, unique salads, panini, and an array of main dishes are combined with a few Pacific-inspired appetizers on the lounge menu. They also offer a gluten-free menu. There are locations in Lihu'e and Kapa'a. The atmosphere is modern, yet warm. The lounge is open till midnight Monday-Saturday and till 10pm on Sunday.

Mexican

Another stop in Nawiliwili is **Mariachi's** (3501 Rice St., 808/246-1570, 8am-10pm daily, $11-20), where basic Mexican food is served up in this Harbor Mall eatery. The menu is quite extensive and offers many common Mexican dishes. This is a decent stop while exploring Nawiliwili Bay if you're in the mood for Mexican food.

Thai and Filipino

At Kalapaki Bay is **Gingbua Thai Restaurant** (3501 Rice St., 808/245-9350, 11am-3pm and 4pm-9pm Mon.-Sat., dinner only Sun., $10-16). The restaurant serves up standard Thai cuisine that can be either really good or just average. Service is usually good but can be slow.

For home-style Filipino cooking, try **Mama Lucy's Kitchen** (4495 Puhi Rd., 808/245-4935, 6am-6pm Mon.-Fri., 6am-4pm Sat., $6-10), where you can get authentic Filipino food served with a smile. The desserts and treats are good too.

WAILUA AND KAPA'A
American

The quaint and simple ★ **Kountry Kitchen** (1485 Kuhio Hwy., 808/822-3511, 6am-1:30pm daily, $6-14) is a perfect place to grab a classic breakfast of eggs, omelets, pancakes, French toast, coffee, and more. The place is a favorite with locals and visitors, and you may have to wait a few minutes on a weekend morning. True to its name, a country theme sets a homey feeling for the decor. Portions are large and service is friendly.

At **Olympic Cafe** (1354 Kuhio Hwy., 808/822-5825, 6am-9pm daily, $6-14), the open-air side of the café overlooks the sidewalk in downtown Kapa'a. Usual breakfast fare like eggs and pancakes are offered for breakfast. Lunch is wraps, burgers, salads, and sandwiches. Dinner offerings include pasta, fish, burgers, Mexican dishes, steaks, and more. The restaurant is known for its large portions. You won't leave here hungry.

Chicken in a Barrel (4-1586 Kuhio Hwy., 808/823-0780, 11am-8pm daily, www.chickeninabarrel.com, $5-15) is famous for its smoked foods and classic barbecue. The

Olympic Cafe

Local Fish

Fresh fish from the waters of Kaua'i is a treat for many. Called *i'a* in Hawaiian, fish is a local staple and fishing is a favorite pastime for islanders. Because many of Hawai'i's fish are also found elsewhere, they have names that will be familiar to you but are usually referred to by their Hawaiian name on a menu. Here's a quick breakdown of local and common names.

- **Mahimahi** is a favorite for fish lovers. Often found in burgers or as an entrée, mahimahi is also known as "dolphin fish." The meat is generally white, flaky, and moist and should not be overdone. The fish is identifiable by its broad head.

- A real island favorite is **ono,** otherwise known as wahoo or king mackerel. A deep-sea fish, the ono is known as one of the all-time best fish to eat, which makes sense considering that *ono* is also a Hawaiian term for delicious.

- The **ulua** is also known as a jack crevalle. Many local fishers test themselves with the ability to catch a large ulua, which can reach over 100 pounds in weight. You may see stickers of the fish on trucks, or even hear the term "ulua hunter." The ulua is also a popular and tasty eating fish.

- The oh-so-popular **ahi** is also called yellowfin tuna. The deep pink meat is another favorite eating fish for many and is great served raw as *poke* (fish salad) or sashimi, or seared.

- The silver *moi* is an especially savored fish, as it can only legally be caught in certain times of the year. Meaning "king" in Hawaiian, *moi* was traditionally reserved for royalty. You probably won't see it in restaurants often, but it is considered an exquisite eating fish by locals.

chicken is known to be tender and moist. Indoor and outdoor seating are available, and the atmosphere is very casual. Try the sampler or the chicken burrito.

Coffee and Bakeries

Situated next to the Moikeha canal in a historic two-story building, **Art Café Hemingway** (4-1495 Kuhio Hwy., 808/822-2250, www.artcafehemingway.com, 8am-2pm and 6pm-9pm Wed.-Sun., $6-22) is a sophisticated and artsy café owned by a friendly German couple. Find your own nook upstairs, downstairs, or on the porch. Table and couch seating is available. The café serves gourmet coffee with a true European feel, and is a testament to the eclectic nature of Kapa'a town.

Sweet describes **Sweet Marie's Hawaii Bakery** (4-788 Kuhio Hwy., 808/823-0227, www.sweetmarieskauai.com, 7am-2pm Tues.-Sat., $1-6), a quaint and cute bakery. The small bakery is in with today's health trends of serving up gluten-free baked goods, desserts, and wedding cakes, as well as gluten-free catering. Freshly baked pastries,

muffins, and cookies are a delightful treat. Try the amazing *liliko'i* (passion fruit) burst. You can even take home some gluten-free muffin mixes and pizza dough. Great for breakfast or dessert.

Java Kai (4-1384 Kuhio Hwy., 808/823-6887, www.javakaihawaii.com, 6am-7pm daily, $2-11) serves locally roasted coffee along with other fair trade varieties. Muffins, scones, croissants, and cookies are baked on-site. Egg sandwiches, bagels, and a decadent waffle pair well with fresh juices and smoothies on the menu. Order at the counter, or order online with pickup ready in 30 minutes.

Hawai'i Regional

Wahooo Seafood Grill & Bar (4-733 Kuhio Hwy., 808/822-7833, www.wahooogrill.com, 11am-2pm and 4pm-9:30pm Wed.-Mon., $13-43) serves a bounty of seafood dishes with a few steak options. Handmade sauces and locally sourced ingredients complement the Pacific-inspired seafood cuisine. Nestled next to a coconut grove, you can enjoy sunset on the lanai with a special sunset menu. Their lounge features a happy hour 4pm-closing and a burger and flatbread menu. There is also nightly entertainment 7pm-9pm.

Escape reality at ★ **Oasis** (4-820 Kuhio Hwy., in Waipouli Beach Resort, 808/822-9332, www.oasiskauai.com, 11:30am-3pm and 4pm-9pm daily, $16-35), which offers oceanfront dining in an environment that is truly an oasis from the outside world. Service is always on point, and the eatery focuses on local cuisine, using 90 percent ingredients from Kaua'i, from veggies to fish. It's the perfect location for a romantic dinner or a celebratory meal. The eatery opens to a white-sand beach. Their main dishes are available in half and full portions. They are open for lunch and dinner with happy hour 4pm-6pm daily. Sunday brunch is 10am-2pm.

Lemongrass Grill (4-871 Kuhio Hwy., 808/822-2888, http://lemongrasshawaii.com, 4pm-9pm daily, $19-27) offers a beautiful atmosphere of island style combined with Asian decor. The menu offers seafood, steak, a full bar, and Thai and American dishes. It's better to sit indoors because the outdoor seating is roadside.

★ **Caffe Coco** (4-369 Kuhio Hwy., 808/822-7990, www.caffecocokauai.com, 5pm-9pm daily, $15-30) is a garden bistro emanating a relaxed island ambience and offering made-to-order gourmet food with a Pacific theme. They specialize in vegan, vegetarian, and gluten-free fare. Enjoy outdoor seating in the courtyard surrounded by numerous fruit trees, tiki torches, delicate lighting, and umbrellas. Indoor seating is offered, and there is also an indoor art gallery. Order at the counter, and don't forget to use the house's "jungle juice" if the mosquitos get bothersome. A full espresso bar and desserts are also available.

Named after the plant that decorates the island, the **Naupaka Terrace** (4331 Kaua'i Beach Dr., 808/245-1955, 6:30am-10:30am and 6pm-9pm daily, $25-40), located in the Aqua Kauai Beach Resort, offers breakfast and dinner overlooking Kaua'i's shore. The open-air restaurant is in a plantation-style building that offers steak and seafood dishes, an abundant salad bar, and vegetarian entrées. The tranquil and elegant environment offers views of waterfalls, ponds, and the ocean. A prime rib and seafood buffet is offered every Friday and Saturday night. Breakfast starts at $9.

Health Food

Rainbow Living Foods (4-1384 Kuhio Hwy., 808/821-9759, www.rainbowlivingfoods.com, 10am-5pm Mon.-Fri., 10am-3pm Sat., $6-14) is an organic, raw, and vegan café offering healthy and gourmet meals like Russian caviar, kale salad, and delicious juices and desserts. Check the daily specials and enjoy the healthy meals.

The Coconut Cup Juice Bar & Cafe (4-1516 Kuhio Hwy., 808/823-8630, www.coconutcupjuicebar.com, 8am-5pm daily, $6-10) is a great stop for a healthy meal on your way to the beach. They serve up sandwiches, bagels, wraps, acai bowls, smoothies, and more. A real treat here is their natural shave ice. Enjoy your meal on the go or at the picnic tables.

A true hole in the wall, ★ **Mermaids Cafe** (1384 Kuhio Hwy., 808/821-2026, www.mermaidskauai.com, 9am-9pm daily, $9-12) is nestled between shops in downtown Kapa'a. The food is delicious, and definitely on the healthy side, although not all vegetarian. The order-at-the-window café serves wraps, burritos, sandwiches, and stir-fry, all with unique twists and most with tofu, chicken, and fresh fish options. They serve breakfast, lunch, and dinner. Check for daily specials. Try the ahi nori wrap and the spearmint and lemongrass iced tea and hibiscus lemonade. There's limited sidewalk seating and a small bar tucked around the side.

Papaya's (4-831 Kuhio Hwy., 808/823-0190, www.papayasnaturalfoods.com, 8am-8pm Mon.-Sat., 10am-5pm Sun.) has an all-day hot bar and salad bar for $7.99 a pound; a deli that makes sandwiches, smoothies, and juices to order; and pre-made foods in the refrigerator. The food is good, organic, and vegetarian, but can feel repetitive if you eat there a lot. The food is served as takeout, but there are seats outside to eat at.

Kauai Juice Company (4-1384 Kuhio Hwy., 808/634-0886, kauaijuiceco.com, 8am-5pm Mon.-Sat., $4-11) offers cold-pressed, local, organic fresh juices. They also have elixirs, bottled kombucha, ili scrub, and hot sauces on the menu. You'll find the small store behind Mermaids Cafe and Java Kai.

Japanese

For spectacular food, stop by ★ **Kintaro** (4-370 Kuhio Hwy., 808/822-3341, 5:30pm-9:30pm Mon.-Sat., $11-21), which has delicious sushi, a full bar, and teppanyaki seating. The fish is local and always fresh, the service is outstanding, and the atmosphere is sophisticated enough to get dressed for an evening. Make reservations for the teppanyaki. Lobster, filet mignon, and other seafood are available for those not in the mood for Japanese food.

In Kapa'a is **House of Noodles** (4-1330 Kuhio Hwy., 808/822-2708, 10am-9pm daily, $7-15). The menu is quite extensive with a lot more than noodles, such as sandwiches, smoothies, and shave ice. The atmosphere is very simple.

Mexican

Monico's Taqueria (4-356 Kuhio Hwy., 808/822-4300, monicostaqueria.com, 11am-3pm and 5pm-9pm Tues.-Sun., $8-17) serves up authentic Mexican food with a local twist. The restaurant is clean and the food is consistent. They also serve meals to go. Try the fish tacos.

Verde (4-1105 Kuhio Hwy., 808/821-1400, www.verdehawaii.com, 11am-9pm daily, $10-17) is located in the Kapa'a Shopping Center. The restaurant is modern and fresh with an urban decor. They proudly source produce, meat, and fish locally and have a bold menu with authentic dishes as well as vegetarian and gluten-free options. For handcrafted cocktails, check out the margarita bar.

Mermaids Cafe

Pizza

Brick Oven (4-4361 Kuhio Hwy., 808/823-8561, http://brickovenpizzahi.com, 11am-9pm daily, $8-33) in Wailua has been a local favorite since 1977. It's very child friendly with the option for the kiddos to have a free ball of dough to play with. Wheat or white crust is offered, as well as the option to have garlic butter brushed on the dough. Thursday night is their signature all-you-can-eat buffet. It's a good place for a group or family dinner or a very casual date.

Ice Cream

Tropical and traditional ice creams and sorbets at **Lappert's** (484 Kuhio Hwy., 808/822-0744, www.lappertshawaii.com, 10am-9pm daily, $4 for a single scoop) are the perfect cool accent to a warm Hawaiian day or night. Originating on Kaua'i, the shop now has outlets statewide. The ice cream contains about 16 percent butterfat in the regular flavors and around 8 percent in the fruit flavors, making for some pretty creamy ice cream. There's an array of delicious flavors, so sample a few before making your decision.

Another option for ice cream is **Cold Stone Creamery** (4-831 Kuhio Hwy.,

808/823-9099, 11am-9:30pm Sun.-Thurs., 11am-10pm Fri.-Sat.). They serve up heaping piles of really good ice cream that they mix with a selection of candies, cookies, and other treats.

Information and Services

VISITORS CENTER

Kaua'i Visitors Bureau (4334 Rice St. #101, 808/245-3971, www.kauai-hawaii.com) offers a wealth of information on all things related to visiting Kaua'i. The information hotline is 800/262-1400 and offers live and up-to-date information. The hotline is available to all 50 states and Canada 6am-6pm Monday-Friday and 6am-2pm on weekends. The KVB can direct visitors to parks and beaches, sites and attractions, local culture, island events, activities and recreation, and all things Kaua'i-made.

POST OFFICES

There are several federal post offices on the east side. U.S. Postal Service post offices can be found in Lihu'e (4441 Rice St., 800/275-8777, 8am-4pm Mon.-Fri., 9am-1pm Sat.), near Wailua (3-4251 Kuhio Hwy., 808/275-8777, 10am-noon Mon. Fri.), and in Kapa'a (4-1101 Kuhio Hwy., 800/275-8777, 9am-4pm Mon.-Fri., 9am-1pm Sat.). The Lihu'e and Kapa'a locations both provide passport application services as well as full shipping and packing services.

INTERNET ACCESS

The **Lihu'e Public Library** (4344 Hardy St., 808/241-3222, 11am-7pm Mon. and Wed., 9am-4:30pm Tues., Thurs., and Fri.) and the **Kapa'a Public Library** (1464 Kuhio Hwy., 808/821-4422, 9am-5pm Mon., Wed., Thurs., and Fri., noon-8pm Tues.) offer Internet access. Visitors can get a temporary card for $5. You must use their computers.

Small Town Coffee (4-1495 Kuhio Hwy., 808/821-1604) in Kapa'a provides Internet access for the public on their desktop or via your laptop with their free wireless Internet. **Akamai Computers** (4-1286 Kuhio Hwy., 808/823-0047) provides Internet access and computer repair.

EMERGENCY SERVICES

Wilcox Memorial Hospital (3-3420 Kuhio Hwy., 808/245-1100) is central in Lihu'e and has a 24-hour emergency room (808/245-1010). The **Kaua'i Medical Clinic Urgent Care** (3-3420B Kuhio Hwy., 808/245-1532, 8am-5pm daily, with 8am-2pm walk-ins and 2pm-4pm appointments by availability daily) is located right by the hospital in Lihu'e.

BANKS

Lihu'e
First Hawaiian Bank (4423 Rice St., 808/245-4024, 8:30am-4pm Mon.-Thurs., 8:30am-6pm Fri.) provides full teller services and a 24-hour ATM. **American Savings Bank** (4318 Rice St., 808/245-3388, 8am-5pm Mon.-Thurs., 8am-6pm Fri.) has teller services and a 24-hour ATM.

Kapa'a
First Hawaiian Bank (4-1366 Kuhio Hwy., 808/822-4966, 8:30am-4pm Mon.-Thurs., 8:30am-6pm Fri.) provides full teller services and a 24-hour ATM. **American Savings Bank** (4-771 Kuhio Hwy., 808/822-0529, 9am-7pm Mon.-Fri., 10am-3pm Sat.-Sun.) has teller services and a 24-hour ATM.

Getting There and Around

CAR

The most convenient way to get to and around the east side is by car. Route 56 heads west straight out of Lihu'e and runs all the way to the end of the road, turning into Route 560 by Hanalei. Rental cars are the best bet here and are available at the airport. Gas prices go up the farther north you go, so it's a good idea to fill up in Lihu'e.

BUS

The **Kaua'i Bus** (808/241-6410, www.kauai.gov/transportation, 5:27am-10:40pm Mon.-Fri., 6:21am-5:50pm Sat.-Sun. and holidays) runs island-wide with numerous stops from Lihu'e to Anahola. The bus is a green, convenient, and affordable way to get around, and even goes to the airport. Fares are $1 for children and seniors, and $2 for the general public. Monthly passes are also available. Bus schedules for the east side are available on the website.

TAXI AND LIMOUSINE

Pono Taxi (808/635-3478, www.ponotaxi.com) in Lihu'e offers taxi, airport shuttle, and tour services island-wide. They provide spacious and clean minivans. **Island Taxi** (808/639-7829) is based out of Lihu'e and provides airport rides as well as rides island-wide. Service is prompt and friendly. Lihu'e's **Ace Kaua'i Taxi Services** (808/639-4310) will take you wherever you need to go. Hawai'i taxi rates are $3 per mile and $0.40 per minute. Prices are per minivan, not per person.

SCOOTERS

Hop onto a moped to zip around the east side and save on gas at **Kauai Car & Scooter Rental** (3148 Oihana St., 808/245-7177, kauaiscooter.com). They are located about a mile from the airport. Call for prices and reservations. **Kauai Mopeds** (3148 Oihana St., 808/652-7407, www.kauai-mopeds.com) rents scooters and mopeds. Mopeds are smaller and designed for a single rider at least 18 years old with a valid driver's license. Daily rates are $65 and decrease the more days you rent the vehicle. Scooters are larger and can seat two people. The driver must be at least 21 years old and have a motorcycle license. The discount scooter starts at $75 per day and the two-seater at $110 per day; prices decrease for every consecutive day. Reserve by phone or online. They will deliver the vehicle to your accommodation.

Princeville and the North Shore

Look for ★ to find recommended
sights, activities, dining, and lodging.

Highlights

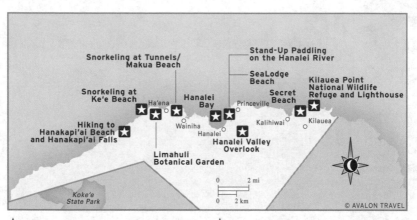

★ **Kilauea Point National Wildlife Refuge and Lighthouse:** Enjoy great views of the coastline, then walk through the lighthouse and learn about the seabird sanctuary (page 71).

★ **Hanalei Valley Overlook:** This overlook provides views of a wildlife preserve and acres of the Hawaiian staple taro and other farmlands (page 73).

★ **Limahuli Botanical Garden:** Take a botanical stroll through history along terraced taro fields used by ancient Hawaiians (page 76).

★ **Secret Beach:** Located at the end of a short downhill hike, Secret Beach offers a refreshing waterfall and fine white sand. Just beyond are crystal clear tide pools and a lovely ocean-side waterfall (page 78).

★ **SeaLodge Beach:** This beautiful and secluded white-sand beach is perfect for sunbathing, swimming, and snorkeling. Picturesque views abound from the trail (page 80).

★ **Hanalei Bay:** Nearly two miles of fine white sand make up this heavenly crescent moon-shaped beach. Enjoy several surf breaks, swimming, and full amenities (page 82).

★ **Snorkeling at Tunnels/Makua Beach:** One of the best snorkeling sites on the island features unique reef formations just off the beach (page 87).

★ **Snorkeling at Ke'e Beach:** Marking the beginning of the Na Pali Coast, Ke'e's protected cove creates a natural swimming pool and spectacular snorkeling (page 87).

★ **Stand-Up Paddling on the Hanalei River:** Rent a board in Hanalei and paddle the calm, long, and winding river that empties into Hanalei Bay (page 91).

★ **Hiking to Hanakapi'ai Beach and Hanakapi'ai Falls:** Enjoy splendid views along the famous Kalalau Trail on the Na Pali Coast. The finale is a majestic waterfall and its icy cold pool. This is the ideal hike for a daylong nature experience (page 97).

The north shore of Kaua'i is one of the most beautiful, intriguing, and naturally preserved locales across the island—even the entire state.

The coast unfolds to the east with undulating bays, white-sand beaches, rocky headlands, and picturesque river mouths until it slams up against the dramatic Na Pali Coast—with cliffs that rise thousands of feet from the crashing waves.

The north shore is a place of both opulence and simplicity. World-class golf courses, a luxury resort, and high-end condominiums give way to a taro fields; a quaint, historic town; and a slow, easy way of life centered around the ocean. Farms abound, seabirds nest on cliffs, and whales breech offshore as winter waves pound the reefs along the coast. All the while, Mount Wai'ale'ale, the wettest place on earth, stands watch over the region, and white ribbons of waterfalls slice through the lush green mountains.

The north shore is raw and unadulterated. It's also soft and inviting as the colors of the sky change from sunrise to sunset, the dichotomy a reflection of its native Hawaiian past, when this region was a place for both *ali'i* (royalty) and commoners.

Today, the north shore is for everyone, though visitors with an eye for nature will no doubt have a hard time leaving. Recreation is the cornerstone of life here.

In the winter, surfers flock to Hanalei Bay to catch long waves. In the summer, snorkelers and divers explore the reefs along the entire stretch of coast. Kayakers and stand-up paddlers take to the river for its calm water.

Hikers relish the challenge of walking the infamous Kalalau Trail, an 11-mile, one-way journey that offers beautiful, timeless views and tests the mind and body. Wherever you trek on the north shore, the verdant mountains frame the view.

ORIENTATION

There is no hard line dividing the east side of the island from the north, as rolling hills, pasture land, and agricultural estates provide the scenery. Heading northwest from Anahola, **Kilauea** is the first town you'll encounter on the north shore. It's home to the **Kilauea Point National Wildlife Refuge**

Previous: fresh eats in Hanalei town; Limahuli Botanical Garden. **Above:** a sunny day at the beach.

Princeville and the North Shore

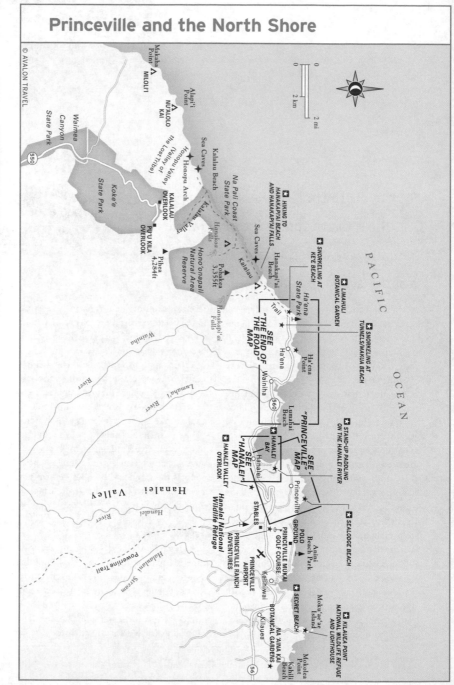

© AVALON TRAVEL

PACIFIC OCEAN

Makaha Point
MILOLI'I
Alapi'i Point
NU'ALOLO KAI
Waimea Canyon State Park
550
Honopu Valley (the Lost Tribe)
Honopu Arch
Sea Caves
Kalalau Beach
KALALAU OVERLOOK
Koke'e State Park
Kalalau Valley
PU'U KILA OVERLOOK
Pihea 4,284ft
Hono'onapali Natural Area Reserve
Na Pali Coast State Park
Hanalou Falls
Pohakea 3,355ft
Hanakapi'ai Falls
Sea Caves

🅷 HIKING TO HANAKAPI'AI BEACH AND HANAKAPI'AI FALLS
Hanakapi'ai Beach
Kalalau Trail

⭐ SNORKELING AT KE'E BEACH
Ha'ena State Park

⭐ LIMAHULI BOTANICAL GARDEN

"SEE THE END OF THE ROAD" MAP

Ha'ena
Ha'ena Point
Wainiha

⭐ SNORKELING AT TUNNELS/MAKUA BEACH

Waimha
Lumaha'i River
Lumahai Beach
560

Wainiha River

"SEE PRINCEVILLE" MAP
⭐ STAND-UP PADDLING ON THE HANALEI RIVER

HANALEI BAY
🅷 HANALEI VALLEY OVERLOOK
"SEE HANALEI" MAP
Hanalei
Princeville

⭐ SEALODGE BEACH

Hanalei Valley
Hanalei River

STABLES
Hanalei National Wildlife Refuge
PRINCEVILLE RANCH ADVENTURES
PRINCEVILLE AIRPORT
PRINCEVILLE GOLF COURSE
POLO GROUND
PRINCEVILLE MAUKA
Anini Beach Park
Kalihiwai

Powerline Trail
Halaulani Stream

56
Kilauea
NA 'AINA KAI BOTANICAL GARDENS
⭐ SECRET BEACH
Moku'ae'ae Island
⭐ KILAUEA POINT NATIONAL WILDLIFE REFUGE AND LIGHTHOUSE
Mokolea Point
Kahili Beach

0   2 mi
0   2 km

and **Lighthouse** as well as marvelous white-sand beaches, secret tide pools, and waterfalls. Nearby, **Kalihiwai** is the access point to beaches like Kalihiwai Beach and Anini Beach. A few miles north is **Princeville** on a high bluff. It's composed of 9,000 acres of planned luxury homes, condos, and a luxury hotel with a view of Hanalei Bay that can't be beat. Descending into Hanalei Valley is historic **Hanalei town,** backed by prominent green cliffs of Mount Waiʻaleʻale, lined with waterfalls. From Hanalei to the start of the **Na Pali Coast** at the end of the road, the coast is made up of some of the state's most spectacular beaches. Beginning at **Keʻe Beach,** the **Kalalau Trail,** leading for miles along the wild and gorgeous Na Pali Coast, leads to waterfalls, secluded beaches, and camping far off the beaten path.

The **Kuhio Highway** (Route 56) is the only highway in this region, so getting around is easy.

PLANNING YOUR TIME

The north shore should not be rushed, and there's no way a day trip from another side of the island will do it justice. The best way to explore this area entails finding accommodations that fit your budget and planning on at least an overnight stay. Three days is sufficient to see the sights, visit a few beaches, get in the water, and even take a hike, but the more time you can muster here, the better.

You'll find the lion's share of the region's accommodations in **Princeville;** however, the locale requires driving out of the resort area to access most of the area's attractions. Luckily, it's not a far drive in either direction to Kilauea or Hanalei. **Hanalei** is a great home base for food, shopping, and supplies. No matter if you're planning a beach day or a day hike, you'll most likely be eating at least one meal in Hanalei. It offers the user-friendliest beaches, and the business district is centrally located in the middle of town. You can literally park and walk to almost all of the restaurants and shops Hanalei has to offer. There is phenomenal snorkeling on the north shore when ocean conditions permit, and you can stand-up paddle up the rivers almost any time of year. **Kalalau Trail** along the Na Pali Coast is the ultimate for avid hikers.

Sights

KILAUEA
★ Kilauea Point National Wildlife Refuge and Lighthouse

A picture-perfect view of a beautiful inlet speckled with white seabirds nesting in the cliffs and gliding overhead, monk seals on the rocks below, and even humpback whales in the winter months, makes the **Kilauea Point National Wildlife Refuge and Lighthouse** (end of Kilauea Rd., 808/828-1413, www.fws. gov/refuge/kilauea_point, 10am-4pm daily) a must-see stop. Upon arrival, the initial view from the cliff-top parking lot is photo-worthy. After this, take a stroll on the narrow peninsula to the Kilauea Lighthouse, a designated National Historical Landmark and visitors center. Originally boasting the world's largest "clamshell lens," which could send a beam of light 20 miles out to sea, it was replaced in 1976 with a small, high-intensity beacon. This is also a great place for dedicated bird-watchers, and people who just enjoy watching wildlife. Permanent and migrating seabirds spend their time here, including the frigate bird, boasting its eight-foot wingspan; and the red-footed booby with white feathers, black-tipped wings, and, of course, red feet; as well as the wedgetail shearwater and red- and white-tailed tropic birds.

Sea turtles, dolphins, and Hawaiian monk seals can all be seen from the cliffs occasionally. The waters here are also part of the Hawaiian Islands Humpback Whale

The Best Day on the North Shore

The best day on the north shore is all about good food, beach-hopping, colorful sunsets, snorkeling, and catching a few waves. It can all be experienced in one day if you begin early (around 9am).

- Begin your day on the north side with views of the **Kilauea Point National Wildlife Refuge.** Gaze down into the clear blue water of the cove, where birds nest and whales make wintertime visits. It's a classic photo opportunity with the lighthouse standing proudly above the cove.

- Head back up to **Kilauea Bakery & Pau Hana Pizza** for a quick but quality breakfast of sweet and savory pastries, coffee, and other treats. If you'd like, you can drop into some other shops here.

- Next, it's off to **Anini Beach** for a beautiful beach walk. The east side of the beach has long strips of white sand that hug the shallow and clear nearshore water. Past the beach park to the west you'll find the white sand dotted with rocks and tide pools, depending on the tide.

- After working up an appetite strolling in the sand, stop at the **Hanalei Valley Overlook** for a photo and then head down to Hanalei for a healthy local lunch at the **Hanalei Taro and Juice Co.** This is a great place to try some healthy Hawaiian dishes.

- Now, to experience what the north shore is all about—go for a surf. There are two easy options: rent a surfboard at **Hanalei Surf Company** or **Backdoor Surf** for a self-guided surf lesson, or if you're more comfortable with a surf school, visit the **Titus Kinimaka Hawaiian School of Surfing** in Hanalei and book a lesson. Another option is renting a stand-up paddleboard and hitting the **Hanalei River** or **Hanalei Bay** if the waves are flat.

- For lunch, stop at **Red Hot Mama's** in Wainiha for some unique burritos and local fish. Enjoy them on a nearby beach.

- If it's summer and the waves are small, **Tunnels Beach** is the next stop for excellent snorkeling, so don't forget your snorkel gear.

- Next, it's time to go spelunking, Kaua'i style. If you parked at Ha'ena Beach Park and walked down to Tunnels Beach, you won't need to drive anywhere. Back at the beach park, cross the highway to the **Maniniholo Dry Cave** and take a quick peek. It's fun to take photos here. After that, stop for photos and dipping your feet in the cold water at **Waikapala'e Wet Cave.** Some people like to swim here, but the cave is rather dark and eerie.

- To end the day, head down to **Ke'e Beach** for more snorkeling in the natural pool, or just relax and enjoy the sunset.

- On the way back, stop in Hanalei at **Postcards Cafe, The Dolphin Restaurant,** or **Bar Acuda Tapas and Wine** for dinner. If you're looking for entertainment, hit up **Bouchons Hanalei** or **Tahiti Nui** for live music.

National Marine Sanctuary, and whales can be seen here during winter and spring. The visitors center holds a wealth of information worth checking out about bird and plant life, the history of the lighthouse, and Hawaiian history. To get here, turn into Kilauea at the Shell gas station near mile marker 23, then down Kilauea Road. Drive straight to the end to the lighthouse, where entrance is free for people 16 and under, and all others cost $5 per person.

Na 'Aina Kai Botanical Gardens

Just past the Quarry Beach access road is **Na 'Aina Kai Botanical Gardens** (808/828-0525, www.naainakai.org, 8am-noon Mon. and Fri., 8am-5pm Tues.-Thurs.), encompassing a whopping 240 acres of tropical hardwoods, fruit trees, ornamental plantings, and statues. Over 100 acres of the property is a tropical hardwood plantation with about two dozen types of trees, including teak, mahogany, zebra wood, rosewood, and cocobolo, along with a lot of tropical fruit trees. The gardens take a creative twist in the central areas, where theme gardens feature various types of plants and 60 lifelike bronze sculptures add life to the experience. Admission may feel a bit pricey, from $25 for a 90-minute walk to $70 for a five-hour walk and tram ride through all areas, but the view from the parking lot is enticing, and it's truly an enjoyable treat. The visitors center and gift shop are a fun stop to explore the gifts, books, and plants. To get here, turn down Wailapa Road after mile marker 21 and go to the end.

PRINCEVILLE
Sunset on the Lawn

In front of the St. Regis Princeville Resort (5520 Ka Haku Rd., 808/826-9644, www. stregisprinceville.com), where the last remnants of a *heiau*'s rock walls can be seen, is a perfect place to end a beautiful north shore day. On any clear day, drop by the lawn to take in the array of colors as the sun sets over Hanalei Bay and the green mountains backing the coast. During winter months, surfers may be seen dropping in on mountainous waves at the same time.

HANALEI
★ Hanalei Valley Overlook

The sights over Hanalei Valley inspire a dreamy feeling that harken back to the days of old Hawai'i. Different photo opportunities present themselves as the soft morning light changes to bright afternoon sun and then to demure sunset hues, all bringing out different colors in the taro patches below. Right after the Princeville turnoff on the left is the Hanalei Valley scenic overlook. This is a view not to be missed. The Hanalei River cuts through the valley until it meets the ocean, and along its banks myriad shades of green radiate from the valley, which reaches back into the 3,500-foot *pali* (cliffs) for almost nine miles. Waterfalls hang in the valley, either as light curtains or heavy torrential falls when rain falls on the mountains. There's a saying on Kaua'i's north shore: "When you can count 17 waterfalls, it's time to get out of Hanalei." Legend says that Pele sent a thunderbolt to split a boulder in Hanalei so that Hawaiians could run an irrigation ditch through the

Kilauea Lighthouse

Princeville

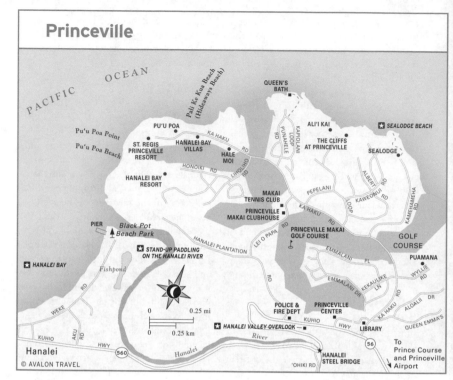

© AVALON TRAVEL

center to their fields. While Princeville was for *ali'i* (royalty), Hanalei was for the "commoners."

Originally Hanalei produced taro, which is evident far back in the valley, where the outlines of the old fields can still be seen. The bay and fishponds produced fish. When the foreigners arrived, they tried and failed at coffee here, then sugar, which didn't last as in other places on the island, and all the while Hanalei was bringing in poi from the Kalalau Valley. The bay was one of the most popular ports for a long time and was also a whaling harbor. Chinese immigrants eventually moved in and re-terraced the valley with rice. Rice was a successful crop until the 1930s, when the valley took a turn back to taro.

Wai'oli Hui'ia Church and Wai'oli Mission House Museum

The **Wai'oli Hui'ia Church** (5-5363 A Kuhio Hwy., 808/826-6253) lies near the west end of

town and stands tall with its colorful stained-glass windows illuminated by sunlight. Wai'oli means "joyful water," and it pays to go inside to look at the windows and take in the open-beam ceiling of the quaint church. Built in 1912, the church was part of a mission station that also included a home for the preacher, a school for Hawaiian boys, and accommodations for the teacher.

Behind and slightly to the right of the church is the **Wai'oli Mission House Museum** (808/245-3202, www.grovefarm.org/waiolimissionhouse, 9am-3pm Tues., Thurs., and Sat., free), which was originally the teacher's house. The lush green parking lot welcomes visitors to the home, which boasts a New England-style interior that was built in 1836 by Reverend William P. Alexander. It was then passed to the Wilcox family, who owned and occupied the house until recently. Wilcox family members founded the Grove Farm in Lihu'e and the nonprofit

Hanalei

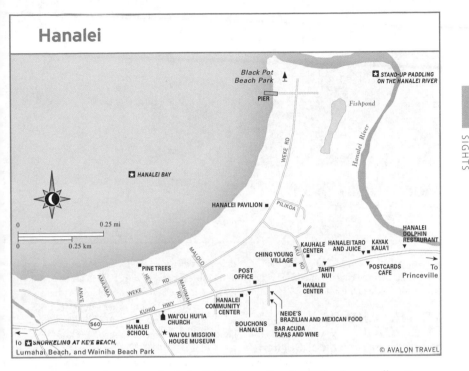

Black Pot
Beach Park

PIER

**STAND-UP PADDLING
ON THE HANALEI RIVER**

Fishpond

Hanalei River

WEKE RD

HANALEI BAY

0   0.25 mi

0   0.25 km

HANALEI PAVILION PILIKOA

HANALEI
DOLPHIN
RESTAURANT

KAUHALE HANALEI TARO KAYAK
CENTER AND JUICE KAUA'I

CHING YOUNG
VILLAGE

MALOLO

AKU RD

PINE TREES

POST
OFFICE

TAHITI
NUI

HANALEI
CENTER

POSTCARDS
CAFE

To
Princeville

HE'E RD

AMA'AMA

WEKE RD

MAHIMAHI

KUHIO HWY

ANAE

HANALEI
COMMUNITY
CENTER

WAI'OLI HUI'IA
CHURCH

BOUCHONS
HANALEI

NEIDE'S
BRAZILIAN AND MEXICAN FOOD

BAR ACUDA
TAPAS AND WINE

560

HANALEI
SCHOOL

WAI'OLI MISSION
HOUSE MUSEUM

To **SNORKELING AT KE'E BEACH,**
Lumahai Beach, and Wainiha Beach Park

© AVALON TRAVEL

organization that operates both the Wai'oli Mission House Museum and the Grove Farm Homestead. Inside you enter the parlor, where Lucy Wilcox taught Hawaiian girls how to sew and paintings of the families are on the walls. Around the house are artifacts including dishes, knickknacks, and a butter churn from the 1800s. It's interesting to note, now that the Hawaiian language has experienced a resurgence, that Abner Wilcox, a missionary, teacher, doctor, public official, and veterinarian, wrote letters to the king urging him to make Hawaiian the first language, with English as the second. Tours are given on a first-come, first-served basis.

Ho'opulapula Haraguchi Rice Mill

The **Ho'opulapula Haraguchi Rice Mill** (5-5070 A Kuhio Hwy., 808/651-3399, www. haraguchiricemill.org, kiosk hours 11am-3pm Mon.-Fri.) is an agrarian museum nestled in the taro fields of the Hanalei Valley within a national wildlife refuge usually not accessible to the public. Dating back to the 1800s, it's listed on the National Register of Historic Places. It was purchased by the Haraguchi Family in 1924, who restored the mill following a 1930 fire, then again after Hurricane 'Iwa in 1982 and Hurricane 'Iniki in 1992. This mill is the last remaining rice mill in all of Hawai'i, although it stopped operating in 1960 when the rice industry ceased to thrive. A nonprofit organization was formed to preserve and share the mill. The Haraguchi family continues to farm taro on nearby land that used to grow rice. Guided tours and private tours are available by reservation on Wednesdays only, so you need to call first. Tours ($87 adults) share Hawai'i's agricultural and cultural history, and visitors can view endangered native water birds and learn about taro cultivation and the uses of taro. A complimentary picnic lunch including taro grown at the farm is offered. When making a reservation, you must choose between a sandwich

The End of the Road

Waikanaloa Wet Cave

★ SNORKELING AT KE'E BEACH

Ha'ena State Park

★ SNORKELING AT TUNNELS/MAKUA BEACH

Ha'ena Beach Park

PACIFIC OCEAN

YMCA CAMP NAUE

Kepuhi Beach

MEDITERRANEAN GOURMET

HANALEI COLONY RESORT

Lumahu'i Beach

Wakoko Beach

KAULU PAOA HEIAU

Ha'ena

560

Wainiha Bay

Kalalau Trail

Maninholo Dry Cave

Mt Makana

LIMAHULI BOTANICAL GARDEN

Wainiha

Wainiha River

RED HOT MAMA'S

WAINIHA GENERAL STORE

560

HANALEI BAY

HIKING TO HANAKAPI'AI BEACH AND HANAKAPI'AI FALLS

Waikapala'e Wet Cave

Lumahai River

0   1 mi

Waipa

© AVALON TRAVEL

0   1 km

To Hanalei

or Hawaiian plate lunch. The entrance kiosk is one mile after the Hanalei one-lane bridge, on the north side of the road.

TO THE END OF THE ROAD
★ Limahuli Botanical Garden

At the **Limahuli Botanical Garden** (5-8291 Kuhio Hwy., 808/826-1053, http://ntbg.org/tours/limahuli, 9:30am-4pm Tues.-Sat.), you'll take a trip back in time to see the native plants that decorated Hawai'i before invasive species moved into the islands. Visitors have a choice of self-guided or guided walking tours. Self-guided tours for children 12 and under are free and cost $15 for ages 13 and up, while on guided tours children under 10 are not allowed, those 10-12 years old are charged $15, and it's $30 for ages 13 and up. Guided tours are 2-2.5 hours, and self-guided ones last 1-1.5 hours. Reservations are required for the guided tour only.

Part of the National Tropical Botanical Garden, the gardens lie in front of Mount Makana (*makana* means "gift") on 1,016 acres that help both ancient and modern plants flourish. The original 14 acres were donated by Juliet Rice Wichman in 1976, then expanded to 17 acres, and the final 985-acre parcel in the above valley was donated by Wichman's grandson, Chipper Wichman,

in 1994. It's a good idea to wear proper shoes, and umbrellas are provided. The visitors center is where the tours begin, and this is where books, crafts, gifts, and other things are on sale. The taro *lo'i* (patches) here are believed to be around 900 years old. The brochure and the tour guide share legends of the valley.

The majority of the preserve lies in the valley and is only available to biologists and botanists for research. To get to the gardens, take a left inland at the Hawaii Visitors Bureau warrior sign about a half mile after mile marker 9. The marker points to the gardens, which are in the last valley before Ke'e Beach. Just past this is the Limahuli Stream, which locals use as a rinse-off spot after swimming. There's only one good spot to pull off the road here. On your way to the Limahuli Botanical Garden, stop at the **Lumahai Overlook** for a view of the Lumahai Beach and a great photo op. After the fifth mile marker you'll notice a small pull-off area where an HVB sign points to the ocean.

Maninholo Dry Cave

Directly across from Ha'ena Beach Park is the wide, low, and deep Maninholo Dry Cave. Take a short stroll inside the cave. There's no water in here, just a dusty dirt bottom, but it can be fun to take photos, especially from the inside facing out. Sometimes walking around in here, you may look at all the footprints on the ground and wonder how long they go undisturbed. Although the cave seems to stay dry, there is no archaeological evidence that it was used for permanent habitation.

Waikapala'e Wet Cave

The earth opens up here to crystal-clear water after you've walked up a short hill to look down into the Waikapala'e Wet Cave. Also known as the "Blue Room" because of another hidden cave here that's accessible only through an underwater tunnel that turns a vibrant blue, the cave is a contradiction. It's beautiful and spacious, but since the trees have grown up and block the light, it exudes a slightly eerie feeling. Visitors will find a tranquil place to spend time, and many people swim in the cold water. It's said that the Blue Room is no longer blue due to a change in the water table height and other environmental changes. To get here, drive about three minutes past Ha'ena Beach. It's on the left just past the big overflow parking lot on your right, and is only identifiable by the obviously worn path up the rocky hill and the pull-off spot across the street. It's about a 1.5-minute walk up, where you can peer into the cave from above

or take a short but steep and slippery trek down into it.

Waikanaloa Wet Cave

The Waikanaloa Wet Cave is clearly seen from the road a little before Ke'e Beach. The cave is a nice sight and another good photo opportunity. There is no swimming allowed, as the sign indicates. Look at the floor of the pond itself to see some interesting patterns.

Kaulu Paoa Heiau and Kaulu O Laka Heiau

To the right of Ke'e are Kaulu Paoa Heiau and Kaulu O Laka Heiau, where it's said that the art of hula was born. Legend says the goddess Laka bestowed hula to the Hawaiians here. At these *heiau* as well as at any others, please respect everything in the area, meaning do not disturb or touch. *Heiau* are the equivalent to a Christian church for Hawaiians, and respect should always be paid when visiting them. The views up here are wonderful, especially during sunrise or sunset when the sky changes to all shades of color. For over 1,000 years the area was used as a valued hula school. At Ke'e Beach look for the trail weaving inland through the jungle up to the *heiau*.

Limahuli Botanical Garden

Beaches

No matter what kind of beach lover you are, Kaua'i's north shore has a beach that will make your day: surfers revel in the world-class waves during the winter months, snorkelers enjoy pristine reefs during the summer, beachcombers can easily find shells and driftwood, and sunbathers will love the white sand and myriad nooks and crannies along the coast to find their own slice of paradise. You can post up next to a lifeguard or spend the day without seeing another soul at Secret Beach. Some beaches, like Hideaways, requires a hike and a thirst for adventure, while others, like Pine Trees, provide the convenience of beachfront parking under the ironwood trees for the perfect beach picnic. North shore beaches are dynamic, raw, and some of the most beautiful beaches in the Hawaiian Islands.

KILAUEA
Moloa'a Beach

Moloa'a means "matted roots" in Hawaiian, and the relevance of the name is apparent at the river mouth, where tree roots are exposed to the elements. Moloa'a Beach is a crescent moon-shaped, white-sand beach. At this lesser-visited beach, black rocks jut out of the water to the far left and right of the large bay. Even though oceanfront houses back the east half of the beach, it still provides an undisturbed haven from the more crowded beaches. The river mouth here usually has rough water flowing out of it, and the water can be murkier than other river mouths in the area. The south side of the beach is nicer than the north, providing shade and safer swimming and bodyboarding than the other end of the beach. As with any beach in Hawai'i, swimming should only be attempted when the waves are very calm. Due to the prevailing trade winds, the water at Moloa'a Beach can be a bit rough and windy. Moloa'a is a perfect place to watch a colorful sunset, which will most likely be enjoyed alone. To get here, turn onto the rough Ko'olau Road between mile markers 16 and 17. Then turn onto Moloa'a Road and follow it to the end to Moloa'a Bay. Parking is very limited here, but signs alert visitors of where it's okay to park.

Larsen's Beach

Named after the former manager of Kilauea Plantation, L. David Larsen, Larsen's offers seclusion and enough space to stroll and see what you can find on the beach. Larsen's is another place where the crowds are usually nonexistent, and many times you will be alone or a good distance from other visitors. The very dangerous Pakala Channel is right before the point on the north end and features an extremely strong current that beachgoers absolutely must stay out of. For the rest of the beach, if the waves are flat and conditions are very calm, snorkeling can be marvelous here. To get to Larsen's Beach, turn down the second Ko'olau Road headed north, right before mile marker 20, and a little over one mile down take the left Beach Access road to the end. After the cattle gate is a trail; it's about a 10-minute walk to the bottom.

★ Secret Beach

Secret Beach is a wonderful treasure at the end of a dirt road and short trail. The beach is very, very long, and when the waves are really small, generally in the summer months, swimming is possible. Conversely, during the winter months the waves pound the shore and the current is extremely strong. Steep, tall cliffs back the beach, and about halfway down the beach you'll find a small waterfall—perfect for rinsing off.

Secret Beach is full of surprises, and depending on the season, wave size, rain, currents, and tides, you may find swimming ponds in the sand or exposed rock and tide pools. The walk down takes about 10 minutes and is a steep trail on roots and dirt. The way back up can be strenuous because of the incline. Secret Beach is also the unofficial nude beach on the north shore. Unofficial because, as signs posted by the police department will tell you, nudity is against the law. However, the signage hasn't entirely stopped dedicated nudists.

Secret Beach is also known as Kauapea Beach, and the Kilauea Lighthouse is visible on the point at the east end. There are awesome, even more secret tide pools and another waterfall farther west past the beach. To get here, turn onto the first Kalihiwai Road heading north and take the first right onto a dirt road. Head to the end of the road; parking is behind large homes.

Kahili/Quarry Beach

A long, fine white-sand beach backed by an ironwood forest, Kahili Beach is also known as Quarry Beach. A popular spot with locals for surfing and bodyboarding, Kahili Beach is gorgeous, but not a good choice for swimming. The ironwood forest growing out of the red dirt backing the beach makes for a fun place to experiment with photography. There are two sides to the beach with a ridge of rock dividing them. The east side serves as an unofficial campsite. It's not a wide section of rock, and crossing over is simple when the waves are small. A river meets the ocean on the west end of the beach, and along the river can be a good, calm zone for swimming. During weekdays, there's a good chance Quarry Beach will be empty, but it's popular with locals on weekends.

Local fishers come here to catch a fish they use for bait called 'o'io. The fish is too bony to fry and eat, but the fishers get the meat off the bones by cutting off the tail, rolling a soda bottle over the body, and then squeezing the meat out of the cut. It's then made into fish balls by mixing it with water, hot pepper, and bread crumbs.

To get to Kahili Beach, head north and turn right onto Wailapa Road between mile markers 21 and 22. Turn left at the yellow post and

cement blocks marking the top of the road and go about a half mile down to the beach.

Waiakalua Beach

The great thing about Waiakalua Beach is that it's usually empty and secluded. Ample shade, soft white sand, a fringing reef, and a spring at the north end add character to this beach. As usual, ocean conditions dictate whether swimming is doable here. To get here, turn onto North Waiakalua Road and turn left onto the dirt road just before you reach the end. Park at the end and walk the trail on the left. Waiakalua Beach is on the left after about a 10-minute mini hike down the steep path. To the right after the large rocks is **Pila'a Beach,** which is reachable after about 15-30 minutes of walking.

KALIHIWAI
Kalihiwai Beach

Kalihiwai is another beautiful bay nestled between two rocky points with a river at the west end that usually offers a perfect place for a refreshing and calm swim. The sand is white and very fine, and the right-hand breaking wave along the cliff at the east end of the bay is a draw for expert surfers. There are no amenities here, but there is sufficient parking under the ironwood trees. Swimming in the river is great for children, but make sure to stick by them. The edge of the water varies from a gradual slope to a steep drop. If you rented stand-up paddleboards or kayaks and have them strapped to your rental car, launch them into the river for a solitary paddle. Kalihiwai is a favorite spot for locals and families because the vibe is low key and the ocean activities are endless.

Coming from the east side, turn down the first Kalihiwai Road to get here. The road ends at the river, where the other side is visible. The road used to connect, but was destroyed in a 1946 tsunami. To reach the other side, take the second Kalihiwai Road and take a right at the first fork. It leads to the other side of the beach, where locals sometimes come to fish or paddle across the river to the beach.

Anini Beach

The seemingly endless white sand of Anini Beach stretches for approximately two miles. Much to the delight of beachgoers who like to laze about in the water, a barrier reef stretches the entire length of Anini and creates a shallow lagoon and great swimming for children and others who appreciate calm waters. The swimmable water here is a highlight. There's really no safer swimming on the north side than at Anini, and the water is surprisingly shallow, even very far out. Along the drive down, various pull-offs on the shoulder dot the road. They are all near small patches of beach where it's likely you'll be alone.

Anini Beach Park, about halfway down the road, is a popular beach with a camping area, restrooms, showers, picnic tables, and barbecue pits. The beach park is almost always crowded. If you're looking for less of a crowd, try any of the beach areas before or after the beach park. Past the beach park, beach access continues until the end of the road, where a stream meets the ocean. The occasional tide pool may be spotted along the way depending on the tide. Feel free to pull over anywhere and take a dip or enjoy the beach. Near the end of the road is a swing hanging from a false kamani tree, a perfect opportunity for an ocean-side swing. To get here, take the second Kalihiwai Road headed north. Keep to the left at the fork in the road (going right leads to the north side of Kalihiwai Beach) and keep driving until you find your patch of beach.

Wyllie Beach

After the stream at the end of Anini Beach is Wyllie Beach, named after the road that accesses it from Princeville. If you want to check it out, park at the end of Anini and walk across the stream. It's the narrow strip of sand before the point and is lined with false kamani trees. The water is very calm here.

PRINCEVILLE
★ SeaLodge Beach

Seclusion, white sand, shade, and a pristine cove of crystal clear water—everything a beach lover could want—are what you'll find at SeaLodge Beach. Accessed by a shaded hike through the trees and then a short walk along the rocky coast, the beach provides good snorkeling when the ocean is calm. There's no lifeguard or amenities here, so it's important to be careful in the water. Located near the SeaLodge condos at the end of Kamehameha Road in Princeville, parking is in the unmarked stalls toward the top of the parking

Kalihiwai Beach

lot. The trailhead is in front of building A and marked with a sign. On the way down you'll find amazing panoramic views worth taking a minute to indulge in and snap a few photos.

Take the dirt trail down past the small stream on the way to the ocean. Once you reach the ocean keep to your left, where you can walk along the black rocks or on the narrow trail a little up on the dirt. After a minute you'll see SeaLodge Beach, nestled in its own cove and backed by a vertical cliff. The back of the beach is lined with trees that provide enough shade that you can spend a few hours at the beach. It's quite an amazing beach and worth the effort. The trail isn't super strenuous, but it is rather steep and can be tiresome on the way up. Bring plenty of drinking water.

Queen's Bath

Queen's Bath is a tide pool at the bottom of a cliff looming above the ocean. Erosion has created an extremely unique and picturesque natural rock pool that is at its best when the waves are small, but big enough to wash into the pool. This spot is extremely dangerous. There's a plaque at the base of the trail with a safety warning stating that as of 2011, 28 people have died here, which speaks for itself. On very calm days, normally during the summer, the pool is crystal clear and swimmable. When the ocean is rough at any time of the year, it's risky. During the winter, when large waves pound the cliff, it's suicidal. A five-minute walk from the bottom of the trail to the pool puts visitors at the edge of the cliff and the pool. The hike down is intriguing in itself and offers several sights along the way, including a river, a couple of waterfalls, and a pool that usually has a few fish resting in it.

To get here, turn right onto Punahele Road and take the second right onto Kapiolani Loop. The parking lot is on the left-hand corner, bordered by a green cement wall. The trailhead is easy to find, marked with a warning sign and another sign giving notice of the shearwater breeding grounds. About 10 to 15 minutes down the dirt trail, it veers to the left at a waterfall pouring right into the ocean. Go left past the warning signs, and almost right on the edge of the cliff is the pond. Remember that during the winter months, from about September through April, the pool is unusable due to the large surf.

Hideaways Beach/Pali Ke Kua

Hideaways is a great beach for snorkeling, as is its sibling beach on the far side of the rocky point on the right. When the surf is small,

Anini Beach

snorkelers will usually see a gorgeous variety of fish and some green sea turtles. As at many other north shore beaches, false kamani trees provide shade, enabling beachgoers to spend quality time here without turning into sun-baked lobsters. The trail down the cliff is very steep, slippery, muddy, and strenuous. Ropes stretch from the top of the trail to where it flattens out for assistance. Although it's a very short hike, it takes agility and balance and is not suitable for young children.

Check ocean conditions before going to this beach. When the waves are big in Hanalei Bay, the surf will be washing far up the beach at Hideaways. The beach is at its best when the winds are light. To get here, take the trail that starts shortly before the St. Regis Princeville Resort gatehouse, next to the Pu'u Poa tennis courts. To reach the other side of the beach, either swim to the right from Hideaways (when conditions allow, of course) or walk the paved trail from the Pali Ke Kua condominiums.

Pu'u Poa Beach

Directly below the St. Regis Princeville Resort is the easily accessible and popular Pu'u Poa Beach. Swimming and snorkeling are both good here when ocean conditions allow. The white-sand beach reaches toward the mouth of the Hanalei River to the left. The ocean right off the beach is a mix of shallow sand and reef. It's the perfect area for beginning snorkelers and children. When the surf is up, the break on the outer reef is where experienced and elite surfers catch some of the biggest waves the north side musters up in the winter. For hotel guests, access is by the hotel pool area. For those not staying at the hotel, there is a small parking area by the guardhouse at the hotel entrance, and a cement path behind the hotel leads to the beach.

HANALEI
★ Hanalei Bay

Hanalei Bay is a crescent moon-shaped, two-mile stretch of unbroken white-sand beach with several different named beaches along the heavenly stretch. The bay was used as one of Kaua'i's three main ports until recently and is still visited by large yachts. Constructed in 1912 for rice transportation, the pier on the right side of the beach is now utilized mostly by children, who love to jump off it, and by fishers, who enjoy lazing on it with a pole.

To the left of the pier is **Queen Reef,** and to the right is **King Reef.** Surfing for both experts and beginners takes place here, along with bodyboarding, sailing, swimming,

Pu'u Poa Beach fronts the St. Regis Princeville Resort.

and stand-up paddling. At the end of Weke Road between the pier and river is **Black Pot Beach Park.** The name refers to the days when a large black pot was always cooking over a fire on the beach here with a big meal for everyone to share. Nearby and *mauka* (on the mountain side) of Weke Road is the headquarters of the Hanalei Canoe Club. You will see the sign when driving in, along with the sign for a shave ice wagon.

West of that is **Hanalei Pavilion** by the pier, recognizable, of course, by the large pavilion on the side of the road. Farther west and roughly in the center of the bay is **Pine Trees,** a popular surf spot for local children and families. Access to Pine Trees is at the end of He'e, Ama'ama, and Ana'e Roads. It's a good place to watch locals surf or take surfing lessons yourself. More access is available near the west end of the bay before the bridge. Hanalei Pavilion and Pine Trees both have lifeguards, and all of these spots are county-maintained and have showers, restrooms, picnic tables, and grills. When in Hanalei, turn off Route 560 onto Aku Road right before Ching Young Village. Turn right onto Weke Street, and near the end you'll see the beach where the pier is. Turn left onto Weke and then right onto He'e, Ama'ama, or Ana'e Roads to reach Pine Trees.

Waikoko Beach

Located at the west end of Hanalei Bay is Waikoko Beach and surf break. Another white-sand beach with black rocks dotting the area in the water and on the beach, it can be a less-crowded place to hang out, perhaps because the number of visitors here is limited by the roadside parking. To get here, look for the small parking area on the side of the road after the bridge and mile marker 4. If a spot is available, look for the short trail through the trees.

TO THE END OF THE ROAD
Lumahai Beach

After Waikoko Beach is the first access to Lumahai Beach. Lumahai is slightly over a mile long, running between mile markers 5 and 6, and has two accesses. The locals call the north end by the river "local" Lumahai and the east end "tourist" Lumahai. Don't be put off by nicknames, as tourist Lumahai has a nice trail down, and this end of the beach is prettier. Heading north, about a mile after the last bridge at the end of Hanalei Bay is a curve in the road with several parking spots alongside. This is before mile marker 5. Look for the trailhead, located where the trees open up to the ocean the most.

Hanalei Bay

To access the north end of the beach, head about a mile past the first access. If you pass mile marker 6 and the bridge, you've gone too far. The best thing about this end of Lumahai is the river. The river is a great place for children to swim and play in the sand, but only upriver from the mouth. Local parents and children spend a lot of time here, and it's a good place to bring beach toys and floats. It's best to stay out of the open ocean here. Lumahai is one of the most dangerous beaches to swim on the north side, and there isn't a lifeguard, so be careful.

Kepuhi Beach

After mile marker 7, ironwood trees line the beach; parking spots under them provide access to the start of Kepuhi Beach. The long white-sand beach can also be accessed at the Hanalei Beach Resort, where parking is free. This long beach isn't good for swimming, especially considering how nice all the other beaches are out here. It is a nice place to eat the food you might get at the Na Pali Art Gallery & Coffee Shop or for a romantic stroll before dinner at Mediterranean Gourmet.

Tunnels/Makua Beach

Named after the surf break on the outer reef, this beach offers some of the best snorkeling on the island, when the waves are flat. Reef fish can usually be found enjoying the waters not far from shore, and the sea caves to the left entertain bigger fish. There is a drop-off farther out that is intriguing, but this area is for experienced snorkelers and divers only, and should only be explored when the waves are small. The surf break is an intense wave for locals and experts only, sending thundering white wash all the way to the beach when the waves are breaking. This part of the beach is generally less crowded than Ha'ena Beach Park on the north end of Tunnels thanks to the limited parking. The beach is beautiful and long and makes a perfect place for a walk or run. Access borders homes located on two narrow side roads past mile marker 8. The first is just short of a half mile past the marker, and the second is slightly farther and most recognizable by the bent metal post with red paint. It is across from the 149th telephone pole, although at press time the 9 was missing so it looks like pole 14.

Ha'ena Beach Park

A picturesque beach with a backdrop of lush green mountains highlighted by perfect

the north end of Lumahai Beach

Counterculture Camp

In 1969, 13 young people from the mainland moved to Kauaʻi. They considered themselves refugees from campus riots, the Vietnam War, and police brutality. After a short time the group was arrested and sentenced to 90 days of hard labor for having no money and no home. Howard Taylor, brother of Elizabeth Taylor, bailed them out and invited them to camp on his oceanfront property right past Haʻena Beach. Taylor then left them with free reign of his property, and soon throngs of hippies, surfers, and Vietnam vets joined the clothing-optional, marijuana-friendly village where people lived in treehouses.

In 1977, the state of Hawaiʻi reclaimed **Taylor Camp** to make it into a state park. The residents of Taylor Camp moved on, and many of them still live throughout the Hawaiian Islands and Kauaʻi. For more information on the intriguing camp, watch *Taylor Camp,* a documentary of interviews with the residents 30 years after the camp came to an end.

surfing waves and a river, Haʻena Beach Park is a must-visit. Before the sand is a grassy lawn for tent camping, along with restrooms, showers, and picnic tables. A river bordering the east end of the park area runs over the road as you drive in. Swimming is good here only when the waves are small, but the river makes a good spot for the kids when it's running onto the beach. The reef has great snorkeling, again, only when the waves are small in the summer. If the main parking lot is filled up, which it often is, there is a bit more parking at the west end right past the showers. For those intending on camping on the north side, Haʻena is one of the most ideal places because of its location, scenery, and surrounding sights. Past the rocks on the west end the beach keeps going, and it's a great long solitary stroll if you're up for it, passing two *heiau* and eventually the area formerly known as Taylor Camp. Haʻena Beach Park is located off Kuhio Highway after mile marker 8 and just before mile marker 9, across from the Maniniholo Dry Cave.

Keʻe Beach

The pot of gold at the end of the road is Keʻe Beach and its large natural swimming pool. The snorkeling here is truly wonderful. Unfortunately, because it's also the start of the Kalalau Trail, the parking lot is almost always full, day or night. You may have to wait in the car for a few minutes for a spot to open up, or drive back up the road to an upper parking lot or even on the side of the road past that. Either way, Keʻe Beach is breathtakingly beautiful, provides amazing photo opportunities, and has full amenities and a lifeguard. Venturing east down the beach will lead you to several *heiau* and the spot where Taylor Camp stood, which makes for a nice beach stroll. To get here, drive to the very end of Route 560; the road turns into a parking area at the beginning of the Na Pali Coast.

NA PALI COAST
Kalalau Trail Beaches

For those who continue on foot and are dedicated to a serious hike, about a two-mile hike from Keʻe Beach is **Hanakapiʻai Beach.** There's a freshwater stream, and it's a favorite campsite for hikers.

After Hanakapiʻai Beach and four more strenuous miles is **Hanakoa Beach,** another good place to camp. The biggest thrill here are the falls that are another half a mile inland. In this area you'll also see wide terraces and wild coffee trees.

Five miles down the coast from Hanakoa is **Kalalau Beach.** It's important to note that this is a serious hike, requiring proper prepping and serious dedication. Kalalau Beach is about a half mile long with a small waterfall, often used by campers for a shower, and portable toilets. Many people who camp here like to pitch tents in the caves for protection from the wind and rain.

Past Kalalau is **Honopu Beach,** and the only legal way to get there is to swim from Kalalau. No surfboards, boats, or other crafts are allowed on shore, but you could paddle in a ways, anchor in the water, and swim up to the beach. Honopu Beach is actually composed of two picturesque, undisturbed beaches separated by an impressive arch. These are perhaps the most magical beaches on the island. You'll find a wonderful waterfall here and a stream to rinse off the saltwater. Vertical cliff walls that are more than 1,000 feet high back these beaches.

Water Sports

SNORKELING AND DIVING

During the summer months—from May through September—or when the ocean conditions in the winter are very calm, the north shore offers great opportunities for snorkeling. When snorkeling, always remember to only go out when the waves are very small or the ocean is completely calm, and it's safest with a partner. In addition to a mask and snorkel, dive fins are always a must, as strong currents are prevalent even on the calmest days.

A water camera or GoPro is always a good idea, and even the disposable ones available at most supermarkets take pretty good photos. Snorkel gear rentals are available at the **Hanalei Surf Company** (808/826-9000, www.hanaleisurf.com, 8am-9pm daily). They offer complete sets for $6 for 24 hours, $14 for three days, $20 for five days, and $22 for seven days. **Pedal-N-Paddle** (in Ching Young Village, 808/826-9069, www.pedalnpaddle.com, 9am-6pm daily) has complete adults' sets for $5 per day and $20 per week, and kids' sets for $4 per day and $15 per week. They also have flotation devices and fins or mask- and snorkel-only rentals. The last chance for snorkel rentals would be the **Wainiha General Store** (5-6607 Kuhio Hwy., 808/826-6251, 11am-6pm daily). They offer complete sets for $9 per day.

Kilauea
ANINI BEACH

The calm water and the long, fringing reef make for great snorkeling at Anini Beach. The water stays shallow shockingly far out and maintains a depth of around four feet. Some of the safest snorkeling on the north side can be experienced at Anini Beach. Snorkelers who head far enough out will see the ledge dropping into the deep sea. To get here, take the second Kalihiwai Road headed north. Keep to the left at the fork in the road (going right leads to the north side of Kalihiwai Beach).

Princeville
HIDEAWAYS BEACH

Hideaways is the best snorkeling in Princeville, as long as the waves are small. Snorkelers will usually be treated to a colorful array of tropical fish. Green sea turtles are known to cruise through the water at a leisurely pace. To get here, take the trail shortly before the St. Regis Princeville Resort gatehouse and next to the Pu'u Poa tennis courts. To reach the other side of the beach, either swim to the right from Hideaways (when conditions allow, of course) or walk the paved trail from the Pali Ke Kua condominiums.

SEALODGE BEACH

For more Princeville snorkeling, hike down to SeaLodge Beach for seclusion and a pretty lively underwater world. There's a reef right off the beach here in a cove, which means some pretty fish will be lingering around. There's no lifeguard here, so don't go out too far. If you haven't rented gear yet, you can buy some at the Princeville Foodland.

To get here, drive to the SeaLodge condos at the end of Kamehameha Road in Princeville; parking is in the unmarked stalls toward the top of the parking lot. The trailhead is in front of building A and marked with a sign. Take the dirt trail down past the small stream on the way to the ocean. Once you reach the ocean, keep to your left, where you can walk along the black rocks or on the narrow trail a little up on the dirt. After a minute or so you will see SeaLodge Beach.

Hanalei
WAIKOKO BEACH

If you're going to check out Waikoko Beach anyway, you can hop in with a snorkel and mask since you're there. The reef draws in fish and it's worth a glance, but it's not the best snorkeling on the north side. This area is rocky, and waves break here quite often. It's at the north end of Hanalei Bay; to get here, look for the small parking area on the side of the road after the bridge and mile marker 4. If a spot is available, look for the short trail through the trees.

To the End of the Road
★ TUNNELS/MAKUA BEACH

To see a rainbow of brightly colored reef fish, hop in the water at Tunnels. With the outer reef, it's no surprise that fish like to wander in here. Reef fish spend their time not far from shore, and the sea caves to the left are a favorite hangout for bigger fish, along with the outside drop-off. The outer area is for experienced snorkelers and divers only, and should only be accessed when the waves are very small or the ocean is flat. Sea turtles, the occasional reef shark, caves, and fish can be seen. Access borders homes located on two narrow side roads past mile marker 8. The first is just short of a half mile past the marker, and the second is slightly farther and most recognizable by the bent metal post with red paint. It is across from the 149th telephone pole, although at press time the 9 was missing so it looks like pole 14.

★ KE'E BEACH

Another location known for spectacular snorkeling, Ke'e offers great underwater views inside the natural pond, where there is usually a crowd of snorkelers. Outside in the open ocean the views get even better, but snorkeling here should only be attempted when

No matter how big the waves are, Ke'e Beach is a great place to snorkel.

RESCUE

Top Kid-Friendly Activities on the North Shore

Kaua'i's north shore has a lot to offer *keiki* (children), from nature excursions to man-made fun. Out of the many beaches lining the coast of the north side, certain ones are safer and more fun for children than others. If you're looking for a *keiki*-safe beach, it's always a good idea to keep an eye on the surf and beach conditions.

- **Kaua'i Mini Golf** in Kilauea has a fun and unique course for the whole family. It takes golfers through a cultural tour of Hawaii.

- In the Kilauea area, **Anini Beach** is hands down the best beach for children. Only the beach park has a lifeguard, but the two-mile stretch of beach is bordered by a fringing reef that keeps big waves out. The seemingly endless stretch of water is only a few feet deep even yards out toward the ocean. Near the end of the beach, past the beach park itself, is a small river that can be fun for kids to wade in; a ways up is a swing hanging from a tree.

- Located at the top of Princeville on the right of the shopping center is a child's wonderland. Near the **Princeville Public Library** is the **Princeville Playground.** It has two playgrounds, one for 5-12-year-olds and a smaller one for toddlers. There's even a pavilion and uncovered tables to picnic at if you want to bring food from Foodland or enjoy an ice cream cone from **Lappert's Hawaii Ice Cream & Coffee.**

- Once you're down in Hanalei, **Kokonut Kids** is a fun shop for the little ones. Colorful and cute clothing for boys and girls decorates the store. Close to it is the **Hanalei Toy and Candy Store,** loaded with wonderful toys and tasty treats. Don't head in here unless you're prepared to buy something, because the kids will want to indulge.

- Also in Hanalei is the surf break called **Pine Trees** at **Hanalei Bay.** It's not only a beautiful beach but also a great place for your kids to watch local surfer kids catch waves or join in themselves at a surf school.

- If the waves are flat, you can snorkel in the natural pool at **Ke'e Beach.** Bring their gear and stick by them as they explore Kaua'i's underwater world.

the waves are flat in the summer months. Advanced snorkelers find that heading a bit to the left and snorkeling along the reef offers the best views. To get here, drive to the very end of Route 560; the end of the road turns into a parking area at the beginning of the Na Pali Coast.

Na Pali Coast

The best and safest way to snorkel along the Na Pali Coast is definitely with a boat tour company. Tours leave from the east side and head down the coast, but many also leave from the west side. The underwater world along the coast is nothing short of amazing: sea turtles, a spectrum of fish, the occasional reef shark, underwater caves, and marine mammals.

Na Pali Catamaran (5-5190 Kuhio Hwy., 808/826-6853, www.napalicatamaran.com) has been launching out of Hanalei Bay for almost 40 years. Guests ride an outrigger canoe to a 34-foot catamaran that takes 16 passengers maximum. They offer snorkeling cruises and provide all the gear. A deli-style meal is provided; visitors have the option of a meat or veggie sandwich. Snack, drinks, and water are also provided. All tours depend on ocean conditions. Adults pay $160, children 5-11 are $130. The office is right next to the Hanalei Post Office.

Also leaving from Hanalei Bay is **Captain Sundown** (P.O. Box 697, Hanalei, HI, 96714, 808/826-5585, www.captainsundown.com). A six-hour Na Pali snorkel sail ($182) takes you down the coast and stops at a sea-turtle cleaning station where triggerfish clean the turtles. Trampoline nets allow great views below to dolphins and other sea life. Captain Sundown also offers a three-hour Na Pali sunset sail ($144) down the coast. Snacks, soft drinks, and bottled water are provided.

Na Pali snorkeling tours leaving from the west side are much higher in number, and include **Holo Holo Charters** (4353 Waialo Rd., Ste. 5A, Eleele, 808/335-0815 or 800/848-6130, www.holoholokauaiboattours.com), which offers a Na Pali snorkel sail ($99-139). The well-established company's cats, one motorized and one sailing, run out of Port Allen Harbor. The company has a reputation for treating guests well.

Catamaran Kahanu (4353 Waialo Rd., Eleele, 808/645-6176 or 888/213-7711, www.catamarankahanu.com) is a Hawaiian-owned tour company offering Na Pali Coast snorkeling combined with a glimpse into Hawaiian culture. Aboard the boat, passengers are treated to craft demonstrations such as basket, hat, and rose weavings, which guests take home as mementos. Rates are $80-122 with special children's rates. They also leave from the west side.

Hanalei Activity Center (kiosk near Big Save, 808/826-1898) will book you on various tours and other activities and can be visited at Ching Young Village.

SURFING AND STAND-UP PADDLING

The coast from Kilauea to the Na Pali Coast is peppered with A+ surf breaks, best suited for expert surfers. The area has also produced a number of professional surfers, including Bruce Irons and his late brother Andy, Bethany Hamilton, and others. If you haven't brought a board, you can rent a surfboard and head out yourself, or take surf lessons. Surf lessons are a good idea if you're a novice to the sport. Besides the goal to eventually surf down the line, there are some basic tips to learn, like how to paddle for a wave and stand up.

If you'd like to learn to stand-up paddle (SUP) or are already a fan of the sport, there are several beaches and rivers ideal for paddling. Rental SUPs are easily found on beaches all around Kauaʻi.

If you're spending time on the north shore, board rentals are available from **Hanalei Surf Company** (in Hanalei Center, 808/826-9000, www.hanaleisurf.com, 8am-9pm daily). They rent beginner surfboards for $20 per day, $50 for three days, $75 for five days, and $90 per week. They also rent

Surfing at Kalihiwai Beach is for experts only.

high-performance surfboards for $25 per day, $60 for three days, $90 for five days, and $110 per week. **Backdoor Surf** (Ching Young Village, 808/826-1900, www.hanaleisurf.com, 8:30am-9:30pm daily) rents stand-up paddleboards with paddles and car racks for $40 per day, $100 for three days, $150 for five days, and $200 for a full week. For lessons, **Hawaiian Surfing Adventures** (5134 Kuhio Hwy., 808/482-0749, www.hawaiiansurfingadventures.com, 8am-5pm daily) and the **Titus Kinimaka Hawaiian School of Surfing** (in the Quicksilver shop, 5-5088 Kuhio Hwy., 808/652-1116, www.hawaiianschoolofsurfing.com) will take you out and most likely get you on a wave. They offer 1.5-hour lessons—group lessons are $65 per person, private lessons are $100 for children under 13 years old and $150 for others, and for families they offer semi-private lessons with two students per instructor for $200 and three students per instructor for $225. **Hanalei Activity Center** (Ching Young Village, 808/826-1898) also arranges surf lessons.

Kilauea
KALIHIWAI BEACH AND QUARRY BEACH

When the conditions and swell direction are right, Kalihiwai Beach has a heavy, right-hand breaking wave off the rocky point on the east side of the bay. Locals surf and stand-up paddle here, and when the surf spot is breaking, the shore break across the beach is usually intense too. The river is an ideal place for stand-up paddling, and paddlers can head up and down the river as well as across from the beach to the end of the second Kalihiwai Road. Quarry Beach offers another good wave for experienced surfers, and is mostly utilized by locals. There are no lifeguards at either beach.

To get to Kalihiwai when coming from the east side, turn down the first Kalihiwai Road. The road ends at the river, where the other side is visible. To reach the other side, take the second Kalihiwai Road and go right at the fork. It leads to the other side of the beach, where locals sometimes come to fish or paddle across the river to the beach. To get to Quarry Beach when headed north, turn right onto Wailapa Road between mile markers 21 and 22. Turn left at the yellow post and cement blocks marking the top of the road and head about a half mile down to the beach.

Hanalei
HANALEI BAY

All of Hanalei Bay is ideal for stand-up paddling, either on waves for experienced paddlers or around the bay when the waves are small. Most of the sea floor across the bay is covered in sand, save for the points on either side, which is a flat and sharp reef. **The Bay,** the outside break stretching from the St. Regis hotel to the pier, is one of the most famous waves on Kaua'i. Located on the east side of the bay, it generally breaks during the winter months when swells arrive from the west and north. This break is for experienced surfers only. The bay is a fast and hollow right-hand point break. Shortboarders prefer to sit farther up the reef and try for the barrels, while longboarders and stand-up paddle surfers prefer the end bowl, which is slopier and breaks right into the channel. Spectators at the pier or Black Pot Beach Park will have a great view of the end bowl, but the wave actually stretches way up the reef. Paddle out in the channel straight out from Black Pot Beach Park. When in Hanalei, turn off Route 560 onto Aku Road right before Ching Young Village. Turn right onto Weke Street, and near the end you'll see the beach.

PINE TREES

Roughly in the center of Hanalei Bay is Pine Trees, a perfect break for all levels of surfers. The waves break right and left over a shallow, sandy bottom. Beginners and kids generally catch waves near the shore where the whitewater is smaller, while more experienced surfers will sit farthest out for the longest rides. When the waves get bigger, Pine Trees becomes very powerful with strong ocean currents. On most days the lineup will probably be packed with kids, so it can be a good idea to paddle out before the nearby elementary school is out for the day (around 2pm). Surfboards rentals are located nearby in Hanalei. When in Hanalei, turn off Route 560 onto Aku Road right before Ching Young Village. Turn left onto Weke and then right onto He'e, Ama'ama, or Ana'e Roads to reach Pine Trees.

★ HANALEI RIVER

The Hanalei River is a favorite for stand-up paddlers. While crossing the Hanalei Bridge into town, you'll probably see paddlers enjoying a leisurely paddle on the river. Morning is a nice time to paddle before it gets too hot, and it's a great way to start the day. You'll first notice the river as you come into Hanalei and drive over the one-lane bridge. **Kayak Kaua'i** (5-5070 Kuhio Hwy., 808/826-9844, www.kayakkauai.com) offers SUP lessons and rentals from their dock up the Hanalei River. It's about a 20- to 30-minute paddle down the river to the ocean. Lessons cost $85, and rentals are $45 per day or $225 per week. Both include leash and, if requested, a car rack.

WAIKOKO BEACH

At the north end of Hanalei Bay is Waikoko Beach. It's a left-breaking rocky reef break.

Although it's not one of the *most* dangerous spots, it's a good idea to leave it alone unless you're an experienced surfer. The break requires walking out on a very shallow and sharp reef, and hopping off at the end of the wave into a shallow reef. To get here, look for the small parking area on the side of the road after the bridge and mile marker 4. If a spot is available, look for the short trail through the trees.

To the End of the Road
TUNNELS/MAKUA BEACH

Right before Ha'ena Beach Park, Tunnels Beach has an epic, right-breaking wave. Tunnels is for expert surfers only. This is where local surfer Bethany Hamilton lost her arm to a shark at the age of 13. If the big waves don't keep you on the beach, that might. The movie *Soul Surfer* was released in 2011, documenting the Kaua'i native's loss and her comeback. The beach at Tunnels is beautiful, and if the waves are good it can be fun just to watch the surfers in the water.

A little west down the beach from Tunnels is the surf break known as **Cannons.** Again, this is another wave reserved for expert surfers due to the intensity of the barreling, left-hand breaking wave as well as the shallow reef

stand-up paddling the Hanalei River

in front of it. This can be another fun spot to watch the surfers from the beach when the waves are good.

Access borders homes located on two narrow side roads past mile marker 8. The first is just short of a half mile past the marker, and the second is slightly farther and most recognizable by the bent metal post with red paint. It is across from the 149th telephone pole, although at press time the 9 was missing so it looks like pole 14.

KAYAKING
Hanalei

Kayak Kaua'i (5-5070 Kuhio Hwy., 808/826-9844, www.kayakkauai.com) offers a leisurely adventure on the Hanalei River with kayak rentals and guided tours where kayakers have the option of a single kayak for $29 or a double for $54.

A tour of the Hanalei River and Hanalei Bay is also offered by **Kayak Hanalei** (5-5190 Kuhio Hwy., in Ching Young Village, 808/826-1881, www.kayakhanalei.com) from March through October. Suitable for all ages, the tour explores the bay and river and takes paddlers snorkeling. A complete sandwich lunch is provided, with vegetarian as an option, and is enjoyed on the beach.

The price for children is $95.38, adults $106.10.

Na Pali Coast

Kayaks can be rented for a trip down the Na Pali Coast ending at Polihale, but only in summer months when seas are calm. **Outfitters Kauai** (2827A Po'ipu Rd., Po'ipu, 808/742-9667 or 999/742-9887, www.outfitterskauai.com, $230) runs a 16-mile sea kayak adventure along the coast. The trip features an exploration of sea caves, opportunities to see waterfalls, dolphins, and sea turtles, and respites on deserted beaches that feel far from civilization. The tour offers tandem, open-cockpit, or sit-on-top self-bailing kayaks with foot pedal controls, and the tour is only available from mid-May until mid-September on Tuesdays and Thursdays.

Kayak Kaua'i (5-5070 Kuhio Hwy., 808/826-9844, www.kayakkauai.com) also offers sea kayaking along the Na Pali Coast. It's a serious adventure only for the very fit and hardy and can only be done in the summer. The kayaking adventure requires 5-6 hours of paddling and runs about $200.

Na Pali Kayak (5-5070 Kuhio Hwy., 808/826-6900, www.napalikayak.com) takes adventurous day-trippers, honeymooners,

kayak rentals in Hanalei

and campers on various trips along the Na Pali Coast. Adventures include guided day kayaking trips, camping along the coast, a honeymoon private charter for two, and private guided tours. Fees vary $200-3,000 for a group charter, so please call for the most up-to-date rates and details.

FISHING
Na Pali Coast

Na Pali Sportfishing (808/635-9424, www.napalisportfishing.com) will take you down the coast, but they leave out of Kikiaola Harbor on the west side. They generally leave at 6am because, according to them, that's when serious anglers fish; that time can be hard to make if you're on the north shore, but they do schedule later trips as well. They take people out on a 35-foot Baja cruiser with a fly bridge and outriggers for a maximum of six people. Boaters must bring their own food and snacks, but the company provides soft drinks, fishing tackle, and zipper-lock bags so guests can take fish home. Half days shared run $135 an angler, full days are $220, and a full-day fishing charter runs $1,050. Check

for other rates and tours. Restrictions include no pregnant women, no recent back surgeries or injuries, and no children under four years old.

WHALE-WATCHING

During the months of December through March or April, humpback whales *(kohola)* spend time in the islands singing and giving birth. After bulking up on weight in Alaska through the summer, the whales don't eat while they're here and may lose up to about one-third of their weight. During these months, keep an eye out any time you look at the ocean. They breech, they spout, and it's one of the best sights to be seen.

From November through March **Bali Hai Tours** (808/634-2317, www.balihaitours.com) heads north from Kapa'a, taking people out to see the whales. Although the boat can handle 12 people, they take no more than six people out on their 20-foot Zodiac with a two-stroke 100 hp Mercury motor. The company provides snorkel gear, floater noodles and bodyboards, dry bags, and snacks. Prices are $155 for adults and $90 for children.

Hiking, Biking, and Bird-Watching

HIKING

The north shore is home to some of the most outstanding hikes on the island. From short walks and secluded beaches, to hidden waterfalls and the 19-mile trek along the Na Pali Coast, the north shore is a hiker's dream scene. Pair ample hiking with pristine beaches and mountain views, and the value of a mile-long beach walk shouldn't go underestimated; it can be one of the most peaceful and memorable experiences to be had on Kaua'i.

Kilauea
SECRET BEACH TIDE POOLS AND WATERFALL

Tide pools and an ocean-side waterfall are the beautiful rewards at the end of this half-hour,

one-mile hike. It's important to note that this hike should only be done during the summer months when the ocean is completely flat. It's actually a combination of two hikes, one down to Secret Beach and another to the falls and tide pools. At the northern end of the beach at the bottom of the access trail, head over the rocks. After the small, sandy area is a pretty spot where the water juts into the cliffs, and you'll need to pass behind this. There's a roughly 10-foot-tall vertical cliff to climb that presents two options: climb up over the cliff and stick to the rocks, or climb up on the end that's over the water.

After passing this, stick to the trail high on the wall that backs the small cove. You'll eventually reach some tide pools. Then, right before another finger of water juts into the cliffs, you'll see the wonderful deep and smooth boulder-bottomed pools. Once you're here it looks like this could be the end, but it's not. There are several five- to six-foot-deep pools. They are beautiful pools that are generally clean and clear, and the rock bottom is smooth. The pool closest to the edge of the cliff needs to be avoided when the waves are anything but flat.

Where the cliff meets the finger, there is another small vertical cliff, about six to eight feet high. For an even better reward, climb it and head a very short distance inland to see the waterfall coming out of a small, lush green crevice, pouring into more tide pools. This is far from Kaua'i's tallest waterfall, but the combination of an ocean-side waterfall with salt tide pools is a unique sight to see and enjoy. The falls pour down onto a fairly flat rock area, and there is a small cave in back of the water perfect for sitting in as long as the falls aren't pouring too heavily. The rock leading to the falls is extremely slippery, so taking your time is important, although walking above the falls and coming back down and around works too. In front of this are several salt tide pools that the freshwater runs into. Please note again that this hike is dangerous when the waves are big and should generally be done only during the summer months. Even when the waves are small, hikers need to be aware of the ocean. There's another, easier way to get here. Take the first Kalihiwai Road and pass the road to Secret Beach, then stop at the yellow fire hydrant. Take the trail here about 10 minutes down to the top of the waterfall. This isn't nearly as exciting as the hike from Secret Beach, but it's shorter and safer.

To get here, turn onto the first Kalihiwai Road heading north and take the first right onto a dirt road. Head to the end of the road, where parking is behind large homes.

Princeville
POWERLINE TRAIL

It takes a powered-up person to attack the entire daylong journey along the roughly 13-mile Powerline Trail. Completing it is only recommended for those who have a ride waiting on the other side, where the trail ends at the Keahua Arboretum in Wailua. The sights range from a few views into Hanalei Valley to an abundance of mountain views, the north and south shores, the center of the island, and the Hanalei region. The trail is hot and dry and lacking in shade. It's best for hikers to go as far as they like but then return to the Princeville trailhead. Around two hours from the start of the trail, the pass is a good place to turn around and head back. To get to the northern trailhead, turn at the Princeville Ranch Stables about a half mile east of Princeville. Head uphill for about two miles until the pavement ends. Go a little farther to the parking area near the green water tank. This is a serious trail for mountain bikers, but it's strenuous. Don't attempt to go four-wheeling here.

Hanalei
'OKOLEHAO TRAIL

This intense 1.5-hour, 2.3-mile hike is a good hike to prep for the Kalalau Trail. 'Okolehao refers to the Hawaiian version of moonshine, made from the ti root planted up here. It's said the literal translation is "iron bottom" for the iron pots used to ferment it. The hike provides a serious workout that will mostly likely be experienced in solitude. The trail gains about 1,200 feet and will have hikers huffing and puffing in no time. The effort is well worth it though. The 'Okolehao Trail offers amazing views of the island that begin about half a mile up. From the end of the trail the Kilauea Lighthouse, Hanalei River, Wai'ale'ale, Hanalei Bay, and the area by Ke'e and as far as Anahola can be seen. When hiking after a rain, be very careful, as the trail gets slippery. To get to the trailhead, turn left immediately after the one-lane bridge into Hanalei onto Ohiki Road. A little over a half mile down the road, there's a parking lot on the left. A small bridge marks the trailhead on the opposite side of the road.

Legends of the Naupaka Shrub

Naupaka shrubs have light green, somewhat waxy leaves and distinctive white flowers; it looks as though half of the flower's petals are missing. There are two species. One species grows along the coast, another in the mountains. Several Hawaiian legends explain their unique appearance.

One legend tells of Pele being so jealous that she turned two lovers into the plant, sending one to the mountains and one to the coast. Legend says that since they were soul mates, the flowers are incomplete, and when they are brought together they form a whole.

A Kaua'i legend tells of the lovers Nanau and Kapaka, who broke a hula *kapu* (taboo) the night before their graduation. It's said they fled across Limahuli Stream and passed Maniniholo Cave while chased by their *kumu* (teacher). When they reached Lumahai Beach, Nanau fled to the cliffs and Kapaka hid in a beach cave called Ho'ohila. As the teacher approached the cliffs, Kapaka tried to block the *kumu* so her lover could escape. The *kumu* was enraged and killed Kapaka, continuing to chase Nanau. Eventually, Nanau was also struck dead, and later that day fishermen at Lumahai discovered a plant they'd never seen before growing where Kapaka had died. The *kumu* noticed the same plant growing where Nanau had died.

Another Pele legend says the goddess was enamored with a young man who was greatly devoted to his lover. No matter what she did, he remained loyal to his lover. Pele was angered and chased the young man into the mountains, throwing molten lava at him. Pele's sisters saw this happen, and to save him they changed him into half of a naupaka flower and sent him to the mountains. Pele went after his young lover and chased her toward the ocean. Again, Pele's sisters stepped in and changed her into the beach naupaka. It is said that if the mountain and the beach naupaka are reunited, the young lovers will be together again.

MOKOLEA TIDE POOLS

The reward for this fairly easy, quarter- to half-mile hike (depending on how far you can drive in) is a dip in cool, refreshing tide pools. The hike is really a slow walk over lava rock along the shoreline. Take your time and be mindful of your footing. You'll notice very weathered metal remnants of sugar mill gear. There are two ways to get here. One is through Quarry Beach Road in Kilauea village, via a partial four-wheel-drive road that leaves only about a quarter mile hike. The other is from the Quarry Beach access off Wailapa Road via a two-wheel-drive road and then a half-mile walk from the river.

Na Pali Coast

The heavenly and harsh Na Pali Coast is where all of nature's wonder joins together, a world that will both amaze and test those who choose to explore it. Other than the ocean, this is the only access to the rugged coastline with sea cliffs, five lush valleys, waterfalls, and camping along the 15-mile stretch from Ke'e to Polihale. The cliffs rise up to 4,000 feet in certain areas, and sea level is found only at the four main beaches along the way. The largest and most magnificent valley here is the Kalalau Valley, where ancient Hawaiians lived and archaeological evidence still remains. Other valleys also hold evidence of inhabited sites, as Hawaiians lived in various locations along the way. Rain falls here in excess, creating an abundance of waterfalls and streams.

The Na Pali Coast State Park comprises 6,175 acres of raw, pristine nature. The remaining cliffs, coastline, and valleys are either state forests or natural area reserves. There is a ranger stationed at Kalalau Valley who oversees the park and who will ask campers for permits. There is a trailhead by Ke'e Beach that you can't miss, and at Kalalau Valley there's a sign-in box. Day-use permits are required to go beyond Hanakapi'ai (where there are composting toilets), about two miles in, and a camping permit is necessary to stay overnight at Hanakapi'ai, Hanakoa, or Kalalau. Camping is permitted for up to five nights total, but two consecutive nights are not allowed at Hanakapi'ai or Hanakoa. Permits are $20 per day per person. Hawai'i residents receive a $5 discount. Permits issued are limited to protect the natural area, and during busy times can sell out a year in advance. The Department of Land and Natural Resources offers an online reservation system (camping.ehawaii.gov) where you can check for availability and purchase permits.

More than the basics are needed to camp out here. You'll need a waterproof tent, mosquito repellent, first-aid kit, biodegradable soap, food, sleeping bag, and whatever else you think you may need and don't mind carrying on your back mile after mile. Water bladders as opposed to water bottles are a good idea, because they're lighter and run a constant line of water to the mouth. Tree cutting is not allowed, and there isn't much natural firewood, so bring a stove if you want to cook. Drinking out of the streams is not advised; doing so can cause serious stomach illness, so boil the water or bring a water filter or purification tablets. Please remember not to litter and to take out what you carried in. Reachable only by boat or kayak, the Nu'alolo Kai can be visited for the day only, and Miloli'i offers camping for a maximum of three nights with very basic campsites. The most accurate idea of what to expect is from hikers who have recently made the journey, because the trail changes with the weather.

THE KALALAU TRAIL

What may be the best way to experience the coast is the 11-mile Kalalau Trail, which begins right at Ke'e Beach. Mother Nature dictates what condition the trail is in, so hikers may find a somewhat dry and firm trail or a narrow trail so steep and wet they must scoot along on a cliff's edge while digging their hands deep into the dirt to hang on. Upon reaching Kalalau Beach, hikers may be welcomed to the beach by nude campers, as some people take advantage of the remote location and leave swimwear in their packs.

The path was originally created by

the Kalalau Trail

Hawaiians as a land route between Kalalau Valley and He'ena. The Kalalau Trail was built in the late 1800s and rebuilt in 1930 for horses and cows to pass over. To experience the trail is to experience what old Hawai'i must have been like, when people lived off the land and close to nature. It usually takes a full day to get to Kalalau Beach, and it's hands down the best hike in the state. The trail is well worn from decades of use, so you're not likely to get off track and lost. Yet roots weave through it, and it gets extremely muddy and slippery during and after rain, a frequent occurrence out here. Small streams fill up to flooding rivers after a heavy rain but they drain out rather quickly, so instead of crossing a dangerous stream it's usually best to wait it out. Mountain climbing out here is a risky and dangerous idea because the dirt easily crumbles. The trail is filled with continuous amazing views. From the impressively tall mountains to the coastal views and lush foliage, this is not the hike to forget the camera in the car.

The currents along the coast are dangerous

too, so stay out of the water from around September through April, when winter swells pound the cliffs and beaches. In summer, the sand usually returns to Hanakapiʻai Beach, the most commonly visited part of the hike, after being swept away by the winter's large surf. Hanakapiʻai, like Queen's Bath, has a list of the names and ages of people who have died at this beach due to the pounding surf often washing over bare rock.

To access the Kalalau Trail, park at the end of the road at Keʻe Beach. The lot is often full, but there is an overflow lot a short walk up the road. You can park overnight, but never leave anything visible in the car to avoid a break-in. Some hikers who have a permit to stay multiple nights choose to hitchhike to and from the trailhead to avoid leaving their car overnight. However, hitchhiking presents its own challenges, like not knowing how long you'll be waiting for a ride. After hiking 22 miles, are you prepared to walk back to your room?

★ HANAKAPIʻAI BEACH AND HANAKAPIʻAI FALLS

It's about two miles and a two-hour hike from Keʻe to Hanakapiʻai Beach. The first mile goes uphill to about 800 feet, with the last mile going down and ending at the beach. Depending on the season, you may get lucky and see some brave and slightly crazy surfers out here. During low tide and only during the summer, people will camp in caves on the beach, but on the far side of the stream up from the beach is the best place to camp.

From the west side of the stream at Hanakapiʻai Beach the Hanakapiʻai Trail starts, leading two miles inland up into the valley to the wonderful Hanakapiʻai Falls, passing old taro fields and crumbling rock walls. The trail crosses the stream several times on the way up, so if the stream looks full and rushing, just turn around and head back. It can be dangerous during high water. If the stream is low, keep going. The hike to the 300-foot-high falls is rewarding and worth it. There is a wonderful ice-cold swimmable pool at the bottom, but don't swim directly under

the falls. From Hanakapiʻai Camp near the beach, the hike should take around 2-3 hours, and it's about 5-6 hours from Keʻe Beach.

HANAKAPIʻAI BEACH TO HANAKOA

It's a strenuous 4.5-mile, three-hour trek from Hanakapiʻai Beach to Hanakoa. The trail climbs steadily and doesn't go back down to sea level until Kalalau Beach nine miles later. Switchbacks lead you out of Hanakapiʻai Valley, and although the trail is heavily utilized, it can be very rough in certain spots. The trail passes through the hanging valleys of Hoʻolulu and Waiahuakua, both parts of the Honoʻonapali Nature Area Preserve and loaded with native flora, before arriving at Hanakoa. In the past, Hanakoa was a major food-growing area for Hawaiians, and many of its terraces are still intact. Wild coffee plants can be seen here. Hanakoa is a bit rainy, but it's intermittent and the sun usually dominates throughout the day. Numerous swimmable pools are born from the stream here. To get to Hanakoa Falls from here, which are even more amazing than Hanakapiʻai Falls, you'll need to take a worthwhile half-mile detour inland. Cross the Hanakoa Stream and hang a left at the trail near the shelter. Walk for about 150 feet or so, take a left at the fork, and continue for 15 to 20 minutes.

HANAKOA TO KALALAU BEACH

From Hanakoa to Kalalau Beach the trek is less than five miles, but it's a tough one and takes around three hours. It's important to start this one early in the morning to get as much time in as possible before the heat sinks in. The trail gets drier and more open as you approach Kalalau, but the views along the way make it all worth it. Out here the mana of the island is strong. Try to clear your head of thoughts and concerns of the outside world and soak in the invigorating beauty and peace of the valley. Around mile marker 7 is land that until the late 1970s was part of the Makaweli cattle ranch. After Pohakuao

Valley is Kalalau Valley, spanning two miles wide and three miles deep. Freshwater pools dot the area and look inviting after the long, hot hike. The valley was cultivated until the 1920s, and fruit trees are abundant in the area. Camping is only allowed in the trees along the beach or in the caves west of the waterfall—not along the stream, its mouth, or in the valley. The falls have a wonderful, refreshing pool. On the far side of the stream is a *heiau* on top of a little hill. If you follow the trail here inland for around two miles you'll find Big Pool, which is really two pools connected by a natural waterslide.

HONOPU, NU'ALOLO KAI, AND MILOLI'I

If you somehow have it in you to keep going, other destinations include Honopu, Nu'alolo Kai, and Miloli'i. Honopu is less than a half mile west of Kalalau Valley, and is known as "Valley of the Lost Tribe" by legend of the small Mu people said to once inhabit the area. The beach is separated by a big rock arch that has been used in at least two movies. You can get to Nu'alolo Kai by staying on the Kalalau Trail; it is right after Awa'awapuhi Valley, about nine miles down the coast. It has a lovely beach and dunes right up against a tall cliff. There's a pair of reefs here that provide good snorkeling opportunities when the water is calm. A community of Hawaiians lived out here until 1919, and their archaeological remnants still exist as stone walls and *heiau* platforms. They cultivated taro in the adjoining Nu'alolo 'Aina Valley, and they reaped the bounty of the ocean as well. Another mile west is Miloli'i, another site inhabited by native Hawaiians. At Miloli'i you'll find a very basic camping area with restrooms and a simple shelter. Down the beach is another *heiau*. Miloli'i only gets about 20 inches of rain a year, a big contrast from the rest of the wet Na Pali Coast.

BIKING

Hanalei and Princeville are the best areas on the north shore for biking. After Hanalei there are numerous one-lane bridges and a narrow winding road to Ke'e that could push bikers into the traffic. Princeville is the safest and most convenient place for a leisurely ride, although the steady incline heading up can be rough. To rent a beach cruiser to explore Hanalei, stop at **Pedal-N-Paddle** (Ching Young Village, 808/826-9069, www.pedaln-paddle.com, 9am-6pm daily) for hybrid road bike and cruiser rentals for $12 daily or $50 for

shearwater and chick at Queen's Bath

the week. Biking accessories are also available, along with water-sport supplies.

BIRD-WATCHING

Birds can be seen all over the island, but there are few official places to go birding on the north shore. Binoculars and patience are good accessories to bring. No matter how you may be exploring the island, there's a good chance you'll see all types of birds throughout the day, such as live plovers, mynah birds, and the Hawaiian nene. Of course, there are always the unavoidable Kaua'i chickens running wild in parking lots, hotel lawns, and shopping centers.

Kilauea

Kilauea Point National Wildlife Refuge (end of Kilauea Rd., 808/828-1413, 10am-4pm daily, www.fws.gov/refuge/kilauea_point), where 31 acres have been set aside for conservation, is one of the best places to bird on the north shore. Red-footed boobies, shearwaters, great frigate birds, brown boobies, red- and white-tailed tropic birds, and Laysan albatrosses, as well as green sea turtles and humpback whales, occupy the refuge. There's

an informational plaque at the top, and if you look down into the trees right in front of this area, birds can often be seen resting in their nests.

Princeville

Shearwaters nest at **Queen's Bath** (go right on Punahele Road and take the second right onto Kapiolani Loop) and can be seen along the trail and cliffs. Dogs are not allowed due to the high number of dog-related bird deaths.

Hanalei

At the 917-acre **Hanalei National Wildlife Refuge** in Hanalei Valley, endangered native water birds such as the Hawaiian coot, black-necked stilt, koloa duck, and gallinule can be spotted, as well as several migrant species that have reclaimed their ancient nesting grounds. The area is decorated with taro *lo'i*, the square patches where taro is grown. Although visitors are allowed in Hanalei Valley, no one is permitted in the designated wildlife area other than for fishing or hiking along the river. After crossing the first one-lane bridge into Hanalei, turn left onto Ohiki Road.

Adventure Sports and Tours

ZIPLINING
Princeville

For the thrill of flying through the air over verdant landscapes on a private ranch, **Princeville Ranch Adventures** (5-4280 Kuhio Hwy., 808/826-7669 or 888/955-7669, princevilleranch.com, by appt.) has three different zipline tours and one zipline and horseback ride tour, which start at $145 per person. The lines travel through valleys with mountain and ocean views and will get your adrenaline pumping. You can't miss the ranch entrance on the north side of Kuhio Highway before Princeville. Tour fees also include a picnic lunch and an experienced guide.

HELICOPTER TOURS
Princeville

Departing out of the small Princeville airport is **Sunshine Helicopters** (Princeville Airport, 866/501-7738, www.sunshinehelicopters.com). A 40- to 50-minute flight will take you over the Na Pali Coast, Waimea Canyon, and many places utilized in Hollywood films. Open seating is priced at $289, and first class is $364.

HORSEBACK RIDING
Princeville

The **Princeville Ranch Stables** (808/826-6777, www.princevilleranch.com, by appt.) offers four different horseback rides and other adventures through a 250-acre working cattle ranch. The tours start at $99 per person and are for people eight years old and up. It's about a half mile east of Princeville Center on the *mauka* (mountain) side of the road.

Hanalei Activity Center (Ching Young Village, 808/826-1898) offers horseback rides out of Princeville. Call for rates and times.

Polo matches are open to the public every Sunday at 3pm across from Anini Beach Park. Spectating makes for a unique Hawaiian experience and a great tailgate party.

Golf and Tennis

GOLF
Kilauea

To take in some lighthearted time on the greens, hit the little white ball around **Kaua'i Mini Golf** (5-2723 Kuhio Hwy., 808/828-2118, www.kauaiminigolf.com, 10am-8pm, last golfer 7:30pm, $18 ages 11 and older, $10 ages 5-10, ages 4 and under free). The miniature golf course can be viewed from the highway in Kilauea and is lacking in clown mouths and other toy-inspired themes. At this course, putters take a trip through Hawaiian history as they move through botanical gardens, each inspired by a different ethnic group found in Hawai'i. It's ideal to take the family or for a honeymoon date.

Princeville

At the **Princeville Makai Golf Course** (4080 Lei O Papa Rd., 808/826-1912, www.makaigolf.com), the excellent course recently underwent a multimillion-dollar renovation. Designed by Robert Trent Jones Jr. in 1971, the course was rated one of the top 25 golf courses in America for 2004-2005 by *Golf* magazine and has been ranked by *Golf Digest* as one of Hawai'i's top courses. From the central clubhouse there are three nine-hole, par-36 courses. The Makai course combines two of them and weaves around lakes, native woodlands, and the coastline with views of Bali Hai and Hanalei Bay.

The 18-hole course plays a par 72 with four different sets of tees. The renovations, also done by Jones, feature seashore paspalum turf grass on all tees, fairways, and greens, making a wonderful playing surface for all levels. All bunkers also underwent a bold reshaping. The cliff-top Ocean 7 is regarded as a tough hole, with a shot over a ravine, and the Lake 9 hole sets two lakes in the way of the shot, but the toughest hole is known to be Woods 6, with a long dogleg into the trade winds. The nine-hole Woods Course is revered as a leisurely course for the casual golfer with family and friends. The practice area at the Makai Golf Club has also been improved and includes two new practice tees, a practice fairway bunker, seven target greens with bunkers, a teaching tee, and a game practice complex. The club provides rentals for men, women, and juniors. Tee time can be booked at the pro shop, and the snack shop offers decently priced sandwiches, burgers, and snacks. Greens fees are $50 for the Woods Course and $140-210 for the Makai Course, with generous discounts for juniors. Various rates are also offered for golf passes and weekly packages. *Kama'aina* rates are also offered with Hawai'i state ID.

The 18-hole **Prince Course** (808/826-5000, www.princeville.com/golf) opened in 1987 on almost 400 acres of golf heaven. The course was renovated in 2012 by the original architect, Robert Trent Jones Jr. and cost $5 million. Named after Prince Albert, the son of King Kamehameha IV and Queen Emma, the course has both ocean and mountain views. It was ranked the number one golf course in Hawai'i and one of America's Top 100 greatest courses by *Golf Digest*. The course is once again being renovated and will reopen in 2016.

TENNIS
Princeville
At **Makai Tennis** (4080 Lei O Papa Rd., www.makaigolf.com/tennis), tennis fans can enjoy the four newly renovated outdoor hard surface courts. Reservations can be made at 808/826-1912, and tennis pros and certified professional instructors can be reached at 808/651-0638 for lessons. Rates run from $20 per hour to $65 for private lessons. Clinics are also available for $18 per hour or $21 for 1.5 hours. Several of the Princeville condos have tennis courts only for guests, so check with your condo.

Yoga and Spas

YOGA
Yoga is a popular form of exercise on the north shore, with studios across the region. Don't forget, you can always find a secluded beach to practice some poses on your own.

Kilauea
Pineapple Yoga (2518 Kolo Rd., 808/652-9009 or 248/765-4914, www.pineappleyoga.com, 7:30am-9:30am Mon.-Sat.) offers private classes in addition to astanga mysore-style classes six days a week. They do not practice on the new and full moons, choosing to rest instead. The studio is at the top of Kilauea behind the Shell gas station. The drop-in fee is $20 per day or $90 for the week.

    Metamorphose Yoga Studio (4270 Kilauea Rd., 808/828-6292, metamorphoseyoga.com, 8am-7pm) has morning and evening classes for all levels every day. The clean and modern studio offers 10 different classes of yoga instruction and has a lovely boutique (noon-6pm Mon.-Sat.) with apparel, yoga gear, and natural bath, body, and home products. You'll find the studio in the Kilauea Plantation Center, a historic lava-stone building caddy-corner from the Kong Lung Historic Market Square. The drop-in rate is $15 for all classes.

Princeville
The spacious Princeville park is a perfect place for some yoga poses, but **Princeville Yoga** (5-4280 Kuhio Hwy., 808/826-6688, www.

Metamorphose Yoga Studio in the Kilauea Plantation Center

princevilleyogakauai.com, classes at 9:15am Mon., Wed., and Fri., 8am Tues., Thurs., and Sat., and 4:45pm Tues. and Thurs.) is located in the Princeville Center above Lappert's Ice Cream for classes. Specializing in the beginning bikram hatha yoga series, several teachers offer public and private classes. A $15 drop-in rate includes the mat.

Hanalei

From Hanalei to the end of the road, any secluded beach spot is there for ocean-side yoga. For classes in town, bikram, astanga, mysore, and hatha yoga are all offered at **Yoga Hanalei** (5-5161 Kuhio Hwy., 808/826-9642, www.yogahanalei.com). Over 30 classes, workshops, and retreats can all be found here, so call or check the website for times. It's on the second level of Hanalei Center. They also have a boutique with yoga accessories and clothing. Single classes range $15-20 per class, and they offer a three-class traveler's special for $55. These rates include a yoga mat.

Past Wainiha, the **Hanalei Day Spa** (808/826-6621, hanaleidayspa.com, 9am-6pm Mon.-Sat.) in the Hanalei Colony Resort also offers private yoga lessons and yoga retreats.

SPAS
Kilauea

Time at **Pure Kaua'i** (4270 Kilauea Rd., Unit D, 808/828-6570 or 866/457-7873, www.purekauai.com) is not your average spa day. The luxury spa creates Hawaiian getaways as well as honeymoon vacations and romantic retreats. Luxurious accommodations, healthy meals prepared by a private chef, spa activities and services, and various sports such as yoga and surfing are all offered here. Unique services such as astrological consultations, life coaching, and relationship coaching are offered in addition to traditional services like massage ($150-195), facials ($135), manicures ($55), and pedicures ($95).

Princeville

To lounge in the lap of luxury, visit the **Halele'a Spa** (5520 Ka Haku Rd., 808/826-9644, www.stregisprinceville.com/spa) at the St. Regis Princeville Resort, where a consultant will customize a wellness regime to fit each person's needs. The spa combines Hawaiian healing traditions with western techniques to create a truly heavenly experience. Massages are offered with various Hawaiian elements, including hot stones with taro butter, traditional *lomilomi*, sports massage, pregnancy massage, and couples massage. Sixty-minute massages start at $165, and 90-minute massages start at $250. Facials combine healing properties to rehydrate and fight aging, while the clay wrap uses Hawaiian plants to detoxify and relax. Scrubs, baths, waxing, manicures, pedicures, salon treatments, and specialized bridal treatments are also offered.

Hanalei

The **Hanalei Day Spa** (808/826-6621, hanaleidayspa.com, 9am-6pm Mon.-Sat., walk-ins allowed if there's availability, otherwise by appt.) is nestled near the ocean in the Hanalei Colony Resort. Beachside and in-spa couples massage, Hawaiian *lomilomi* massage, facials, waxing, body wraps and scrubs, and Ayurveda healing treatments are all offered with the sound of the ocean in the background. Retreats, wedding services, and private yoga lessons are also offered. Fifty-minute massages are $110, 80-minute deep tissue massage is $345, and packages start at $220.

Shopping

KILAUEA
Kilauea Plantation Center

The Kilauea Plantation Center on Kilauea Road is home to the **Healthy Hut** (4480 Ho'okui Rd., 808/828-6626, www.healthyhut-kauai.com, 8:30am-9pm daily), where you'll find organic produce, fruit, and other natural foods. There are natural home wares and gifts, along with a health and beauty section, vitamins, and natural baby products. A very small wine and beer selection is also available.

Kong Lung Historic Market Square

Also on Kilauea Road is the **Kong Lung Historic Market Square** (2484 Keneke St., 808/828-1822, konglungkauai.com). The shopping center began when the Kilauea Sugar Plantation rented one of its buildings on the current market site to a Chinese businessman named Lung Wah Chee, who opened an all-in-one general store with merchandise, a barber shop, butcher shop, diner, and post office. The original wood-frame building was replaced in the 1940s by the stone building that stands there today. The building is now listed on the National Register of Historic Places for its role in the town's development.

The market square is home to an array of shops and eateries, including the **Lotus Gallery** (808/828-9898, www.jewelofthe-lotus.com, 10am-5pm daily), selling a spectrum of antique and modern Asian art and elegant jewelry made from pearls, opals, black diamonds, jade, and other stones, as well as Hawaiian *kahelelani* and sunrise-shell jewelry. Much of the jewelry is set in gold and is designed by the owners, who share a history in jewelry design and gemology. The shop is also stocked with carvings, garden art, and various artifacts. Lotus Gallery pulls you in from the outside with its outdoor waterfall and tranquil pond, and sets a high-end museum mood.

Exploring **Coconut Style & Tugu**

(808/828-6899, www.coconutstyle.com, 9:30am-5:30pm Mon.-Sat., 11am-5:30pm Sun.) leaves no one wondering why the shop was cited by *Architectural Digest* as one of Kaua'i's must-stop shopping spots. Exclusive hand-painted shirts, sarongs, bedding, and other clothing adorn the shop, which holds the title of having the largest collection of each in Hawai'i. Each piece is a marriage between Hawaiian and Balinese style.

Island Soap and Candle Works outlets (808/828-1955, www.islandsoap.com, 9am-8pm daily) can be found around the island. The Kilauea location is not only a retail shop, but also a working factory where visitors can watch the soap being made by hand. The shop offers a full line of all-natural products. The scents of the lotions, sugar scrubs, beeswax candles, balms, and more will make you long for a spa day.

Kong Lung Trading (808/828-1822, www.konglung.com, 10am-6pm Mon.-Sat., 11am-6pm Sun.) offers a spectrum of quality Pacific-inspired clothing, gifts, art, and more. It's a great place to window-shop, make a purchase to bring home, or absorb decor representing the various cultures in the islands.

PRINCEVILLE
Princeville Center

A variety of shops to fit most needs can be found in the **Princeville Center** (5-4280 Kuhio Hwy., 808/826-9497, www.princev-illecenter.com). **Foodland** (808/826-9880, 6am-11pm daily) offers the usual supermarket foods, as well as a drugstore section, beach and snorkeling supplies, and other basic needs. The large air-conditioned market is usually crowded and also has a pharmacy and a DVD vending machine requiring only a credit or debit card. The other big staple is **Island Ace Hardware** (808/826-6980, www.islandacehardware.com, 7:30am-5:30pm Mon.-Sat.), which has the gamut of hardware needs including keys and duct tape, and even fishing and tackle supplies.

Visit the **Hawaiian Music Store** (808/826-4223, www.hawaiianmusicstore. com, 9am-9pm daily) to find a soundtrack for your trip. It's actually a kiosk near the Foodland entrance. Listening to the music back at home will always take you back to Kaua'i. The kiosk usually has local music playing on speakers, adding an element of island style to the shopping center.

For a select bottle of wine, the **Princeville Wine Market** (808/826-0040, 10am-7pm Mon.-Sat., 1pm-7pm Sun.) holds an array of wines, something for every connoisseur's palate. Pick up a bottle for a romantic night at your accommodation or to enjoy a sunset beverage on the beach.

At the **Magic Dragon Toy & Art Supply** (808/826-9144, 9am-6pm daily), a compilation of unique and educational toys, games, activities, and kites can be found. Great art supplies are also available.

For local art check out **Naturally Hawaiian Gallery** (808/826-5354, 9am-8pm daily), a contemporary Hawaiian art gallery specializing in original paintings from nature artist Patrick Ching, as well as prints and locally made jewelry. **Fish Eye Kauai** (808/631-9645, 9am-6pm daily) features local underwater photography and art.

HANALEI
Kahaule Center

In the **Kahaule Center** (4489 Aku Rd.), on the ocean side of the road, **The Bikini Room** (808/826-9711, www.thebikiniroom.com, 10am-6pm Mon.-Sat., 11am-5pm Sun.) is where unique and quality Brazilian bathing suits can be found. They're stylish, small, and fit for both sunning and surfing, so this is a must-stop when bikini shopping. A sale rack can often be found in front of the shop, and the staff is especially helpful with insight on what suits are best for swimming or sunning.

The Root (808/826-2575, 9:30am-7pm Mon.-Sat., noon-6pm Sun.) has an array of fun, funky, simple, sweet, and trendy women's clothing. From dressy to relaxed, it's of high quality and pretty.

Hanalei Center

The historic **Hanalei Center** (5-5121 Kuhio Hwy.), on the *mauka* side of the highway, has an array of shops and eateries. **Harvest Market Natural Foods and Cafe** (5-5161 Kuhio Hwy. #F, 808/826-0089, http://harvestmarkethanalei.com, 9am-7pm Mon.-Sat., 9am-6pm Sun.) brings healthy food to Hanalei. The shelves are stocked with organic and natural food, produce, body products, and vitamins. Pre-made meals are in the refrigerator at the back of the store, and a salad bar offers an array of food. They also offer freshly made soup, hot entrées, fruit smoothies, and fresh sandwiches and wraps, as well as bakery goods and tea and coffee.

At the west and back side of the center is **Havaiki Oceanic and Tribal Art** (5-5161 Kuhio Hwy. #G, 808/826-7606, www.havaiki-art.com, 10:30am-6:30pm daily), where a visit feels like an exploration through the Pacific. The collection resembles what you may find while visiting a museum, with all the most prized gifts the area has to offer. Interesting and amazing artifacts, statues, carvings, jewelry, and much more pack this store full, ranging from affordable to outrageous. Every piece tells a story.

The **Yellowfish Trading Company** (808/826-1227, 10am-8pm daily) is an interesting store that feels like a journey through Hawaiian history and memorabilia. The store is loaded with Hawaiiana, collectibles, hula girl lamps, aloha shirts, carvings, swords, candles, jewelry, and so much more.

At the far east end of the old Hanalei school building is the **Hanalei Surf Company** (808/826-9000, www.hanaleisurf.com, 8:30am-9pm daily), which sells and rents boards and water gear, along with a good stock of clothing and swimwear for the whole family.

Ching Young Village

The bustling **Ching Young Village** (5-5190

Kuhio Hwy., 808/826-7222, www.chingyoungvillage.com) has many shops, including **Divine Planet** (808/826-8970, www.divineplanet.com, 10am-6pm daily) and **Aloha From Hanalei** (same phone and hours), which are two connected shops, but with different themes. The former features bamboo women's clothing, beads, Asian-themed collectibles, and pretty and fun paper star lanterns. The latter shop has a unique array of local gems, handmade creamy soaps and lotions made by a local goat dairy, and Hawaiiana.

Robin Savage Gifts & Gourmet (808/826-7500, 8:30am-7pm daily) may be the most fun gift shop in Hanalei. Local cards, children's clothing, books, lotions, home and kitchen wares, and gourmet foods fill the shop. The shop is stocked with an abundance of products, and it's almost hard to move, but there are a lot of good finds.

Hula Moon Gifts (808/826-9965, 10am-6pm daily) offers local trinkets, jewelry, shirts, and house decorations. Located on the back strip of shops, the store also offers island-inspired products and souvenirs.

On the east end of the shopping center is **Backdoor Surf** (808/826-1900, www.hanaleisurf.com, 8:30am-9:30pm daily). It rents and sells surfboards, and offers a large array of men's, women's and children's swimwear, surf gear, and clothing.

The **Village Variety Store** (808/826-6077, 9am-6:30pm Mon.-Sat., 10am-5pm Sun.) has an interesting array of souvenirs, housewares, and a random array of things. The cashiers are usually of the no-muss no-fuss type, and the store is fun to dig around in.

Colorful and cute describes the clothing in **Kokonut Kids** (808/826-0353, www.kokonutkidskauai.com, 10am-6pm Mon.-Sat., 10am-5:30pm Sun.), which offers all things local for children. From play clothes to dress clothes, Kokonut Kids can deck out the children for the whole trip.

Speaking of kids, the **Hanalei Toy and Candy Store** (808/826-4400, 10am-6pm daily) offers just that, and has a unique selection of quality toys. It's a good idea not to bring the little ones in here unless you're prepared to buy something.

Big Save (808/826-6652, 7am-9pm daily) is also here for all the basic supermarket needs. In addition to food and liquor, beach gear and school supplies are available, along with ice for the cooler and an ATM.

Ching Young Village

Hanalei Colony Resort

Na Pali Art Gallery & Coffee Shop (5-7132 Kuhio Hwy., 808/826-1844, www.napaligallery.com, 7am-5pm daily) is a wonderful art gallery filled with local art, jewelry, house decorations, tribal carvings, and more. The collection of Niʻihau and sunrise-shell jewelry at the back of the small shop should not be missed. Paintings, scratch-board art, and local shell puzzles decorate the place. Coffee, smoothies, and bagels are offered too.

Entertainment

The very best entertainment on the north shore may very well be the waves, snorkeling, or the sunset. But for those looking for a little more action, there are a few places in town with live music.

PRINCEVILLE

At the **St. Regis Lobby Bar** (inside the St. Regis Princeville Resort), those looking for a mellow social evening or date night will find a 180-degree view of Hanalei Bay accented by local music. Live jazz or Hawaiian music highlights the evening. The bar is open 3:30pm-10:30pm daily.

HANALEI

Hanalei Gourmet (808/826-2524, www.hanaleigourmet.com, 8am-10:30pm daily) in the Hanalei Center often has live music at night, but is more of a bar scene than a nightclub. Call for music schedules.

At **Tahiti Nui** (5-5134 Kuhio Hwy., 808/826-6277, www.thenui.com, dinner and music 6pm-8:30pm, late music 9:30pm-1am) dinner is offered nightly, but more importantly, it's the only place that could be considered a real nighttime entertainment venue in Hanalei, featuring karaoke and Hawaiian music. Check the website for monthly schedules.

Bouchons Hanalei (5-5190 Kuhio Hwy., 808/826-9701, www.bouchonshanalei.com) in Ching Young Village has live music Thursday-Sunday nights. Call for hours and music selection.

TO THE END OF THE ROAD

The oceanfront *luʻau* at **Mediterranean Gourmet** (5-7132 Kuhio Hwy., 808/826-9875, www.kauaimedgourmet.com, 6pm-8:15pm Tues.) offers the opportunity to fill your belly with a buffet dinner of traditional Hawaiian food while taking in hula dancing, fire knife dancing, and local music. Some of the mouth-watering buffet highlights include *lomilomi* salmon, traditional *kalua* pork, *haupia*, coconut cake, and, of course, Hanalei poi. Because it's limited to 80 guests, reservations are required, so call to get your spot. The adult charge is $69, which includes a drink, those ages 12-20 pay $59, and for children 11 and under it's $35.

Food

KILAUEA
Quick Bites

★ **Banana Joe's** fruit stand (5-2719 Kuhio Hwy., 808/828-1092, www.bananajoekauai.com, 9am-6pm Mon.-Sat., 9am-5pm Sun.) is a family-run, small yellow shop that sells smoothies, fresh fruit, baked goods, and local honey. The variety of fruit here makes Carmen Miranda's hat look boring. It's a perfect place for a pre-beach snack stop, a gift run, or an after-scenic-route stop.

Thai 2 Go (Kauai Pacific School parking lot, 4480 Ho'okui Rd., 808/652-3699, 11am-8pm Mon.-Sat., $9-10) serves up Thai food quickly out of a lunch wagon. The Thai chefs are very health conscious. The food is MSG- and GMO-free, and the chicken they use is hormone- and antibiotic-free. Try the green papaya salad and take your meal on the road or enjoy it at the on-site picnic table.

The roadside **Moloa'a Sunrise Fruit Stand** (right after mile marker 16 on Kuhio Hwy., 808/822-1441, 7:30am-5pm Mon.-Sat., 10am-5pm Sun.) is a tasty and easily accessible place to pick up smoothies, sandwiches, a variety of coffee drinks, juices, granola, and smoothies. Although it's a roadside stand, it sits on a well-kept piece of property with a grassy lawn and coconut trees. There are seats on the porch or you can take your food to go.

Seafood

"There's a whole lot more than fish in store" is the self-described motto of the **Kilauea Fish Market** (Kilauea Plantation Center, 4270 Kilauea Rd. #F, 808/828-6244, 11am-8pm Mon.-Sat., $10-30), and it's true. Free-range beef, salads, and plate lunches are also available, along with vegetarian specials. Enjoy the outdoor seating area or take it to go for a room or beach meal.

Health Food

At the **Healthy Hut** (Kilauea Plantation Center, 4270 Kilauea Rd., 808/828-6626, www.healthyhutkauai.com, 8:30am-9pm daily) you will find local produce, health and beauty supplies, and other natural groceries. A very small wine and beer selection is also available. They don't offer any pre-made meals; the only ready-to-eat food is fruit and snacks.

Kauai Juice Company (Kilauea Plantation Center, 4270 Kilauea Rd., http://kauaijuiceco.com, 8am-5pm Mon.-Sat.) offers cold-pressed, organic juices made from locally sourced ingredients. Start your day or rehydrate with one of their delicious and fresh concoctions. They also have elixirs and kombuchas.

Hawaiian

The Bistro (Kong Lung Historic Market Square, 2484 Keneke St., 808/828-0480, www.lighthousebistro.com, noon-2:30pm and 5:30pm-9pm daily, happy hour 5:30pm-6pm daily, $8-26) is near the lighthouse, not right by it. This is the closest to fine dining in Kilauea, but it isn't entirely formal; you can dress up for fun or go low-key. Lunch includes garden and fish tacos, garden and beef burgers, fish sandwiches, soups, and salads and runs $7.50-10 or $15 for all-you-can-eat pasta. Dinner includes ginger-crusted fresh catch, shrimp parmesan, coconut-crusted pork, ribs, and a lot more, along with salads and another all-you-can-eat pasta bar. Vegetarians will have plenty of options here. Wine, beer, and cocktails are available.

Deli, Pizza, and Bakery

★ **Kilauea Bakery & Pau Hana Pizza** (2484 Keneke St., 808/828-2020, www.kilaueabakery.wordpress.com, 6:30am-9pm daily, $15-33) in the Kong Lung Historic Market Square serves up satisfying breakfasts and coffee along with tasty pizzas. Mornings usually bring a line of loyal locals coming in for the sweet and savory breakfast pastries. Pizzas go in the oven at 10:30am and come with a heap of toppings.

Farmers Market
Sunshine Farmers Market at the **Kilauea Neighborhood Center** (4:30pm Thurs.) offers fresh produce and fruits. You can also find an abundance of locally made crafts, some ready-to-eat food, and other locally made food. Bring your own shopping bag.

PRINCEVILLE
American
CJ's Steak & Seafood (5-4282 Kuhio Hwy., 808/826-6211, www.cjssteak.com, lunch 11:30am-2:30pm Mon.-Fri., dinner 5:30pm-9:30pm daily, $15-38) is a steakhouse in the Princeville Center with a Pacific twist to most dishes. As at many steakhouses, saddles and other Western-themed decorations are found throughout. The open-beam ceiling restaurant has seating indoors or on the lanai. Lunch and dinner are both offered with a wide array of pupu. Lunch consists of hot and cold sandwiches, burgers, and salads, ranging $10-12. Dinner offers a salad bar, freshly caught local fish, lobster, and prime rib. A senior and children's menu offers a discount for their meals.

The **Kaua'i Grill** (808/826-9644, www.kauaigrill.com, 5:30pm-9:30pm Tues.-Thurs., 5:30pm-10pm Fri.-Sat., $32-72) inside the St. Regis Princeville Resort offers sweeping views of beautiful Hanalei Bay. The eatery stays true to its surroundings with a nautilus shell-spiraling ceiling. Chef Colin Hazama, who was recently recognized by the James Beard Foundation as a finalist in the Rising Star Chef of the Year category, cooks up a tasting menu, unique salads, a vegetarian menu, and lamb, meats, and fish, all with a unique island twist. A kids' menu helps keep the prices down.

Makana Terrace (808/826-2746, www.stregisprinceville.com, breakfast 6:30am-11am, lunch 11:30am-2pm, dinner 5:30pm-9pm Thurs.-Mon.) inside the St. Regis Princeville Resort offers breakfast ($12-35), lunch ($24-35), dinner ($26-48), and a Sunday champagne brunch. The Thursday Mailani Dinner Show brings Hawaiian chant, hula, and storytelling to diners for $135.

Sweet Treats
In the **Princeville Center** (5-4280 Kuhio Hwy., 808/826-9497) is **Hihimanu Shaved Ice** (8am-7pm Mon.-Sat., 8am-6pm Sun.), which doesn't sell just shave ice. They also offer fruit smoothies, coffee, and waffles. Twists like acai berries or spirulina powder can be added to the smoothies.

Also in the Princeville Center, for a more traditional cold treat, is **Lappert's Hawaii Ice Cream & Coffee** (808/335-6121, 10am-9pm daily, $4 for a single scoop), which scoops and serves some really good ice cream. Walk in and try a cone of ice cream, choosing from a rainbow of flavors from traditional to Hawaiian.

Thai
Lotus Garden Thai and Chinese Cuisine (Princeville Center, 5-4280 Kuhio Hwy., 808/826-9999, 11:30am-8:30pm Thurs.-Tues., $9-20) diners will enjoy authentic Thai food that even comes with a vegetarian and vegan meal. Entrées include soups, curries, fried rice, and vegetable, meat, and seafood dishes. Appetizers include spring rolls and green papaya salad. Inquire about delivery.

Mexican
★ **Federico's Freshmex Cuisine** (Princeville Center, 5-4280 Kuhio Hwy., 808/826-7177, 10:30am-8pm Mon.-Sat., $6-15) offers big portions of authentic Mexican fare. Carnitas, carne asada, and al pastor are favorites at this busy little family-run restaurant. From tortas to tacos, the fresh food is accompanied by a fresh salsa bar. Be prepared to wait a few more minutes than usual for your food because each meal is prepared to order. They also have a great kids' menu. For a few extra cents you can request biodegradable wares.

Pizza
Hideaways Pizza Pub (5300 Ka Haku Rd.,

Hanalei Fish Market

808/378-4187, www.hideawayspizzapub.com, 5pm-10pm daily, $16-36) is located in the Pali Ke Kua condo community. If you're staying in the area, it's a great option for a casual dinner without driving to Princeville Center. The Italian restaurant offers contemporary and traditional dishes as well as delicious pizza creations with local flair. Even better, they have a wide selection of beer on tap.

Supermarket

Foodland (Princeville Center, 5-4280 Kuhio Hwy., 808/826-9880, 6am-11pm daily) is the area's quintessential big-box grocery store. They also offer deli foods like fried chicken, macaroni and cheese, fries, freshly made sushi, and much more. The made-to-order sandwiches are tasty and good-sized for about $6, perfect for a beach day.

HANALEI
Cafés and Breakfast

The scent alone in **Java Kai** (5-5161 Kuhio Hwy., Ste. 210, 808/823-6887, www.javakai.

com, 6:30am-6pm daily, $8-13) in the Hanalei Center will make anyone who enters want to try the local coffee. The coffee is great, and the food is limited but includes a really good Belgian waffle, papaya and bagels, and a small selection of breakfast dishes including a breakfast burrito. Eat and run or drink your cup of joe on the porch.

Hanalei Wakeup Cafe (5-5144 Kuhio Hwy., 808/826-5551, 7am-11am daily, $5-7) in Kauhale Center keeps it simple, serving coffee, egg breakfasts, various pastries, and a papaya bowl. The decor is surf, with plastic chairs, but the breakfast gets the job done.

Harvest Market Natural Foods and Cafe (5-5161 Kuhio Hwy. #F, 808/826-0089, http://harvestmarkethanalei.com, 9am-7pm Mon.-Sat., 9am-6pm Sun.) also has coffee, tea, pastries, and other baked goods in the morning.

Japanese and Seafood

★ **Bouchons Hanalei** (5-5190 Kuhio Hwy., 808/826-9701, www.bouchonshanalei.com, 11:30am-9:30pm daily, lunch $9-15, dinner $11-30) delivers Pacific-American cuisine. The lunch menu, served 11:30am-4pm, features a range of foods from burgers and ribs to taco salads and chicken dishes. Dinner is served 5:30pm-9pm and includes exquisite sushi, a Pacific-themed menu, ribs, burgers, and other Asian dishes. An array of drinks and live music on certain nights are also offered. The restaurant is the best of two previous ones fused together by the owner.

Just after entering Hanalei you'll see ★ **The Dolphin Hanalei** (5-5016 Kuhio Hwy., 808/826-6699, www.hanaleidolphin. com), consisting of the restaurant, a fish market, and sushi lounge. The restaurant (lunch 11:30am-3pm daily, $10-16, dinner 5:30pm-9pm daily, $20-35) serves an array of Pacific Rim salads, burgers, and seafood in all of its glory. Enjoy your meal at the riverside tables or in the open-air restaurant. You can go casual here, but it's also nice enough to dress up. The sushi lounge (5:30pm-9pm daily) has a wonderful array of sushi and a good sake selection. The **Hanalei Fish Market** (10am-7pm daily) offers a wide selection of fresh fish and pre-made sushi rolls. You'll find a good variety of seafood, specialty cheeses, organic produce, beef, and desserts.

Hawaiian

The family-run ★ **Hanalei Taro and Juice Co.** (5-5070A Kuhio Hwy., 808/826-1059, www.hanaleitaro.com, 11am-3pm daily, $4-10.50) serves up a modern take on traditional Hawaiian food. Established in 2000, the company is part of the Haraguchi family farm (of the rice mill) and creates the meals with local foods and taro. They put a new twist on Hawaiian food, as with the taro smoothie and taro veggie burgers, while staying traditional with *kalua* pig, *laulau*, poi, *lomilomi* salmon, and a whole lot more.

★ **Postcards Cafe** (5 Kuhio Hwy., 808/826-1191, http://postcardscafe.com, 6pm-9pm daily, $18-38) is a vegetarian's (or seafood lover's) dream, with a spectacular menu of gourmet vegetarian and seafood cuisine. No meat, poultry, or refined sugar is used here, which makes the abundance of organic ingredients and local produce stand out. Many dishes are vegan or can be made vegan. If you like lobster, try the fennel-crusted lobster tail.

Health Food

Harvest Market Natural Foods and Cafe (Hanalei Center, 5-5161 Kuhio Hwy. #F, 808/826-0089, http://harvestmarkethanalei.com, 9am-7pm Mon.-Sat., 9am-6pm Sun., hot bar $7.99/pound) brings healthy food to Hanalei. The shelves are stocked with organic and natural food, produce, and body products. Pre-made meals are in the refrigerator at the back of the store, and a salad bar offers an array of food. Coffee and pastries are available in the morning, and the deli takes orders off their menu. Slightly on the pricey side, but it's healthy.

To the left of Ching Young Village is the **Aloha Juice Bar** (808/826-6990, $5), where you can find veggie and fruit juices along with acai bowls and chocolate-dipped bananas.

American

At **Bubba Burgers** (5 Kuhio Hwy., 808/826-7839, www.bubbaburger.com, 10:30am-8pm daily, $3.50-7.25) the food isn't necessarily spectacular, but the burgers are good and filling, and seem to remain so on a regular basis. The burgers come in different weights, and they even offer a garden burger. They use only grass-fed Kaua'i beef and have the usual burger joint sides, like shakes, sodas, and

Aloha Juice Bar

chicken sandwiches. It's on the *mauka* side of the highway in the center of Hanalei; you can't miss it.

Hanalei Gourmet Cafe, Bar, and Delicatessen in the Hanalei Center (5-5161 Kuhio Hwy., 808/826-2524, www.hanaleigourmet.com, 8am-10:30pm daily, lunch $7.50-13, dinner $10-27) offers a variety of restaurants in one. It's in the old school building, which adds a historical element to the laid-back atmosphere. Happy hour is 3:30pm-5:30pm daily. Dinner is 5:30pm-9:30pm. Early-bird specials are offered 5:30pm-6:30pm, and selected sports are available on cable TV. A really unique thing about this place is that they offer picnic services. They will help you pack your food and wine into insulated backpacks or coolers so you can hike the Na Pali Coast or paddle up a river. The meal selection is varied, from appetizers of seafood, nachos, and the tasty artichoke dip to dinners of pork loin, poultry, steak, and pastas, many with a Pacific twist. Salads are available in abundance, as well as sandwiches and burgers. This place has plenty of vegetarian options. There are two sides to the café, a sit-down restaurant and a take-out kitchen. Check the chalkboard out front for the daily specials.

Brazilian and Mexican

★ **Neide's Salsa and Samba** (Hanalei Center, 808/826-1851, 11:30am-2:30pm and 5:30pm-9pm daily, $10-20) serves up some really good margaritas, as well as unique dishes. The head chef from Brazil has a unique take on South American food, like adding cabbage and carrots to the dishes. The service is very laid-back, and there is outdoor and indoor seating. It can be a good place to bring kids because the porch seating lies on a yard-like area with a picnic table and garden, so children can roll around while you enjoy a really tasty, strong, and slightly pricey margarita. Vegetarians will not leave here with an empty belly.

Tropical Taco (5-5088 Kuhio Hwy., 808/827-8226, www.tropicaltaco.com, 8am-8pm Mon.-Fri., 11am-5pm Sat.-Sun., $5-14) is in the green Halele'a Building on the ocean side of the highway, the green being similar to the green lunch wagon the owner ran the business out of for 20 years. The tacos, burritos, and tostadas are tasty, simple, and can be grabbed on the run or enjoyed sitting at the location. Vegetarians will find a sufficient meal here. It's very popular, so expect a bit of a wait. The Baja-style fish tacos are the bomb.

Tapas

★ **Bar Acuda Tapas and Wine** (808/826-7081, www.restaurantbaracuda.com, bar 5:30pm-10:30pm daily, dinner 6pm-9:30pm daily, $6-16) in the Hanalei Center may be home to the most modern decor in Hanalei. They serve tapas, which are defined on the menu as a variety of small, savory dishes typically shared communally among friends. To never have a boring month, the menu here changes by the week and the season; offerings include local honeycomb with goat cheese, short ribs, local fish, salads, desserts, and a great wine menu.

Desserts and Snacks

Don't walk into **Pinks Creamery** (4489 Aku Rd., 808/826-1257, 11am-5pm daily, $4-7) in the Kauhale Center unless you are ready to be overcome by the scent of all things sweet, such as ice cream, shakes, and other treats. The single scoop in a cone is a little on the pricey side but so wonderful.

Pizza

Hanalei Pizza (808/826-1300, www.hanaleipizza.com, 11am-8:30pm daily, $12-25) in the Ching Young Village sells pizzas by the slice or the whole pie. They offer white or whole-wheat crust, which they make daily, and whole pies can sometimes require a wait.

Farmers Market

The **Waipa Ranch Farmers Market** (5-5785A Kuhio Hwy., 808/826-9969, 2pm-4pm Tues.) is loaded with local produce, fruit, jewelry, and other crafts. It's a good idea to get here at the start, as the good stuff sells out fast.

TO THE END OF THE ROAD
Mexican

★ **Red Hot Mama's** (808/826-7266, 11am-5pm daily but sometimes closes on Sun., $8-11) is a hole in the wall and thankfully one of the last stops before the end of the road. The food always comes in a hefty serving, and fresh local fish is almost always an optional addition. Vegetarians can always find a substantial meal here. The owner has enough postings around the eatery to let you know *not* to linger right in front and keep asking if your meal is done. Browse the neighboring shops or hang in the grass to the left and she will come out and call you.

Cafés

Na Pali Art Gallery & Coffee Shop (5-7132 Kuhio Hwy., 808/826-1844, www.napaligallery.com, 7am-5pm daily, $2-5) on the Hanalei Colony Resort property provides a last chance for smoothies, bagels, and coffee—in addition to extraordinary local art, jewelry, and gifts. Note that credit card purchases require a $10 minimum.

Mediterranean

★ **Mediterranean Gourmet** (5-7132 Kuhio Hwy., 808/826-9875, www.kauaimedgourmet.com, 11am-3pm and 4:30pm-8:30pm Mon., 11am-3pm and 6pm-8:15pm (*lu'au* only) Tues., 11am-3pm and 4pm-8:30pm Wed.-Sat. with happy hour 4pm-6pm, $17-65) was voted by *Honolulu* magazine as the best new restaurant on Kaua'i in 2007 and best restaurant on Kaua'i in 2008, 2009, 2010, and 2011. If that doesn't speak for itself, then the oceanfront location paired with the menu will amaze you. Lebanon native and chef Imad Beydoun and his wife, Yarrow, feature Greek, French, Spanish, Italian, and Lebanese-influenced dishes for lunch or dinner. Dinner reservations are recommended, and music is provided each night. Monday features guitar, on Tuesday a *lu'au* is offered 6pm-8:15pm, Wednesday is jazz and half-price wine night, Thursday is belly dancing, and Friday and Saturday offer more guitar. Try the homemade sangria or a mojito. Lunch includes wraps, vegetarian dishes, fish, and more. For dinner, there are vegetarian, lamb, beef, fish, chicken, and vegetarian dishes, along with their famous rack of lamb for two.

Information and Services

POST OFFICES

In Kilauea, the **Kilauea Post Office** (Kaneka St., 808/828-1721, 9am-4pm Mon.-Fri., 10:30am-noon Sat.) offers the usual post office shipping and packaging services. They also offer general delivery services for those in need of receiving mail but staying temporarily. To sign up for general delivery, you must go to the post office and register.

The **Princeville Post Office** (5-4280 Kuhio Hwy., 808/828-0217, 10:30am-3:30pm Mon.-Fri., 10:30am-12:30pm Sat.) offers basic shipping services. No general delivery services or passport services are offered here.

The **Hanalei Post Office** (5-5226 Kuhio Hwy., 800/275-8777, 9am-4pm Mon.-Fri., 10:30am-noon Sat.) provides shipping, basic packaging materials, and general delivery. Passport services are also available here.

LIBRARY

At the **Princeville Public Library** (4343 Emmalani Dr., 808/826-4310, www.princevillelibrary.com, 10am-5pm Tues., Thurs., Fri., and Sat., 1pm-8pm Wed.), you can find Internet access along with book and video rentals. Visitors can get a library card with proof of temporary address.

GAS STATION

The last gas station on the north side is in Princeville. So when you're headed to Hanalei from another locale, make sure to fill up. It's a bit of a drive from here to the end of the road, not a place you want to run out of gas.

Getting There and Around

CAR

The most convenient way to get to and around the north shore is by car. Route 56 heads west straight out of Lihu'e and runs all the way to the end of the road, turning into Route 560 by Hanalei. Rental cars are the best bet here and are available at the airport. Gas prices go up the farther north you go, so it's a good idea to fill up in Lihu'e.

BUS

The **Kaua'i Bus** (808/241-6410, www.kauai. gov/transportation, 5:27am-10:40pm Mon.-Fri., 6:21am-5:50pm Sat.-Sun., and holidays) runs island-wide with several stops through Kilauea, Princeville, and Hanalei. The bus is a green, convenient, and affordable way to get around. The last stop is in Hanalei at the old Hanalei courthouse. Fares are $1 for children and seniors, and $2 for the general public. Monthly passes are also available.

TAXI AND LIMOUSINE

Pono Taxi (808/634-4744, www.taxihanalei.com) offers taxi, airport shuttle, and tour services in Hanalei to any destination. **North Shore Cab Co.** (808/639-7829, northshorecab.com) provides rides to and from the airport and island-wide, and offers sightseeing tours. Hawai'i taxi rates are $3 per mile and $0.40 per minute. Prices are per minivan, not per person.

For a more upscale ride, **Kaua'i North Shore Limousine** (808/828-6189, www.kauainorthshorelimo.com) offers limousine service for a special date, wedding, or corporate travel.

SCOOTER

Hop onto a moped to zip around the north side and save on gas at **Island Scooter Rental** (5-5134 Kuhio Hwy., Kilauea, 866/225-7352, www.mobilemopeds.com, 9am-5pm daily). If you rent by the week the company offers free airport pickup, and they even offer four-hour tours for $100. Call for prices and reservations.

Po'ipu and the South Shore

There's a not-so-secret phenomenon that is known by locals and returning visitors alike: For an almost guaranteed sunny beach day, just head to Poʻipu and the south shore.

Even if it's raining on the north shore or windy and overcast on the east side, it's always sunny here. In fact, if it's pouring in the mountains, rain stretches down to historic Koloa town, where the showers abruptly turn off, as if there is a line in the sand.

This region tends to be dry and hot, and the cactus and succulents that line the road and open spaces confirm that. There's even a beautiful succulent botanical garden at the Outrigger Kiahanu Plantation planted back in the 1930s that still thrives today.

The south shore holds claim to an important part of state history: It was home to the first successful sugar mill in Hawaiʻi. Located in Koloa, the mill brought together seven different ethnic groups, the main source of labor on the plantations, shaping the state's diverse cultural demographic. The sugar mill was the central feature of society and life on the south shore. From 1835 to 1880, Koloa was Kauaʻi's most densely populated area. Koloa Landing, down in Poʻipu, was among the top three most active whaling ports in the entire state, and

sugar was a booming business for well over a century. The newest mill, the McBryde Sugar Co. Koloa Mill, shut its doors in 1996, ending the sugar dynasty on Kauaʻi. Its remains can still be seen off Mahaʻulepu Road.

Today, resorts, golf, ocean recreation, and dining are what you'll find in the region, with Poʻipu holding the lion's share of the amenities. While Koloa has evolved into a quaint and quiet residential town, Poʻipu has expanded with massive development over the last couple decades. Visitors who stayed on the south shore 10 years ago might not recognize the coastal locale, as luxury developments and high-end resorts now line the beach and spread inland to Koloa. There might not be as much open space as there once was, but the beaches remain beautiful and the water invitingly clear.

ORIENTATION

The south shore includes **Kalaheo, Koloa, Lawaʻi,** and **Poʻipu,** stretching from the dry and sunny shoreline surrounding Poʻipu to

Previous: Lawaʻi Bay, National Tropical Botanical Garden; monk seal on Poʻipu Beach. **Above:** Spouting Horn.

Look for ★ to find recommended sights, activities, dining, and lodging.

Highlights

★ **Tunnel of Trees:** Eucalyptus trees form a natural tunnel over Maluhia Road, creating a beautiful sight and great photo opportunity (page 118).

★ **Spouting Horn:** Saltwater erupts through a hole in the lava sea cliffs at the south shore's claim to fame (page 118).

★ **Sunset in Po'ipu:** End a lovely south shore day by watching the spectacular sunset in Po'ipu. Several locations offer great views from the beach or sand-free lawns (page 121).

★ **National Tropical Botanical Garden:** The only tropical plant research facility in the United States boasts two gardens with a vast array of plants. Informative tours speak to the history of the region (page 121).

★ **Kukui O Lono Park:** This lovely park is perfect for a stroll through Japanese gardens. It's also a quiet place to picnic with an ocean view (page 122).

★ **Maha'ulepu Beaches:** Visiting these sunny beaches is the closest you'll get to venturing into the wild on the south shore. The long dirt road keeps many people out, and the expansive beaches offer space for everyone (page 123).

★ **Po'ipu Beach Park:** A joy for all beach-goers, this beach offers protected swimming and a manicured park perfect for picnicking and relaxing. It's a wonderful place for children (page 125).

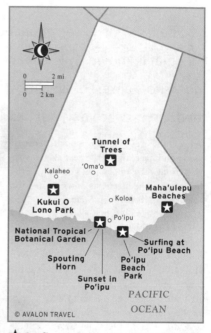

★ **Surfing at Po'ipu Beach:** This is the only beach in the region where the surf is very accessible for novices. Lessons are available, and you'll find expert surfers and surf schools pushing kids into waves in close proximity (page 129).

Po'ipu and the South Shore

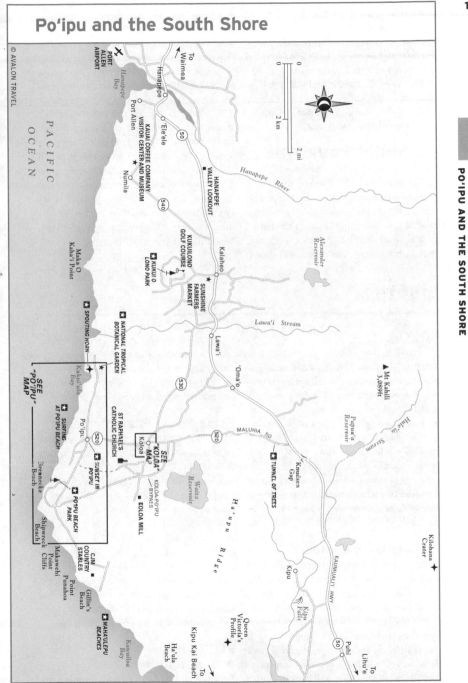

© AVALON TRAVEL

PACIFIC OCEAN

To Waimea

PORT ALLEN AIRPORT

Hanapepe Bay

Hanapepe

Port Allen

'Ele'ele

50

Numila

540

KAUAI COFFEE COMPANY VISITOR CENTER AND MUSEUM

HANAPEPE VALLEY LOOKOUT

Hanapepe River

Alexander Reservoir

Maka O Kaha'i Point

KUKUIOLONO GOLF COURSE

KUKUI O LONO PARK

Kalaheo

SUNSHINE FARMERS MARKET

Lawa'i Stream

SPOUTING HORN

NATIONAL TROPICAL BOTANICAL GARDEN

530

Lawa'i

'Oma'o

▲ Mt Kahili 3,089ft

Papua'a Reservoir

Kukui'ula Bay

SEE "PO'IPU" MAP

Po'ipu

520

SURFING AT PO'IPU BEACH

ST RAPHAEL'S CATHOLIC CHURCH

SUNSET IN PO'IPU

Koloa

SEE "KOLOA" MAP

520

MALUHIA RD

Waita Reservoir

TUNNEL OF TREES

Knudsen Gap

Hulë'ia Stream

Kilohana Crater

Brennecke Beach

PO'IPU BEACH PARK

KOLOA-PO'IPU BYPASS

KOLOA MILL

Shipwreck Beach

Makawehi Point Cliffs

CJM COUNTRY STABLES

Point Punahoa

Gillin's Beach

MAHA'ULEPU BEACHES

Kawailoa Bay

Ha'upu Ridge

Kipu

Queen Victoria's Profile

Kipu Falls

KAUMUALI'I HWY

Ha'ula Beach

Kipu Kai Beach

To

Puhi

50

To Lihu'e

0

2 km

0

2 mi

the thick jungles above Kalaheo. Kalaheo, Koloa, and Lawa'i are quiet, residential towns. The bulk of the accommodations, shops, restaurants, and sights are in Po'ipu. Po'ipu is also where you'll find all the ocean activities.

If you're headed to the west side, you'll inevitably pass through and Lawa'i and Kalaheo because the **Kaumuali'i Highway** (Route 50) is the only road that leads west.

PLANNING YOUR TIME

The south shore can be a day trip if you're staying up on the north shore or east side, or it can be a destination all to itself. For daytrippers, the appeal is hanging out at **Po'ipu's beaches,** soaking up the sun, and visiting the **National Tropical Botanical Garden** or **Spouting Horn.** The region is known to be dry and hot, so botanical garden explorers should plan their tours in the morning and head to the beach in the afternoon where they can cool off in the water.

Visitors staying in Po'ipu will find ample accommodations, including condos, bed-and-breakfasts, vacation rentals, and hotel rooms. The variety of condos and vacation rentals makes it easy for long-stay travelers to stock up the kitchen with food to avoid eating every meal out. While you might be able to see all the sights in a day or two, this is also a great home base for day trips to the west side and Waimea Canyon. Visitors who want to arrive at their accommodation, put the car keys away, and play at the beach every day will love what this region has to offer.

Sights

KOLOA
★ Tunnel of Trees

Entering Koloa via Maluhia Road takes you through the Tunnel of Trees, a natural tunnel of eucalyptus trees bending over the road, branches and leaves laced together. The trees were brought in from Australia by the Knudsen family to stabilize the road. If you can find a safe pull-off spot along the road, this is a wonderful photo opportunity if you can get a traffic-free shot. On very sunny days, the tunnel is especially intriguing as diamonds of light shine through the leaves overhead.

Koloa History Center

At the quaint **Koloa History Center** (Building 10 in the Waikomo Shops on Koloa Rd., www.oldkoloa.com, 9am-9pm daily, free), you can get some insight into the history of Koloa via artifacts and photographs from the plantation era. The center is small, yet the displays and photographs are a good place to start a south side visit for a deeper understanding of the region and its agricultural history. Near the Waikomo Stream, the center is at the former site of an old hotel and provides picnic tables and a small garden to enjoy in the courtyard, which is shaded by a very old and impressive monkeypod tree.

Koloa Sugar Plantation

All that's left of the foundation of Koloa town is the remnants of the old sugar mill, the first successful mill in Hawai'i. The mill, which was established in 1835, is located across from the shops at the end of Maluhia Road. A plaque gives a brief history and explains the significance of the mill and sugar industry. You can see and touch about 12 different varieties of sugarcane that grow on-site. A bronze sculpture pays respect to the seven ethnic groups that worked on Hawai'i's plantations: Hawaiians, Chinese, Japanese, Puerto Ricans, Filipinos, Koreans, and Portuguese. If you're shopping in Koloa, it's worth a quick stop.

PO'IPU
★ Spouting Horn

Near the end of Lawa'i Road, shortly after

The Best Day on the South Shore

Spouting Horn

You can easily experience the best of the south shore in one day without missing out on anything. While the best days on other parts of the island require visitors to move quickly through many activities, you can see the best of the south shore in a more relaxed manner. If you start with breakfast around 8am, you should be able to get it all done by sundown.

- Begin your day with breakfast at **Kalaheo Cafe.** Sit down or order takeout; either way you'll have plenty of time for the day. If you prefer takeout, head over to **Kukui O Lono Park** and enjoy breakfast amid a Japanese garden overlooking the ocean.

- Enjoy a walk through the **National Tropical Botanical Garden.** With two gardens and tours to choose from, you could easily spend anywhere from an hour to half a day exploring the exquisite gardens.

- While you're in the immediate vicinity, stop at **Spouting Horn.** Wait for a couple of big bursts from the blowhole, snap a few photos, and then it's on to the next stop.

- Head down the road to **Po'ipu Beach** for a surf. If you're an experienced surfer, renting a board is easy, or beginners can take a lesson. Make sure to book the lessons in advance. Afterward, grab lunch at **Living Foods Market and Cafe** in **The Shops at Kukui'ula.**

- For a relaxing time with full amenities, bask in the sun and salt at **Po'ipu Beach Park.** This is an especially good option if you have children. For a much more secluded beach time, make the drive to the **Maha'ulepu Beaches.**

- To end the day, enjoy the sunset in Po'ipu. Watch the sunset over the boats and Spouting Horn from **Kukui'ula Small Boat Harbor** or from the **Beach House Restaurant.**

- For dinner, stay at the **Beach House Restaurant,** or head back to The Shops at Kukui'ula in Po'ipu and take your pick between five excellent, high-quality restaurants. There's even **Lappert's** ice cream for dessert.

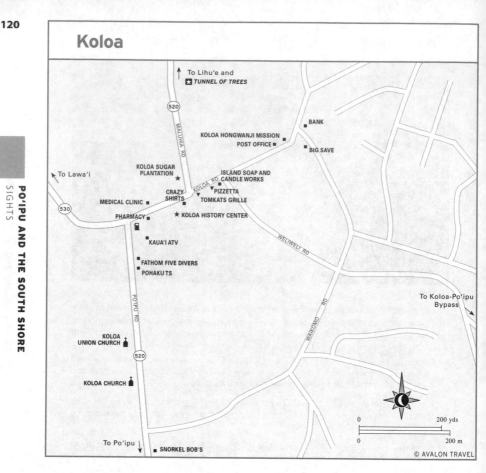

Koloa

the National Tropical Botanical Garden, is the south side's claim to fame, the explosive Spouting Horn. Saltwater erupts through a hole in the lava sea cliffs, bursting high into the air (the bigger the waves, the bigger the spray). Listen for a low moaning sound following each eruption from another hole that blows only air. Hawaiian legend says that a huge lizard called Mo'o (*mo'o* is Hawaiian for lizard) lived in this area. The lizard would eat anyone who tried to fish here. A man named Liko made that mistake, and Mo'o attacked him, only to get speared in the mouth and stuck where the blowhole is. According to the legend, the noise is the sound of the lizard's pain.

There is ample parking, a grassy lawn, and a picnic table along with souvenir and jewelry booths. The main viewpoint is from the gated area just in front of the spout, where everyone huddles together to get the best shot. Don't forget your camera for this one, and do not go down to the blowhole.

Koloa Heritage Trail

To learn about five million years of the south side's natural and cultural history, follow the 10-mile-long Koloa Heritage Trail. Don't be fooled by the name, as the trail is actually along the coast in Po'ipu. Weaving along the trail by car, foot, or bicycle, you will visit 14 cultural, historical, and geological sites of

The People's Prince

Prince Jonah Kuhio Kalanianaole was raised in Koloa. He was a worldly prince who attended the Royal School on Oʻahu and studied at St. Matthews College in California for four years. He also attended the royal Agricultural College in England and eventually graduated from a business school there. King David Kalakaua, also Kuhio's uncle, appointed Kuhio to a seat on the royal cabinet. Not long after, the Hawaiian Kingdom was overthrown in 1893. Kuhio joined with fellow Hawaiians to restore the monarchy, but the attempt was unsuccessful. He was sentenced to a year in prison while other activists were executed for treason. After being released, Kuhio left the islands and traveled in South Africa for a few years with a vow to never return to his homeland as long as it was inhospitable to its native people. When he came back to Hawaiʻi, it had been annexed as a territory of the United States.

For his efforts to help his people and work toward conserving the Hawaiian culture, Kuhio was nicknamed Ke Aliʻi Makaʻainana, meaning "prince of the people." Prince Kuhio served as Hawaiʻi's delegate to Congress from the early 20th century until his death in 1922. While part of Congress, he was a leader in the passage of the Hawaiian Homes Commission Act, which provides land for native Hawaiians to live on. He was loved and respected by his people for his efforts in working for the respect and rights of Hawaiians.

significance to the area. Each site has a numbered marker, and it's a good idea to pick up the *Koloa Heritage Trail* guide, which offers descriptions of each site as you follow the trail. Call 888/744-0888 to pick up the trail guide or visit www.poipubeach.org/local-resources/visitor-info/koloa-heritage-trail to download a copy. The self-guided tour stretches from Spouting Horn to Makawehi and Paʻa Dunes to the east, and then to Koloa town.

★ Sunset in Poʻipu

Poʻipu has a clear view west, and there are many places to watch the vibrant and colorful sunset. An ideal spot is at the **Beach House Restaurant** (5022 Lawaʻi Rd., 808/742-1424, www.the-beach-house.com, 5:30pm-10pm daily, $26-48) on Lawaʻi Beach. The open-air restaurant serves dinner, pupu, and drinks overlooking the ocean. For sunset worshippers, a waterfront lawn offers tiki-torch-lit outdoor lounging while watching the sunset and surfers at PK's. Although many locals and visitors like to spend the evening on the lawn here without eating at the restaurant, the lawn is technically part of the restaurant grounds.

At the very end of Lawaʻi Road is **Kukuiʻula Small Boat Harbor.** Here you will find a pavilion, a lawn backing a small strip of sand, picnic tables, and a small pier to watch the sunset over Spouting Horn. Swimming here isn't recommended, but it is a great place to end the day watching boats bob in the harbor as the sun sets on the horizon.

Prince Kuhio Park and Hoʻai Heiau

Across from the ocean on Lawaʻi Road and across from Hoʻona Road is the birthplace of beloved Prince Kuhio. The well-maintained monument and park has a large lawn, a pond, a pavilion, Hoʻai Heiau, and foliage. The beautiful area is a great place for culture and history buffs. The *heiau* (sacred rock structure) is in great condition.

★ National Tropical Botanical Garden

Composed of McBryde and Allerton Gardens, the **National Tropical Botanical Garden** (visitors center, 4425 Lawaʻi Rd., 808/742-2623, www.ntbg.org, 8:30am-5pm daily,) in Poʻipu is the only tropical plant research facility in the United States. With three gardens on Kauaʻi, one on Maui, and one in Florida, their mission is to enrich life through discovery, scientific research, conservation, and education by perpetuating the survival of plants, ecosystems, and cultural knowledge of tropical regions.

Over 6,000 tropical plant species flourish at the 259-acre **McBryde Garden.** Here you can explore a seemingly infinite array of plants and flowers ranging from bamboo to orchids. The gardens are divided into sections dedicated to medicinal and nutritional plants, herbs and spices, endangered species, fruits, and much more. Trams take visitors into McBryde Garden every hour 9:30am-2:30pm daily; self-guided tours cost $20 for those 13 years old and up, $10 for children 6-12, and children 5 and under are free.

The 80-acre **Allerton Garden** is named after the garden's creator, John Allerton, a member of a mainland cattle-raising family that founded the First National Bank of Chicago. The garden dates back to the 1870s, when Queen Emma first planted here at one of her summer vacation homes. In 1938, Robert Allerton bought the property, and for the next two decades he and his son John cleared the land. John traveled the Pacific extensively, bringing back exotic plants to Kaua'i. Cutting through the property is the Lawa'i River, and small garden rooms and pools make it quite an enchanting experience. The garden is complete with statuary and fountains. Guided tours start at 9am, 10am, 1pm, and 2pm Monday-Saturday. Reservations are necessary, and you'll want to make them about a week in advance as they are often booked up, especially during holiday seasons. The fee is $45 for those 13 years old and up and $20 for children 8-12. Children under eight are not allowed on the tour. Even for those who aren't generally interested in botany, this is an informative tour that covers the history of the area, Hawaiian culture, art, and design.

Drop by the visitors center across from Spouting Horn to check out the gift shop and displays in the restored plantation manager's house. They have Hawaiian crafts, Ni'ihau shell lei, and books about Hawai'i. Around this center, which was constructed in 1997 after the last center was destroyed in Hurricane 'Iniki, are the demonstration gardens, which are worth exploring even if you aren't going on a tour. Tours leave from the visitors center. Be prepared with water, comfortable walking shoes, and your camera.

KALAHEO
★ Kukui O Lono Park

Oftentimes public parks aren't exceptional places to visit, but **Kukui O Lono Park** (Pu'u Rd., 6:30am-6:30pm daily) is quite an

Kukui O Lono Park

enjoyable experience. A unique combination of Japanese gardens, rocks used by Hawaiians for various purposes, abundant plumeria trees, and a public golf course, the park is beautiful and has a great ocean view. It was given to the people of Kaua'i in 1919 by plantation owner Walter D. McBryde. After entering through the large stone and metal gate, go straight to find the gardens and memorial, or take the right at the fork in the road to find the golf clubhouse about a half mile up. The views in every direction are amazing. Pink plumeria flourish here, and the collection of rocks used by Hawaiians for various functions is quite interesting. If you're a runner, this is a great place to get some exercise. There is even designated parking for joggers.

To get here, turn onto Papalina Road in Kalaheo. About two miles in, turn right at the large gate on the second Pu'u Road.

LAWA'I

Along the hillside at **Lawa'i International Center** (3381 Wawae Rd., 808/639-4300, www.lawaicenter.org, free, donations accepted), 88 Buddhist shrines replicate the 88 temples along the thousand-mile trail and pilgrimage route in Shikoku, Japan. The center opened in 1904 in a small, lush valley that had been used by Hawaiians as a place of worship and then by Japanese Taoists and Shintoists. The area had become rundown and ignored until the 1960s, when a local woman organized the repair and eventual acquisition of the property. The area is lush with tropical foliage and dotted with orchids. During the tour you'll learn the history of the property and enjoy tea and local pastries. The tour begins through a small cave and leads to the miniature shrines, where previous visitors have left jewelry, shells, coins, and other offerings. The shrines can be viewed on the second and last Sunday of each month with tours taking place at 10am, noon, and 2pm.

Beaches

Some of Kaua'i's best beaches are found on the south side. They're blanketed in fine white sand and range from popular and crowded to secluded and rarely visited. All of the beaches are in the Po'ipu area, as Koloa, Kalaheo, and Lawa'i are all inland areas. The beaches are great for all kinds of ocean activities, such as snorkeling, surfing, swimming, and sunbathing.

PO'IPU

★ Maha'ulepu Beaches

Adventure into the outskirts of the south side and drive out to the Maha'ulepu Beaches at the east end of Po'ipu. You'll travel down a long and bumpy dirt road through undeveloped land with great views of the green mountains inland. The road is fit for two-wheel-drive cars but is usually pocked with ruts and potholes. Fortune favors the brave, though. Drive slowly and eventually you'll get to the long strip of beaches. Gillin's Beach is the first you come to, Kawailoa Bay is the second, and the third and most secluded is Ha'ula Beach. To get here, drive past the Grand Hyatt Kauai until the road turns to dirt. You'll see the CMJ Stables sign as the road turns to dirt and a gate. The access is privately owned, and the gates are locked at 6pm. Respect the area and pack out everything you brought in.

Gillin's Beach is accessed via a short trail through some dense shoreline brush. Parking is out of sight from the beach, so bring your valuables to the beach or leave them at home. The beach is very, very long with fine white sand. It's a nice beach for swimming, but be careful and use good judgment as the conditions are often windy and strong currents prevail. Although the beach is very long, it's not the widest from dunes to ocean. As

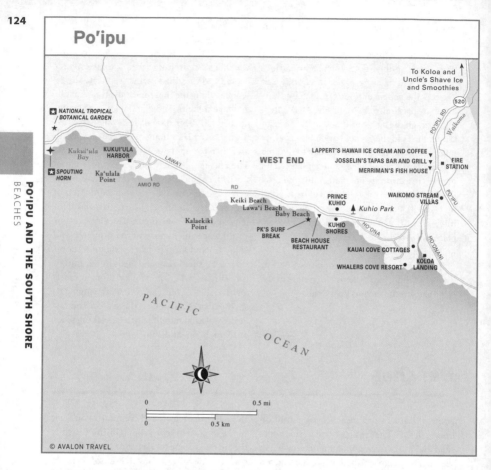

Po'ipu

the tide gets higher the sand gets narrower, and you will most likely see sunbathers bordering the dunes. To the right of the beach after Elbert Gillin's house is the Makauwahi Sinkhole, which is fun to explore. The open sandstone sinkhole has some fun elements to check out including unearthed archaeological finds.

Swimming is best east of Gillin's at **Kawailoa Bay,** where the water is most protected. To get here, drive past Gillin's and you'll see Kawailoa Bay from the roadside, or walk from Gillin's east around the bend, but it's a bit of a walk. The cove is calmer here than anywhere else on the beach, but the beach isn't quite as nice as the rest. Since the beach is in a semi-protected cove, the whipping winds can be less offensive here.

To get to **Ha'ula Beach,** walk for a while along the lithified cliffs. The cliffs look wild and prehistoric; they're rough, and you'll want shoes for this beach walk. After about 15 minutes of walking, you'll reach Ha'ula Beach. Swimming out here is always dangerous, but secluded beachcombing and sunbathing is ample. Serenity and isolation is the main appeal of making the trip.

Shipwreck Beach

Shipwreck Beach fronts the Grand Hyatt Kaua'i Resort and Spa. Named after an old shipwreck that used to rest on the eastern end,

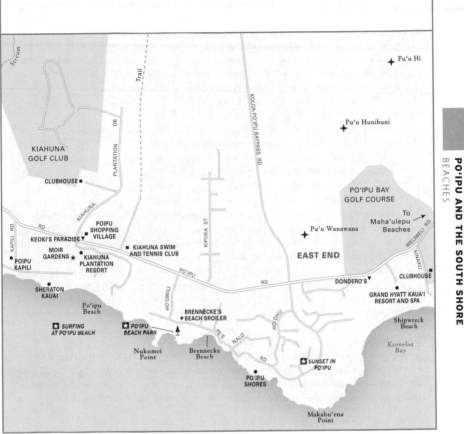

the beach is generally crowded because of its location. It offers plenty of space with about a half mile of sand, but the ocean here is usually too rough for swimming except for those who are experts in the water. Local surfers and bodyboarders congregate on the east end of the beach and surf the waves along the outer reef. Also on the eastern end is Makawehi Point, the high cliff that locals like to jump off for fun. To get here, drive toward the Hyatt on Weliweli Road and turn right onto Ainako Road. Park in the small parking lot at the end.

★ Po'ipu Beach Park

Po'ipu Beach Park (at the end of Kuai Road) is hands down the most ideal beach for families and children on the south side. A protected swimming area, playground, full amenities, and grassy lawn come together to create everything necessary for a full day at the beach. It's often crowded with visitors and local families, a testament to its popularity. The shallow ocean pool is semi-enclosed by a short rock wall, providing calm water within the rock barrier. It's a great swimming pool for children to float and play. The water isn't as protected on the west side of the beach, but if the waves are small it's safe and a great zone for swimming and snorkeling. Monk seals frequent the beach too, so if you see a seal, please respect all signs and safety zones and give the seal plenty of space to snooze in the sun.

An elaborate playground for children is located at the east side of the park alongside a shade-offering tree. Picnic tables dot the grassy lawn, showers and bathrooms are on-site, and there are lifeguards on duty. There is parking available across the street from the beach, but on most days the spots are full. Get there early to grab a spot or be prepared to wait for someone to leave.

Just east of Po'ipu Beach Park is **Brennecke Beach.** The waves are great for bodyboarding and bodysurfing. Surfboards are not allowed. Beginners can rent a bodyboard from **Nukumoi Beach & Surf Shop** (2080 Ho'one Rd., 808/742-8019, www.nukumoisurf.com, 8am-6:30pm daily) across the street and charge the little waves. To get here, turn down Ho'owili Road off Po'ipu Road. The beach is right at the bottom along Ho'one Road.

Po'ipu Beach

Also known as Sheraton Beach (because it fronts the Sheraton Kaua'i) and Kiahuna Beach, Po'ipu Beach is a popular, and therefore a generally crowded, beautiful beach. The swimming just offshore is usually pretty mellow thanks to the outer reef where the surfers find great waves. Surf lessons are also given

here. It's also a good spot for snorkeling if the ocean is calm, so bring your gear. There are restrooms at the grassy lawn above the sand. Parking here and along the street can be tight, so keep a lookout for several parking areas along the road. The beach is at the end of coastal Ho'onani Road.

Baby Beach

True to its name, Baby Beach is perfect for small children and babies. The small beach is nearly always calm, still, and shallow. The water here feels more like a saltwater swimming pool than the open ocean. There is a narrow strip of white sand descending into the water, leading to a rocky bottom. Hawaiian rocks can always be a bit tough on the feet, so bringing water shoes is a good idea. Kids will love jumping around in the water with floats here. To get here, turn off Lawa'i Road onto Ho'ona Road and look for the beach access sign. The beach is behind the oceanfront homes.

PK's

Located right across from the Prince Kuhio monument, hence the name PK's, the narrow strip of sand is most notable by the surf break to the right of the Beach House Restaurant.

Brennecke Beach

The wave here is also called PK's. Snorkelers will find a lot of fish here since the bottom is so rocky, but the ocean surface is usually rough. It's best to snorkel when the waves are very small and the wind is calm. The beach is narrow and just off the road, so it's less than ideal for a day at the beach. Drive down Lawa'i Road and you'll see the small beach below the roadside rock wall directly across from the monument.

Lawa'i Beach

A small white-sand beach in an almost always sunny area, Lawa'i Beach offers swimming and decent snorkeling along a narrow strip of white sand. The grounds of the Beach House Restaurant jut out on the left side of the beach, while condominiums act as a backdrop across the road. Across the street is a small parking lot with restrooms and a small shop. This is a popular hangout for local surfers, who enjoy a few beers at day's end while watching the waves at PK's. Head down Lawa'i Road and you can see the beach from the street right past the Beach House Restaurant.

Keiki Beach

A few yards down from Lawa'i Beach is Keiki Beach. A secluded and very small strip of sand just below the road, the small beach is accessible by hopping over the rock wall and stepping down past a few boulders. There's a little tide pool here that's good for a very shallow dip or for kids, only at low tide. The nice thing about this spot is that it's nearly always uninhabited. During high tide you'll find yourself sitting up against the rock wall, so it's best at low tide. Although small, Keiki Beach is a change from Lawa'i Beach just because it's usually empty.

Lawa'i Bay

Bordering the National Tropical Botanical Garden is Lawa'i Bay. The bay is usually only reached by those with a passion for serious ocean adventuring. If you kayak about a mile west from **Kukui'ula Small Boat Harbor** you will reach it. Those who make it there are asked to be respectful and not enter the gardens. Needless to say, you'll most likely be alone here if you make the trip. Park your vehicle at Kukui'ula Small Boat Harbor at the end of Lawa'i Road. Hop in the water with your kayak and paddle about a mile west down the coast.

Po'ipu Beach

Water Sports

SNORKELING AND DIVING

The south side has great snorkeling at several popular beaches. One of the highlights underwater is the large number of green sea turtles that feast on the seaweed that covers the shoreline rocks. They move slowly and are gentle creatures. Green sea turtles are a federally protected species, and it is against the law to touch them.

Po'ipu

BEACHES

Hop in the water at **Lawa'i Beach** and you'll see colorful reef fish. The water is clear and the bottom is rocky, which means fish are attracted to the area because they eat the seaweed and algae growing on the rocks. Just east of Lawa'i Beach and across from the Prince Kuhio monument is **PK's.** The snorkeling conditions are very similar to Lawa'i Beach, but the beach is rarely visited because it's right off the road. Down the road, **Po'ipu Beach Park** is a good option for snorkeling. There's usually something to see at either end of the beach, and the water is often calm here. The beach park is heavily used, so be prepared to rub shoulders with other snorkelers.

SNORKELING AND DIVING GEAR RENTALS

You can rent or buy snorkel gear at **Nukumoi Beach & Surf Shop** (2080 Ho'one Rd., 808/742-8019, www.nukumoisurf.com, 8am-6:30pm daily). They rent all kinds of beach gear, including complete snorkel sets for about $6 per day and $20 per week. At **Snorkel Bob's** (3236 Po'ipu Rd., 808/742-2206, www.snorkelbob.com, 8am-5pm daily) you'll find a wide variety of gear for rent. They offer complete sets including a mask, snorkel, and net gear bag with grade A surgical-quality silicone for ultimate comfort and water seal. The adult package goes for $35 per week or $22 per week for children. The budget crunch package offers a basic mask, snorkel, fins, and dive bag for $9 per week. A unique rental package is what they call The 4 Eyes RX Ensemble, to compensate for nearsightedness while snorkeling. This includes a mask with a

checking the surf at PK's

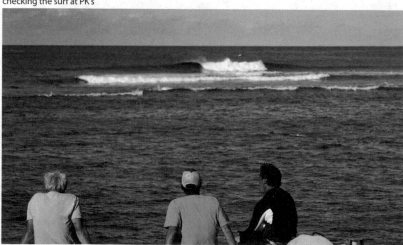

Top Kid-Friendly Activities on the South Shore

Although just about every site and activity on the south shore is fit for kids, there are a few high-lights for them, especially outdoor activities.

- The south shore is filled with beaches galore, but take the kids to **Po'ipu Beach Park.** There isn't a more perfect beach for kids than this, with its protected, shallow area for swimming, a playground, showers, and a grassy park.

- At **Spouting Horn** kids love watching the ocean water blast through a hole in the lava rock. There are also picnic tables on a well-manicured lawn and plenty of chickens to chase.

- **Surf lessons at Po'ipu Beach** will make any Kaua'i trip complete. Kids will love a chance to try to catch some waves.

- There is a really nice **playground** on Omao Road. Swings, slides, a small rock-climbing wall, a large field, a picnic table, and more make for a nice break from the car. Heading up from the bottom of the road, the playground is around three-quarters of the way up on your right.

- Kids love pizza, and **Brick Oven Pizza** in Kalaheo is a great place for lunch or dinner. Stop by on Monday and Thursday nights for an all-you-can-eat buffet.

prescription lens for $44 per week for adults and $32 for kids.

Fathom Five (3450 Po'ipu Rd., 808/742-6991, www.fathomfive.com, 7am-6pm daily) offers everything you could need for casual snorkeling to professional diving. They rent complete snorkel sets for $6 daily. For diving, the company has over 26 boat dive locations and a few shore dives. A complete list of their dives is featured on their website, with exceptional detail about each dive. If you need to rent dive equipment, shore dives start at $130, and two-tank boat dives start at $170. Their boats leave from Kukui'ula Small Boat Harbor. **Boss Frog's** (5022 Lawa'i Rd., 808/742-9111, www.bossfrog.com, 8am-5pm daily) has rental snorkel gear for $8 per day or $30 per week. It's at Lawa'i Beach in the same building as the Beach House Restaurant.

SURFING AND STAND-UP PADDLING
★ **Po'ipu**
BEACHES
The break at **Po'ipu Beach,** also known as Waiohai, is a great wave for beginners and intermediate surfers. It breaks best when it's head high or smaller and breaks right and left.

The lefts break into a very shallow section of the reef on the inside that is a favorite for bodyboarders. It can get crowded with locals and visitors staying in the surrounding hotels. For a local spot with both left- and right-hand breaking waves, paddle out to **PK's** in front of Lawa'i Beach. The waves here mostly break left, but the section directly in front of the restaurant breaks as a right sometimes. Paddle out from the beach, but keep an eye out for sections of shallow reef. The wave is a local favorite, so be mellow and respectful. During the right swell, a powerful and intense right-hand breaking wave called **Acid Drops** is to the west of PK's. This wave is heavy, but a coveted wave for experienced surfers.

SURF LESSONS AND GEAR
Po'ipu is a hot spot for surfing, and a Hawaiian vacation wouldn't be complete without at least trying to catch a few waves. If you haven't surfed before, a lesson is the way to go. The instructor will teach you the basics of the sport and current ocean conditions. Several surf schools offer lessons at Po'ipu Beach. Experienced surfers can simply rent a board and hit the surf.

For lessons from a company started by

a true surf pioneer, try **Surf Lessons by Margo Oberg** (808/332-6100, www.sur-fonkauai.com) at Po'ipu Beach. You'll have the option of group lessons ($68), semiprivate lessons ($90), or private lessons ($125). The surf school is known for satisfying customers and was recently named in *National Geographic Traveler Magazine* as one of the top 25 things to do on Kaua'i. Lessons begin with a short instruction on land to learn the basics of the sport along with ocean safety. Soft boards and protective booties are provided. Instructors are locals who are previous or current professional surfers.

Also offering lessons at Po'ipu Beach is the **Garden Island Surf School** (808/652-4841, www.gardenislandsurfschool.com). They offer group lessons for $75 and private lessons for $150, or $120 for two students. All lessons are two hours in duration at 8am, 10am, and noon and require reservations. For something different try outrigger canoe surfing, where you'll catch waves in a canoe. They also give stand-up paddle lessons; 90-minute classes are $70. You'll find their kiosk at the Ko'a Kea Hotel & Resort poolside kiosk. The entrance to the resort is off Po'ipu Road.

Kaua'i Surf School (808/651-6032, www.kauaisurfschool.com) offers lessons at Po'ipu Beach as well as weeklong surf clinics. For 1.5-hour group classes of no more than four people they charge $75 per person; a one-hour private lesson costs $100, while a two-hour private lesson is $175; and a two- to three-person semiprivate lesson is $240. They provide a beginner surfboard, protective booties, and a rash guard.

To rent a board, contact **Poipu Surf** (2829 Ala Kalanikaumaka Rd., Ste. H-151, 808/742-8797, 9am-9pm daily). Located in The Shops at Kukui'ula, they rent high-performance surfboards for $25 per day or $110 per week and bodyboards for $8 per day with fins or $25 per week. **Nukumoi Beach & Surf Shop** (2080 Ho'one Rd., 808/742-8019, www.nukumoisurf.com, 8am-6:30pm daily) rents soft longboards for $25 per day and $75 per week, epoxy shortboards for $30 per day and $90 per week, and stand-up paddleboards starting at $60 per day and $250 per week. They charge $6 for soft surfboard racks for the duration of your rental.

KAYAKING
Po'ipu
You can kayak the south shore's coastline with **Outfitters Kauai** (2827A Po'ipu Rd., 808/724-9667, www.outfitterskauai.com) on their kayaking and whale-watching secluded beach adventure, which is available Tuesday-Saturday from mid-September through May. They use tandem, open cockpit, or sit-on-top-type self-bailing kayaks with foot-pedal-controlled rudders to explore the coast. You'll paddle to secret beaches and snorkel and bodysurf at beaches that are only accessible by water. Because the tours are done in the wintertime, whale sightings are common, as well as dolphin and sea turtle sightings. Price for adults is $162 and children 12-14 are $131.

Adventure Sports and Tours

ATVS
Koloa
Ride ATVs with **Kaua'i ATV** (3477-A Weliweli Rd., 866/482-9775, www.kauaiatv.com, 7:30am-5pm daily, $113-170). They have a large collection of vehicles and can take family groups or individuals. They offer two tours: the Waterfall Tour, a four-hour, 23-mile adventure that includes a stop at a waterfall with a pool and lunch, and the Koloa Tour, a three-hour tour on 22,000 acres of private land with mountain and ocean views. They have clothing to loan, so you don't have to get yours dirty. They also offer *'ohana* (family) buggies to ride with your group. Reservations are required.

The Kaua'i Cave Wolf Spider

The blind Kaua'i cave wolf spider is only found in three caves in the Koloa-Po'ipu area on the south shore. Discovered in 1973, the harmless spider has no eyes. It's both rare and unusual because it's blind, unlike other wolf spiders on the island. To the left of the second fairway at the Kiahuna Golf Course are a couple of caves that are home to the spider. It's believed that the spider is at risk because of the pesticides seeping into the cave.

Wolf spiders get their name from being fast runners. Rather than catching their victims in webs like most spiders do, they chase their prey and catch it. Once they catch the prey, they bite the victim and inject poison through their fang-tipped chelicerae—which resemble miniature elephant tusks when seen through a lens. The venom paralyzes the prey and also deteriorates its tissues, breaking them down to a liquid, which the spider can suck out and swallow through its small mouth. They feed on insects like beetles and ants, leaving humans alone.

ZIPLINING
Lawa'i

Adrenaline junkies can fly through the air with **Just Live** (3416 Rice St., 808/482-1295, ziplinetourskauai.com, 7am-5pm daily). The adventure sports company offers three different zipline ecotours as well as a ropes course. The Zipline Treetop Tour covers seven different zipline courses and lets you walk over four canopy bridges for $120. The ziplines run up to 800 feet long and are suspended 60-80 feet in the air. The Wikiwiki Zip Tour utilizes three different ziplines, two of which are over 700 feet long, and three bridge crossings for $79. The Zipline Eco Adventure combines three ziplines, three bridges, rappelling, a monster swing, and rock-wall climbing for $125. Tours include a snack and water.

BOAT TOURS
Po'ipu

Several boat tour companies cruise Po'ipu waters. They also offer **whale-watching** from December through April. **Captain Andy's Sailing Adventures** (4353 Waialo Rd., 808/335-6833, www.napali.com) offers various boat cruises, and each one includes whale-watching in season. During the winter months, combine whale-watching with the two-hour Po'ipu Sunset Sail, which takes you down to the secluded Maha'ulepu Beaches and Kipu Kai. Adults cost $69, children $49, and kids under two are free. The sail includes live Hawaiian music, appetizers, beer, and wine. In season, whales and dolphins are a common sight.

Blue Dolphin Charters (4354 Waialo Rd., 808/335-5553, www.kauaiboats.com) offers a two-hour South Side Sunset Sail in the Po'ipu area. Food, cocktails, and romantic sunsets are enjoyed on this tour, along with whales in season. This company prefers December through March as whale season, and rates run $72 for adults 18 and up, $67 for youth 12-17, and $53 for childrens 2-11.

GUIDED HIKING TOURS
Koloa

Kaua'i Nature Tours (808/742-8305, 888/233-8365, www.kauainaturetours.com) offers guided hikes in the Maha'ulepu area on the east end of the south side. They also offer hikes in other parts of the island. The guides, authors of *Kaua'i's Geologic History,* share insight into the island's geological formation and history. On this hike you'll see wildlife and enter a sinkhole where fossil-filled sediment speaks to the island's history. The 2.5-mile coastal walk begins after a 9am pickup at Po'ipu Beach Park. They provide lunch after a four-hour walk to a private beach cove, and snorkeling and swimming in Kawailoa Bay. The rate is $135 for adults and $105 for children 5-12.

HORSEBACK RIDING
Po'ipu

A down-to-earth and peaceful way to explore the south side is with **CJM Country Stables** (1831 Po'ipu Rd., 808/742-6096, http://cjm-stables.com, 8am-5pm daily for reservations). Located on the east end of Po'ipu, they offer scenic horseback rides through the forest and along the coast. Journeying into the undeveloped Maha'ulepu area, you'll ride along secluded beaches as well as into the green interior of the land. The Mahaleapu Beach Ride includes beverages for $110, but you must bring your own lunch. The two-hour ride is offered at 9:30am and 2pm daily except Sunday. They also offer the Secret Beach Picnic Ride for $140. After riding to a secluded beach, the guide makes a picnic lunch. The three-hour tour is available at 1pm on Wednesday and Friday. Experienced riders can request private rides for $130 per hour.

Golf and Tennis

PO'IPU
Po'ipu Bay Golf Course

Golf fanatics will love the **Po'ipu Bay Golf Course** (2250 Ainako St., 808/742-8711, www.poipubaygolf.com) at the Grand Hyatt Kaua'i Resort and Spa. Designed by course architect Robert Trent Jones Jr., the high-end course offers fabulous surroundings, mountain and ocean views, and open space on 210 oceanfront acres. The 18-hole course consists of 85 bunkers, five water hazards, and wild trade winds that are Mother Nature's way of testing a player's game and patience. A sacred *heiau* is on the grounds, along with ancient stone walls. Modern amenities are offered like in-cart satellite navigation systems, an on-course beverage court, and daily professional clinics. The ocean-links-style course has over 30 acres of tropical plants and flowers with wonderful views. The large clubhouse is home to a golf shop open 6:30am-6:30pm daily, locker room facilities, a restaurant and lounge, and club storage.

Tee times can be made up to 30 days in advance. First tee time is at 7am, and everyone must be off the course by 6:15pm. The general

golf course in Po'ipu

public rate is $240, hotel guests pay $160, after noon the rate drops to $145, and after 2:30pm it's $85. Club rentals are $55 and include Callaway, Titleist, Cobra, and TaylorMade. Carts are mandatory, and appropriate attire is required.

Kiahuna Golf Club

The **Kiahuna Golf Club** (2545 Kiahuna Plantation Dr., 808/742-9595, www.kiahuna-golf.com) inland in Po'ipu offers 18 holes on a course also designed by Robert Trent Jones Jr. The course, which is more affordable than Po'ipu Bay Golf Course, features remnants of ancient Hawaiian structures and good mountain views with glimpses of the ocean. Notable sights on the course include the endangered state bird, the nene goose, which you may see wandering around the greens. The Hawaiian stilt and moorhen may also be seen here. To the left of the 15th fairway are the remnants of a house where a Portuguese immigrant lived during the early 19th century. Nearby is the crypt where he and his family were laid to rest.

The first tee time is at 7am and the last is at 4:30pm, with players required to be off the course by 7pm. Play 18 holes with a cart for $103. After 2pm the price drops to $72. Golfers 17 and under can spend a day on the greens for $47. They offer a bounce-back rate of $88 for the duration of your stay, cart included. Club rentals are offered for $52 for 18 holes and $32 for nine holes.

Kiahuna Swim and Tennis Club

At the **Kiahuna Swim and Tennis Club** (2290 Po'ipu Rd., 808/742-2111, www.kiahunacondos.com/swim-tennis-club.html, 6am-7pm daily) is open to the public, and players can utilize eight courts. Contact them to reserve court time, for rates, and for lessons from a tennis pro.

Grand Hyatt Kaua'i Resort and Spa

The **Tennis Garden and Sports Center** at the **Grand Hyatt Kaua'i** (1571 Po'ipu Rd., 808/240-6391, 8am-noon and 1pm-6pm daily) offers tennis clinics, lessons, and equipment rentals. One hour of court time daily is complimentary to all guests. Additional court time is available at $30 per hour. Call for other rates.

KALAHEO
Kukuilono Golf Course

The nine-hole **Kukuilono Golf Course** (854 Pu'u Rd., 808/332-9151, $9 adults, $3 under 17, cash only) is a very affordable place to spend the day on the greens. Donated to the state by Walter McBryde in 1919, the course was the second built on Kaua'i. McBryde loved the course so much that he was buried by the eighth hole. A Japanese garden, many fragrant plumeria trees, and a Hawaiian rock collection are also on-site. The course has wonderful ocean views. Carts can be rented for $6 per day. The course doesn't book tee times; it's first-come, first-served, with the first tee time starting at 6:30am. For those renting clubs, the last tee time is at 3pm, while those who brought their own can tee off at 4:30pm.

Yoga and Spas

KOLOA

Yoga is offered at a variety of places on the south side. For practice with an instructor who offers classes at several locations, try **Yoga at Koloa Hongwanji** (5521 Koloa Rd.) for hatha yoga. Classes are offered here Monday and Thursday at 8:30am for $15 visitors and $12 *kama'aina*. The same instructor also leads classes at the Grand Hyatt Kaua'i's **Anara Spa** (1571 Po'ipu Rd., 808/240-6440, www.anaraspa.com) in Po'ipu on Monday and Thursday mornings at 10:30am and Wednesday mornings at 9:30am. The spa grounds are beautiful and exotic, and practice takes place in an open-air yoga pavilion. For more information, contact Paul Reynolds at 650/773-3422 or check out his site at www.unlimited-ideas.com.

PO'IPU

Pure luxury can be indulged in at **Anara Spa** (1571 Po'ipu Rd., 808/240-6440, www.anaraspa.com, 7am-8pm daily) at the Grand Hyatt Kaua'i. Services are offered both indoors and outdoors in the enchanting Lokahi Garden with waterfalls, soaking pools, and open-air bungalows. You can find a full-service salon here, a spa boutique, a garden Vichy shower, a lap pool, steam rooms, saunas, and more. Hawaiian healing methods are integrated into the treatments as well as tropical scents. Relax in the lap of luxury and receive ultimate pampering here. Anara Spa offers massage in a variety of modalities ranging $160-235, including Hawaiian *lomilomi* and maternity.

Facials with tropical scents and ingredients range $105-250. Body treatments run $165-320. Luxurious spa packages are also available and are pricey. Salon services cover all general services from nails to bridal styling and even kids' treatments for mother and daughter time.

Located in the Ko'a Kea boutique hotel is **The Spa** (2251 Po'ipu Rd., 808/828-8888, www.koakea.com/spa-experience, 9am-5pm daily). The spa has five treatment rooms and a romantic couples suite that draw inspiration from the natural beauty of the island; it focuses on natural and indigenous ingredients in its treatments and products. Massages range $75-135 and include Swedish, deep therapy, *lomilomi*, hot stone, and pregnancy. Their couples 50-minute massage starts at $240. Facials and scalp treatments start at $120. They also have a Sun Kissed Rescue Wrap for $105 if you've overdone it in the sun. They offer a handful of body treatments starting at $75 for a sea salt coconut body polish.

KALAHEO

Inland in Kalaheo is **Kalaheo Yoga** (4427 Papalina Rd., 808/652-3216, www.kalaheoyoga.com), with a wide variety and broad schedule of classes and yoga traditions provided daily. Check the website for scheduling. An up-to-date calendar lists all classes, and you can reserve a space online. Single classes run $18, a 3-class card costs $48, and a 10-class card costs $120. Workshops are also offered.

Shopping

Shopping on the south side is contained to several areas where shops are clustered together. The area is filled with many boutiques, galleries, souvenir shops, and clothing stores. Most daily shopping needs are found in nearby Lihu'e.

KOLOA
Clothing

For a unique array of clothing, check out **Jungle Girl** (5424 Koloa Rd., 808/742-9649, 9am-9pm daily). They also have a collection of accessories and housewares. There are some locally made items as well as creations from around the world. If you're looking for aloha wear, drop into **Pohaku Ts** (3430 Po'ipu Rd., 808/742-7500, www.pohaku.com, 10am-6pm Mon.-Sat., 10am-5pm Sun.). They offer cotton aloha shirts that are designed, cut, and sewn on Kaua'i for men, women, and children. Bikinis galore decorate the inside of **South Shore Bikinis** (3450 Po'ipu Rd., 808/742-5200, 9am-7pm daily), where they specialize in the tiny-backed Brazilian bikini. They also offer a variety of other suits along with beachwear for all ages, hats, sandals, and other accessories. A huge spectrum of Kaua'i and Hawai'i souvenir shirts can be found in **Crazy Shirts** (5356 Koloa Rd., 808/742-7161, www.crazyshirts.com, 10am-9pm). A chain found throughout the islands, they sell shirts and a few other items for men, women, and children with a heavy Kaua'i and Hawai'i theme.

Gifts, Crafts, and Souvenirs

Island-style souvenirs and gifts can be found at **Hula Moon Gifts** (5426 Koloa Rd., 808/742-9298, 9am-9pm Mon.-Sat., 10am-9pm Sun.). They sell unique locally made crafts, gifts, and jewelry. At the **Emperor's Emporium** (5330 Koloa Rd. #3, 808/742-8377, 9am-9pm daily) you will find a resort-style store offering jewelry, gifts, and clothing. The fragrant scents emanating from **Island Soap and Candle Works** (Koloa Rd., 808/742-1945, www.kauaisoap.com, 9am-9pm daily) will draw you in. The locally run store has shops island-wide where they manufacture natural Hawaiian botanical products, beeswax candles, and other gifts. While shopping you'll get a behind-the-scenes look into how it's all made.

Wine

The lovely **Wine Shop** (5470 Koloa Rd., 808/742-7305, www.thewineshopkauai.com, 10am-7pm Mon.-Sat.) in Koloa offers a great selection of wine along with other spirits. Fun and cute wine accessories, gift baskets, and gourmet foods are also available.

General Store

The Koloa **Big Save** (5516 Koloa Rd., 808/742-1614, 6am-11pm daily) offers a lot more than food. They have a decent array of basic fishing gear and poles, limited snorkel gear, beach gear, stationery, and other basic needs.

PO'IPU

Most of Po'ipu's recommended shops are located within **The Shops at Kukui'ula** (2829 Ala Kalanikaumaka St., 808/742-9545, www.theshopsatkukuiula.com, 10am-9pm daily), the south shore's premier high-end outdoor mall, home to award-winning restaurants, boutiques, and contemporary art galleries.

Galleries

Admire the work of local crafters and artists at **Halele'a Gallery** (The Shops at Kukui'ula, Ste. K, 808/742-9525, www.haleleagallery.com, 10am-9pm daily), a chic boutique gallery. Island artisans and designers showcase their creations, like wall art, jewelry, photography, koa furniture, and apparel. A wonderful source for locally made products is **Palm Palm** (The Shops at Kukui'ula, Ste. H157, 808/742-1131, www.palmpalmkauai.com,

10am-9pm daily). It's well stocked with fashionable clothing, bath products, high-end jewelry, and quality accessories. The owner has been in the jewelry industry for a decade and brings style to the shop.

Clothing, Accessories, and Swimwear

Also found at The Shops at Kukui'ula are a handful of clothing boutiques ranging from surfwear and resortwear to unique island-style apparel. For high-quality aloha wear, stop at **Tommy Bahama** (The Shops at Kukui'ula, Ste. A107, 808/742-8808, www.tommybahama. com, 10am-9pm daily). The store offers high-end casual island wear for men and women. Swimwear, beachwear, and classy women's clothing is available at **Olivine Beach Boutique** (808/742-7222, www.olivinekauai. com, 10am-9pm daily), where you can find bikini cover-ups, beach accessories, jeans, name brands, and local one-of-a-kind designs.

Hopefully you brought sunglasses to Kaua'i, because you'll need them. If not, there's the **Sunglass Hut** (The Shops at Kukui'ula, Ste. E129, 808/742-9065, www.sunglasshut.com, 10am-9pm daily), which offers a huge selection of sunglasses for men and women. **Quicksilver** (The Shops at Kukui'ula, Ste. F131, 808/742-8088, 10am-9pm daily) has a great selection of men's, women's, and children's surf-themed clothing for in and out of the water. Accessories like sunglasses, hats, and sandals are available with other surf accessories.

Arts, Crafts, and Jewelry

At the intriguing **Red Koi Collection** (The Shops at Kukui'ula, Ste. G143, 808/742-2778, www.redkoicollection.com, 10am-9pm daily) you'll find fine arts, from hand-painted silks to original paintings, to koa furniture and jewelry. The high-end products make it feel like a hip and modern island museum combined with the home decor of a wealthy world traveler. Expect high prices. Amazing Kaua'i

outdoor photography decorates **Scott Hanft Photography** (The Shops at Kukui'ula, Ste. H155, 808/742-9515, www.scotthanftoutdoorphotogallery.com, 10am-9pm daily), showcasing wonderful air, underwater, nature, and landmark shots from around the island. Originals and prints are available, along with magnets, cards, jewelry, and more.

Local island jewelry can be found at **Ocean Opulent Jewelry** (The Shops at Kukui'ula, Ste. G141, 808/742-9992, www.oceanpoipu. com, 10am-9pm daily). Look for freshwater pearls and island-themed jewelry among the gold, silver, and platinum.

Bath and Beauty

Malie Organics (The Shops at Kukui'ula, Ste. F133, 808/332-6220, www.maile.com, 10am-9pm daily) is a locally owned line of organic and all-natural Hawaiian luxury spa products. They capture the glorious, decadent scents from the islands with their skin care line, hand soaps, and other pampering products. They use organically grown ingredients.

LAWA'I
General Store

The small **Lawai General Store** (3586 Koloa Rd., 808/332-7501, 6am-11pm daily) sells snacks, beer, ice, and some general store needs. The shop is tiny and local, and much of the stock is covered in dust. They're known for their Spam *musubi*.

KALAHEO
Music

In Kalaheo, **Scotty's Music** (2-2436 Kaumuali'i Hwy. #A3, 808/332-0090, 11am-4pm Mon.-Sat.) offers an array of instruments, guitars, and ukuleles. Ukuleles are a great take-home souvenir for music lovers.

Liquor Store

Kujo's Mini Mart (2-2459 Kaumuali'i Hwy., 808/332-9220, 5am-11pm daily) has the usual array of beer, beverages, and snacks.

Entertainment

PO'IPU
Lu'au

If you're in the mood for dinner and a show, Hawaiian style, check out the **Grand Hyatt Kaua'i Lu'au** (1571 Po'ipu Rd., 808/240-6456, www.grandhyattkauailuau.com, 5:15pm-8pm Thurs. and Sun.). Guests are treated to cocktails, music, and a *lu'au* dinner with traditional foods from Hawai'i and the Pacific, along with arts and crafts and bar drinks. This includes a Polynesian dancing show, hula, and fire knife dancing.

Bars and Live Music

The Grand Hyatt Kaua'i (1571 Po'ipu Rd., 808/742-1234, www.grandhyatt-kauailuau.com) is also home to several lounges and bars, including **Stevenson's Library** (808/240-6456, 5:30pm-midnight daily), which features sushi and live jazz nightly 8pm-11pm. Minors are permitted 6pm-9pm. There is also live music at the **Seaview Terrace** (808/240-6456, 4:30pm-10pm daily). The evening begins with a torch-lighting ceremony, and performances may include a Hawaiian soloist, Hawaiian duet, or a children's hula show.

Surrounded by flaming tiki torches and the Moir Gardens of the Outrigger Kiahuna Plantation Resort, the **Plantation Gardens Bar and Restaurant** (2253 Po'ipu Rd., 808/742-2121, www.pgrestaurant.com, 5pm-9:30pm daily) mixes classic elegance with tropical nights. The restaurant and full bar feature a unique and delicious Pacific Rim menu with a Hawaiian flair. You can sit outside on the lanai and enjoy specialty cocktails, tropical drinks, wine, and beer.

KALAHEO
Live Music

Kalaheo is quiet at night, but **Kalaheo Steak and Ribs** (4444 Papalina Rd., 808/332-4444, www.kalaheosteakandribs.com, 4pm-10pm Tues.-Sun.) has live music every Thursday and Sunday at 7pm and karaoke on Friday and Saturday nights at 7pm. Their happy hour is 4pm-7pm.

Food

KOLOA
Italian

If you're in the mood for really good pizza, head over to ★ **Pizzetta** (5408 Koloa Rd., 808/742-8881, www.pizzettarestaurant.com, 11am-9pm Mon.-Fri., 11am-10pm Sat.-Sun., $12-25) for great pizza and other wonderful Italian dishes, such as calzones and chicken parmigiana. Nestled in a historic clapboard Koloa building, the restaurant is central in Koloa town and the atmosphere is laid-back. In honor of Kaua'i's wild chickens, Pizzetta offers Rooster Brew, a custom beer brewed specifically for the eatery. Pizzetta uses homemade sauces. Try the spinach artichoke dip.

Seafood and Local Cuisine

Koloa Fish Market (5482 Koloa Rd., 808/742-6199, 10am-6pm Mon.-Fri., 10am-5pm Sat., $8-11) offers fish, of course, along with plate lunches and other local dishes like *laulau, poke,* cucumber salad, and sashimi. The selection is limited, but it's really popular with locals. The market is takeout only, great for a snack on the beach.

Local-style **Sueoka's Snack Shop** (5392 Koloa Rd., 808/742-1112, 9am-8pm Tues.-Sat., 9am-4pm Sun., $5-10) is a quick stop to pick up local food. They serve teriyaki burgers, curries, chili, and plate lunches. They also have sliced-up fruit available in the same style as small New York City delis. Drinks, chips, and the usual convenience store snacks are also available. This is another affordable option for a beach lunch.

Local quick eats are available at the **Big Save** (5516 Koloa Rd., 808/742-1614, 6am-11pm daily), which provides groceries along with ready-made sushi rolls, hard-boiled eggs, bentos, rice, and a few other ready-to-eat meals.

Ice Cream and Shave Ice

For a treat, try **Koloa Shave Ice** (Po'ipu Rd., 808/651-7104, 9am-9pm daily). Located in the Old Koloa Town shops, they serve up a very finely shaved cone, which is the make-or-break aspect with shave ice.

Koloa Mill Ice Cream and Coffee (5424 Koloa Rd., 808/742-6544, www.koloamill. com, 7am-9pm daily, $4 for a single scoop) serves up items to satisfy the sweet tooth and provide a caffeine fix. They pride themselves on serving only Hawaiian-made foods, such as Kaua'i coffee, ice cream made on Maui, and locally made baked goods and snacks. The ice cream shop atmosphere is classic and offers free wireless Internet.

Farmers Market

Sunshine Farmers Market in the **Koloa Ball Park** (Maluhia Rd., noon, Mon.) offers fresh produce and fruits. You can also find an abundance of locally made crafts and locally made and ready-to-eat food.

PO'IPU
Steak and Seafood

A beautiful, tropical atmosphere and great food are found at ★ **Keoki's Paradise** (2360 Kiahuna Plantation Dr., 808/742-7534, www. keokisparadise.com, 11am-10:30pm daily, $22-35), where ponds, a small waterfall, greenery, and a large beautiful tree create a very relaxing vibe. You'll find a mix of visitors and locals enjoying a drink at the bar. Service is friendly, and the Pacific cuisine menu features several dishes with locally sourced ingredients. Steak and seafood are the specialties. Keoki's is in the Poipu Shopping Village with covered, open-air seating.

Overlooking the ocean is the ★ **Beach House Restaurant** (5022 Lawa'i Rd., 808/742-1424, www.the-beach-house.com, 5pm-10pm daily, $26-48). The open-air restaurant has a prime oceanfront location on Lawa'i Beach with a front lawn dotted with tiki torches—the perfect spot for watching

the view from Beach House Restaurant

Hawai'i Regional Cuisine

In August 1991, 12 notable Hawai'i chefs developed a Hawaiian fusion style of cooking that combines diverse ethnic styles with local Hawai'i ingredients and flavors. Sam Choy, Philippe Padovani, Roger Dikon, Gary Strehl, Roy Yamaguchi, Amy Ferguson Ots, Jean-Marie Josselin, George Mavrothalassitis, Beverly Gannon, Peter Merriman, Mark Ellman, and Alan Wong formed a nonprofit organization and trademarked the term Hawai'i Regional Cuisine. Rooted in sustainable agricultural and fishing practices, their goal was to connect local ranchers and farmers with chefs to develop a cuisine that is a reflection of Hawai'i's culture and flavors, from past to present. You'll find this fantastic fare on the south shore at Roy Yamaguchi's Eating House 1849, Peter Merriman's Merriman's Fish House and Merriman's Gourmet Pizza & Burgers, and Jean-Marie Josselin's self-titled Josselin's Tapas Bar & Grill.

the sunset. Open for dinner, the Beach House serves seafood, steaks, and even a roasted duck dish. It can get pretty crowded, so reservations are a very good idea. They also have a great wine list.

Brennecke's Beach Broiler (2100 Ho'one Rd., 808/742-7588, www.brenneckes.com, 11am-10pm daily, $14-30) is right across from Po'ipu Beach. With an open-air dining room on the 2nd story of the building, the restaurant offers great views during lunch and dinner service. They serve up seafood and steak, pastas, and burgers. You could say they're famous for their *kiawe*-broiled meat and chicken, as well as for being right across the street from the beach.

The peaceful tropical atmosphere at **Plantation Gardens Restaurant and Bar** (2253 Po'ipu Rd., 808/742-2121, www.pgrestaurant.com, 5:30pm-9pm Mon.-Sat., $25-37) accompanies great food. They serve up seafood and steaks for dinner and have a variety of Pacific-themed appetizers. Surrounded by the tiki-torch-lit Moir Gardens at Kiahuna Plantation Resort, the small restaurant is comfortable and homey, and offers mostly outdoor seating. They have a nice wine list and full bar along with tasty desserts. All of their produce is said to be organically and locally grown.

The Dolphin Poipu (The Shops at Kukui'ula, Ste. A100, 808/742-1414, www.hanaleidolphin.com, 11:30am-3:30pm and 5:30pm-9:30pm daily, $20-35) serves exotic sushi, local fish, and steak entrées. The fish market sells fresh fish, choice-cut steaks, and pre-made sushi rolls and is open 10am-7pm daily—perfect for a meal back at the condo.

Hawai'i Regional

Two farm-to-table sister restaurants by Chef Peter Merriman are **Merriman's Gourmet Pizza & Burgers** (The Shops at Kukui'ula, Ste. G147/149, 808/742-8385, www.merrimanshawaii.com, 11am-10pm daily, $13-18), which is downstairs, and ★ **Merriman's Fish House** (808/742-8385, 5:30pm-9pm daily, $15-59), located upstairs. Delicious fare and sustainability are combined to produce high-quality, Hawai'i regional cuisine. Both eateries utilize locally grown or caught ingredients, constituting 90 percent of the food they use. The downstairs café offers casual dining, while the upstairs fish house offers mountain and ocean views with a full bar.

Consistency is key at ★ **Eating House 1849** (The Shops at Kukui'ula, Ste. A201, 808/742-5000, www.eatinghouse1849.com, 5pm-10pm daily, $13-38), where Chef Roy Yamaguchi offers his dynamic and modern version of plantation cuisine inspired by the region's past. The menu changes nightly, depending on the fresh local fish, produce, meats, and game that are available that day. The menu is small and the service is excellent. Reservations can be made by phone or online.

Italian

At the elegant ★ **Dondero's** (1571 Po'ipu Rd., 808/240-6456, 6pm-10pm Mon.-Sat., $15-44) in the Grand Hyatt Kauai, you will be treated to a wonderful meal with a romantic and high-end atmosphere. You can sit outdoors under the stars, overlooking the ocean, or enjoy your meal inside with Italian decor of murals and tiles. A robust wine list complements their fresh local fish, veal, pastas, and decadent desserts. Resort casual wear is required.

Spanish

The food might not be entirely Spanish, but the style certainly is. ★ **Josselin's Tapas Bar & Grill** (The Shops at Kukui'ula, Ste. F207A, 808/742-7117, 5:30pm-9:30pm daily, $8-39) inspires sharing with friends and family by serving up tapas, a variety of small dishes designed to be shared. Chef Josselin has won numerous awards with his Pacific-inspired eateries, from fresh fish tapas to tapas made in the wood-burning oven. The exotic array of small dishes includes scallops, oxtail, vegetarian tapas, duck, fish, and so much more. They also serve lovely *liliko'i* and pomegranate sangrias and other signature drinks.

Ice Cream and Shave Ice

Tropical and traditional flavored ice cream and sorbet are on offer at ★ **Lappert's Hawaii Ice Cream and Coffee** (The Shops at Kukui'ula, Ste. K160, 808/741-1272, www.lappertshawaii.com, 6am-10pm daily, $4 for a single scoop). The shop originated on Kaua'i and now has outlets statewide. Its regular flavors have about 16 percent butterfat while the fruit flavors have 8 percent, making it very creamy ice cream. You can purchase freshly scooped pints, and this location sells coffee too.

For a local treat, head to ★ **Uncle's Shave Ice and Smoothies** (The Shops at Kukui'ula, Ste. K158B, 808/742-2364, www.uncleskauai.com, 11am-9pm daily, $4-8). They offer 25 shave ice flavors with extras like cream caps, fruit, and ice cream. They also sell other snacks like caramel apple bites and popcorn. Sugar-free syrups sweetened naturally with stevia are a progressive option here.

Quick Bites

The south shore's **Savage Shrimp** (The Shops at Kukui'ula, Ste. K158A, 808/742-9611, 11am-9pm daily, $12) serves up shrimp plates, fish tacos, shrimp tacos, fish and chips, and fried shrimp. A favorite with beach-going

Merriman's sister restaurants at The Shops at Kukui'ula

locals, it used to be in a lunch wagon and now has a permanent home.

Below Brennecke's Beach Broiler is **Brennecke's Beach Deli** (2100 Ho'one Rd., 808/742-1582, www.brenneckes.com 7am-9pm, $5-10), which serves up made-to-order sandwiches, cold beer, breakfast burritos, snacks, and coffee. A meal from here is best enjoyed across the street at the beach. They offer picnic lunches for those who call ahead to take on a hike or long day at the beach.

The popular Kaua'i eatery **Bubba Burgers** (The Shops at Kukui'ula, Ste. L163, 808/742-6900, www.bubbaburger.com, 10:30am-9pm daily, $4-8) is family owned and operated and serves Kaua'i grass-fed beef, chicken, fish, and vegan burgers. The burgers are priced by weight. They also have the usual burger joint sides like shakes, fries, and soda.

Living Foods Market and Cafe (The Shops at Kukui'ula, Ste. D124, 808/742-2323, www.livingfoodskauai.com, 7am-9pm daily) offers local and organic prepared foods, salads, smoothies, produce, and groceries. They also have homemade breads and dips, made-to-order pizzas, sandwiches, and more. The shop is spacious and elegant, but it's rather expensive. They have a good array of wines and liquors. Outside tables are provided, or you can take away for a picnic at the beach or dinner back at the condo. The café closes at 8pm.

KALAHEO
American

The always-good ★ **Kalaheo Cafe** (2-2560 Kaumuali'i Hwy., 808/332-5858, www.kalaheo.com, 6:30am-2:30pm Mon.-Sat., 6:30am-2pm Sun., dinner at 5pm Tues.-Sat., $2-13) is the south side's answer to the cute, local, friendly café where you can relax reading the paper or have Sunday brunch with 10 friends. Order at the counter and then choose a table,

but there's no rush to get out of the spacious hardwood floor café, which is adorned with local art and music. Coffee is served with eggs, breakfast burritos, waffles, pastries, and sides. Salads and off-the-grill specialty sandwiches are available for lunch, along with bottled beer. Vegetarians can find a decent array of meat-free options.

The name says it all at **Kalaheo Steaks and Ribs** (4444 Papalina Rd., 808/332-4444, www.kalaheosteakandribs.com, Tues.-Sun. 4pm-10pm, dinner 5pm-9:30pm, $16-33). For three decades the restaurant has been serving ribs, steaks, fresh fish, pastas, appetizers, and salads. A full bar, the Saloon, adds to the fun. The atmosphere also fits the name with a knotty pine interior with the usual steakhouse theme. At the Saloon, happy hour is held 4pm-7pm daily with a selection of appetizers.

Italian

A local favorite is ★ **Brick Oven Pizza** (2-2555 Kaumuali'i Hwy., 808/332-8561, http://brickovenpizzahi.com, 11am-9pm daily, $10-33). It's great for family night or a casual date. Also very kid-friendly, it offers free dough for kids to play with during dinner. They offer a selection of pizza, beer, and wine, and you can get your crust in white or wheat dough as well as basted with garlic butter. The decor has a country feel, and the walls are covered in license plates from around the country that almost all say something Hawaii-related on them. All-you-can-eat buffet nights are 5pm-9pm Monday and Thursday.

Farmers Market

Sunshine Farmers Market in the **Kalaheo Neighborhood Center** (4480 Papalina Rd., 3:30pm Tues.) offers fresh produce and fruits. You can also find an abundance of locally made crafts and locally made and ready-to-eat food. Bring your own shopping bag.

Information and Services

POSTAL SERVICES

There are two U.S. post offices on the south side: **Kalaheo Post Office** (4489 Papalina Rd., 808/332-5800, 9am-3:30pm Mon.-Fri., 9am-11:30am Sat.) and the **Koloa Post Office** (5485 Koloa Rd., 800/275-8777, 9am-4pm Mon.-Fri., 9am-11:30am Sat.). Both post offices offer the usual shipping needs and basic packaging.

INTERNET ACCESS AND PHOTO SERVICES

Wireless Internet is available with your own computer at **Koloa Mill Ice Cream and Coffee** (5424 Koloa Rd., 808/742-6544, www.koloamill.com, 7am-9pm daily) and at **Starbucks** (2360 Kiahuna Plantation Dr., 808/742-5144, 5am-8pm daily) in Poipu Shopping Village. You can also bring your laptop to **Kalaheo Cafe** (2-2560 Kaumuali'i Hwy., 808/332-5858, www.kalaheo.com, 6:30am-2:30pm Mon.-Sat., 6:30am-2pm Sun., dinner at 5pm Tues.-Sat.).

For instant vacation memory gratification, try **Poipu One Hour Photo** (3450 Po'ipu Rd. #C, 808/742-8918). Located in the Poipu Plaza, they develop prints off of memory cards.

Getting There and Around

CAR

The most convenient way to get around the south shore is by car. **Route 50** heads west straight out of Lihu'e and runs through Kalaheo all the way to the end of the road on the west side. To get down to Koloa and Po'ipu, you can turn down Maluhia Road and drive through the Tunnel of Trees, or turn down Koloa Road and drive through lush Lawa'i. Rental cars are the best bet here and are available at the airport. Gas prices go up the farther west you go, so it's a good idea to fill up in Lihu'e.

BUS

The **Kaua'i Bus** (808/241-6410, www.kauai.gov/transportation, 5:27am-10:40pm Mon.-Fri., 6:21am-5:50pm Sat.-Sun. and holidays) runs island-wide with many stops in Kalaheo, Koloa, and Po'ipu. Check the website for bus stops and times. The bus is a green, convenient, and affordable way to get around. Fares are $1 for children and seniors, and $2 for the general public. Monthly passes are also available.

TAXI

No matter which company you choose, Hawai'i's standard taxi rates apply ($3/mile and $0.40/minute, per van). **South Shore Taxi** (808/742-1525) offers island-wide tours along with services for individual and large groups. **Pono Taxi** (808/634-4744, www.ponotaxi.com) will take you on a south side sightseeing tour as well as the usual taxi runs.

Waimea and the West Side

Look for ★ to find recommended
sights, activities, dining, and lodging.

Highlights

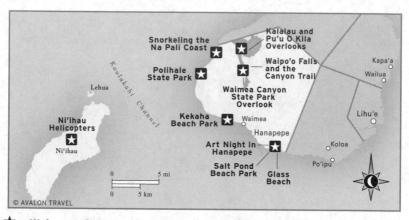

Snorkeling the Na Pali Coast ★
Polihale State Park ★
Kalalau and Pu'u O Kila Overlooks ★
Waipo'o Falls and the Canyon Trail ★
Waimea Canyon State Park Overlook ★
Kekaha Beach Park ★
Ni'ihau Helicopters ★
Art Night in Hanapepe ★
Salt Pond Beach Park
Glass Beach

Lehua
Ni'ihau
Kaulakahi Channel
Kapa'a
Wailua
Lihu'e
Waimea
Hanapepe
Koloa
Po'ipu

0   5 mi
0   5 km

© AVALON TRAVEL

★ **Waimea Canyon State Park Overlook:** The views from this overlook into the vast and deep red Waimea Canyon are not to be missed. Make sure to take Waimea Canyon Drive inland, because the sights from there are just as valuable (page 151).

★ **Kalalau and Pu'u O Kila Overlooks:** Feast your eyes on dramatic and pristine vertical mountain cliffs reaching down to the sea from two overlooks in Koke'e State Park. They are regarded as the best views in the Pacific (page 153).

★ **Glass Beach:** This unique beach has a colorful, sparkling layer of beach glass atop dark sand (page 153).

★ **Salt Pond Beach Park:** The family-friendly beach is an ideal place for children to swim and frolic in the protected swimming area, an oversized sand-bottom tide pool. A large lawn, lifeguards, and restrooms make it perfect for a picnic (page 153).

★ **Kekaha Beach Park:** Marking the beginning of 15 miles of white sand, Kekaha Beach Park offers all the amenities for a full day at the beach:

pavilions, picnic tables, a barbecue pit, and a lifeguard (page 156).

★ **Polihale State Park:** This is the epitome of tropical Hawai'i paradise, with endless fine white sand and bright blue water framed by sacred cliffs. The western-most end of the main Hawaiian Island chain, Polihale State Park has the best sunset-viewing in the entire state (page 156).

★ **Snorkeling the Na Pali Coast:** Hop on a boat with Captain Andy's Sailing Adventures or any of the other outfitters in Port Allen for an unforgettable snorkeling trip (page 157).

★ **Waipo'o Falls and the Canyon Trail:** Hikers who endure the trek to Waipo'o Falls are rewarded with an 800-foot double waterfall (page 161).

★ **Ni'ihau Helicopters:** Virtually the only way to explore Ni'ihau's beaches is on a tour with Ni'ihau Helicopters. The company offers beach-combing and snorkeling tours (page 165).

★ **Art Night in Hanapepe:** Check out the local art scene as a plethora of galleries open their doors 6pm-9pm every Friday (page 170).

Locally known as the west side, Kaua'i's leeward coast is a world unto itself.

Miles of white-sand beaches wrap the island to the north where the vertical cliffs of the Na Pali Coast strike down to meet the ocean, and dramatic canyons cut deep into the island's interior. Small towns seem frozen in the plantation era, and red dirt covers everything. The west side is as local as it gets. From the artists in Hanapepe who relocated to the area to paint Kaua'i's beauty to the west-side born-and-raised Hawaiians in Waimea, the people are warm and friendly.

Hanapepe town and Port Allen welcome visitors to the west side. Hanapepe, which means "crushed bay," originally thrived as a hub for taro cultivation and later evolved into a rice-farming community, then became a bustling town from the early 1900s until just after World War II. At one point the town was an economic center and, shockingly, one of the biggest towns on the island. In the 1940s, thousands of GIs were trained here before being sent away for duty. Today, the riverside town offers country charm and artisan creations that can be experienced via a stroll or walking tour of the historic buildings, over 40 of which are listed in the National Register of Historic Places. In historic Old Hanapepe, art galleries have a monopoly on the main strip.

Waimea town, to the west of Hanapepe, has a story all its own—a moment in time that changed the course of Hawai'i's history. Captain Cook first set foot in Hawai'i on the beach in Waimea on January 20, 1778, and is remembered by two monuments in the small town. Once home to the last great king of Kaua'i, Kaumuali'i, Waimea was for many years a bustling town and port until the Nawiliwili and Port Allen harbors were created and the sugar mill closed in 1969.

Waimea is also the portal to Waimea Canyon, which has been called the "Grand Canyon of the Pacific," and Koke'e State Park. Koke'e State Park is known for its amazing trails, a high-elevation swamp ecosystem found nowhere else in Hawai'i, and majestic lookouts over the Na Pali Coast. Back down on the coast, Kekaha marks the 15-mile stretch to the end of the road and the Na Pali Coast's sacred cliffs at Polihale State Park. Out here, the silence is broken only by the picturesque and dangerous waves that crash on the beach and lull campers to sleep.

Previous: Kalalau Overlook; Waimea town. **Above:** Waimea Canyon.

Waimea and the West Side

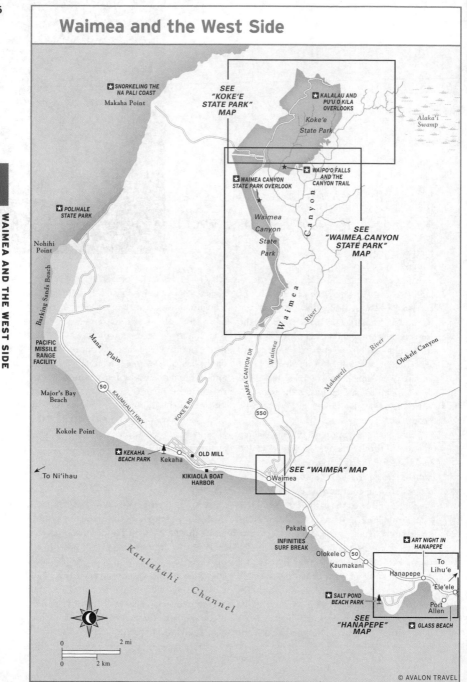

SEE "KOKE'E STATE PARK" MAP

SNORKELING THE NA PALI COAST

Makaha Point

KALALAU AND PU'U O KILA OVERLOOKS

Koke'e State Park

Alaka'i Swamp

WAIPO'O FALLS AND THE CANYON TRAIL

WAIMEA CANYON STATE PARK OVERLOOK

POLIHALE STATE PARK

Nohihi Point

Waimea Canyon State Park

SEE "WAIMEA CANYON STATE PARK" MAP

Barking Sands Beach

Waimea Canyon

Waimea River

PACIFIC MISSILE RANGE FACILITY

Mana Plain

Olokele Canyon

Major's Bay Beach

50 KAUMUALI'I HWY

KOKE'E RD

WAIMEA CANYON DR

Waimea River

Makaweli River

Kokole Point

550

KEKAHA BEACH PARK

Kekaha

OLD MILL

SEE "WAIMEA" MAP

To Ni'ihau

KIKIAOLA BOAT HARBOR

Waimea

Pakala

ART NIGHT IN HANAPEPE

INFINITIES SURF BREAK

Olokele

50

To Lihu'e

Kaumakani

Hanapepe

'Ele'ele

Kaulakahi Channel

SALT POND BEACH PARK

Port Allen

GLASS BEACH

SEE "HANAPEPE" MAP

0   2 mi

0   2 km

© AVALON TRAVEL

ORIENTATION

The west side stretches from 'Ele'ele all the way to the Na Pali cliffs at the end of the road in Polihale State Park. It includes **Port Allen,** from where many of the sightseeing tours to the Na Pali Coast depart, **Hanapepe,** which carries the moniker "Kaua'i's Biggest Little Town," historic **Waimea** town, **Waimea Canyon** and **Koke'e State Parks, Kekaha Beach Park,** and **Polihale State Park.**

The **Kaumuali'i Highway** (Route 50) is the main thoroughfare along the coast all the way to the end of the road. Waimea Canyon is accessed by **Waimea Canyon Drive** (also known as Route 550) in Waimea town, and **Koke'e Road** in Kekaha.

PLANNING YOUR TIME

There are a few options for accommodations on the west side, but most travelers make day trips to this region. From Po'ipu it takes approximately 20 minutes to get to Waimea town and another 20-30 minutes to get to the Waimea Canyon State Park Overlook. From the north shore, it takes about 1 1.5 hours to get to Waimea town, depending on traffic in Kapa'a and Lihu'e.

Some visitors camp on the beach at Polihale State Park or in the cool forests in Waimea Canyon and Koke'e State Parks. It is a long and slow drive to both of these remote

locations. Once you've arrived at your destination, whether it's a secluded beach or a canyon lookout, you'll probably be ready to have a snack and stretch your legs before getting back in the car. Be prepared with food and water at these remote locations. Serious hikers could spend their entire vacation just hiking the state park trails in this region.

If you'd like to explore the towns as well, stop in historic Waimea town or artsy Hanapepe after your day at the beach or in the mountains. Have a meal, then explore without rushing since you've already accomplished your big sightseeing goals. For those not interested in the great outdoors, a day trip of sightseeing at Waimea's historic sites and Hanapepe's art galleries, paired with a trip to the plantation at Kaua'i Coffee, will hold your attention for a full day. Those who wish to stay out of the sun, have a hard time walking in sand, or dislike eroded, washboard dirt roads should avoid Polihale altogether. The sunset may be "the best" from Polihale, but it's still amazing from anywhere along the west side's long and drawn-out coastline.

If you've booked a tour along the Na Pali Coast, most of which are at least half-day adventures, you'll need to make your way to either Port Allen or Waimea, where the tours depart from. Upon your return, check out nearby Hanapepe and make it a full day.

Sights

Sights from Hanapepe to the end of the road share two common themes: history and natural wonders. They're generally all easily accessible and very camera worthy.

HANAPEPE
Hanapepe Valley and Lookout

As you come around the bend from Kalaheo and first lay eyes on the Port Allen area, a Hawai'i Visitors Bureau sign points out an overlook pull-off for Hanapepe Valley. It offers a peek down into the valley and is easily

accessible. The vast and beautiful valley is a reminder of the geological activity that shaped the Hawaiian Islands and is home to some overgrowth and small taro fields. It's good for a quick look since it's so easy, but the valley is tiny in comparison to Waimea Canyon.

Hanapepe Swinging Bridge

Extended over the Hanapepe River, this wooden plank footbridge runs between the historic town and the inland side of the river. With enough bounce and shake to inspire a

The Best Day on the West Side

Waimea Canyon State Park Overlook

The best of the west can be experienced in one day if you start early, but be prepared to spend much of the day driving.

- Your one-day Kaua'i western adventure begins with a quick stop at **Glass Beach,** where you can take a morning dip in the tide pool before heading up to **Old Hanapepe** to browse local art, walk on the swinging bridge, and have breakfast at **Grinds Cafe.**

- Head farther west and inland to the **Waimea Canyon State Park Overlook.** It's a good idea to hit the Big Save for snacks and drinks before heading up Waimea Canyon Road (the views are much better along this route compared to Koke'e Road). Remember to keep an eye out for the waterfall at the 1,500-foot elevation sign.

- After taking in the sweeping views up the red-earth canyon, head back down to the coast or visit the **Kalalau and Pu'u O Kila Overlooks.** If it's cloudy and misty at the Waimea Canyon Overlook, chances are the weather will be the same or worse at the other overlooks. Either way, take Koke'e Road back down to the coast and turn left to Waimea town for lunch at **Island Tacos,** then take a break from the heat with a **Jo-Jo's Clubhouse** shave ice. If you're out of snacks and drinks, you'll want to restock before heading out to **Polihale State Park** for the rest of the afternoon.

- Once on the road into Polihale, you'll come to a fork in the road at the big tree about three miles in. From here you can go right to the parking area with showers and restrooms, or you can go left about a tenth of a mile to **Queen's Pond.** At Queen's Pond, swimming is generally safe and suitable for kids. Since you most likely will need a break from the car, spend the remainder of the day at the beach and watch the sun set over Ni'ihau. Maybe you'll see the elusive green flash just as the sun drops below the horizon.

- Head back to Waimea for dinner. For a good steak or vegetarian pasta dish, try **Wrangler's Steakhouse.**

Hanapepe

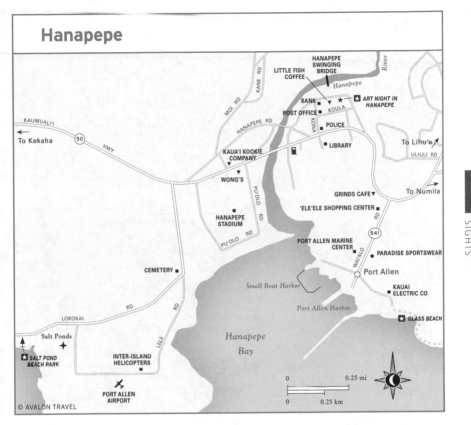

© AVALON TRAVEL

little excitement as well as a lovely view down the river, the Hanapepe Swinging Bridge is fun to take a walk on. It's easily accessible from the town and free. Originally built to run a water line across the river and into town, the bridge ends nearly in someone's backyard. Once off the bridge take a left to walk the levee back to the old vehicular bridge and come back into town along Hanapepe Road. A stroll across the bridge fits in easily with any stroll through town.

Kauai Coffee Company Visitor Center and Museum

The first coffee to be cultivated in the Hawaiian Islands was planted in this region over 150 years ago as the state's first coffee plantation. Years later, only little success was achieved and coffee production ceased in

Kaua'i and moved to the Big Island at Kona. Today, coffee is grown not only on the Big Island, but also on Maui, Moloka'i, O'ahu, and again on Kaua'i. It's actually been so successful that in 2011, Italian coffee giant Massimo Zanetti Beverage bought Kaua'i Coffee Company, which grows Hawaiian arabica coffee bean plants on its 3,400-acre drip-irrigated property and produces roughly four million pounds of coffee a year.

Harvest is done mechanically and takes place September through November, which is the busiest time of year on the estate. The largest single coffee estate in Hawai'i, Kaua'i Coffee has a hold on about 60 percent of the Hawaiian coffee market. If you use Route 540, and especially if you love coffee, stop at the **Kaua'i Coffee Company Visitor Center and Museum** (1 Numila

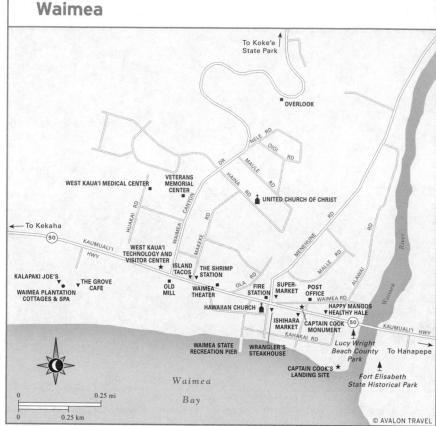

Waimea

To Koke'e
State Park

OVERLOOK

West Kaua'i Medical Center

Veterans Memorial Center

United Church of Christ

To Kekaha

West Kaua'i Technology and Visitor Center

Kalapaki Joe's

The Grove Cafe

Waimea Plantation Cottages & Spa

Island Tacos

The Shrimp Station

Old Mill

Waimea Theater

Fire Station

Super-market

Post Office

Hawaiian Church

Happy Mangos Healthy Hale

Ishihara Market

Captain Cook Monument

Waimea State Recreation Pier

Wrangler's Steakhouse

Captain Cook's Landing Site

Lucy Wright Beach County Park

To Hanapepe

Fort Elisabeth State Historical Park

Waimea Bay

0   0.25 mi
0   0.25 km

© AVALON TRAVEL

Rd., 808/335-0813 or 800/545-8605, 9am-5pm daily, free). A refurbished plantation building houses the gift shop and museum. Historical artifacts are available for viewing, and information explains how coffee is handled and processed at each stage. Gifts, clothing, food items, and, of course, coffee can be purchased and tasted.

WAIMEA
Fort Elisabeth State Historical Park

Just before the Waimea River and right past mile marker 22 is Fort Elisabeth State Historical Park. The shape of this Russian fort somewhat resembles an eight-pointed star. It dates back to 1817, when, according to traditional history, a German doctor named Georg Anton Schaeffer constructed it in the name of Czar Nicholas of Russia and named it after the czar's daughter.

However, in 2002, University of Hawai'i at Hilo anthropologist Peter R. Mills studied the fort and drew the conclusion that "Hawaiians had been left out of their own history." Mills used hundreds of firsthand accounts along with field research to show that the fort was originally built and used by Hawaiians as a *heiau*, a Hawaiian sacred site. He shows that after the Russians' departure, Hawaiians continued to use the fort, but in ways that reflected an ongoing transformation of cultural values as a result of contact with outsiders and the development of multiethnic communities in Waimea and other port settlements throughout the Hawaiian chain. For more information, read Mills's book *Hawai'i's Russian Adventure.*

History goes on to say that Schaeffer, an agent for the Russian-American Company, built two other forts on the island, one on the bluff at Princeville and another farther down in Hanalei Bay. It's said that Czar Nicholas never quite warmed up to Schaeffer's work and withdrew official support. Eventually Schaeffer was banned from Kaua'i, sent to Honolulu, and then forced to leave the islands altogether. No longer maintained and cared for, the fort fell apart and was dismantled in 1864 when 38 guns were removed. The walls were once 30 feet thick and are now rubble left to erode by the elements. Brochures are usually available at the entrance, and plaques on the board tell the history.

Captain Cook Monuments

The Captain Cook monuments pay tribute to James Cook, the explorer who is credited with "discovering" the Hawaiian Islands (for the western world). A life-size statue of Cook is located on the strip of grass that is Hagaard Park, between Waimea Road and Route 150. Benches are nearby if you'd like to have a seat and enjoy a snack. The other monument is a plaque attached to a boulder at Lucy Wright Beach Park.

West Kaua'i Technology and Visitor Center

At the bottom of Waimea Canyon Drive, audiovisual displays, books, and wall displays at the **West Kaua'i Technology and Visitor Center** (9565 Kaumuali'i Hwy., 808/338-1332, www.westkauaivisitorcenter.org, 10am-4pm Mon.-Fri.) offer visitors a glimpse into the history of the town and surrounding areas. There is some Ni'ihau shell jewelry on display, and other artifacts tell the story of the area's sugar past and technological present. Brochures for Waimea businesses and restaurants, books,

Internet access, and printing services are also available.

★ Waimea Canyon State Park Overlook

Waimea Canyon State Park Overlook and the drive up offer a series of majestic sights of the canyon. The canyon's colors change throughout the day as the sun moves across the sky, so if you gaze into the 10-mile-long, 3,000-foot-deep canyon for any length of time, different photo opportunities usually present themselves. Make sure to take Waimea Canyon Drive rather than Koke'e Road (which the street sign in Waimea recommends). This road provides clear views of Ni'ihau, multiple valley lookouts, and a small waterfall flowing over bright red dirt at the 1,500-foot elevation sign. Each lookout holds different views of the canyon, and you will probably be able to spend some time at one by yourself. To get there, take Waimea Canyon Drive and stick to the right at the fork in the road at the Koke'e State Park sign. At the top there is a lookout with wheelchair accessibility, bathrooms, and often a snack and gift tent. On the way back down, take Koke'e Road just to see the other views. At the bottom are several gift shops and a general store.

Koke'e Natural History Museum

The **Koke'e Natural History Museum** (3600 Waimea Canyon Dr., after mile marker 15, 808/335-9975, www.kokee.org, 10am-4pm daily, suggested donation of $1) offers several displays. The museum calls the outdoors the real plant displays, but inside is an exhibit called Treasury of Trees, Resources of a Traditional Lifestyle. The exhibit is on forest trees and their traditional Hawaiian uses. It's interesting to visualize how the Hawaiians utilized their natural resources. Game animals that were introduced to the island are also on display, including a wild boar, a stag, goats, game birds, and trout. A weather exhibit focuses on devastating Hurricane 'Iniki.

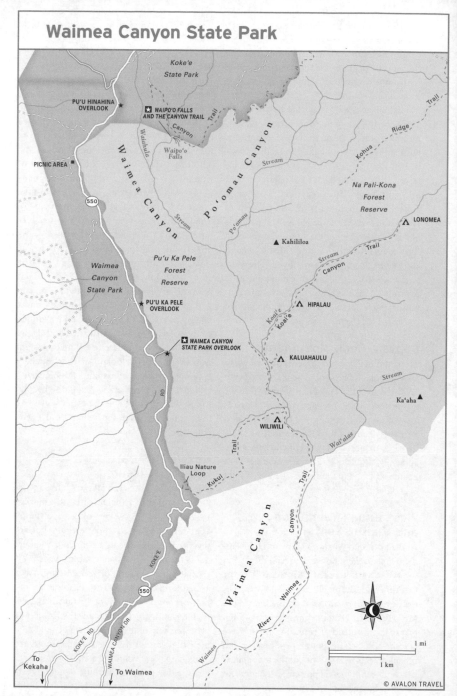

Waimea Canyon State Park

Koke'e State Park

PU'U HINAHINA OVERLOOK ★

★ WAIPO'O FALLS AND THE CANYON TRAIL

Waialoha

Canyon

Waipo'o Falls

PICNIC AREA ■

550

Waimea Canyon

Stream

Po'omau Canyon

Po'omau Stream

Kohua Ridge

Trail

Na Pali-Kona Forest Reserve

▲ Kahililoa

LONOMEA Λ

Waimea Canyon State Park

Pu'u Ka Pele Forest Reserve

Stream

Canyon

Trail

★ PU'U KA PELE OVERLOOK

Koai'e

Koai'e

Λ HIPALAU

★ WAIMEA CANYON STATE PARK OVERLOOK

Λ KALUAHAULU

Stream

RD

Ka'aha ▲

Trail

Λ WILIWILI

Wai'alae

Iliau Nature Loop

Kukui

KOKE'E

550

Waimea Canyon

Canyon Trail

Waimea

River

Waimea

KOKE'E RD

WAIMEA CANYON DR

To Kekaha

To Waimea

0   1 mi

0   1 km

© AVALON TRAVEL

Perhaps the most interesting display is a collection of land and sea shells from Ni'ihau and Kaua'i. A large whale vertebrae and a sea turtle shell are quite intriguing. The museum staff can help you choose which of the 19 trails and hikes in the park are right for you, which is very helpful. Detailed hiking maps are also available.

★ Kalalau and Pu'u O Kila Overlooks

Many regard these two overlooks as the best views on Kaua'i, and even the best in the Pacific. At mile marker 18 the Kalalau Overlook opens to an expansive view over Kalalau Valley, the biggest valley on the Na Pali Coast. The valley was inhabited until the beginning of the 1900s.

About a mile down the road is the even better Pu'u O Kila, which offers a window into Kalalau Valley, from the Alaka'i Swamp to Mount Wai'ale'ale. If you get there on a cloudy day, there's a chance the views won't be visible at all. Earlier in the day is better, or if scheduling allows, check the weather and go when it looks best. To get here, go past the Koke'e Lodge and onto a road that turns into potholes and broken-up pavement.

Beaches

Kaua'i's west coast is the driest side of the island, which makes its bountiful beaches all the more inviting. They range from sufficient to spectacular, narrow to wide, black to white, remote to popular, and, depending on Mother Nature's mood, swimmable to unsafe. The Pacific is easily accessible from many areas along the coastline. Peruse all the beaches on offer and find your own nook to enjoy this often overlooked side of the island. Just like at any beach, do not leave valuables in your car. You'll be on your own most of the time, so stay out of the water if the waves are big or if you're unsure about the ocean conditions. If in doubt, don't go out.

HANAPEPE
★ Glass Beach

The saying "one person's trash is another's treasure" describes Glass Beach to a tee. On this small, black- and gray-sand beach, colored beach glass blankets the sand, making a colorful landscape that sparkles in the right light. The amount of glass varies with the tide and ocean conditions, but there's usually a good amount. Located near a former dumpsite and right in front of large gas tanks in an industrial area, the small beach is actually quite nice and easily accessible. The water is not necessarily inviting; it's darker than at other beaches because of the underlying reef, but you can still enjoy a dip in the natural tide pool almost directly in front of the beach access. At high tide, small waves rush into the pool, but at low tide it provides safer swimming than the rest of the beach. It's not uncommon for monk seals to frequent the beach. To get here, head west on Route 50 from Po'ipu and turn left onto Waialo Road toward Port Allen. Turn left onto Aka Ulu then right at the fork in the dirt road and you will see the beach.

Wahiawa Beach

Wahiawa Beach is less than a half hour east from Glass Beach on foot. This beach has black and gray sand and is a popular fishing spot with locals, but it doesn't offer much for swimming or sunbathing. To get here, head east down the coast past the Chinese cemetery.

★ Salt Pond Beach Park

Salt Pond Beach Park offers the best of Hawai'i's beaches: white sand, black rocks, tide pools, a protected swimming area, and a large lawn. This beach is popular with visitors and locals, so it can be crowded. It has

Top Kid-Friendly Activities on the West Side

Kaua'i may be a small island, but every parent knows that restrained car time while sightseeing makes children bored and antsy. The west side has an array of children-focused options to mix it up for kids. Here's a list of eateries, parks, beaches, and fun for kids, whether it's for the day or just a short break from the car.

- **Glass Beach** may not have the best swimming for the little ones, but children love treasure hunting the beach glass. They may even get lucky and see an endangered Hawaiian monk seal.

- **Salt Pond Beach Park** in Hanapepe is a perfect beach for children. The protected swimming area offers calm and shallow water with lifeguards. There is a grassy lawn to run around on and play games, and a tide pool on the west end of the beach.

- Turning right onto Kona Road off Kaumuali'i Highway leads to a park and **playground** on the left side. Located in the center of town, the playground has slides and swings for the kids to let out some energy.

- Hanapepe is home to the **Children's Media Center and Storybook Theatre of Hawaii** (3814 Hanapepe Rd., 808/335-0712, www.storybook.org), which offers a varied schedule of puppet shows, music, storytelling, and additional activities on Art Night. Drop by or call for scheduling and events, and visit the Children's Garden of Peace adjacent to the theater.

- In Waimea, **Jo-Jo's Clubhouse** offers 60 flavors of shave ice to choose from. After this treat, the little ones might need a change of clothes.

- The safest swimming for tots in Waimea is at the **Kikiaola Boat Harbor,** where the protected swimming area is very calm. There are also picnic tables, but, unfortunately, no lifeguard.

- At **Faye Park** in Kekaha, a playground and ball field is available for public use. Turn inland off Route 50 onto Alae Road and the park is on the left.

restrooms, showers, and lifeguards. A lunch wagon even stops by on a regular basis. It's easily accessible and convenient if you don't have time to venture out farther west. It's also great for children and swimmers who prefer calm and safe ocean conditions.

Its name comes from the nearby salt ponds, where locals harvest salt (*pa'akai*, in Hawaiian, translating to "firm sea from evaporative basins scraped out of the earth"). Utilized for generations, the basins are lined with black clay, and after drying they're filled with seawater. When the seawater evaporates, salt is left behind and harvested. The salt is spoken for, so please don't take any if you see it. The rock salt with a reddish tint from the red dirt is called *alae*. To get here from Route 50, turn onto Route 543 at the street sign pointing toward the ocean, then go right on Lele Road.

Pakala's

A three-minute walk through brush and trees takes you to Pakala's. The river-mouth beach is roughly 500 yards long and is composed of compact dark sand. It's remote and quiet, although not as picturesque as other west-side beaches. Its length makes it a great place for a morning stroll, and the compact sand is perfect for a jog or a few yoga poses. The beach is a favorite for surfers who surf the long left-hand point break along the reef. The small rock pier to the left is a good place to enjoy the morning sun and watch surfers catch waves. The water here is murky because of the sand flowing in from the river. To get here, park on the side of the road just after mile marker 21. There is a trail by the guardrail and fence.

WAIMEA

The Waimea district lies along a black-sand beach. It is long, narrow, and made of fine black sand mixed with river sediment and green olivine. Rivers are common in this area and during heavy rain cause the surrounding ocean to become murky with the red dirt, resulting in less-than-perfect swimming conditions. The beaches are still worth checking out, and are great for a picnic or walk.

Lucy Wright Beach County Park

Named after the first native Hawaiian schoolteacher, who passed away in 1931, Lucy Wright Beach Park is located at the mouth of the Waimea River on the western bank and is home to Captain Cook's landing site. Consisting of a small ball field, restrooms, and a couple of picnic tables, the black-sand beach is usually covered in driftwood. It's a popular hangout for locals; a canoe club launches here. Swimming isn't recommended along this entire beach. The history of the area is the main attraction. To get here, turn left after

the bridge just as you enter Waimea town. Looking west down the beach, the Waimea State Recreation Pier juts off the beach into the ocean. It's a good place for picnicking and a popular spot for pole fishing. To access the pier, walk along the beach or down a back street behind the Waimea Library.

Kikiaola Boat Harbor

Kikialoa Boat Harbor is not a sprawling white-sand beach with crystal-clear bright blue water, but it offers calm, protected swimming for children and others looking to relax without worry from open-ocean waves. The harbor has covered picnic tables and a small sandy area on the west end, as well as a larger sand area to the left. Many of the Na Pali Coast tours leave from here. To get to the harbor, head west out of Waimea and look for the sign after mile marker 24.

THE WILD WEST

This is where dreamy, seemingly endless beaches begin and stretch all the way to the Na Pali Coast. You'll encounter miles of soft sand and a multitude of opportunities for oceanside four-wheel-driving, camping, surfing, and sunbathing.

Salt Pond Beach Park

★ Kekaha Beach Park

Kekaha Beach Park marks the beginning of about 15 miles of white sand that stretches to the Na Pali Coast. Pavilions, picnic tables, portable toilets, and a barbecue pit set the stage for a complete day at the beach. Riptides are frequent and dangerous when the surf is up, but when the ocean conditions are calm, it's great for swimming. Locals hang out, fish, and surf here, and it's a good place to spend the day if you don't want to drive another 30 or 40 minutes to Polihale. This is the last beach with a lifeguard on duty, something to keep in mind when deciding where to post up for a beach day. Ni'ihau is in full view from here. Kekaha Beach Park stretches west for a few miles, but this is the last area with facilities until Polihale. The beach is at mile marker 27.

Pacific Missile Range Facility

Pacific Missile Range Facility (PMRF, 808/335-4229, http://cnic.navy.mil/PMRF/index.htm) begins about six miles past Kekaha Beach Park and consists of a long strip of beach and large sand dunes, surf breaks, and the beach known as Barking Sands. The U.S. Navy operates PMRF, a training facility for sea warfare, and all sectors of the U.S. military utilize the base. It covers 42,000 square miles to the west and south with another 1,000 square miles under the sea. NASA officials chose it because the local weather provides 360 clear days each year, creating perfect flying conditions in unobstructed air space. PMRF is not open to the public. The beach is only accessible to those carrying a valid military ID or certified Kaua'i residents who pass a thorough background check.

★ Polihale State Park

Imagine sitting on a long white-sand beach, a distant island in view, clear blue sky overhead, looming cliffs behind you, and waves rolling in as your soundtrack. This is Polihale. At the very end of the beach, where the cliffs meet the ocean, is **End of the Road** and **Echoes,** popular surf breaks for only the most experienced surfers. The sand gives way to cliffs that fall into the ocean, which marks the beginning of the Na Pali Coast. The area is also home to the Polihale Heiau. This sacred spot is said to be where the souls of the dead leap off the cliffs to the land of the dead, a mythical underwater mountain a few miles off the coast. Polihale is also popular for four-wheel-driving and camping. For the adventurous who make the trek and plan to stay till dark, the reward

Kekaha Beach Park

is the most amazing sunset over the "forbidden" island of Ni'ihau.

To get to Polihale, drive until the pavement ends on Route 50 and turn left onto the dirt road at mile marker 33. It's about a 3.5-mile, or 20- to 30-minute drive to the big tree at the fork in the road. The left fork leads to **Queen's Pond,** where a fringe reef creates a protected swimming area. Look for a dirt parking lot and walk down to the beach. The right fork leads to another section of beach and facilities. Drive another tenth of a mile and near the north end of the beach you'll see a dirt parking area with covered picnic tables, restrooms, and showers. Park where the ground is firm. You can walk as far up or down the beach as you'd like. Lifesaving devices are attached to a post near the back of the beach in this area.

For those setting out for the end of the road, the final three miles of dirt road become very treacherous due to erosion and soft sand. A Four-Wheel-Drive Only sign is posted at the beginning of the road for good reason. It is not recommended to drive a two-wheel-drive vehicle past this area. For rental vehicles, driving on the dirt road will void any insurance you've signed for. Two-wheel-drive vehicles get stuck all the time. In this situation, you'll either have to wait for a local with a vehicle that can assist you or call for a tow truck, which is extremely expensive. Also, most cell phones do not get reception here. For those who are willing to take a chance and drive a two-wheel-drive vehicle on the dirt road, do not drive any faster than 5 miles per hour. If you're in doubt about the surface of the road, exit the vehicle and check for soft sand before proceeding on. For better or worse, you'll most likely be on your own at the end of the road.

Water Sports

SNORKELING AND DIVING

Beach snorkeling on the west side isn't the best on Kaua'i, but remember that almost anywhere the sea is calm it is worth it to hop in the water with your snorkel gear. In Hawai'i's lively waters there's always the chance of seeing a green sea turtle or some tropical fish. Numerous boat tour companies that leave from the west side offer guided trips along the Na Pali Coast for spectacular snorkeling. Fish, sea turtles, and reef life can be seen while snorkeling, and dolphins and whales in the winter and early spring months can be seen from the boat. Port Allen and Kikiaola Boat Harbor are the main mooring and departure points for Na Pali cruises.

Hanapepe
SALT POND BEACH PARK
West-side snorkeling is best at Salt Pond Beach Park. The water is almost always calm and the area is protected from open ocean waves, making it a great place for children and beginners to check out the underwater life. Snorkeling is best out by the rock wall, but it's worth it to swim all over and see what's below.

★ Na Pali Coast
BOAT TOURS FROM PORT ALLEN
Holo Holo Charters (Port Allen Marina Center, 4353 Waialo Rd., Ste. 5A, 808/335-0815 or 800/848-6130, www.holoholokauai-boattours.com) offers the only tour available to the island of Ni'ihau ($190 adults, $124 children 6-12). (This tour lets visitors explore the Ni'ihau reefs. To visit Ni'ihau itself, book a tour with Ni'ihau Helicopters.) They also offer a 3.5-hour Na Pali sunset tour ($104 adults, $84 children 5-12) as well as a five-hour Na Pali snorkel sail ($134 adults, $94 children 6-12). The company has two catamarans, one 50 feet long and another with a shaded cabin and large bar area, to get oceangoers to their destination from the Port Allen Harbor. They provide a deli-style buffet for lunch along with

soft drinks, beer, and wine. The company has a reputation of treating guests well.

Captain Andy's Sailing Adventures (Port Allen Marina Center, 4353 Waialo Rd., 808/335-6833 or 800/535-0830, www.napali.com/kauai_sailing) boasts a 55-foot catamaran and three tours. They offer a snorkeling and barbecue sail ($169 adults, $119 children), a snorkeling and picnic sail ($149 adults, $109 children), and a sunset or dinner cruise along the Na Pali Coast ($119 adults, $89 children). Discounts are available by booking online at their website.

Catamaran Kahanu (Port Allen Marina Center, 4353 Waialo Rd., 808/645-6176 or 888/213-7711, www.catamarankahanu.com) is a Hawaiian-owned, 22-year-old tour company offering a year-round, five-hour Na Pali Coast swimming and snorkeling tour ($145 adults), a whale-watching/snorkel tour ($79), and a sunset dinner tour ($89) available December through April. On the boat they give visitors a glimpse into Hawaiian culture with craft demonstrations such as basket, hat, and rose weavings, which guests take home as mementos. They also offer private charters, and online rate specials are available at their website.

Kaua'i Sea Tours (Port Allen Marina Center, 4353 Waialo Rd. #2B, 808/826-1854 or 800/733-7997, www.kauaiseatours.com), operating for over 29 years, offers dinner or snorkeling power sailing catamaran tours aboard the 60-foot *Lucky Lady* and ocean raft snorkeling tours aboard rigid-hulled inflatables. The catamaran has a maximum of 49 passengers. Half-day morning snorkeling tours are $156 adults, $146 children 13-17, and $116 children 3-12; the afternoon snorkeling and dinner cruise is offered May through September for the same rate as the morning tour; and the four-hour sightseeing sunset dinner cruise is $120 adults, $110 children 13-17, and $95 children 3-12. There are four raft tours: a 5.5-hour morning or afternoon snorkel picnic tour, a four-hour sightseeing tour that will take you up to the cliffs and sea caves, and a 6.5-hour

tour with a beach landing that's available April through October. The raft tours start at $115 adults, $105 children 13-17, and $75 children 7-12. Rate specials are available at their website.

To explore the outskirts of Ni'ihau, try **Bubbles Below Scuba Charters** (Port Allen Marina Center, 4353 Waialo Rd., 808/332-7333 or 866/524-6268, www.bubblesbelowkauai.com) for unique three-tank diving experiences in the waters of Ni'ihau and Lehua Island ($345), and two-tank dives along the Na Pali Coast and Mana Crack ($245), including a night crustacean dive and a twilight dive. Mana Crack is an 11-mile-long sunken barrier reef of finger coral and is home to the largest eel in the world. They offer private boats and instruction as well.

Blue Dolphin Charters (Port Allen Marina Center, 4353 Waialo Rd., 877/511-1311, www.kauaiboats.com) offers a variety of tours, and scuba diving is available on all of them, no experience necessary. A Na Pali snorkel tour ($156 adults, $145 children 12-17, $113 children 2-11) and a Na Pali snorkel tour with a snorkeling stop on Ni'ihau ($196 adults, $169 children 12-17, $137 children 5-11) is available, along with a Na Pali sunset and dinner cruise ($117 adults, $106 children 12-17, $90 children 2-11), a Na Pali rafting with snorkeling tour ($137 adults, $126 children 12-17, $94 children 8-11), and a whale-watching tour from December through March. The company uses a 63-foot and 65-foot catamaran with freshwater showers and provides all gear needed for snorkeling. Check the website for discounted rates.

BOAT TOURS FROM WAIMEA

Na Pali Explorer (9643 Kaumuali'i Hwy., 808/338-9999 or 877/335-9909, www.napaliexplorer.com, $105-149 with children's rates) is in Waimea right next to Island Tacos and offers various tours on their rigid-hulled inflatable boats, called RHIB. These under-30-foot boats are maneuverable and get up close to the natural geography and wildlife on the Na Pali Coast. Their expeditions include dolphin and whale-watching (Nov.-Mar., $69), shore landings to an ancient fishing village and sea cave explorations (Apr.-Sept., $149 adults, $129 children 8-12), and a 4.5-hour snorkeling tour (year-round, $139 adults, $119 children 5-12).

Kaua'i native Liko Ho'okano is the captain at **Liko Kaua'i Cruises** (4516 Alawai Rd., 888/732-5456, www.liko-kauai.com, $140 adults, $95 children 4-12), where a five-hour Na Pali snorkeling and sights tour is available year-round. Dolphin-watching is included, and whale-watching is part of the tour during the season. A deli lunch and soft drinks are included aboard the 49-foot powered catamaran. A morning and afternoon tour depart daily.

Na Pali Riders (intersection of Hwy. 50 and Hwy. 550, 808/742-6331, www.napaliriders.com, $150 adults, $120 children 5-12) uses Zodiac rafts for a tour combining snorkeling, dolphin and whale-watching, and sea cave exploration. Departing from the Kikiaola Boat Harbor in Waimea, the four-hour tour covers all 17 miles of the Na Pali Coast. They reach the north shore's Ke'e Beach before turning around and heading back west. They offer a $20 discount for cash payments.

SURFING AND STAND-UP PADDLING

Some of the most intense and powerful barreling waves can be found on the west side, especially during the winter months. Westside waves in general are suited for expert surfers due to their size, strong currents, and the lack of lifeguards. Chances are, if you are planning on surfing on the west side, you have your own board, you know where to go, and you have a few local friends to paddle out with. For the beginner or intermediate traveling surfer, your best option is to stick to the more user-friendly waves on the south shore. A good slogan to live by, whether you're surfing or swimming, is if in doubt, don't go out. If you have your heart set on getting on a board, your best bet is to stand-up paddle along the

Waimea River where it is calm and flat. You'll need to come equipped with your own board and paddle though.

Hanapepe

Salt Pond Beach Park is a calm place for stand-up paddling. There are no rentals on the beach, so you'll need to come ready with your own board and paddle. To get here from Route 50, turn onto Route 543 at the street sign pointing toward the ocean, then go right on Lele Road.

Waimea

Infinities (between mile markers 21 and 22) is a long, left-hand breaking wave located at Pakala's Beach. The popular surf break is almost directly in front of the small rock pier at the east end of the beach, just past the river mouth. The wave's name refers to the seemingly endless ride surfers get out here. Although Infinities isn't the most dangerous wave, only experienced surfers should venture out. It's a very localized break, and only those with thorough knowledge of surf etiquette and respect should paddle out.

FISHING

From trout to sport fishing, visitors have the option to reel in some fish in either freshwater or saltwater.

The Wild West

Na Pali Sportfishing (7923 Bulili Rd., Kekaha, 808/635-9424, www.napalisportfishing.com, 8am-7pm daily) leaves out of the Kikiaola Boat Harbor and offers the captain's lifetime of Hawai'i fishing experience catching mahimahi, ahi, wahoo, blue marlin, and more. The fish caught on the trip become property of the captain, but he will send you home with fillets. You must bring your own lunch on this boat. Make sure to inquire about departure time because the first cruise leaves at 6am. The half-day shared rate is $135 per angler and the full-day shared rate is $220 per angler. Half-day charters are $650 and full-day charters are $1,050. The company also offers a five-hour Na Pali sightseeing cruise ($150/person).

Koke'e State Park

Rainbow trout can be found in the **Pu'u Lua Reservoir** on the west side of Koke'e. Koke'e trout season is from the first Saturday in August for 16 consecutive days, then weekends and holidays until the end of September. Call the **Division of Aquatic Resources, Department of Land and Natural Resources** (3060 Eiwa St., Lihu'e, 808/274-3344) for any questions. **Cast and Catch** (located in Koloa, 808/332-9707) provides guided freshwater fishing trips. Fishing licenses can be obtained from **Lihu'e Fishing Supply** (2985 Kalena St., Lihu'e, 808/245-4930).

Hiking and Biking

HIKING
Waimea Canyon State Park

Waimea Canyon State Park is home to vast, breathtaking canyons and decorated with numerous trails weaving through the forest from ridgeline to the canyon floor, ranging from serious hikes to short walks. Once you've gazed at the views on the drive up, take a walk or a long hike to immerse yourself in the natural splendor of the canyon.

ILIAU NATURE LOOP

A perfect family walk, the Iliau Nature Loop begins off Koke'e Road and also marks the beginning of the Kukui Trail. Pull all the way off the road between mile markers 8 and 9 to access the easy, quarter-mile-long trail, which takes about 15 minutes to complete. Views of Waimea Canyon and Wai'alae Falls open up about midway along the loop. The trail is at an elevation of about 3,000 feet and is home to its namesake, the *iliau* plant. The *iliau* is a relative of the silversword, which grows high on Haleakala on Maui, and the greensword, which grows on the Big Island. This rare plant grows only on the dry mountain slopes of western Kaua'i. White-tailed tropic birds and the brown-and-white *pueo* (Hawaiian owl) are known to fly through the area.

KUKUI TRAIL

The Kukui Trail leads down into Waimea Canyon and is the trailhead for the Iliau Nature Loop as well, so begin at the same location between mile markers 8 and 9. This 2.5-mile trail takes about 60-90 minutes to complete the walk in. It is strenuous as it descends over 2,000 feet very quickly, which of course you have to climb up on the way out. Don't forget to bring plenty of water if you're planning on hiking all the way down and up. There are gorgeous views of the canyon along the way. The Wiliwili Campground marks the end of the Kukui Trail. You can set up camp for the night (permit required) and continue on other trails or head back out the same day.

KOAI'E CANYON TRAIL

From the end of the Kukui Trail, serious hikers can head up the Waimea River for about a half mile and then cross the river to find the trailhead for the three-mile-long Koai'e Canyon Trail. This trail has about a 720-foot change in elevation. If the river water is high and rushing, do not cross it. Flash flooding is always a concern. The trailhead is near the Kaluahaulu Campground on the east side of the river. The trail leads you to the south side of Koai'e Canyon, where there are many freshwater pools, which have higher water levels in the winter. The canyon was once used for farming. There are two more campsites at the end of this trail. It is strongly advised to avoid this trail during rainy weather.

WAIMEA CANYON TRAIL

If you head south from the Kukui Trail, you can connect with the 11.5-mile, strenuous,

Waimea Canyon Trail

Koke'e Natural History Museum (3600 Waimea Canyon Dr., after mile marker 15, 808/335-9975, www.kokee.org, 9am-4pm daily) offers trail maps and information. A basic trail map called *Trails of Koke'e* can be picked up at **Na Pali Explorer** (9643 Kaumuali'i Hwy., 808/338-9999 or 877/335-9909, www.napaliexplorer.com) in Waimea, but much more thorough trail maps are Hawaii Nature Guide's *Koke'e Trails* map and *Northwestern Kaua'i Recreational Map* by Earthwalk Press.

THE CLIFF TRAIL

For an easy family trail, take a 10-minute walk on the Cliff Trail. Located off Halemanu Road, it's a leisurely stroll and leads to a wonderful viewpoint overlooking Waimea Canyon. From the lookout you may see some wild goats hanging out on the canyon walls. This trail also accesses the Canyon Trail.

★ WAIPO'O FALLS AND THE CANYON TRAIL

The semi-strenuous 1.8-mile Canyon Trail branches off the Cliff Trail and leads to the upper section of the 800-foot Waipo'o Falls before going up and along the edge of the canyon. It takes about three hours and could be done by a family, if the family is up for a bit of a challenge. Wonderful views of the canyon are offered on this popular trail, and the reward of swimming in freshwater pools makes it a choice hike. The trail goes down into a gulch and then weaves along the cliff to the Koke'e Stream and the falls. It follows the eastern rim of the canyon. Parking is at the Pu'u Hinahina Lookout between mile markers 13 and 14. The trailhead is at the back of the parking lot. The trail ends at the Kumuwela Lookout, where you can head back on the Canyon Trail or walk back on Kumuwela Road.

FAYE TRAIL

At the end of Halemanu Road is the 0.1-mile Faye Trail, which crosses a wooded valley and accesses other trails in the Halemanu area.

and usually hot and dry Waimea Canyon Trail. This is a lengthy trail that parallels the Waimea River through the canyon. It can also be reached by hiking eight miles inland from Waimea town. This trail is popular with serious hikers who enjoy a challenge, but many regard the trail as lacking in sights and views. The hike is well worn and passes back and forth over the river, which usually has plenty of water. Note that river water needs to be boiled or treated before drinking.

Koke'e State Park

There are about 45 miles of trails in Koke'e State Park that vary in difficulty. Most of the hikes begin along Koke'e Drive or the dirt roads that veer off it. The trails generally fall into five categories: Na Pali Coast overlook trails, Alaka'i Swamp trails, forest trails, canyon overlook trails, and even a few birdwatching trails. Remember to bring good hiking shoes, lots of water, sunblock, food, and even swimwear, depending on which trail you take.

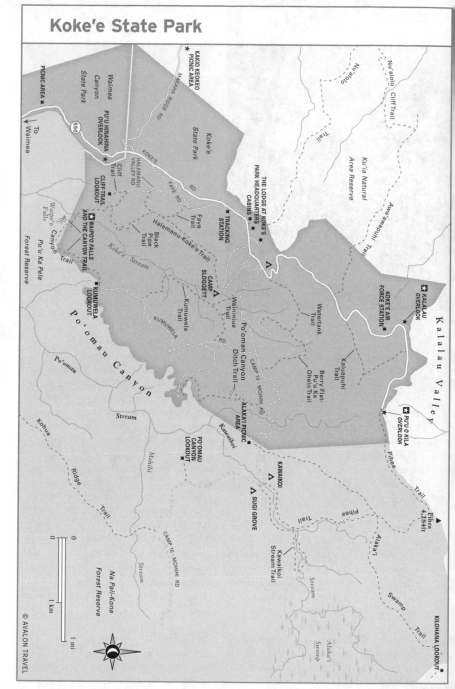

Koke'e State Park

The trail brings you to an undrivable section of Faye Road, which leads left and back up to the highway, not far from the Halemanu Road turnoff. Take a right at Faye Road to end up on the highway below the state park cabins.

NATURE TRAIL

A good trail for children is the 0.1-mile Nature Trail. Starting behind the Koke'e Natural History Museum, it parallels the meadow. It's an easy and enjoyable walk through forest and offers good examples of native vegetation. Before beginning the trail, pick up a free copy of a plant guide at the museum. This trail takes about 15 minutes to complete.

KUMUWELA TRAIL

Off Mohihi Road is the Kumuwela Trail (1.6 miles round-trip). It takes about one hour on the way in and offers lush native vegetation and fragrant flowers. It's a good birding trail, and you can connect to the Canyon Trail at Kumuwela Road at the end of the trail.

PU'U KA OHELO/BERRY FLAT TRAIL LOOP

Near park headquarters is pole #320, which marks the beginning of Camp 10-Mohihi Road. This is generally a four-wheel-drive road, but occasionally two-wheel-drive cars can make it if the weather has been really dry. Numerous trails start here and head into the forest along ridges with canyon views, crossing a couple of minor streams. The roughly 1.6-mile loop called the Pu'u Ka Ohelo Berry Flat Trail is a semi-strenuous trail that has a beautiful forest of sugi pine, California redwoods, Australian eucalyptus, and the valuable native koa as well as the 'ohi'a tree. Small, red strawberry guava with a thick flesh and edible seeds grows here, and this is a popular spot for locals to harvest the fruit. Picking season is midsummer, so it's important to check with park headquarters before snacking on the fruit while hiking. To access this trail, begin at the Pu'u Ka Ohelo trailhead near some cabins about a quarter mile up a road off Camp 10-Mohihi

Road, and hike clockwise, which will take you downhill.

PO'OMAU CANYON DITCH TRAIL

The beautiful Po'omau Canyon Ditch Trail is less than a half mile past the Berry Flat Trail. Developed to maintain the Koke'e irrigation ditch, this trail is less than four miles long round-trip. It's fairly strenuous and deserves plenty of time to be completed. This trail leads to wonderful views of the Po'omau Stream, lush green forests, and a great view of two waterfalls from a peninsula of land that extends out into the canyon. If you bring a picnic lunch you'll find a grassy overlook to rest and enjoy the views. Take Waineke Road across from the Koke'e Museum to Mohihi Road. You will need to park well before the trailhead on Mohihi Road, a little over 1.5 miles from Route 550. Walk about three-quarters of a mile to an unmarked trailhead on your right.

PIHEA TRAIL AND ALAKA'I SWAMP TRAIL

Beginning at the end of Waimea Canyon Drive at the Pu'u O Kila Overlook is the Pihea Trail, about 3.8 miles in length. It leads to the Alaka'i Swamp Trail, about 3.5 miles long. The Pihea Peak, accessed by a very steep trail, is about 1.3 miles after the lookout. This trail runs along the back edge of the Kalalau Valley, and you will be treated to wonderful views into the valley and out to the ocean. About 1.6 miles in, a wooden boardwalk has been constructed to help keep hikers from getting submerged in mud. When you hit the Alaka'i Trail take a left, and it's about two miles to the end. A majestic, gorgeous, and unique trail, the Alaka'i Swamp Trail heads down toward the Kawaikoi Stream and then up a ridge across boggy forestland to the Kilohana Overlook, the trail's ultimate destination. When you can catch a very clear day, which can be tough, the views of the Wainiha and Hanalei Valleys are awesome.

The approximately five-million-year-old swamp is about 4,500 feet above sea level, and is one of the most distinctive experiences on the island. The environment is otherworldly. Mossy trees, birds, and fog create an ecosystem different from anywhere else in the state. It's a great birding trail, but the views are iffy with the lingering mist and clouds of the area. The entire trail totals about eight miles.

NU'ALOLO LOOP/ NU'ALOLO CLIFF TRAIL/ AWA'AWAPUHI TRAIL LOOP

For a daylong hike with spectacular views, explore the Awa'awapuhi/Nu'alolo Loop. This trail offers some of the most fantastic views on the island, and it's a must-do if you are up for a strenuous and long hike. It's nearly 10 miles long, about 11 if you walk the paved road back to your car at the end, but the views on this trail are picturesque and sublime. Most hikers do the full loop, beginning on the Nu'aloalo Trail then turning right (north) about 3.2 miles in onto the Nu'alolo Cliff Trail, which connects with the Awa'awapuhi Trail. At the end, take a left for amazing views from a narrow ridge. A highlight is the thin finger of cliff where you can look down at the sea and a vibrant valley 2,500 feet below. From here, hike uphill back to the road, gaining 1,500 feet in elevation. Along the hike bright red wild berries called thimbleberries (resembling raspberries) are edible, along with the sweet and sour *liliko'i*, or passion fruit. The damage Hurricane 'Iniki did to the area is still evident in this upland forest.

There are no views until the end of the trails. Because they are on the western slopes of Koke'e, it gets extremely hot and sunny in the afternoon, so it's a good idea to begin around 9am or earlier. It's a tough hike. Take your time, bring plenty of water and food, and expect to spend half to a full day on the hike. The trailhead for the Nu'alolo Loop is at the Koke'e Ranger Station. The museum parking lot is probably safer for your car than the trailhead, and walking down the road after you emerge from the Awa'awapuhi trailhead back to the museum is easier than hiking up the road to your car.

Bird-Watching Trails

For bird-watching in Koke'e, try one of the following trails:

- **Alaka'i Swamp Trail** (7 miles round-trip)
- **Kaluapuhi Trail** (4 miles round-trip)
- **Pihea Trail** (7.6 miles round-trip)
- **Halemanu-Koke'e Trail** (2.4 miles round-trip)
- **Kumuwela Trail** (1.6 miles round-trip)

KALUAPUHI TRAIL

The Kaluapuhi Trail is 4 miles round-trip and one of the flattest trails on Kaua'i. The easy hike is a forest trail from start to finish, passing through moist forest where native birds can be seen. Walk in as far as you'd like to go and then return on the same trail to avoid walking back on the highway. To get to the trailhead from the Koke'e Museum, drive 1.9 miles north on Route 550. There is a small pull-off on the right side of the road at the trailhead. The trail ends a quarter mile past the Kalalau Lookout.

HALEMANU-KOKE'E TRAIL

Take a stroll on the Halemanu-Koke'e Trail for birding in native koa forest. The round-trip hike to Halemanu Valley and back is 2.4 miles. The trail climbs 300 feet through koa forest, follows the ridge, and then drops into the valley. To get to the trailhead, turn right onto the dirt road that leads to YMCA Camp Sloggett and park near the Camp Sloggett sign. Walk toward the cabins. The trailhead is by the first cabin on the right.

BIKING

Sunrise and sunset group bike tours are offered for an 11-mile downhill ride, but of course you can always take the ride on your own. Starting in the cool mountain air along the rim of Waimea Canyon at around 3,600 feet, the ride skirts the rim and then heads down the roller coaster foothills to the coast at Kekaha. All of the tours are groups, and participants are given a helmet and jacket to wear. Cruiser bikes with comfortable seats are available for the half-day tour. Refreshments and information on Hawaiian culture are offered. Sunglasses, sunscreen, and sometimes pants are a necessity. A sag wagon follows for bikers who need a rest and to alert traffic from behind. If you'd like to spend about five hours on a bike tour, contact **Outfitters Kauai** (2827 Po'ipu Rd., Po'ipu, 808/742-9667 or 999/742-9887, www.outfitterskauai.com). The rate is $110 for adults, $90 for children 12-14, and van riders are $55.

For the serious mountain biker, the **Waimea Canyon Trail** is an adventure. This eight-mile trail leads back down to Waimea town via an old dirt track and crosses through a game management area. Because of this, a special permit is required to walk though the area and is available at the trailhead. You can connect to the Waimea Canyon Trail by going south from the Kukui Trail. This trail is for dedicated mountain bikers only.

Adventure Sports and Tours

West-side tours explore Kaua'i's coffee industry, history, and nature. Get a glimpse of history through town walking tours, gain insight into the tropical flora and fauna in Koke'e, explore the beaches of Ni'ihau, and see Kaua'i from a bird's-eye view. Unique to the west side is the opportunity for skydiving, offered nowhere else on the island. The adventure sports add some real action to an otherwise mellow locale.

SKYDIVING
Skydive Kauai (Port Allen Airport, Kuiloko Rd., 808/335-5859, www.skydivekauai.com, $239) will help you free-fall out of a plane to 4,500 feet, where the chute opens and you glide back to the airfield. The ride only takes people 18 and older and under 200 pounds. They offer video or photo packages of your experience starting at an additional $70.

HELICOPTER TOURS
★ Ni'ihau Helicopters
Virtually the only way to visit the beaches of Ni'ihau unless invited by an islander is via a **Ni'ihau Helicopters tour** (877/441-3500, www.niihau.us, 8am-2pm Mon.-Sat., $385 including lunch and refreshments), which will take you there for a half day on the beach to

snorkel and sunbathe. A safari/hunting excursion is also offered ($500-1,750). Owned and operated by the owners of Ni'ihau, the company offers free-chase hunting for boars, sheep, and oryx. Five people are required for both tours, and you reach the island in a twin-engine Agusta 109A helicopter that was originally set up to provide medical services for Ni'ihau residents.

Island Helicopters
Movie and waterfall buffs will enjoy a trip to **Manawaiopuna Falls,** which was used in Steven Spielberg's 1993 blockbuster *Jurassic Park* and is located on land that is said to belong to the Robinsons, the same family that owns Ni'ihau. The nearly 400-foot-tall falls are hidden in a valley near Hanapepe and have been restricted to the public for years. Around five years ago the owner and pilot at **Island Helicopters** (Ahukini Rd., Lihu'e, 808/245-8588 or 800/829-5999, www.islandhelicopters.com) began pursuing permits from the state and county to land at the falls. He was successful and now flies people to the remote location five days a week for a 25-minute landing at the falls as part of an 85-minute circle island tour for a regular rate of $371 with online discounted fares.

Ni'ihau: Hawai'i's "Forbidden Island"

Known as Hawai'i's "Forbidden Island," Ni'ihau is a privately owned island passed down through generations by the Robinson family. A cattle and sheep ranch until 1999, today it is home to approximately 120 pure-blooded Hawaiians who are allowed to come and go as they wish. Some even commute daily from Ni'ihau to Kaua'i for work or health care. Outsiders can only come on shore if they are fortunate enough to have an invitation by the owners, a resident, or via a tour with **Ni'ihau Helicopters.** Surfers sometimes manage to sneak in now and then by boat to catch a wave off Lehua Island, by the northern tip of Ni'ihau. For a small island it boasts an array of unique features: the state's two largest lakes, several perfect surf breaks, rare animals like the tall horned oryx, and, of course, the island's famous shells.

The 17-mile Kaulakahi Channel separates the island from the western tip of Kaua'i and is a popular hangout spot for whales. The island can be seen from the shores of Kaua'i's west side from Waimea to Polihale. Measuring just 18 miles long by 6 miles wide, Ni'ihau has a total area of 70 square miles, and the surrounding waters are popular with scuba divers and spear fishers. The highest point on the island, Pani'au (1,281 feet) lies on the east-central coast. Because Ni'ihau is so low and lies in lee of Kaua'i, it gets only about 30 inches of rain each year. It's said that the low rainfall has led to a lack of flowers on the island, and this is the reason Ni'ihau Hawaiians replaced flowers with shells in lei making.

Hawaiian legend says Ni'ihau was born after the goddess Papa and her husband Wakea reconciled after he was caught with another lover while Papa was visiting Tahiti. Kaua'i was born from this pregnancy, and Ni'ihau came out as the afterbirth, along with Lehua and Ka'ulu, the last of the low reef islands. Because of the lack of rain and poor soil, Ni'ihau was never as populated as the other islands. The islanders traded their abundant fish catches with Kaua'i peoples for poi and other necessities. Ni'ihau mats made from *makaloa* also became highly valuable. Today, Ni'ihau Hawaiians raise livestock, produce the famous Ni'ihau shell lei, and work on Kaua'i for their income.

Kaua'i and Ni'ihau became part of the Kingdom of Hawai'i under Kamehameha the Great. Ni'ihau was passed down to his successors, and in 1864 Kamehameha V sold the island for $10,000 to the Sinclair family. It's said that the king offered them a swampy beach area on O'ahu, but the Scottish family didn't want it. It turns out the swampy beach was Waikiki, which means they could have had a much better investment. Through marriage, Ni'ihau became property of the Robinson family.

Today the population on Ni'ihau is slowly declining as the young residents choose to live elsewhere. There's no electricity on the island, and generators power refrigerators, TVs, and computers. Horses and old pickups are the popular mode of transportation. In the main community of Pu'uwai, there is one elementary school. Teenagers attend high school on Kaua'i.

WALKING TOURS

Hanapepe

A self-guided walking tour through Hanapepe town can be done with or without the *Historic Hanapepe Walking Tour Map* that is available without charge in many of the shops in town. The map provides background information on the historical buildings and churches. For map-free walkers, plaques with information can be found on the front of most of the buildings.

The **Kaua'i Coffee Company** (800/545-8605, www.kauaicoffee.com, 9am-5pm daily), the largest single coffee estate in Hawai'i, offers a free walking tour where visitors can learn about Kaua'i coffee. The tour includes interpretive signs that identify the five different varieties of coffee as well as the entire coffee bean growing process, from initial blossoming through harvesting and processing, to the final roasting and into your cup.

Waimea

A local volunteer offers two tours in Waimea free of charge. A walking tour of Waimea town is offered on Monday and begins at the **West Kaua'i Technology Center** (9565 Kaumuali'i Hwy., 808/338-1332) at 9:30am. She also guides a tour on Saturday of a plantation neighborhood dating back to the 1900s; it meets at the lobby of the **Waimea Plantation Cottages** (9400 Kaumuali'i Hwy., 808/338-1625). Reservations are required and can be made by calling 808/337-1005.

Shopping

High-end fashion and big-box stores are absent on the west side. Small boutiques, local crafts, jewelry, and art are abundant. The west side offers some unique souvenirs, from Ni'ihau jewelry to local art.

HANAPEPE

Art galleries featuring photography, paintings, drawings, sculptures, glass, and more line the streets of Hanapepe. The town is always worth a stroll through, whether window shopping or purchasing a masterpiece.

Art Galleries

Kaua'i Fine Arts (3905 Hanapepe Rd., 808/335-3778, www.brunias.com, 9am-5pm daily) calls a small white building on the eastern end of Old Hanapepe home. The shop has the feel of an antiques store, as much of its stock is previously used items. Prints by local artists, shell jewelry, maps, books, antique maps, carvings, and other art objects make up the shop's unique collection.

Giorgio's Gallery (3871 Hanapepe Rd., 808/335-3949, www.giorgiosart.com, 11am-5pm daily) is an extravaganza of color reflecting the beauty of the islands in landscape, floral, and abstract paintings. Using a method called plein air, Giorgio creates palette knife oil paintings, often on location around Kaua'i. You will usually find a friendly staff member overseeing the spacious gallery during business hours, who's happy to chat about the island and art. The walls are covered in bursts of color that seem to leap off the canvas.

If you look to your left as you enter **Banana Patch Studios** (3865 Hanapepe Rd., 808/335-5944, www.bananapatchstudio.com, 10am-4:30pm Mon.-Thurs., 10am-9pm Fri., 10am-4pm Sat.) you will see art being made through a large window looking right into the studio. This is a great place for souvenirs such as ceramic tiles saying "please remove shoes," and "aloha." Owner Joanna Carolan creates the tiles, an array of jewelry, and nature-inspired paintings. Island-style trinkets and home decor from other crafters are also in stock.

Traditional watercolors and incredible island photography capturing nature's spectacular moments can be found in the

Arius Hopman Gallery (3840C Hanapepe Rd., 808/335-0227, www.hopmanart.com, 10:30am-2pm Mon.-Thurs., 10:30am-2pm and 6pm-9pm Fri.), where the artwork can be printed up to 12 feet long. Both the paintings and photos reflect Kaua'i's beauty, life, and energy. Hopman's artistic ability is in his blood; his mother was a world-renowned artist who was commissioned to sculpt Mahatma Gandhi twice. The native of India moved to Hawai'i in 1985 and lives in Hanapepe.

Crafts and Books

There's something warm and cozy about independently owned bookstores, and **Talk Story Bookstore** (3785 Hanapepe Rd., 808/335-6469, www.talkstorybookstore. com, 10am-5pm Mon.-Thurs., 10am-9:30pm Fri., noon-5pm Sat.) doesn't disappoint. The family-run business is Kaua'i's only new and used bookstore and is located in the historic Old Yoshiura Store. Over 40,000 used, rare, and collectible books are available, along with Hawaiian gifts, crafts, records, and Hawaiian slack-key and ukulele lesson courses. Any books you want to unload can be traded in for in-store credit. The shop stays open late on Art Night, offering live entertainment.

Crafts and jewelry decorate **JJ Ohana** (3805-B Hanapepe Rd., 808/335-0366, www. jjohana.com, 8am-6pm Mon.-Thurs., 8am-9pm Fri., 8am-5pm Sat.). The highlight here is the Ni'ihau shell jewelry made by the owner, whom you may find overseeing the shop. She makes beautiful earrings, necklaces, and bracelets that are some of the most valuable Kaua'i souvenirs.

PORT ALLEN
Clothing

At the **Red Dirt Factory Outlet** (4350 Waialo Rd., 800/717-3478, www.dirtshirt. com, 9am-5pm daily) in Port Allen, a natural resource has been used to create one of the most famous Kaua'i souvenirs. The shirts are dyed with real Kaua'i red dirt, and there's an interesting story behind the making of the shirts.

When Hurricane 'Iniki unleashed its fury on Kaua'i in 1992, the staff at Paradise Sportswear returned to the shop to find the warehouse roof completely torn off. The storm left a large stock of shirts dyed red from the island's dirt. What could have led to a bleak future for the company suddenly became a blessing as a person with a glass-half-full outlook on life said, "These shirts look pretty cool." Next thing you know, the Red Dirt Shirt

Giorgio's Gallery

Ni'ihau Shell Jewelry

Diamonds and platinum may be a sign of luxury in the U.S. mainland, but in Hawai'i it's Ni'ihau shell jewelry. The rare and highly valued shells (*kahelelani, laiki, momi,* and *kamoa*) are found on the beaches of Ni'ihau and crafted by the island's residents into various styles of lei, earrings, and bracelets, equaling one of Polynesia's most precious art forms. Captain Cook returned from Hawai'i with a Ni'ihau shell lei that now resides in the British Museum. The jewelry is mostly sold on Kaua'i, though some of it makes it to shops on other islands.

The shells wash up on the beaches from October to March, when winter swells bring waves big enough to wash them ashore. This is when islanders rush to gather the shells and either make the jewelry on the island or send the shells to family on Kaua'i to craft. The tiny shells are sorted by size and color, and only the best are kept; around 80 percent are thrown away. Many of the pink *kahelelani* that are found are a dull flesh color, worn rough, or are broken. The shell colors include bright pink, deep red, white, yellow, blue, and gold. Holes are delicately drilled into the small shells, and they are strung in a traditional fashion to make various types of jewelry. Most common are the necklaces and lei. The lei are usually a combination of many strands, either hanging below each other or spiraling around each other.

To see a museum-type collection of Ni'ihau shell work, visit the Hawaiian Trading Company in Lawa'i, visible from Route 50. For a rare and valuable souvenir, Ni'ihau jewelry is the perfect thing. The best book on Ni'ihau jewelry is *Ni'ihau Shell Leis,* by Linda Paik Moriarty, published by the University of Hawai'i Press.

was created and is maintained by local families taking regular old white shirts home and dipping them in vats of Kaua'i's red dirt. They bring them back and other locals apply silk-screen designs on shirts that are distinct from one another because the color ranges from deep reddish brown to a light orange. Self-guided tours are available at the factory store 9am-noon and 1pm-4pm daily to watch the silk-screening process. There is also a smaller red dirt store in Waimea and on each island.

WAIMEA
Gourmet Treats and Beauty Products

Known as one of the tastiest tropical flavors and used across the culinary board from desserts to entrées, the *liliko'i,* or passion fruit, is used in all of its glory at **Aunty Liliko'i** (9875 Waimea Rd., 808/338-1296, www.auntylilikoi.com, 10am-6pm daily). The sweet and sour fruit is the highlight in jams, jellies, mustards, dressings, syrups, and even skin-care products. Drop by the quaint shop in Waimea to pick up a snack.

Antiques

Antiques from around the islands can be found at **Collectibles and Fine Junque** (9821 Kaumuali'i Hwy., 808/338-9855). An array of Hawaiiana, books, trinkets, jewelry, and so much more fills the small shop to the brim. The staff is usually happy to talk story with shoppers, and even just browsing here can be fun. The small building that houses the shop is an antique itself. Those looking for it may question if the rundown building is being utilized, but the historic look adds to the shop's spirit.

THE WILD WEST
Souvenirs

Located at the bottom of Koke'e Road is the Waimea Canyon Plaza, with a **Menehune Food Mart** (808/337-1335, 6am-8pm Mon.-Sat., 6am-6pm Sun.), **Waimea Canyon General Store** (808/337-9569, 9am-5:30pm daily), and **Thrifty Mini Mart** (808/337-1057, 8am-9pm daily). These markets are good for last-minute souvenir shopping.

Stargazing

Stargazing can be done anywhere on Kaua'i, but few take advantage of this opportunity. Joining a group of stargazers once a month is an inspiration to relax outdoors at night and revel in the light of the sparkling stars (*hoku* in Hawaiian). From June to September, the **Kaua'i Educational Association for Science and Astronomy** (808/332-7827, www.keasa.org) gathers stargazers together at the Kaumakani ball field to watch a celestial cinema. Heading west from Hanapepe, look for the Thrifty Mart Bakery in Kaumakani, take a right at the Kaumakani sign, then turn right again to the ball field. With no city lights around, the stars burn bright.

Entertainment

If you're looking for nightlife, the west side isn't where you'll find it. Art Night in Hanapepe is really the only action at night other than a dinner out or stargazing on the beach (which is quite enjoyable).

★ ART NIGHT IN HANAPEPE

Around 16 art galleries open their doors for a night of art celebration 6pm-9pm each Friday on Hanapepe Road. Art Night is an opportunity to socialize with locals and other visitors, explore the town, and meet artists. The night can be enjoyed casually if you're coming straight from the beach, but it can also be an opportunity to dress up for a night out on the small, historical town. You'll find live music on the boardwalk, artists working away at their latest masterpieces, and plenty of food and refreshments. If you're considering purchasing a piece of local art, meeting the artist can often provide context and a deeper story to the work that is fun to share with family and friends

back home and creates a connection to your time in the islands.

CINEMA

The historic **Waimea Theater** (9691 Kaumuali'i Hwy., 808/338-0282, www.waimeatheater.com) was built in 1938. It closed in 1972 and was converted to a warehouse and later survived damage from Hurricane 'Iniki in 1992. The building was leased in 1993 by West Kaua'i Main Street to prevent the owner from tearing it down, and this marked the beginning of a seven-year effort to save the landmark theater. In 1996 the County of Kaua'i purchased the building, and after years of restoration it was opened in 1999 as a functioning movie theater that now accommodates 270 patrons. Featuring a small stage, movie screen, sound system, and snack bar, it's the only movie theater from here to Lihu'e. A night at the Waimea Theater isn't just movie night, it's experiencing a part of the west side's history. Call or check the website for show times and movie listings.

Food

Good food isn't hard to find out west. There are a number of *ono* (delicious) places to eat, from snacks and desserts to local brews and dinner. For such small towns there's a wide array of cuisines and a decent number of vegetarian dishes scattered through the eateries.

HANAPEPE
Cafés
The roadside **Grinds Cafe** (4469 Waialo Rd., 808/335-6027, www.grindscafe.net, 5:30am-9pm Mon. and Fri.-Sun., 6am-3pm Tues.-Thurs., $5-22) serves their entire menu all day long. They offer pizzas, sandwiches, pasta, salads, and more. Breakfast options start at $5, while dinner entrée options range $13-20. Indoor and patio seating is available, where you will find a mix of locals picking up a cup of coffee and visitors passing through.

Grab a smoothie, coffee, bagel, acai bowl, salad, or a fresh sandwich at **Little Fish Coffee** (3900 Hanapepe Rd., 808/335-5000, 6:30am-5pm Mon.-Sat., $3-11). The artsy café has indoor seating and patio seating in the backyard. The coffee is fair trade, organic, and roasted by Kauai Roastery. The kitchen closes at 3pm, and they're open till 9pm during Hanapepe Art Night. Check the Little Fish Coffee Facebook page for more information.

Groceries
For groceries, alcoholic beverages, and local deli food, drop into the **Big Save** (808/335-3127, 6:30am-10pm daily) in the 'Ele'ele Shopping Center (4469 Waialo Rd.). Stock up on extra drinks or snacks before heading out on a boat cruise or jetting off to Ni'ihau for the day. The store offers limited pre-made food such as sushi and other local-style dishes to eat on the road.

Local Food
Located on Kaumuali'i Highway, you can't miss **MCS Grill** (1-3529 Kaumuali'i Hwy.,

808/431-4645, www.mcsgrill.com, 10:30am-8:30pm Mon.-Fri., 5pm-9pm Sat., $10-21) with the red flame logo on the front of the restaurant. It serves breakfast, lunch, and dinner and offers a few vegetarian items. MCS Grill is best known for its saimin as well as its plates, served with rice as well as potato, macaroni, or tossed salad.

Bobbies (3820 Hanapepe Rd., 808/335-5152, 10am-3pm Mon.-Wed., 10am-2:30pm and 5pm-8pm Thurs.-Sat., 10am-2:30pm and 5pm-8:30pm Fri., $9-15) serves local food at its best: loco moco, chicken katsu, saimin, pulled pork sandwiches, and ahi salad. Don't forget, everything comes with rice and mac salad. Eat at the no-frills eatery or take away. Either way, the portions are big.

Treats and Desserts
Chocolate, especially local, is enough of a reason to stop at the **Kaua'i Chocolate Company** (4341 Waialo Rd., 808/335-0448, www.kauaichocolate.us, 10am-6pm Mon.-Fri., 11am-5pm Sat., noon-3pm Sun.). Serving up truffles, macadamia nuts, and ice cream, the shop will either fill your belly on the spot or your suitcase for gifts at home. The small shop is like a mini version of Willie Wonka's factory, and it's nearly impossible to leave without a treat.

Wong's (13543 Kaumuali'i Hwy., 808/335-5066, www.wongsomoide.com, 8am-9pm Tues.-Sun.) claims to serve up Kaua'i's best *liliko'i* (passion fruit) pie. Wong's is a Chinese restaurant, but they are best known for the pie and other pastries. The light *liliko'i* chiffon pie is delicious, and it actually tastes like real *liliko'i*. Stop in and enjoy a piece for under $3, or take a whole pie to go.

The tropical- and traditional-flavored ice creams and sorbets at ★ **Lappert's Ice Cream** (1-3555 Kaumuali'i Hwy., 808/335-6121 or 800/356-4045, www.lappertshawaii.com, 10am-6pm daily, $4 for a single

Kaukau: Favorite Local Dishes

There's really no better way to experience a culture than to *kaukau* (pidgin slang for "eat") the food of the people. Most of these foods are available in restaurants, supermarkets, and delis. When you stumble across one of these local favorites, give it a try:

- *Poke:* Cubed raw fish with seasonings. The fish of choice is usually ahi (yellowfin tuna), but it's not un-common to find *poke* made with *tako* (octopus), other types of tuna, or other fish. Seasonings are usually a combination of chopped onion, soy sauce, oil, sea salt, seaweed, and garlic. With *poke,* the fresher the fish the better the dish.

- **Poi:** A form of taro that has been cooked, pounded, and fermented. The consistency of this Hawaiian sta-ple can be runny or thick. There is "two-finger" and "three-finger" poi, referring to how many fingers it takes to eat it depending on how thick it is.

poke

- *Huli huli* chicken: Barbecued chicken, Hawaiian style. *Huli huli* chicken is often roadside-roasted. (*Huli* means "to turn," a reference to the rotisserie whole chicken continuously turning during cook-ing.)

- **Plate lunch:** A local favorite composed of two scoops of rice, one scoop of macaroni salad, and a main meat course, often served on a disposable plate. Lunch wagons usually serve plate lunches.

- *Kalua* pig: A flavorful dish, cooked in an *imu,* or earth oven, that is usually found at cel-ebratory gatherings. Birthday parties, *lu'au,* and other holiday feasts are usually reason to go through the long process, which entails hours of slow cooking.

- **Loco moco:** A bowl of rice topped with a meat patty, egg, and gravy. In Pacific Rim cuisine, the modernization of *loco moco* with unique ingredients is becoming a trend.

- *Lomilomi* salmon: A popular side dish consisting of raw salmon and tomatoes. It's called "massaged" (*lomilomi*) salmon because the fish is massaged by hand with ingredients including salt, onions, and sometimes chili pepper.

scoop) are the perfect cool accent to a warm Hawaiian day. Originating on Kaua'i, the shop now has outlets statewide. The ice cream has about 16 percent butterfat in its regular flavors and around 8 percent in its fruit flavors, mak-ing for some pretty creamy ice cream.

The **Kaua'i Kookie Company** (1-3529 Kaumuali'i Hwy., 808/335-5003, www.kauai-kookie.com, 8am-4pm Mon.-Fri., 11am-4pm Sat.-Sun.) is another local treat that makes a great snack or gift. At the Hanapepe factory outlet they sell their macadamia shortbread,

Kona coffee, guava macadamia, and coconut krispies cookies. The cookies are also distrib-uted around the island and can be purchased by mail order.

Farmers Market

A year-round, open-air market, the **Hanapepe Farmers Market** provides local produce and crafts. Located behind the Hanapepe fire station in **Hanapepe Park,** the market happens 3pm-5pm every Thursday. Remember to bring your own

Little Fish Coffee

reusable shopping bag or a pre-used plastic bag from another store.

WAIMEA
American

The decor is true to the name at ★ **Wrangler's Steakhouse** (9852 Kaumuali'i Hwy., 808/338-1218, www.wranglersrestaurant.com, lunch 11am-4pm Mon.-Fri., dinner 4pm-9pm Mon. Sat., $18-33), where the restaurant is decorated with cowboy trinkets and gear. Indoor and outdoor seating are offered. Wrangler's is known for their great steaks, and they offer a salad and soup bar with each meal. A full bar is stocked with a variety of liquors, wines, and beers to please any palate. The menu offers a hefty assortment of red meats, poultry, and seafood. Service is friendly, and there is also a small *paniolo* (Hawaiian cowboy) museum as well as shell jewelry for sale.

To peel, or not to peel, that is the question at ★ **The Shrimp Station** (9652 Kaumuali'i Hwy., 808/338-1242, 11am-5pm daily, $11-12), where shrimp is served up in a number of ways. At this very laid-back eatery, seating is at picnic tables under a tent right on the side of the main road. The menu includes shrimp entrées, drinks, desserts, and ice cream. It's located across from Island Tacos.

Kalapaki Joe's (9400 Kaumuali'i Hwy., 808/338-1666, http://kalapakijoes.com, 7am-10pm daily, $11-19), the westernmost sports bar in the United States, is open for breakfast, lunch, and dinner and has a wonderful selection of beers on tap. It offers a steak and seafood menu with plenty of bar-food appetizers like nachos and spinach dip, mixed with local pupu favorites like *poke, kalua* pork, and pork wontons. Joe's has happy hour 3pm-6pm daily with $2 off drafts and house wine, $3 fish tacos, $1 shrimp tempura, and 25-cent wings.

Groceries

For usual supermarket needs there is a **Big Save** (9861 Waimea Rd., 808/338-1621, 6am-10pm Mon.-Sat., 6am-9pm Sun.) in Waimea. They carry limited pre-made deli food, groceries, snorkel and dive gear, and baby products.

Ishihara Market (9894 Kaumuali'i Hwy., 808/338-1751, 6am-7:30pm Mon.-Thurs., 6am-8pm Fri.-Sat., 6am-7pm Sun.) offers the usual supermarket finds, but they are well known with locals for their wide variety of local deli foods. Check out the deli in the back for *poke,* sandwiches, sushi, ribs, and a whole lot more. They even sell plain already-made rice and have a substantial selection of bowls, cups, and utensils, making it perfect for a last-minute camping stop. The store smells a little funky and fishy, but locals love the food.

Local Treats

Finely shaved ice and 60 flavors can be found at ★ **Jo-Jo's Clubhouse** (9734 Kaumuali'i Hwy., across from mile marker 23, www.jo-josshaveice.com, 11am-5:30pm daily, $3-6). The line can be long, but it's a testimony to their great shave ice. Try some local flavor combos like lychee and coconut or *liliko'i* and *melona*.

Mexican

★ **Island Tacos** (9643 Kaumuali'i Hwy., 808/338-9895, www.islandfishtaco.com, 11am-5pm daily, $3-12) in Waimea is a simple order-at-the-counter taco stand with seating, reminiscent of roadside taco stands in Mexico. The large menu offers local fish, pork, chicken, and even a wide variety of satisfying vegetarian and vegan options. Portions are large, with unique toppings like a wasabi-spiked aioli sauce and the option of fat-free dishes. Perfect for a quick stop on a drive through Waimea or to satisfy a craving after camping at Polihale, this place is really good. They even serve fresh homemade tortillas.

Health Food

Organic, vegetarian, vegan, and natural breakfasts, lunches, smoothies, and desserts can be found at the family-run ★ **Happy Mangos Healthy Hale** (Alawai Rd., 808/338-0055, www.happymangos.com, store 6:30am-5pm Mon.-Fri., 7am-3pm Sat., café 6:30am-4pm Mon.-Fri., 7am-2pm Sat., $3-9). The owners serve freshly made food along with natural and organic groceries and produce. Located in a small plantation-style building across from Lucy Wright Beach Park, the health-food store is the only natural and organic choice in Waimea. They serve non-vegetarian sandwiches too.

G's Juicebar (9681 Kaumuali'i Hwy., 808/634-4112, 10am-4pm Tues.-Sat., $4-10) serves smoothies, fresh juices, and acai bowls and offers monthly specials. If you're into chocolate for breakfast, check out the Rambla Bowl with acai, cacao powder and nibs, almond milk, banana, almonds, hemp seed, and honey. They also have a shot menu for daily natural energy boosts.

An easy and healthy breakfast or snack in the hotel room or while camping can be found at **Kaua'i Granola** (9633 Kaumuali'i Hwy., 808/338-0121, www.kauaigranola.com, 10am-5pm Mon.-Sat., 10am-3pm Sun.). Unique flavors like Hawaiian zest and guava crunch are available and sold along with Waimea-made chocolate-dipped coconut macaroons, dried fruit, cookies, and pastries. Nestled in a small shop next to Island Tacos, grab some for a treat back home.

KOKE'E STATE PARK
Local Food

Breakfast and lunch are served daily at the restaurant of the **Lodge at Koke'e** (808/335-6061, www.thelodgeatkokee.net, 9am-2:30pm daily, $6-8). The soups accent the cool

The Lodge at Koke'e in Koke'e State Park

weather, and their banana bread and Koke'e corn bread make a great treat. Meat entrées are common, but there are a few vegetarian options too, along with local dishes like *kalua* pork and *loco moco*. Wine, beer, and cocktails are also on the menu. The next eatery is about 15 miles away unless you bring a picnic lunch.

THE WILD WEST
Farmers Market
On Saturday a farmers market happens 9am-11am at the **Kekaha Neighborhood Center** on Elepaio Road. Drop by on the way to the beach to see the assortment of local crafts, fruits, vegetables, and other local specialties. The market is open year-round.

Groceries
Located at the bottom of Koke'e Road is the Waimea Canyon Plaza and **Menehune Food Mart** (808/337-1335, 6am-8pm Mon.-Sat., 6am-6pm Sun.), **Waimea Canyon General Store** (808/337-9569, 9am-5:30pm daily), and **Thrifty Mini Mart** (808/337-1057, 8am-9pm daily). Each market offers basic small-supermarket finds. These markets are good for cooler stocking before heading out to Polihale or when entering or leaving the parks.

Information and Services

BANKS
Hanapepe
In the 'Ele'ele Shopping Center is a **First Hawaiian Bank** (808/335-3161, www.fhb.com, 8:30am-4pm Mon.-Thurs., 8:30am-6pm Fri.), offering walk-in and 24-hour ATM services and a notary service.

Bank of Hawaii has an ATM in the Big Save in the 'Ele'ele Shopping Center and the McDonald's at the shopping center.

In Old Hanapepe is an **American Savings Bank** (4548 Kona Rd., 808/335-3118, www.asbhawaii.com, 8am-5pm Mon.-Thurs., 8am-6pm Fri.). The branch offers walk-in services and a 24-hour ATM.

Waimea
There are several banks in Waimea. **First Hawaiian Bank** (4525 Panako Rd., 808/338-1611, www.fhb.com, 8:30am-4pm Mon.-Thurs., 8:30am-6pm Fri.) offers walk-in and 24-hour ATM services and a notary service.

POSTAL SERVICES
Hanapepe
At Hanapepe's **U.S. Post Office** (3817 Kona Rd., 808/335-3641, 9am-1pm and 1:30pm-4pm Mon.-Fri.), regular shipping services are offered.

Waimea
There is a **U.S. Post Office** (9911 Waimea Rd., 808/338-9973, 9am-1pm and 1:30pm-4pm Mon.-Fri., 9am-11am Sat.) in Waimea. They provide shipping services, limited packaging materials, and stamps.

INTERNET SERVICES
Waimea
Internet is available at **Aloha-n-Paradise** (9905 Waimea Rd., 808/338-1522, 7am-noon Mon.-Fri., 8am-noon Sat.), where you can surf the net on their computers or bring in your own laptop and use their wireless. The **Waimea Public Library** (9750 Kaumuali'i Hwy., 808/338-6848, noon-8pm Mon. and Wed., 9am-5pm Tues. and Thurs., 10am-5pm Fri.) and the **West Kaua'i Visitor and Technology Center** (9565 Kaumuali'i Hwy., 808/338-1332) both offer Internet access. Printing is available at each location.

EMERGENCY SERVICES
Waimea
A **fire station** is located along the highway at the bottom of Menehune Road. A short distance up Waimea Canyon Drive, **West Kaua'i Medical Center** (4643 Waimea Canyon Dr., 808/338-9431) and its clinic (808/338-8311) is

the only hospital on the west side and offers 24-hour emergency services.

CLASSES
Waimea

There's no better way to experience local culture than to learn some of the traditions. Hula and art classes give visitors a unique window into the Hawaiian culture and the island's natural beauty.

Hula at **A Hideaway Spa** (9400 Kaumuali'i Hwy., 808/338-0005, www.ahideawayspa.com) will expose you to an art that is a foundation of the Hawaiian culture. Located on the property of Waimea Plantation Cottages, the 90-minute classes are a perfect way to relax, learn, and have fun on your vacation. Call for a class schedule.

Create your own souvenir at **Kaua'i Art Classes** (808/631-9173, www.kauaiartclasses. com). All materials are provided for creating silk paintings, acrylics, and pastels at Waimea Plantation Cottages. Classes are offered at multiple locations on the west side, so check the website for directions and addresses.

To get the most out of your photo opportunities on Kaua'i, take a **digital photography class** from Hanapepe painter and photographer Arius Hopman (808/335-5616).

Getting There and Around

AIR

After arriving at the **Lihu'e Airport,** visitors have the choice of catching the bus around the island, renting a car, having a friend pick them up, or even hitchhiking. Most visitors will arrive in Lihu'e via a stopover in Honolulu, where they will connect from their large commercial airline to a local regional carrier.

CAR

The most convenient way to get around the west side is by car. **Route 50** heads west straight out of Lihu'e and runs all the way to the end of the road to Polihale. Rental cars are the best bet here and are available at the airport. Gas prices go up the farther west you go, so it's a good idea to fill up in Lihu'e.

BUS

The **Kaua'i Bus** (808/241-6410, www.kauai. gov/transportation, 5:27am-10:40pm Mon.-Fri., 6:21am-5:50pm Sat.-Sun. and holidays) runs island-wide as far west as Kekaha, and is a green, convenient, and affordable way to get around. But with Kekaha as the last stop, and no routes up to the parks, taking the bus out west means you are far away from the biggest draws of the west side—the far west beaches and the state parks. It does stop at the Kaua'i Coffee Company Visitor Center and in Hanapepe, allowing for a visit to the art galleries. Fares are $1 for children and seniors, and $2 for the general public. Monthly passes are also available.

TAXI

Pono Taxi (808/634-4744, www.ponotaxi. com) offers west shore sightseeing and dining tours. Hawai'i taxi rates are $3 per mile and $0.40 per minute. Prices are per minivan, not per person.

HITCHHIKING

Hitchhiking is legal on Kaua'i, as long as you stay off the paved part of the road, but if you try to thumb it all the way out to Polihale, there's a good chance of walking a very long way in the scorching sun. For safety reasons, it is recommended that women and children do not hitchhike alone.

Where to Stay

On Kaua'i, you'll find an array of vacation rentals, condominiums, resorts, bed-and-breakfasts, smaller hotels, and mainstream, big-name resorts situated on the south, east, and north shores.

Budget travelers and outdoor enthusiasts looking for nothing more than a hot shower and a place to sleep can find suitable, lower-priced accommodations. Camping is also an affordable way to enjoy the best of Kaua'i's natural beauty, even if just for one night. Visitors who prefer relaxing at their accommodations may find a large resort or luxury condominium to their liking. Families and large groups should consider vacation rentals, which include residences with the usual amenities a home has to offer. Whatever option you choose, make accommodation reservations well in advance, especially if you're visiting in the busy season. Planning ahead could mean the difference of a room with a view of the ocean instead of the parking lot.

For those who are making their first visit to the island and planning on exploring all sides of Kaua'i, consider a place in Kapa'a or Lihu'e, in the island's most central region. Both towns are located on the east side, which generally offers more affordable accommodations than the north or south shore. This will cut down on the time you spend on the road and in traffic, no matter which direction you travel.

Wherever you choose to stay, from Po'ipu to Hanalei, oceanfront properties are the norm. Even if you select a garden-view room to save a little money, the beach will be a short walk away. Most hotels and resorts near the beach have a kiosk where you can rent or purchase snorkel and beach gear, even kayaks and stand-up paddleboards. Most vacation rentals also have beach gear like beach chairs, umbrellas, and bodyboards that you can use free of charge.

Previous: The St. Regis Princeville Resort; vacation rentals on Anini Beach. **Above:** fruiting banana tree.

East Side

WAILUA
Under $100

Easy on the wallet is the **Rosewood Kaua'i Bunk House** (872 Kamalu Rd., 808/822-5216, www.rosewoodkauai.com, $75-85), where you can choose from three studios with kitchenettes and private entrances with shared bathroom and outdoor shower. Very cute and clean with hardwood floors and bright white walls. Two rooms rent for $75 a night and one for $85, each with a $45 cleaning fee and a three-night minimum.

On three acres on the Sleeping Giant mountain is **Lani Keha** (848 Kamalu Rd., 808/822-1605, www.lanikeha.com, $55-65), which offers very casual accommodations perfect for the traveler who is looking to meet others. They offer three rooms with a communal kitchen and living room. You can rent one room at $55 a night for a single or $65 for a double, or the whole house for $250 with a two-night minimum. No frills but nice, simple, and clean.

The ★ **Kaua'i Sands Hotel** (420 Papaloa Rd., 808/822-4941 or 800/560-5533, www.kauaisandshotel.com, $80-152) offers a perfect blend of simple island style and great affordability in 200 rooms on six oceanfront acres. Reminiscent of a 1970s hotel in the simple style and color mix, the hotel is quite nice, although simple with no frills. Each room has a small refrigerator, TV, air-conditioning, and either one king-size, two queen beds, or two double beds. Service is always friendly, and out by the pool the lawn opens up to the ocean. The hotel is extremely affordable, with standard and mountain/garden-view rooms going for $80-89 a night, pool views for $98 a night, ocean views for $116 a night, and a studio suite with kitchenette for $152 a night.

$100-200

The lovely **Sleeping Giant Cottage** (5979 Heamoi Pl., 505/401-4403, www.wanek.com/sleepinggiant, $109) is a one-bedroom simple cottage with three lanai nestled in a lush yard. It's about a 10-minute drive down to the ocean, and they require a three-night minimum. The rate is $109 a night, but they offer specials for weekly and monthly stays with a one-time $75 cleaning fee. It has a homey, simple island style with full bathroom and kitchen, cable TV, washer and dryer, some beach gear, gas grill, king-size bed, and a queen-size sleeper sofa.

Opaeka'a Falls Hale (120 Liahu St., 800/262-9912, www.bestbnb.com/OpaekkaUpper.html, $130) has two units as part of their B&B. The upper is called the Royal Palm, and the Queen Emma is on the lower level. Both have a $50 cleaning fee and require a five-night minimum. There's a beautiful pool on-site, and it's a short drive from the ocean. Both have a full kitchen, lanai, and washer and dryer and offer a Hawaiian continental breakfast.

The **Fern Grotto Inn** (4561 Kuamo'o Rd., 808/821-9836, www.ferngrottoinn.com, $150-190) consists of three cottages and a house. All are remodeled, simple, plantation-style homes with shared laundry and either full or limited kitchens. The friendly owners live on-site, and it's near the Wailua River. All the accommodations are decorated with a clean island style. The River Cottage is a cute and clean studio for $190 a night with a $125 cleaning fee. The Canal Cottage is divided into two studios, both renting for $150 a night with a $100 cleaning fee.

A privately owned apartment dubbed the **Traditional Rooms** (808/822-5216, www.rosewoodkauai.com, $145) is located in the hills of Wailua in a residential neighborhood. It is an immaculately maintained unit with a private bathroom. You'll wake up to breakfast each morning here. It sleeps two for $145 a night with a three-night minimum and $75

Where to Stay on the East Side

Name	Type	Price	Features	Why Stay Here	Best Fit For
Aloha Hale Orchid	studio	$55	mini fridge	on orchid farm, affordable	budget travelers
★ Aston Aloha Beach Hotel	hotel	$113-195	pool	affordable, good location	families, couples
Courtyard Kaua'i at Coconut Beach	hotel	$179-239	pool, business center	friendly service	families, couples
Fern Grotto Inn	cottages	$150-190	kitchens	privacy	families, couples
Garden Island Inn	small inn	$134-143	kitchenettes, beach gear	affordable, central location	couples
Hale Lani B&B	B&B	$135-195	breakfast, hot tub	privacy, home-cooked meals	couples
Honu'ea International Hostel Kaua'i	hostel	$25-70	common kitchen area	affordable	budget travelers, young people
Hotel Coral Reef	hotel	$125-245	pool	oceanfront	couples
Kaha Lani	condos	$188-268	tennis court, pool	oceanfront	families, couples
Kapa'a Sands	condos	$135-225	pool, barbecue	oceanfront, affordable	families, couples
Kaua'i Beach House Hostel	hostel	$33-75	kitchen area	near the water	budget travelers
Kauai Beach Villas	condos	$145-185	pool, jet spa, tennis	beachfront	families on a budget
Kauai Country Inn	B&B	$179-219	breakfast	Beatles museum	couples

Name	Type	Price	Features	Why Stay Here	Best Fit For
Kaua'i Inn	small inn	$129-189	pool	free breakfast	budget travelers
★ Kaua'i Marriott Resort	large resort	$309-459	full resort amenities, childcare	full-service resort	families, couples
Kaua'i Palms Hotel	budget hotel	$79	free muffins and coffee	affordable	budget travelers
★ Kaua'i Sands Hotel	budget hotel	$80-152	pool	oceanfront, affordable	budget travelers
★ Lae Nani Resort Kauai	condos	$189-359	pool, tennis court	oceanfront	families, couples
Lani Keha	rooms	$55-250	communal kitchen	affordable	budget travelers
★ Motel Lani	hotel	$64	showers	affordable	budget travelers
No Ka Oi Studio	studio	$125	beach gear, barbecue	affordable	budget travelers, couples
Opaeka'a Falls Hale	vacation rental	$130	pool	affordable	couples
Pono Kai Resort	condo	$110-155	pool, tennis, jet spa	walking distance to beach, shops, restaurants	families, budget travelers
Rosewood Kaua'i Bunk House	rooms	$75-85	kitchenettes	affordable	budget travelers
Sleeping Giant Cottage	private home	$109	beach gear, grill	privacy	couples
Traditional Rooms	apartment	$145	breakfast	affordable	couples
Wailua Bayview	condos	$155	pool, ocean views	affordable	couples

cleaning fee. It's a gorgeous room with an elegant island style.

Four clean cottages make up the **Hale Lani B&B** (283 Aina Lani Pl., 808/823-6434, www.halelani.com, $135-195). Kanoa's Cottage has a private hot tub and costs $175 a night. Melia's Suite is a two-bedroom with kitchenette and private hot tub for $160 a night or $195 for four adults. Nani's Retreat is a studio with kitchenette for $145 a night. Lani's Studio is $135 a night. All have private entrances, personalized gift baskets, and home-cooked meals left outside your door in a cooler if you choose. Three-night minimums are required for all. When available they offer a half-day rate of $45 if you have a late return flight home.

A great deal is **Kapa'a Sands** (380 Papaloa Rd., 808/822-4901 or 800/222-4901, www.kapaasands.com, $135-225), along the ocean with under 30 units. It's just off the beach with a nice lawn between the units and the ocean, and you'll find a pool, barbecue area, and free Internet access. Oceanfront and ocean-view studios and two-bedroom units are available with lanai and maid service. Studios can be rented for $135-167, and two-bedrooms that can house up to four people are $175-225. A three-night minimum stay is required April 16-December 14, and a seven-night minimum stay is required December 15-April 15. There is also a $50 service fee per studio and $75 service fee per two-bedroom.

A steal of a deal is at **Wailua Bayview** (320 Papaloa Rd., 800/367-5242, www.wailuabay.com, $155), where fewer than 50 units are located just off the beach. All units are oceanfront and face the ocean. Condominium amenities include pool, free Internet access, and a barbecue area. One-bedroom units are $155. A four-night minimum stay is required.

At the **Courtyard Kaua'i at Coconut Beach** (650 Aleka Loop, 808/822-3455, www.courtyardkauai.com, $179-239) in Kapa'a, you'll find very nice accommodations. The rooms have a modern, island-style feel with lovely furniture made from coconut wood and really comfortable beds. They have a business area with free Internet access and a computer and printer for guests. It was renovated in 2011. The property is along the ocean, and rooms have ocean or mountain views. Mountain-view rooms start at $179 and ocean-view rooms start at $229. A pool, spa, tennis courts, fitness center, and lounge decorate the centrally located hotel.

Backing the wonderful Lydgate Beach Park is the ★ **Aston Aloha Beach Hotel** (3-5920 Kuhio Hwy., 808/823-6000 or 888/823-5111, www.abrkauai.com, $113-195). The location is great for anyone who loves swimming in the calm ocean, especially families. Consisting of 216 rooms, the hotel boasts two pools, a tennis court, a jet spa, an on-site restaurant, fitness room, high-speed Internet, and coin-operated laundry. Rooms have sliding doors but no balcony and offer small refrigerators. Two-room cottages are also available. One wing has bathtubs while the other has showers. Garden views run $113, ocean views $123, junior suites $139, one-bedrooms $195, and cottages $169.

$200-300

Between the Wailua golf course and Lydgate Beach Park, location is just one of the appeals of **Kaha Lani** (4460 Nehe Rd., 808/822-9331, www.castleresorts.com, $188-268). The complex is luxury on the ocean, but with ample space between the units and the water. There is a pool and lighted tennis court, and all units have full kitchens and a lanai and are either oceanfront or ocean view. One-bedroom units rent for $188-210 and two-bedrooms for $239-268. Prices vary slightly between seasons.

A real treat is the condominium ★ **Lae Nani Resort Kauai** (410 Papaloa Rd., 866/733-0599, www.outriggeratlaenanicondo.com, $189-359). An Outrigger property, the nicely decorated units have full kitchens, a lanai, TVs, and one and a half baths. Guests are also treated to a pool, poolside grill, and tennis court. The price for a one-bedroom ocean-view room is $189, one-bedroom oceanfront $235, two-bedroom ocean-view $305, and two-bedroom oceanfront $359. A minimum stay of two nights is required.

KAPA'A
Under $100

Proof of a round-trip ticket or continuing voyage is required to stay at the **Honu'ea International Hostel Kaua'i** (4532 Lehua St., 808/823-6142, http://kauaihostel.com, $25-70), which offers bunk beds ($25/night), private rooms with shared bathroom ($50/night), and deluxe rooms and a suite ($60/night). For $65 you'll get hallway bedrooms or the master bedroom with a private bathroom in the main house. Office hours are 11am-9pm daily; check-in begins at 3pm and checkout by 11am. The kitchen and common areas are open 7am-9pm, and it's lights out at 11pm. Keys and linens are issued without a deposit. Bring your own bath supplies and towels; use of the communal kitchen (including utensils) is included. There is an in-office safe, and the hostel is well kept and clean, with free parking, kayaks, Wi-Fi, cable TV, and coin-operated washer and dryer.

Most rooms at **Kaua'i Beach House Hostel** (4-1552 Kuhio Hwy., 808/652-8162, www.kauaibeachhouse.net, $33-75), a converted beach house, look across a lawn and onto the water. There is a separate mini kitchen area for guest use. One person in a shared dorm bed is $33 per night; when a couple shares a large bed in the shared dorm, the second person pays $20. Private rooms for one and two people rent for $75 a night; each extra person in a private room is an additional $20. Females and couples have priority for beds that have complete privacy and curtains in a dorm. There are shared bathrooms and a gathering place on the second-level lanai.

The **Aloha Hale Orchid** (5087-A Kawaihau Rd., 808/822-4148, www.yamadanursery.com, $55) offers simple and clean accommodations for the low price of $55 a night with a three-night minimum. It's a very simple and affordable studio with a queen-size bed, shower and tub, fan, TV, and mini refrigerator. It's located on a functioning orchid nursery.

$100-200

Hotel Coral Reef (1516 Kuhio Hwy., 808/822-4481 or 800/843-4659, www.hotelcoralreefresort.com, $125-245) was one of the first hotels in Kapa'a. The hotel is rather small with around 20 rooms and a pool. It sits right on the ocean, and the rooms have a modern island style. All rooms have air-conditioning, microwaves, in-room refrigerators, and flat-screen TVs, and guests receive a continental breakfast. Mountain-bike rentals and barbecue facilities are also offered. Standard guest rooms start at $125, oceanfront guest rooms $245, and economy suites $175. Check the website for their "eSpecials."

Meaning "the best" in Hawaiian, the **No Ka Oi Studio** (4691 Pelehu Rd., 808/651-1055, www.vrbo.com/125884, $125) has a two-night minimum and an $85 cleaning fee. It's a studio that can fit up to three people. It is comfortable with a kitchenette, videos and books, barbecue, great ocean views, and beach gear for guest use. It also offers a weekly rate of $825.

Located by Kapa'a Beach Park, **Pono Kai Resort** (4-1250 Kuhio Hwy., 808/822-9831, http://ponokairesort.com, $110-155) is a beachfront condominium with vacation rental units available on 11 acres. The community offers a swimming pool, whirlpool tub, tennis, two saunas, golf putting greens, and the convenience of walking to shops and restaurants in Kapa'a town. There are one- and two-bedroom units with fully equipped kitchens. Free Wi-Fi access is available in the lobby and pool areas. In-room Wi-Fi is dependent on the owner of the unit.

The **Kauai Country Inn** (6440 Olohena Rd., 808/821-0207, www.kauaicountryinn.com, $179-219) has a unique twist—it's the only private Beatles museum in the United States! A simple continental breakfast is supplied every morning, and all units have private entrances and bathrooms and a full kitchen or kitchenette. Wireless Internet is available in each of the four gorgeous suites. The Green Rose, Plumeria Suite, and Yellow Ginger rent

Condos, Vacation Rentals, and Bed-and-Breakfasts

Vacation rentals can be found island-wide. They range from small studios to large luxury beach-front homes. When booking a vacation rental, take into account the minimum-night requirement and the cleaning fee when determining the cost. For vacation rental listings and reservations, visit **www.vrbo.com** for a huge selection of reliable and legal, tax-paying vacation rentals island-wide. The site has thorough listings, detailed information, availability calendars, and plenty of photos. Another option is **www.vacationrental.com,** with sufficient information to help you with your choice. **Summit Pacific Inc.** (www.summitpacificinc.com) also lends booking help and has information for Kaua'i vacation rentals.

R&R Realty and Rentals (800/367-8022, www.r7r.com) has a variety of oceanfront and inland accommodations with the usual amenities for $630-1,500 a week. Many come with a pool, sauna, and kitchen and are near the beach. For one- to five-bedroom rentals, contact **Garden Island Rentals** (800/247-5599, www.kauairentals.com). They have units all over Po'ipu and offer a range of options as well as prices and bookings. **Kauai Vacation Rentals** (800/367-5025, www.kauaivacationrentals.com) offers assistance with booking low- to mid-range condos and mid- to upper-level vacation rentals on the south side.

High on a bluff, **Princeville** is loaded with condominiums. Many are privately owned and have been turned into timeshares. Since there isn't just one central management company for all of them, to get the best rates and up-to-date information, go online and work with one of the recommended booking companies. A reliable source for Princeville condos, **Pacific Vacations** (800/800-3637, www.princeville-vacations.com) has a thorough listing of vacation rentals and condos on Kaua'i. They will help you with availability and reservations. Another source is **Rentals on Kaua'i** (800/222-5541, www.kauai-vacation-rentals.com). **Hanalei Vacations** (www.800hawaii.com) is a great source for vacation rentals and condo listings. They'll book you and give you travel info. Remember that most condos require a minimum number of nights and charge a cleaning fee. Try **www.oceanfrontrealty.com** for lots of options.

For a lengthy listing of condos and to make reservations, visit **www.astonhotels.com/kauai.** Another option is **www.diamondresorts.com,** also reachable at 808/742-1888. Both websites have information on condos and vacation rentals. At **www.greathawaiivacations.com** there is a wealth of options for the south side. This site offers condos ranging $84-1,650 a night. You'll find overview photos, reviews, and room info. **Poipu Connection Realty** (800/742-2260, www.poipuconnection.com) can connect visitors with an array of condos ranging 1-3 bedrooms all over Po'ipu. They also have up-to-date information on all of Po'ipu.

For thorough listings of vacation rentals and condominiums, consult **Kauai Vacation Rentals and Real Estate** (800/367-5025, www.kauaivacationrentals.com). They have over three decades of experience with visitors. **Garden Island Properties** (800/801-0378, www.kauaiproperties.com) is a source for vacation rentals and condos on the east side. They manage vacation rentals and can help you find the right place.

Bed-and-breakfast fans should check out **Hawaii's Best Bed and Breakfasts, Private Inns, and Vacation Rentals** (800/262-9912, www.bestbnb.com). They provide thorough listings of the aforementioned types of accommodations on the island with bookings of three nights or longer. From the north to the west, this site offers an array of beautiful homes to stay in while on Kaua'i.

for $219 a night, and the Orchid Suite rents for $179. Check the website for discounted rates.

LIHU'E
Under $100
The ★ **Motel Lani** (4240 Rice St.,

808/245-2965, $64), consisting of only eight rooms, provides bare bones, very simple rooms with a shower only, and no TV or phone. They only take cash and it's very affordable. This is the type of place to stay if you are planning on being outdoors all the time and a very good option for leaving your belongings while hiking for days along the Kalalau Trail, since you don't want to risk anything valuable getting stolen out of your car at the trailhead parking lot. They don't have a website; just call.

The **Kaua'i Palms Hotel** (2931 Kalena St., 808/246-0908, www.kauaipalmshotel.com, $79) offers very simple and affordable rooms with few amenities. There are full kitchens in the higher-priced rooms. This is another good option for travelers looking for a simple place to sleep or keep their belongings, since the hotel itself doesn't offer the lap of luxury. There's free wireless Internet throughout the property and a coin-operated laundry. They offer complimentary muffins and coffee in the lobby in the mornings. Amenities include refrigerators and TVs, and some rooms have air-conditioning, so check when booking. Rooms have a standard rate of $79 for one king-size bed or two queens.

$100-200

Kauai Beach Villas (4330 Kauai Beach Dr., 800/241-1000, www.gardenislandinn.com, $145-185) is an oceanfront condominium resort vacation rental with a pool, jet spa, tennis courts, and a beautiful beach fronting the property. Just a few minutes' drive from the airport, the property has one- and two-bedroom rooms with fully equipped kitchens that accommodate 2-6 guests. They offer daily and weekly rates. Search the available units at the website to find one with the amenities to suit your needs.

You'll feel the aloha at the **Garden Island Inn** (3445 Wilcox Rd., 800/648-0154, www.beachvillaskauai.com, $134-143), which offers 21 simple rooms at a decent price. Flat-screen TVs, kitchenettes, air-conditioning, and complimentary use of a variety of beach gear are what you'll find. Rooms have a modest tropical decor, and discounts are offered for three nights or more. It's located near Kalapaki Beach.

Located on the south end of Lihu'e past Nawiliwili Bay, the **Kaua'i Inn** (2430 Hulemanu Rd., 800/808-2330, www.kauai-inn.com, $129-189) is another rather simple place. Rooms include a small refrigerator, microwave, and air-conditioning. There's a shallow swimming pool, and ground-floor rooms have a lanai. There is a free continental breakfast each morning. Mountain views are seen from the property. Rooms have a king, queen, or two double beds. There is also a soaking tub suite for $189 a night.

Kaua'i Marriott Resort

Over $300

The ★ **Kaua'i Marriott Resort** (3610 Rice St., 808/245-5050, www.marriott.com, $309-459) overlooks beautiful Kalapaki Bay and is fronted by the large beach, with two more smaller ones nearby. The immaculate resort makes a home on hundreds of acres over the bay with nearly 600 rooms on-site and the high-end Kaua'i Lagoons Golf Course, offering world-class golf on 18 holes. The hotel offers a complimentary airport shuttle. You'll find a spa, fitness center, and six restaurants right there, including the option for private cabana dining. The hotel is within walking distance to some shopping and other eateries. All rooms offer high-speed Internet access, mini refrigerators, and safes. There is a huge, centrally located swimming pool where you can easily spend the entire day lounging and sunning. Guests have the option of one king or two double beds in the rooms, many with balconies. They offer childcare on-site. Features include a business center, tennis courts, and wedding services, and the hotel has a smoke-free policy. Garden-view rooms start at $309, partial ocean-view rooms $409, and ocean-view rooms $459.

North Shore

KILAUEA

You won't find large hotels or condominiums in quiet Kilauea. Accommodations here are limited to vacation rentals and small cottages, which maintains the country feel. Staying in Kilauea is convenient and enables guests to be very close to everything the north shore has to offer, but be within a shorter driving distance to the other sides of the island.

Under $100

Enjoy the scent of citrus at **Green Acres Cottages** (5-0421 Kuhio Hwy., 808/651-6173 or 866/484-6347, www.greenacrescottages.com, $75-90), where three freestanding studios (no shared walls) are nestled among 300 citrus trees. Each studio has a queen-size bed with a kitchenette, wireless Internet, cable TV, and barbecue supplies, as well as access to beach gear and a shared hot tub. You'll find complimentary danishes, coffee, and teas inside and can help yourself to picking fruit on-site. They don't charge cleaning fees, and two of the cottages (16 by 20 feet) both sleep two for $75 per night while the third cottage (around 500 square feet) sleeps up to four for $90 a night.

$100-200

Self-proclaimed ecotourism destination **North Country Farms** (808/828-1513, www.northcountryfarms.com, $160), located just east of Kilauea, offers two cottages on a four-acre farm. A stay on the farm enables guests to stroll the land and pick fruit to eat and flowers to enjoy. Both cottages are cute, clean, and decently priced for the north shore. There is a $95 cleaning fee, a preferred three-night minimum, and children under 18 stay free and are welcome.

Cozy up near the fireplace at the **Bamboo at Kalihiwai** (808/828-0812, www.surfsideprop.com, $200), a one-bedroom just east of Kilauea that is located above the owner's home. Private facilities are offered, and it's a short walk to the beaches, with ponds and a waterfall in the lush yard. The home has a full kitchen, TV, and wireless Internet access, and the bathroom has a spa tub. It rents for $200 a night with a three-night minimum or $1,350 a week. The Bamboo Cottage also offers guests the use of beach gear. There is a $150 cleaning fee.

Over $300

The secluded homes **Plumeria Moon Cottage** and **Hideaway Bay** (4180 Waiakalua St., 888/858-6562, www.kauaivacationhideaway.com, $335-795) are perfect for romantic getaways. Located on a three-acre farm, the cottage has a hot tub, and, uniquely, long-distance calls to the mainland and inter-island are free. Hideaway Bay is a two-bedroom vacation home with everything a visitor could want, including a spa tub in the bathroom. Lovely ocean views can be taken in from the home. It's decorated with elegant yet relaxed Asian Pacific decor. Plumeria Moon Cottage has a deck for sunning with great ocean views and a hot tub. The home has full amenities, including a washer and dryer and a barbecue on the deck. The cottage rents for $335 per night, the main house is $495 per night, and the rate is $795 per night for both properties.

The **Plumeria at Anini Beach** (808/828-0812, www.surfsideprop.com, $375) is just 300 yards from Anini Beach, which usually has peaceful, calm waters. The three-bedroom, two-bath home has a master suite, a loft bedroom, and a den with more sleepers. A lanai wrapping around three sides of the home offers a place for enjoying the sunsets and a screened-in area for dining. There is a private outdoor shower. The home rents for $375 per night with a five-night minimum or $2,500 a week, offers use of beach gear and bicycles, and sleeps up to five people. There is a $175 cleaning fee.

PRINCEVILLE

Princeville accommodations include luxury hotel rooms and condominiums. As with most accommodations, prices are lower in the off-season. One might assume that with so many condos in one area, finding a place to stay would be easy. But since there isn't one main booking agency, one condominium complex can have a high number of booking agents, all with different contact info and rates. With each condo privately owned, it's up to the owner to find someone to manage it. With so many condos in Princeville, the Internet is the best resource to explore the wealth of condos. One thing to remember with condos is that you'll most likely have a minimum-night requirement and a cleaning fee.

$100-200

For condominiums with an unbeatable ocean view of the cliffs of Princeville, try ★ **SeaLodge** (3700 Kamehameha Rd., 866/922-5642, $110-175), which offers nearly 100 units along the cliffs, most with great ocean views. A real treat here is the location near SeaLodge Beach, a wonderful hidden cove below the cliffs. It's accessible via a 15-minute hike down a dirt path and along the coast. Features include a pool, places to barbecue, coin-operated laundry and washer and dryer in many units, Internet access, and full kitchens. One- and two-bedroom units are available.

Mauna Kai (3920 Wyllie Rd., search for Mauna Kai on www.vrbo.com, starting at $125) isn't on the cliffs and doesn't have an ocean view but offers a pool and is within walking distance of the Princeville Center and Anini Beach.

Puamana (3880 Wyllie Rd., search for Puamana on www.vrbo.com, starting at $100) has a pool but no views and offers one-, two- and three-bedroom units. There are 26 units and a clubhouse in the collection of condos, and a few are right on the golf course.

With great ocean views, the ★ **Ali'i Kai** (3830 Edward Rd., 877/344-0692, www.aliikairesort.com, starting at $110) offers proximity to Hideaways Beach and Queen's Bath. All units are two-bedroom, two-bath, with full kitchen, washer and dryer, lanai, and living room. On-site facilities include a barbecue area, tennis courts, and a pool. Rates vary between units and booking agencies but run from a real steal of $110 per night up to $200 from VRBO.

At the bottom of Princeville are the **Hanalei Bay Villas** (5451 Ka Haku Rd., 800/222-5541, search on www.vrbo.com, starting at $165). Lovely mountain views can be taken in from these two-story villas offering two- and three-bedroom options in stand-alone homes. Two-bedrooms start at $165 a night and three-bedrooms start at $200. The rental company offers the seventh night for free with weekly rentals. Location is the

Where to Stay on the North Shore

Name	Type	Price	Features	Why Stay Here	Best Fit For
★ Ali'i Kai	condos	starting at $110	pool, tennis	location	couples, families
Bamboo at Kalihiwai	apartment	$200	spa tub, kitchen	privacy	couples
Bed, Breakfast and Beach at Hanalei	B&B	$120-170	breakfast	location	couples
The Cliffs at Princeville	condos	$324-414	pool, tennis	views, location	couples, families
Emmalani Court	condos	starting at $125	pool, barbecue	affordable	couples
Green Acres Cottages	B&B	$75-90	studios	location, affordable	budget travelers
★ Hanalei Bay Resort	condos	starting at $109	pool, tennis courts	location, decent price	families, couples
Hanalei Bay Villas	stand-alone homes	starting at $165	mountain views	location	families, couples
★ Hanalei Colony Resort	condos	$279-479	pool	oceanfront location	honeymooners, couples
Hanalei Inn	motel	$149-159	barbecue, TV, hammock	simple, location	couples
Kaua'i Coco Cabana	private home	$175-190	outdoor shower, beach gear	location	couples

appeal here, with a short drive to the lovely beaches of the north shore and Hanalei town.

At the affordable **Emmalani Court** (5200 Ka Haku Rd., 808/826-7498 or 808/826-9675, www.kauai-vacations-ahh.com, starting at $125) you'll find a pool, hot tub, and barbecue area. The one- and two-bedroom units are individually owned, so decor will vary. Rates change slightly with the season. Discounts are offered for weeklong and monthlong rentals. Check rates on VRBO as well.

★ **Hanalei Bay Resort** (5380 Honoiki Rd., 808/826-9775 or 800/826-7782, www.hanaleibayresort.net, starting at $109)

offers privately owned condo units as vacation rentals on over 20 acres in Princeville. Accommodations range from studios to three-bedroom plus loft, adding up to nearly 300 rooms. There are eight tennis courts on-site with a full-time tennis pro, as well as a swimming pool with a small waterfall. The suites have the added convenience of kitchens. The resort is located sort of behind the St. Regis Princeville Resort, and guests have access to the white-sand Pu'u Poa Beach. Just about any type of beach gear can be rented on-site, including chairs. Rates vary greatly, from $100 without taxes and cleaning fees

Name	Type	Price	Features	Why Stay Here	Best Fit For
Mauna Kai	condos	starting at $125	pool	affordable	families, couples
North Country Farms	cottages	$160	orchard	location, kid-friendly	nature lovers
Plumeria Moon Cottage and Hideaway Bay	cottage and main home	$335-795	hot tub, beach gear	privacy	couples
Plumeria at Anini Beach	private home	$375	near beach	privacy	couples, families
Puamana	condos	starting at $100	pool	affordable	families, couples
The River Estate	private homes	$275-295	hot tub	location	couples, families
★ SeaLodge	condos	$110-175	pool, barbecue	location, price	couples, families
★ St. Regis Princeville Resort	luxury resort	$552-747	pools, beach, restaurants, spa	luxurious stay	lovers of luxury
Westin Princeville Ocean Resort Villas	villas	$369-686	pools	resort amenities	luxury-seeking families and couples
YMCA Camp Naue	cabins, tents	$15	oceanfront	affordable, simple	budget travelers

up to $550, and most have a three-night minimum.

Over $300

The high-end **The Cliffs at Princeville** (3811 Edward Rd., 808/826-6219 or 800/367-8024, www.cliffsatprinceville.com, $324-414) offers one-bedroom units with two bathrooms, fully equipped kitchens, large living rooms, and two lanai. You'll be treated to on-site tennis, swimming pool, hot tub, putting green, volleyball court, recreation room, laundry room, and barbecue pavilion near the ocean. One-bedroom garden-view suites are $324 nightly and sleep four; with the loft they sleep six for $384 per night. Ocean-view suites are $354 and with the loft are $414 nightly.

The **Westin Princeville Ocean Resort Villas** (3838 Wyllie Rd., 808/827-8700, www.westinprinceville.com, $369-686) is an elaborate collection of units. The grounds feature many amenities, including a main pool, a kid's pool, hot tub, a kid's club, fitness center, plunge pool, and more. Entertainment is offered by the pool nightly, barbecue areas are offered for your enjoyment, and they even have daily activities like hula. Rates for the one-bedrooms and studios vary greatly depending on seasons and specials. The lowest-priced studios are 512 square feet with a lanai, one-bedrooms are 799 square feet with a lanai, and the two-bedroom villas are 1,311 square feet with a 132-square-foot lanai.

The ★ **St. Regis Princeville Resort** (5520 Ka Haku Rd., 808/826-9644, www.stregisprinceville.com, $552-747), the north shore's premier resort, is a destination in itself. It rests above Hanalei Bay, which is in full view from the ocean-view rooms. Other rooms look out to a garden or the lush green mountains. Venture off the hotel property for surfing, hiking, and exploring nearby historical Hanalei town, or remain in Princeville to stay cool in the pool while the kids play in the adjacent children's pool, sun on the white-sand beaches in front of the hotel, play a round of golf while the children are looked after by the on-site Keiki Aloha program, or indulge in ocean-side spa treatments. Other features include childcare, three restaurants and bars, a spa lounge, ballrooms, boardrooms, and valet parking.

The mountain- and garden-view rooms offer approximately 540 square feet of modern Hawaiian decor. Each room has a queen- or king-size bed, marble bathroom, oversized tub, double vanity, and unique transparent glass electronically controlled for views or privacy. These rooms are located on floors two through seven and nine. Rooms with the same views and features are also available with a terrace on floors one, four, nine, and ten.

Ocean-view rooms offer beautiful Pacific and garden views. Features are similar to the other rooms but include a sitting room. Located on floors two through seven and nine, these rooms offer an oversized tub and shower combination. The ocean-view rooms with terrace are the beginning of the high-end rooms. Located on the ground floor at pool level, with wonderful views of the ocean and gardens, you'll have either two queen beds or a king bed covered with 300-thread-count linens. The rooms have a sitting area with a loveseat and coffee table. Each of these rooms offers an entertainment console that contains a 42-inch HD flat-screen TV, and business travelers will be happy to find an elaborate workspace with a large desk and high-speed Internet access. Privacy is enhanced with a glass partition between the bathroom and sleeping area that can be electronically controlled, and plush bathrobes and slippers wait here for guests.

The premium ocean-view rooms have many of the same features and decor as the

the Westin Princeville Ocean Resort Villas

World Wide Opportunities on Organic Farms (WWOOF)

Become one with nature by WWOOFing on your Kaua'i vacation. World Wide Opportunities on Organic Farms (WWOOF) is a worldwide program that offers accommodations and food on organic farms in trade for volunteer work. Visit www.wwoofhawaii.org to sign up for the program. It's only $25 a year per person or $40 a year for a couple. There are around 20 farms on Kaua'i that serve as WWOOF host farms, and more throughout the islands. They usually ask for a certain amount of hours of volunteer work in exchange for a place to stay and meals. Accommodations can vary from pitching a tent on the property to a basic cabin. It's a good idea to try and book a couple of months in advance as the spots can fill up quickly. Check out the website for host information.

garden-view rooms, along with spectacular views of Hanalei Bay. In front of the large window looking out on the ocean is a seating area perfect for taking in the breathtaking views and relaxing. These rooms are located on floors four through eleven.

The top-tier suites are nothing short of amazing. The Prince Junior Suite has a foyer, bedroom, entertainment system, sitting and dining area, and bath suite all serviced by a 24-hour butler. The suites climb through four more levels of luxury to the St. Regis Ocean View Suite, the Bali Hai Signature Suite, the Presidential Suite, and finally to the Royal Suite, all with butler service. The Royal Suite is more like a high-end apartment, with a large walk-in shower for two, a royal spa with a whirlpool bathtub, an entertaining room, master bedroom, kitchen, wet bar, and more.

Room prices start from $552 per night for mountain views and go up to $747 per night for premium ocean views. Suites start at $957 per night for the Prince Junior Suite and top off at $4,852 per night for the Royal Suite.

HANALEI TO THE END OF THE ROAD
$100-200

Hanalei Inn (5-5468 Kuhio Hwy., 808/826-9333 or 877/769-5484, www.hanaleiinn. com, $149-159) offers five quaint and simple rooms one block from beautiful Hanalei Bay. The rooms provide queen-size beds, homey local-style decor, air-conditioning, TV, and a covered lanai to take in the mountain views.

Rooms with a kitchenette are priced at $149 and with a fully equipped kitchen go for $159. The great thing about the Hanalei Inn is that it's in Hanalei, just minutes from snorkeling, hiking, and the spectacular north shore beaches at the end of the road. In the yard you'll find hammocks and a barbecue pit. There is a pay phone outside, but no phones in the rooms. This is a good choice for those who intend to remain on the north shore. A small discount is offered for booking four nights or longer. There is no minimum-night requirement, but an additional $20 fee is charged for a single-night stay.

Great location and a tasty breakfast are the highlights at **Bed, Breakfast and Beach in Hanalei** (5095 Pilikoa Rd., 808/826-6111, www.bestvacationinparadise.com/bandb. htm, $120-170), which is near Hanalei Beach but doesn't offer ocean views. A maximum of two guests can stay in each of the three rooms. The three-story house with a large lanai is a good choice if you don't mind meeting others. Breakfast (daily 8:30am-9am) includes local fruit, banana pancakes, and lemon coconut coffee cake. Beach gear is available. The Country Cedar room ($120, two-night minimum) has a queen bed and a private bath steps outside the door. The Pua Lani room ($135, two-night minimum) has a king bed and a private bath. The 700-square-foot Bali Hai suite ($170 a night, three-night minimum), on the 3rd floor, has a king-size bed and a large private bath.

The location is unbeatable at the **Kaua'i**

Coco Cabana (4766 Ananalu Rd., 866/369-8968, www.vrbo.com/153703, $175-190), a one-bedroom, one-and-a-half-bath home on a lush two acres in Wainiha, toward the end of the road. The fully equipped home, located along the Wainiha River (which you can swim in) sleeps up to two people. It's great for those who want to enjoy the solitude of the Hanalei area and beaches near the end of the road. It's also a short drive from Hanalei and the Na Pali Coast. The home is not suitable for children but is great for honeymooners, with a private outdoor shower, hammock, and beach gear. There is a four-night minimum.

$200-300

Two glorious homes make up **The River Estate** (Ala Eke Rd., 800/390-8444, www.riverestate.com, $275-295), situated on lush green land along a stream. The two-bedroom, two-bath Guest House is perfect for honeymooners for $275 a night for two. Additional guests are allowed for $15 a night. The River House is a three-bedroom, two-bath home with a hot tub on a screened-in lanai for $295 a night. Both are gorgeous, perfectly kept, unique, and fun with a great location. Located in Wainiha, the land itself is green, vibrant, and a tropical experience of its own. Everything you could need can be found here.

Over $300

Nearing the end of the road and all of the north shore's wonderful beaches is the ★ **Hanalei Colony Resort** (5-7130 Kuhio Hwy., 808/826-6235 or 800/628-3004, www.hcr.com, $279-479). The hotel stakes claim as one of the best locations to stay. Here you will find 48 condominium units on five oceanfront acres with ocean or mountain views. Each condo features the same size and floor plan with a full kitchen, dining and living room area, two bedrooms with sliding louver doors (one has twin beds), and one and a half or two bathrooms. Each

unit has a lanai and large picture windows and is decorated with a relaxed and classy island theme. You are very close to the ocean no matter what room you're in, but the premium ocean-view units are just a few yards from the sand. To enhance the experience of Kaua'i's raw nature, the units do not have televisions, stereos, or phones, although pay phones are located outside. Cell phones generally work out here but may be a little unreliable. High-speed wireless is available. There is a pool, a long beach out front, and many other beaches in the immediate area. Rates change throughout the year, and every seventh night is free.

Camping

Unless you're motivated to haul camping gear miles across the Kalalau Trail, there are two main campsites on the north shore. **Anini Beach Park** on Anini Road offers ample camping space with bathrooms, barbecue pits, and showers. The campgrounds can get pretty crowded, and daily beachgoers fill up the area fast. Past Hanalei nearing the end of the road is ★ **Ha'ena Beach Park** with showers, bathrooms, and a covered pavilion. Daily beachgoers crowd this beach park also, but it's an ideal place to camp because you'll be close to all the north shore beaches, Hanalei, and the Na Pali Coast for hiking. The campgrounds can get crowded too, but the gorgeous beach makes it worth it. You'll need camping permits for both of these spots.

Not far past the Hanalei Colony Resort, between mile markers 7 and 8, is **YMCA Camp Naue** (808/246-9090, www.ymcaofkauai.org) in Ha'ena. It's a quick stroll to the wonderful snorkeling of Tunnels Beach. You'll be able to spend the night in bunk-bed-filled structures with a toilet area and cooking facility on-site. Reservations are only taken for groups of 20 or more; smaller groups are served on a first-come, first-served basis. Bunking or tent camping costs $15 per night per person.

South Shore

The south shore is Kaua'i's resort area. Luxury resorts line the coast with condominiums and vacation rentals in close proximity. The relaxed small town of Kalaheo has modest and generally affordable accommodations, and Koloa has a few cottages if you'd like to avoid the large resorts in nearby Po'ipu. Po'ipu is the place to stay if you're looking for that walk-to-the-beach-from-your-room experience.

KALAHEO
Under $100

Sea Kaua'i (3913 Ulualii St., 808/332-9744, www.seakauai.com, $75-95) offers affordable studios. The modestly decorated and clean Ti Room ($75/night) is a roomy studio with living area, kitchenette, lanai, and king-size bed. It's a great deal and perfect for those who want to explore what nature has to offer on the south or west side. The Ti Room is right next to the Seaview Suite, and the two can be rented together. The simply decorated Seaview Suite has a large full kitchen, two-person shower, and a king bed with two convertible twin beds. It rents for $95 a night with a three-night minimum and has a clean, spacious interior.

In laid-back Kalaheo, the ★ **Kalaheo Inn** (4444 Papalina Rd., 808/332-6023, www.kalaheoinn.com, $82-156) offers 15 private suites in a lush garden setting. Studios with a kitchenette go for $82, a one-bedroom with a kitchenette for $92, a one-bedroom with a kitchenette and lanai for $103, a two-bedroom with a kitchenette and lanai for $125, and a three-bedroom, two-bath house with a full kitchen for $156. Rooms are simple with a quaint island theme, and the inn rests in very quiet and small Kalaheo town, a short drive from the beaches of Po'ipu and not too far from the west side. Seventh-night-free specials are available for certain months, and other discounts depend on the length of your stay.

$100-200

A mix of island style and elegance, **Kauai Garden Cottages** (5350 Pu'ulima Rd., 808/332-0877, www.kauaigardencottages.com, $145-165) is on two acres with a small stream. The two suites are in an elevated home with separate access. The one-bedroom Torch Ginger Suite measures about 500 square feet and offers lovely views from the lanai. The one-bedroom Orchid Suite is over 400 square feet. Both suites have wireless Internet, full bathrooms, and kitchenettes. Each room opens onto a large, shared open lanai with valley and treetop views. Beach gear is available for guest use. Each suite rents for $165 a night for 3-6 nights, and $145 a night for 7-13 nights. Special rates are available if renting both rooms or for more than two weeks.

There are a variety of accommodations with **Classic Vacation Cottages** (2687 Onu Pl., 808/332-9201, www.classiccottages.com, $70-150), which offers nine different accommodations—a combination of cottages, vacation rentals, and studios. Each place has a kitchen or kitchenette and lanai and sleeps 1-7 people. Rates range $70-150 a night depending on season. All have TV, free use of beach towels, chairs, and mats, snorkel gear, tennis gear, golf clubs, bikes, barbecues, coolers, boogie boards, hot tub, and unlimited free use of the tennis courts at the Kiahuna Swim and Tennis Club in Po'ipu.

KOLOA
Under $100

A very short drive from historic Koloa town, the **Boulay Inn** (4175 Omao Rd., 808/742-1120, www.boulayinn.com, $85) is a private, one-bedroom, 500-square-foot unit. It is at the owner's home but is on top of the garage, so it has a private entrance and no shared walls. Free beach gear use is available. There

Where to Stay on the South Shore

Name	Type	Price	Features	Why Stay Here	Best Fit For
Boulay Inn	apartment	$85	beach gear, private room	affordable	budget travelers
Classic Vacation Cottages	vacation rentals	$70-150	beach gear, hot tub	lots of options	families, couples, groups
Grand Hyatt Kaua'i Resort and Spa	resort and spa	$448-1,136	two pools, golf course, restaurants, spa	location, luxury	families, couples
Hale Kua	B&B	$120-175	kitchenettes, beach gear	private units	families, couples
Hideaway Cove Villas	high-end villas	$185-725	Jacuzzi tubs, kitchens, beach gear	high end, amenities	luxury lovers
★ Kalaheo Inn	inn	$82-156	kitchenettes	affordable, location	families, couples
Kaua'i Banyan Inn	private suites	$155-230	kitchenettes	location	families with children 10 and older
Kaua'i Cove Cottages	cottages	$129-239	kitchens	honeymoon cottages	couples
Kaua'i Garden Cottages	private home suites	$145-165	lanai	privacy	couples
★ Kiahuna Plantation Resort	cottages	$269-415	gardens, restaurant	lovely grounds	couples

is a three-night minimum and the place rents for $85 a night with a $50 cleaning fee. Weekly and monthly rates are also available.

$100-200

Five options are available at **Hale Kua** (800/440-4353 or 808/332-8570, www.hale-kua.com, $120-175), just minutes from Poipu Beach. The Vacation Cottage is a full house and sleeps four. The Coral Tree has three bedrooms and sleeps six. The Gardenia Unit sleeps four and overlooks a citrus farm. The Banana Patch has a wraparound lanai and sleeps four with a separate bedroom. The Taro Patch sleeps four and has a separate bedroom and a wraparound lanai. All have kitchenettes and access to beach gear and barbecue facilities.

Overlooking lush Lawa'i Valley is **Marjorie's Kaua'i Inn** (P.O. Box 866, 808/332-8838 or 800/717-8838, www.marjorieskauaiinn.com, $170-225), where all rooms include breakfast. The Sunset View Room fits two people and has a lovely view, mini kitchen, and queen bed with pullout couch. It rents for $225 a night. The largest room at Marjorie's is the Valley View Room for $190 a night. The Trade Wind Room rents for $170 a

Name	Type	Price	Features	Why Stay Here	Best Fit For
Kuhio Shores	condos	$150-300	oceanfront	location	families, couples
Marjorie's Kaua'i Inn	B&B	$170-225	pool, hot tub	affordable	couples
Nihi Kai Villas	condos	$145-625	heated pool, oceanfront, hot tub, tennis	full amenities	families, couples
Poipu Kapili	condos	$320-650	pool, oceanfront	luxury	families, couples
Poipu Shores	condos	$290-389	pool	location	families, couples, honeymooners
★ Prince Kuhio	condos	$85-155	pool, barbecue	affordable, location	families, budget travelers
Sea Kaua'i	rooms in home	$75-95	kitchenette	location, affordable	groups, nature lovers
Sheraton Kaua'i	resort	$339-746	two pools, spa, shopping	full-service resort	families, couples
Turtle Cove Cottage	private home	$275-285	lanai, full home	close to beach	families, couples
Waikomo Stream Villas	condos	$130-270	pool, hot tub, kiddie pool, tennis	amenities	families, couples
★ Whalers Cove	condos	$366-975	pool, hot tub, oceanfront	location	couples

night and has a mini kitchen. On the grounds of the inn you'll find a pool, hot tub, Bali-style hut bar, surfboard, bikes, and use of a kayak and snorkel gear.

Located on one acre in Lawa'i is the **Kaua'i Banyan Inn** (3528-B Mana Hema Pl., 888/786-3855, www.kauaibanyan.com, $155-230). There are five self-contained private suites on the property. All are clean, with an elegant Hawaiian-style decor. No children under 10 years old are allowed to stay. All have kitchenettes and wireless Internet access. The Ali'i suite is $230 a night with a $55 cleaning fee, the Ulu is $175 per night with a $45

cleaning fee, and the Koa, Pueo, and Nani Loa are $155 per night with a $45 cleaning fee for each.

PO'IPU
$100-200

Bordering Prince Kuhio Park is ★ **Prince Kuhio** (5061 Lawa'i Rd., 800/367-5025 or 808/245-8841, $85-155), which offers studios and one-bedroom units close to beaches with a five-night minimum stay. The grounds are nice, and there's a pool and barbecue area. It's a great location to enjoy sunsets. Units run $85-110 per night for studios and $135-155 per night for one-bedrooms. Rates tend to be higher from December through April.

Decorated like luxury island jungle escapes, the accommodations at **Kaua'i Cove Cottages** (2672 Pu'uholu Rd., 808/742-2562 or 800/624-9945, www.kauaicove.com, $129-239) are ideal honeymoon cottages. The Plumeria cottage has woven bamboo on the walls, full kitchen, canopy bed, and a tasteful tropical decor. The Wild Orchid has an island decor, nice tiled bathroom, and kitchen. The Hibiscus is a studio with a canopy bed, kitchen, and porch with barbecue. Per-night rates vary throughout the year, and there is a $50-85 cleaning fee.

The condominium complex called **Waikomo Stream Villas** (2721 Po'ipu Rd., 808/742-2000 or 800/742-1412, www.parrishkauai.com, $130-270) is a small place of 60 units with a pool and hot tub. It's not on the ocean but a short walk, drive, or bike ride from it and is directly across from a shopping center. One- and two-bedroom ($270) units with one or two bathrooms are available with covered lanai, along with several barbecue areas, a three-foot-deep kiddie pool, and tennis courts. Units range in size 1,000-1,500 square feet and include free parking. A nice accent is toiletries from the local Malie

Organics line. The Parrish Collection manages the majority of units.

$200-300

The **Nihi Kai Villas** (1870 Ho'one Rd., 808/742-2000 or 800/742-1412, www.parrishkauai.com/kauai-condos/nihi-kai-villas, $145-625) are steps away from the ocean, just a bit over 300 yards to Brennecke's Beach and Po'ipu Beach Park. Here you'll be treated to a large heated oceanfront pool and hot tub, along with tennis courts, paddleball court, and barbecue area. Units are individually owned, so interior decoration varies, but The Parrish Collection manages the majority. Units range 1,000-1,800 square feet with oceanfront, ocean-view, or garden-view options, including one-bedroom ($145-238), two-bedroom ($159-380), and three-bedroom ($300-625) units.

On the water is **Kuhio Shores** (5050 Lawa'i Rd., 800/543-9180 or 808/742-7555, www.kuhioshores.net, $150-300). One-bedroom ($150-260) and two-bedroom ($200-300) condos are available, and many beaches and a surf break are nearby. There isn't a pool here, but it is near the beach.

The exquisite units at **Hideaway Cove Villas** (2307 and 2315 Nalo Rd.,

Kiahuna Plantation Resort

866/849-2426, www.hideawaycove.com, $185-725) are extremely nice options. Smaller studio units go for $185 per night and up with a $140 cleaning fee, while one-bedrooms with one bath cost $230 a night and up with a $165 cleaning fee, and two-bedrooms with two baths are $275 and up with a $210 cleaning fee. Larger units are offered with three bedrooms and three baths for $425 a night and up with a $325 cleaning fee, and with five bedrooms and four baths for $725 a night and up with a $495 cleaning fee. Features include kitchens with granite countertops, entertainment centers, whirlpool tub in the bathrooms, high-speed wireless Internet, covered lanai, barbecues, beach chairs and towels, and coolers.

Just 80 feet from the ocean is **Turtle Cove Cottage** (831/479-3885, www.vrbo.com/292422, $275-285), a plantation-style cottage that was built in 1992, with ocean views from the kitchen, living room, and deck. The neighborhood is peaceful and close to Po'ipu's lovely beaches, including Lawa'i Beach for snorkeling, Baby Beach for children, and PK's for surfing. You'll find queen beds here along with a full kitchen, barbecue grill, wireless Internet, linens, and washer and dryer. The home is wheelchair accessible.

There is a $150 cleaning fee, a $500 deposit, and a four-night minimum.

Over $300

The lovely ★ **Kiahuna Plantation Resort** (2253 Po'ipu Rd., 866/733-0587, www.outriggerkiahunaplantationcondo.com, $269-415) is operated by Hawai'i's own Outrigger, although some units are managed by Castle Resorts and Hotels. Before the grounds opened to the public in 1972, they were the estate and gardens of Mr. and Mrs. Hector Moir, a manager of the Koloa Sugar Company. What is now the reception building was once the owner's private home, and the dining area of the Plantation Garden Restaurant is located in the home's living room and other rooms. In the yard is the Moir Garden, where succulents and tropical flowers flourish. On 35 acres, the gardens have over 3,000 types of tropical flowers, trees, and plants. Just over 300 units make up the resort. Because each unit is individually owned, they are all decorated differently. They have queen or full-size beds. Each unit has its own lanai with patio furniture, one bedroom or two, bathroom, living room, and dining area. Concierge service can book anything on the island, and there's daily maid service. Room rates vary between

Sheraton Kaua'i

seasons; garden-view one-bedrooms start at $269 without tax. All the rooms are a very short walk to the beach.

The **Sheraton Kaua'i** (2440 Ho'onani Rd., 808/742-1661 or 800/782-9488, www.sheraton-kauai.com, $339-746) is wonderfully placed on Po'ipu Beach. The 394 rooms boast a casually upscale, island-style decor. Each has a private lanai. The hotel was one of the last to reopen after the devastating effects of Hurricane 'Iniki in 1992. The resort is elegant but not over the top, and is also home to retail shops, a fitness center, and two freshwater pools. The Beach Pool, near Po'ipu Beach, has a hot tub, while the Garden Pool is slightly inland and surrounded by koi ponds and a waterfall. Both pools have a children's pool. Two restaurants, childcare, a spa, and beach rentals and gear are available on-site. High- and low-season prices vary greatly.

At **Poipu Kapili** (2221 Kapili Rd., 888/699-0354, www.poipukapili.com, $320-650) you'll find one- and two-bedroom condos and suites. It's high class, well maintained, and luxurious. The oceanfront property has a large pool. Prices change with the season, but one-bedrooms start at $320 a night, two-bedrooms start at $405 a night, and penthouse suites cost $500-650 a night. All rates depend on views and season. Well-equipped kitchens are offered in each, along with free wireless Internet, cable, and queen or king beds. The beach is a short walk away.

Poipu Shores (1775 Pe'e Rd., 808/742-7700 or 800/367-5004, www.castleresorts.com/Home/accommodations/poipu-shores, $290-389) offers one- and two-bedroom condo units with a swimming pool and is very close to the ocean. Units are individually owned, so upkeep varies, but they're generally

well kept. There's a penthouse available for around $500 a night.

Recently renovated Po'ipu's **Grand Hyatt Kaua'i Resort and Spa** (1571 Po'ipu Rd., 808/742-1234 or 800/633-7313, www.grandhyattkauai.com, $448-1,136) boasts a luxurious air. The four-level hotel is home to 602 rooms but isn't any taller than the swaying palm trees. The hotel has shops, four restaurants, and bars that offer excellent food and nightly entertainment. Fresh- and saltwater pools are found on the ocean-side grounds, complete with slides, waterfalls, and whirlpools. Rooms are entered through heavy hardwood doors and boast minibars, entertainment centers, robes, and lanai sitting area with Hawaiian quilts. You can even kayak the hotel's lagoons. You will find iPod docks and stereos in the room. On-site childcare, golf, and a luxury spa are available. There are many types of rooms available, from garden views to the presidential suite; one unique choice is the hypoallergenic room. All rooms come with the option of two beds or one king. Prices vary greatly between seasons. Pool-view rooms start at $448. Suites start at $1,136 per night.

At ★ **Whalers Cove** (2640 Puuholo Rd., 800/225-2683, www.whalerscoveresort.com, $366-975) you'll find condos right on the ocean. On-site treats include a heated pool, hot tub, and barbecue area. The individually owned units have free wireless Internet and whirlpool tubs, and are all well kept. Spring and fall have lower rates, with one-bedroom ocean-view rooms starting at $366; in summer it's $399 and in winter $418. Two-bedroom ocean-view units start at $503 and top out at $579 in winter. The resort also offers a three-bedroom penthouse starting at $750 per night.

West Side

Hotel and vacation rental accommodations on the west side are limited, but the region does offer some of the best places to camp, from secluded beaches to mountain forests.

HANAPEPE
Under $100

For those who appreciate quiet locales, **Hanapepe Riverside** (4466 Puolo Rd., 808/261-1693, www.affordable-paradise.com, $85), located on the Hanapepe River, is a newly built upstairs one-bedroom hideaway that boasts river views. It includes a full kitchen, a bedroom with king-size bed, a living room with a sofa bed that sleeps two, and a washer and dryer. Salt Pond Beach Park is only about a half mile down the road. Rates start at $85 daily with a three-night minimum.

$100-200

A "green" option is **Coco's Kaua'i Bed and Breakfast** (P.O. Box 169, Makaweli, HI 96769, 808/338-0722, www.cocoskauai.com, $120-140). Owned by the Robinson family, the owners of Ni'ihau, the two-room bed-and-breakfast offers single or double occupancy on the 12-acre estate. A private 600-square-foot guest room has a king-size bed, kitchenette, a living room area, and a connecting private full bath. Another bedroom across the hall is perfect for two people, and futons can be put on the floor for children. Wireless Internet, laundry, barbecue facilities, and use of beach gear are included. Coco's is off the electrical grid and uses hydroelectric power, compact fluorescent lightbulbs, and plant-based cleaners. Rates are $120 a night without breakfast or $140 a night with breakfast.

WAIMEA
Under $100

The Boathouse (4518-A Nene St., 808/332-9744, www.seakauai.com, $85) is a private studio with an extra-large wraparound lanai to enjoy wonderful west-side sunsets. The studio has a kitchenette, full bathroom, and an extra-large outdoor shower as well. There is a king-size bed and light fishing tackle for guests. It rents for $85 a night with a three-night minimum.

Waimea Plantation Cottages & Spa

Where to Stay on the West Side

Name	Type	Price	Features	Why Stay Here	Best Fit For
The Boathouse	studio	$85	kitchenette, fishing tackle	affordable	budget travelers
Coco's Kaua'i Bed and Breakfast	B&B	$120-140	breakfast, off grid	unique	green travelers
Hale Puka 'Ana	suites in home	$95-235	private rooms, communal living area	location	couples
Hanapepe Riverside	apartment	$85	full kitchen, washer and dryer	affordable, location	budget travelers
Inn Waimea	B&B	$120-150	lanai, near beach	friendly service	couples
★ The Lodge at Koke'e	cabins	$93	wood-burning stoves, cooking utensils	affordable, in nature	outdoors types or budget travelers
Monolithic Dome	private home	$95	lanai, kitchenette	private and relaxing	solitude-seekers
PMRF Beach Cottages	cottages	$80-95	barbecue, restaurant	oceanfront	budget travelers, military
★ Waimea Plantation Cottages & Spa	hotel	starting at $149	pool, oceanfront	historic, unique	families, couples
West Inn Kaua'i	small hotel	$199-349	kitchens in some rooms	location	families, couples
YMCA Camp Sloggett	tents, cabins	$15-225	fireplace, kitchen	time in nature	outdoors types

A uniquely designed place to stay is the **Monolithic Dome** (808/651-7009, www.vrbo.com/204885, $95), a one-bedroom, one-bath home that sleeps up to two people. It has a kitchenette and is very quiet and private. A river lines the back of the property, and it has TV, a washer shared with the main house, queen bed, lanai, and wireless Internet. It is a good location for relaxing in solitude and spending time on the west-side beaches. The home rents for $95 a night with a three-night minimum and $75 cleaning fee.

$100-200

Sprawling across 30 acres of oceanfront land adorned with coconut trees, ★ **Waimea Plantation Cottages & Spa** (9400 Kaumuali'i Hwy., 808/338-1625, www.

West Side Camping

One of the best ways to get in touch with the island's natural rhythms and beauty is by camping, and the west side is the perfect place. Camping is possible island-wide, but the west side's drier weather and clear skies make it the ideal location to be hotel free. And, unlike on the rest of the island, on the west side you can camp up in the mountains or down by the sea.

In **Koke'e State Park,** tent camping is allowed with a permit that costs $5 per campsite and can be obtained at the state parks office in Lihu'e (https://camping.ehawaii.gov/camping/welcome.html). Picnic tables and toilets are available in the area, and two forest reserve campgrounds are located along Camp 10-Mohihi Road. There are four very basic campgrounds in Waimea and Koai'e Canyons that can be utilized as long as you have a permit from the State Division of Forestry and Wildlife, which are free. The main camping area is in the open meadow past the museum. Campers can spend up to three days at Sugi Grove off the road in Koke'e, and the Pihea Trail leads to the Kawaikoi campsite.

In **Waimea Canyon State Park,** the Kukui Trail leads to the Wiliwili campsite. About a half mile up the Waimea River from here is the Kaluahaulu Camp at the beginning of the Koai'e Canyon Trail. Three miles past this are the Hipalau and Lonomea campsites. These require substantial hikes to reach, so hauling in food, water, and other gear is a must.

Along the coast on the west side, camping is allowed by permit at the county parks of **Salt Pond Beach Park** in Hanapepe and **Lucy Wright Beach Park** in Waimea. Lucy Wright Beach Park isn't the most ideal camping area. It's directly off the highway, and there are much prettier and more secluded places to camp. At these parks, restrooms, cold-water showers, grills, pavilions, and drinking water are provided.

By far the nicest beach camping is at **Polihale State Park.** Waking up early at Polihale is to wake up to a silence and feeling of peace in the world that will stay with you forever. An early stroll down the beach is a great way to start the day, especially before the sun comes over the cliff. When it does, it instantly brings an intense heat. Polihale has cold showers, bathrooms (you'll want to bring your own stash of toilet paper), pavilions, picnic tables, and trash cans. Camping in a vehicle is allowed here, and campsites are on top of the dunes at the back of the beach. Shade is one of the most important things for camping at Polihale. Unless you plan to leave in the morning, some form of shade, either an EZ Up or another pop-up tent, is a necessity. The sun out here is scorching by midmorning and lasts till midafternoon.

The state requires that tents be used at these campsites instead of camping under the stars, although many locals sleep in the back of trucks. Permits ($3 per adult per night for non-residents, free for Hawai'i residents and children under 17), which are obtained at the **Division of Parks and Recreation** (4444 Rice St., Pi'ikoi Bldg., Ste. 350, Lihu'e, 808/241-4463, 8:15am-4pm Mon.-Fri.), are good for up to seven days. Those under age 17 must camp with at least one adult over age 18. More information can be found at www.kauai.gov, under the Camping Information link on the Visiting page.

Camping permits for Polihale or Koke'e are obtained at the **Department of Land and Natural Resources** (Division of State Parks, 3060 Eiwa St., Rm. 306, Lihu'e, 808/274-3444, www.hawaii.gov/dlnr/dsp, 8am-3:30pm Mon.-Fri.). Permit costs vary, so please call for more information.

waimeaplantation.com, starting at $149) is a combination of contrasting elements and styles. A collection of original sugar plantation cottages from the 1900s, the homes exude a unique blend of history and elegance, island style, and luxurious comforts. The homes still have their original layout, style, and wood but have been refurbished. Set along a black-sand beach and swimming pool where hammocks stretch from one original plantation coconut tree to another, cottages range in size from one to five bedrooms, providing guests with the space and privacy of their own home and fully equipped kitchen, with the comforts and ease of being guests. Live in the lap of luxury lounging at the pool, napping in an ocean-side hammock, indulging at the spa, and exploring the hotel's museum. You can go low-key and local style with a backyard barbecue in the yard with an old mango tree, watch the sunset over Ni'ihau from your porch while sipping a locally brewed beer from the on-site Waimea Brewery, or make dinner in a classic plantation kitchen in your own home. One-bedroom cottages start at $149 and range in size and price up to a five-bedroom ocean-front home for $892.

Nestled in the small town of Waimea, **Inn Waimea** (4469 Halepule Rd., 808/338-1814, www.westkauailodging.com, $120-150) offers four quaint suites near the ocean. This former home was renovated into an inn in 2001. A lanai allows guests to take in the breeze, and it's a short walk to the ocean, although the beach here isn't ideal for swimming. The Banana Suite ($150/night) holds one king bed and a whirlpool tub. The ocean-view Bamboo Suite ($135/night) has one queen bed. In the Hibiscus Suite ($120/night) you'll find one queen bed and a mountain view. The Taro Room ($135/night) has a king bed and renovated bathroom. All rates require two-night minimum stays. All rooms have living rooms, Internet access, coffeemakers, and small refrigerators. The Hibiscus Suite and Taro Room have TVs.

Located in the very relaxed west-side neighborhood of Kekaha is **Hale Puka 'Ana** (8240 Elepaio Rd., 808/652-6852, www.kekahakauaisunset.com, $95-235), a large home with three suites for rent. While the rooms are private, the communal areas include a living and dining area and ocean-view lanai. The Ali'i Suite has a king bed, private bathroom, and private entrance. A highlight here is the large double-head shower. The Hoku Suite has a king bed, private bath, and private entrance. It's an ocean-view suite, and sliding glass doors open to the ocean and a large private lanai. The Ku'uipo Suite has a queen bed, private bath, and private entrance. Rates vary for each unit depending on the season.

$200-300

The **West Inn Kaua'i** (9690 Kaumuali'i Hwy., 808/338-1107, www.thewestinn.com, $199-349) is directly across from the historic Waimea Theater. It has a two-night minimum (it will take guests for one-night reservations but only on short notice the day before). Rates vary by the season, and a room with a king bed or two double beds ranges $199-249, a one-bedroom suite with one king bed and a kitchen ranges $219-249 with a seven-night minimum, and the two-bedroom suite with two king beds and a kitchen rents for $239-349 with a seven-night minimum.

KOKE'E
Under $100

In the cool mountain air is ★ **The Lodge at Koke'e** (3600 Koke'e Rd., 808/335-6061, www.thelodgeatkokee.net, $93), offering cabins in Koke'e State Park. The wooden cabins are nice and clean with wood-burning stoves and mattresses and often remind visitors of mainland mountain cabins. Hot showers, cooking utensils, bedding, and wood for the stoves are provided. There is a five-night maximum stay and two-night minimum stay if one night is a Friday or Saturday, which can be perfect for hiking and enjoying overlooks in the park. The cabins cost $93 a night and provide all you need for a simple, frills-free weekend in the forest. Call between 9am and 3:30pm to make a reservation.

Camping

At **YMCA Camp Sloggett** (Kumuwela Rd., 808/245-5959, www.campingkauai.com, $15-225) you'll find different options for spending the night in nature in Kaua'i's mountains. Built in 1925 by the Sloggett family for a personal mountain retreat, the camp offers a beautiful and relaxing escape from the busyness of everyday life. It's a great place to stay for a break from the beach and heat, and for those who plan to explore many of the Koke'e's trails and hikes. For $15 per person ($5 children 6-12, ages 5 and under free), you can pitch your own tent on the campgrounds and have access to a kitchenette and bath facilities. It's the same price per person for a night in the simple Weinberg bunkhouse. Here you'll spend the night on bunk-style beds and have access to a kitchenette and bath facilities. No-frills mattresses are provided, but it's the guest's responsibility to bring a sleeping bag and towels.

Also at the camp, up to four people can stay in the Mokihana studio with two double beds for $160 per night Monday-Thursday and $180-200 per night Friday-Sunday. You'll also have access to the kitchenette and bath facilities in the Weinberg bunkhouse.

The Cottage, a cabin with a king bed, a queen sofa sleeper, a complete kitchen, wood-burning fireplace, and a bathroom with shower, is available for four guests for $125-150. This accommodation provides linens and towels. The Sloggett Lodge houses up to 15 people, who stay in two bedrooms, each with a double bed and a bunk bed, and a main living room with sleeping couches and mattresses. There is also an 800-square-foot covered patio for dining and recreation, a complete kitchen, wood-burning fireplace, and a bathroom with shower. You'll need to bring your own blankets and towels, but mattresses are provided.

Prices range from $200 a night Monday-Thursday to $225 Friday-Sunday. Really large groups can rent the entire grounds for $720 a night Monday-Thursday and $880 Friday-Sunday. If you're planning on anything other than a tent, try to book a few weeks in advance because the cabins fill up often. There is a two-night minimum requirement for the Lodge, Cottage, and Mokihana. Check the website for various organization-related discounts.

THE WILD WEST
Under $100

For those who belong to the armed forces, **PMRF Beach Cottages** (1293 Tartar Dr., 808/335-4752, $80-95) is a great option. Nineteen cottages are located right on the beach at the PMRF military base. For those who have access to the base, this is a great and affordable place to stay. Barbecues are provided, along with free wireless Internet and computers at the restaurant. A tennis court is on the grounds, along with a driving range, fitness center, pool, racquetball, handball, and a restaurant. Each cottage stands alone, with air-conditioning in the bedrooms, and is about 1,000 square feet for only $80-95.

Background

The Landscape

As the eldest of the main Hawaiian islands, time and erosion have shaped Kaua'i's lush green mountains, creating nutrient-rich, fine red dirt. Crashing, powerful waves produced amazing long beaches covered in fine white sand. The island lies 100 miles northwest of O'ahu and is the northernmost and westernmost of Hawai'i's eight main islands. The Garden Island is the fourth largest of the islands, measuring approximately 33 miles long and 25 miles wide. With 90 miles of coastline, Kaua'i is the most circular of all the islands. In fact, the good news for beach lovers is that nearly half of the coastline is beautiful white-sand beach. You'll find many of Hawai'i's best beaches on Kaua'i, and much more sand than on the Big Island or Maui. The coast is also dotted with sections of vertical sea cliffs, bays, a port, and crashing waves.

Approximately 90 percent of Kaua'i's land is unlivable thanks to the mountainous interior. This means that the population lives along the coast, with a very small number of people residing in Koke'e State Park on long leases. It's believed by some that Ni'ihau, a separate and smaller private island off the coast of Kaua'i's west side, may have once been connected to Kaua'i. Legend says the small island was the afterbirth from Kaua'i being born.

Built by one huge volcano that became extinct about five million years ago, Kaua'i was once farther south, on the hot spot that is now under the Big Island. The hot spot erupts magma and builds islands. As the Pacific plate moves, so do the islands. That's why Kaua'i sits at the top of the island chain, and the Big Island, still growing thanks to active Kilauea Volcano, is at the bottom of the island chain.

Hawaiian legend recounts the geological activity through the myth of Pele. It tells of the fire goddess as a young and beautiful woman who visits Kaua'i during a hula festival and falls in love with Lohiau, a handsome and mighty chief. She wants him as a husband and determines to dig a fire-pit home where they can reside in contented bliss. However, her unrelenting and unforgiving sea-goddess sister pursues her, forcing Pele to abandon Kaua'i and Lohiau. So Pele wandered throughout the islands and sparked volcanic eruptions on O'ahu, Maui, and Kilauea Crater on Hawai'i, where she now resides.

GEOGRAPHY

The interior of Kaua'i is a high and wet mountainous area. The two highest points on Kauai, **Mount Kawaikini** (5,243 feet) and **Mount Wai'ale'ale** (5,148 feet), are thought to be the western rim of the island's collapsed main volcanic crater. Mount Wai'ale'ale's claim to fame is being the wettest spot on Earth, boasting 450 inches of rain per year. The only way to look in the crater is by helicopter, and the views are exceptional.

A hospitable environment to flora and fauna found nowhere else on Earth, the **Alaka'i Swamp** draws water from the abundant rain on Mount Wai'ale'ale. Old 'ohi'a trees and unique tropical flowers decorate the enchanting swamp. Bordering the swamp on the west is **Waimea Canyon,** where weather and geological activity have worn a 3,000-foot-deep, two-mile-wide canyon aptly nicknamed the Grand Canyon of the Pacific. The **Waimea River,** which runs through the floor of the canyon, is just under 20 miles long and is the island's longest river. The Wailua River is the only truly navigable waterway; however, passage by boat is restricted

---

Previous: Na Pali Coast; Po'ipu Beach.

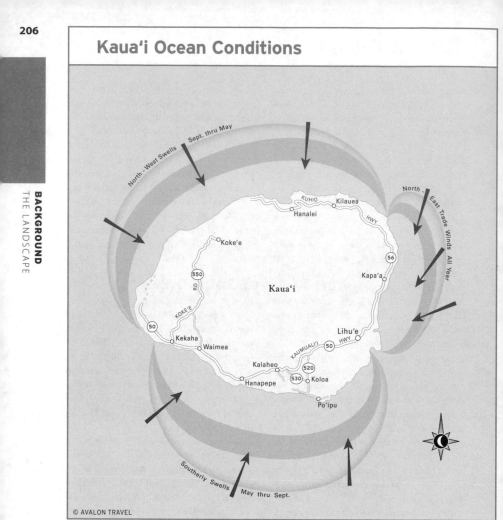

Kaua'i Ocean Conditions

© AVALON TRAVEL

(although it's a popular place to explore in a kayak).

Towering over the ocean near Waimea Canyon is the stunning and pristine **Na Pali Coast,** where amazing cliffs reach up to 4,000 feet high over the Pacific. Deep lush valleys, caves, secluded beaches, and waterfalls sit above some of the best snorkeling in Hawai'i.

Inland, north of Koloa, is the human-made **Waita Reservoir,** which is the largest body of freshwater in Hawai'i, covering 424 acres with a three-mile-long shoreline.

A few unique mountain formations in Kaua'i have been identified by their notable shapes. Some say the **Ha'upu Ridge** (elevation 2,000 feet), which divides the south side and Lihu'e, forms a profile of Queen Victoria. Resting above Wailua is the Sleeping Giant, traditionally known as the **Nounou Range,** which takes the shape of a man resting on his back.

Between O'ahu and Kaua'i is the **Kaua'i Channel.** It reaches a depth of almost 11,000 feet and is 72 miles wide. The channel is

Hurricane Statistics

Various types of storm systems find Hawai'i, isolated in the Pacific. A **tropical depression** is a storm system characterized by a large low-pressure center accompanied by thunderstorms that produce strong winds and heavy rain. A **hurricane** is defined as a storm with violent winds exceeding 64 knots or 74 miles per hour. Heavy rains, huge waves, high water, and storm surges usually come along with hurricanes.

Hawai'i has an elaborate warning system for natural disasters, community alarms for tsunamis, hurricanes, and earthquakes. They are tested the first day of every month very early in the morning. So if you hear a siren, check the date; if it's the first of the month, you're probably safe. Below are the major hurricanes that have occurred in Hawai'i since 1950:

Name	Date	Islands Affected	Damages
Hiki	Aug. 1950	Kaua'i	1 death
Nina	Dec. 1957	Kaua'i	$100,000
Dot	Aug. 1959	Kaua'i	$5.5 million
Fico	July 1978	Big Island	$200,000
'Iwa	Nov. 1982	Kaua'i, O'ahu	1 death, $234 million
Estelle	July 1986	Maui, Big Island	$2 million
'Iniki	Sept. 1992	Kaua'i, O'ahu	8 deaths, $1.9 billion

the deepest and widest in all of Hawai'i. Off the west side of Kaua'i, between Kaua'i and Ni'ihau, is the nearly 4,000-foot-deep **Kaulakahi Channel**, a favorite place for humpback whales to spend time while visiting the islands. The two islands are just 17 miles apart.

CLIMATE
Temperatures and Rainfall

The average temperature is 75-85 degrees Fahrenheit in the spring and summer, and dips only a few degrees down to 75-80 degrees the rest of the year. From Lihu'e heading west is the warmest area, and it gets increasingly dryer in that direction. It's not uncommon for nights to drop 10-15 degrees, and they can even get down to the upper 50s in the wintertime, even along the coast.

Although the west side appears to be very dry, there is significant rainfall on the arid Mana Plain before Polihale Beach in the west. The dry west side is home to the wide and perennial Waimea River. From the south shore to the Po'ipu beach resort area, rainfall runs 5-20 inches per year, and to the east precipitation increases; Lihu'e receives about 30 inches of rain a year. North toward Kapa'a and around the coast past Kilauea toward Hanalei, rainfall becomes more frequent at about 45 inches per year, which is evident in the vibrant green jungle and waterfalls cascading down the back of Hanalei Valley. Farther along the northern shore, precipitation may reach 75 inches per year, raining more during the winter months.

Due to the **trade winds** (breezes from the northeast that blow 15-35 mph), temperatures in Hawai'i are constant and moderate. Blowing an average of 300 days a year, the trade winds are a factor in keeping down the humidity. The **Kona winds** (hot winds coming from the south) blow less often and bring hot, sticky air and vog (volcanic fog).

Hurricanes

Severe damage was done to the island during Hurricanes 'Iwa and 'Iniki. On Thanksgiving of 1982, **Hurricane 'Iwa** brought 80-mph winds and was the fourth storm of this severity to be recorded in Hawai'i. Kaua'i sustained a total of $200 million in damage from 'Iwa. Homes were destroyed and beaches washed away.

A decade later, on September 11, 1992, **Hurricane 'Iniki** struck Kaua'i with unimaginable force and top wind speeds of 175 miles an hour, destroying everything it hit. A third of the homes on the island were demolished, boats were thrown about, and over 4,000 hotel rooms were destroyed. In Hawaiian, *'iniki* can mean either piercing winds or pangs of love. Director Steven Spielberg and the cast of *Jurassic Park* were stuck inside the hotel that is now the Kaua'i Marriott Resort, weathering the storm with other guests and hotel staff. While trying to heal the island and its people, the mayor of Kaua'i and her staff worked in her office, which was missing its roof, while trying to help with the recovery. Eight people were killed, although many people were emotionally scarred from the trauma and their losses.

ENVIRONMENTAL ISSUES
GMOs

A GMO (genetically modified organism), also known as a genetically engineered or transgenic organism, is created by a scientist in a laboratory, where they insert foreign genes into an organism to create new traits, such as insect resistance. GMO crops are a common sight on Kaua'i, with many acres on the west side planted with GMO corn grown for feed and seed. Kaua'i residents are split on how they feel about GMOs. Many people aren't comfortable with the idea of living by these crops where many chemicals are frequently sprayed and carried in the wind. Others say the chemical companies that grow these crops provide jobs for the community.

Hawai'i has more experimental field trials of genetically engineered crops than any other state in the nation. Also on the west side you'll notice the large and looming workplaces of the GMO manufacturers, and many Kaua'i residents are extremely unhappy about the number of them on the island. West-side residents speak of sicknesses and water pollution as by-products of the GMO crops in the area. Another point anti-GMO activists make is that the corn feed is shipped out of state and fed to animals; they feel the acreage involved should be used to grow food for people instead.

Plants and Animals

Originally landmasses of barren lava 2,000 miles from the nearest continent, the Hawaiian Islands gradually eroded, slowly creating soil. Eventually, Polynesian settlers arrived with 27 varieties of plants that would feed them, serve as medicines, and provide other necessities for survival. Around 90 percent of the plants found on the Hawaiian Islands today were introduced after Captain Cook first set foot in the islands. Flowers were few; coconuts weren't found here; and vegetables, fruits, edible land animals, mangroves, and banyans didn't exist in the chain. Today, Hawai'i's indigenous plants and animals have the highest rate of extinction on the planet. At the beginning of the 21st century, native plants growing below 1,500 feet in elevation were almost completely extinct, replaced by introduced species.

Some of Hawai'i's indigenous and endemic plants existed on the island long before the first Hawaiians arrived, while others were brought over on ocean vessels with the first settlers. The majority of flora considered "exotic" to visitors was introduced by Polynesians or white settlers. Polynesians brought foodstuffs such as bananas, coconuts, taro, breadfruit, and pigs. Others brought mangos, papayas, passion fruit, pineapples, and other

Marijuana

Marijuana has been a lucrative industry in the Hawaiian Islands for nearly half a century, and business is still booming. Puna on the Big Island, certain parts of Maui, and areas of Kaua'i have been home to marijuana growing more than other parts of the islands. Known in Hawaiian as *pakalolo*, marijuana has found an environment very hospitable to its needs in the islands. Even though it's still illegal, marijuana is a large and profitable cash crop in the islands. Hawai'i is one of the top five marijuana-producing states in the country.

On Kaua'i, marijuana started off as a hippie crop, with hippies in the communes and living on the north shore in the early days cultivating in the jungle and even in their yards. Locals wanted a part of the profits and soon learned how to grow it. There were times that staking claim to a crop became an outright battle. One person would plant and maintain it, and others would come along and simply help themselves to it. Stories of booby-trapped crops are true, and of growers guarding a near-harvest crop with guns. If you happen to stumble across a crop while hiking (you probably won't these days), just keep on moving.

tropical fruits and vegetables that are now associated with the islands.

TREES

The beautiful koa tree still exists on Kaua'i. The **koa**, a form of acacia, is Hawai'i's most valuable native tree and can grow to over 70 feet high, with a strong, straight trunk that can measure 10 feet in circumference. The pricey wood is used to make furniture and other crafts. Koa is believed to have originated in Africa, and when it came to the Pacific islands, it broadened its leaf stem into sickle-shaped, leaf-like foliage that produces a pale yellow flower. Historically, koa was used mainly for the construction of canoes, paddles, spears, and surfboards, and today it is considered excellent and quite expensive furniture wood. It resembles eucalyptus.

The beautiful native *'ohi'a* can live in wet, lush areas as well as dry lands covered only in lava, and therefore is the most abundant of all the native Hawaiian trees. Red is the most common color of the flowers on the *'ohi'a* tree, but yellow and orange *'ohi'a* blossoms do exist, although they are much rarer. Their shape varies too; many trees are narrow and straight, while others have large, far-reaching branches. These trees are often the first life in new lava flows. Legend says that Lehua and Ohia were lovers, and out of

jealousy Pele turned them into the flower and tree. Whenever a lehua blossom is picked, legend says it will rain because the two lovers are crying because they've been separated.

The multipurpose **kukui** tree can grow to a height of 80 feet. Historically, its nuts, bark, and flowers were ground into salves to treat skin ulcers and cuts as an antibiotic, or to be taken internally for various reasons. The nuts were used as candles, the oil holding a steady flame, and they were also ground and eaten as a condiment called *'inamona*. The nuts are also sanded and polished and strung into lei, something you'll most likely come across while shopping around Kaua'i.

GECKOS

Accepted by Hawai'i residents as a friendly roommate is the gecko. Known as *mo'o* in Hawaiian, geckos have become a symbol for Hawai'i. They generally don't get in your way, and they flock to lights at night to feast on insects. You'll notice two main types of geckos: the traditional, light gray or brownish gecko, which comes out at night, and the Madagascar gecko, which has quickly become dominant in the islands and is noticeable by its bright green color and orange spots on its back.

MAMMALS

Hawai'i has only two indigenous mammals: the Hawaiian monk seal and the Hawaiian hoary bat. **Hawaiian monk seals** (*'ilio holu i ka auau*) travel alone and are infrequently seen, but you may get lucky and see one on a beach. They like to sunbathe on the beach, sleeping, relaxing, and being left alone. Females are somewhat larger than males and can weigh up to 600 pounds and measure up to 8 feet long. There are around 1,500 throughout the island chain, and they enjoy Kaua'i beaches just like human visitors. If you see one, please stay at least 10 feet away and do not disturb the seal.

The **Hawaiian hoary bat** (*'ope'ape'a*) is a relative of the North American bat, which flew to the islands long ago, over time evolving into a new species. Small populations of the bat are found on Maui and Kaua'i, but most are on the Big Island. They have a wingspan up to 13 inches wide, and they are solitary creatures that live in trees. Hoary means frosted, which refers to the white tips of the body hairs. They are found in both wet and dry areas from sea level to about 13,000 feet.

Humpback whales migrate to Hawai'i every year from November to May, where they relax, mate, give birth, and care for their young until returning to food-rich northern waters in the spring. Watching them breach, their large yet graceful bodies emerging from the ocean before splashing down, is one of the greatest sights on Kaua'i. An uncommon but not rare treat is hearing their songs from shore at night. Unlike fish, which were given individual names for each species, whales had only two general names in Hawaiian: *kohola*, meaning whale, and *palaoa*, meaning sperm whale. Dolphins are called *nai'a*.

BIRDS

Birds can be seen all over Kaua'i, which is home to the largest number of indigenous birds in Hawai'i, even though they are endangered. An estimated 70 native species of birds existed before the arrival of humans on the island, and since Captain Cook arrived in 1778, a significant number have become extinct or endangered. The island is on a bird migratory route, and wildlife refuges have been reserved for the well-being of these birds. Along with the wildlife refuge centers, the inland regions surrounding Mount Wai'ale'ale and Alaka'i Swamp provide a natural sanctuary for Hawai'i's birds. There are multiple factors for the decline in bird species in Hawai'i, ranging from ancient Polynesians—who used the feathers for *kahili* fans (which indicated rank among the elite), lei, feather capes, and helmets—to rats and disease.

Hawaiian monk seal

Kaua'I's Wild Chickens

feral rooster and hen

The mystery of Kaua'i's feral roosters and hens is addressed in a couple of urban legends. Some say the chickens multiply and roam free because there aren't any mongoose on Kaua'i. Others say that Hurricane 'Iniki set the chickens free from their cages and they just haven't been contained since.

No matter what the reason, the reality is that Kaua'i is covered in wild chickens, roosters, hens, and chicks, running amok. They're at the beach, around the hotels, in shopping center parking lots, on golf courses, pretty much everywhere. You'll see a colorful variety of roosters and many mother hens finding food for their chicks. They can be noisy, but they mind their own business.

Kaua'i upland forests are still home to many Hawaiian birds. You may be lucky and get to see some of the following: Hawaiian owl *(pueo), 'elepaio, 'anianiau* (found only in Kaua'i's native forests), or *nukupu'u.* Some extremely rare species are found in Alaka'i Swamp, such as the *'o'u,* Hawaiian creeper, and *puaiohi.*

Along with the birds that live inland, beautiful seabirds fly offshore, and many can be seen at Kilauea Point National Wildlife Refuge. Some Kaua'i seabirds include the Laysan albatross, wedge-tailed shearwater, red-footed booby, white-tailed tropic bird, great frigate bird, Hawaiian stilt, Hawaiian coot, Hawaiian duck, and Hawaiian gallinule. Many of these birds live in areas you can visit, while others are rare and very difficult to spot.

History

Kaua'i is the first of the Hawaiian Islands in many ways. Besides being the oldest main island geologically, Kaua'i was possibly the first island to be populated by Polynesian explorers. Even Pele had chosen Kaua'i as her first home until her sister drove her away, and she took her fires with her.

DISCOVERY OF THE ISLANDS

Anthropologists believe that Kaua'i was the first of the Hawaiian Islands to be settled by Polynesian explorers. It's believed that the island was first settled as early as AD 200, although what's considered the first "deliberate migrations" from the southern island are believed to have been as early as AD 500 to 800. As new archaeological discoveries are made, academics keep pushing the date back. Old Hawaiian chants tell of return voyages to Tahiti, believed to be the homeland of the people who became Hawaiians. The travelers were great oceangoing people, using the stars, the sun, and the winds to navigate their way across the Pacific.

Archaeological evidence has led researchers to believe that voyagers were originally from Taiwan, and the people began their voyage into the Pacific on bamboo rafts with outriggers, which resembled early Polynesian outrigger canoes. Crossing the Pacific from Taiwan across the Polynesian Triangle and eventually reaching Hawai'i has been estimated to have taken them 35,000 years.

They lived on the islands for 500 years, creating an advanced civilization. Travel back and forth between Hawai'i and Polynesia was a regular occurrence and has been proven by archaeological evidence. In the 12th century, voyagers from Tahiti made their way to Hawai'i and conquered the islands. A Tahitian priest named Pa'ao introduced the god Ku and brought the *kapu* system of rigid taboos. Travels between Tahiti and Hawai'i continued for around a century but then stopped. Hawai'i returned to being an isolated chain of islands.

Almost 500 years of isolated tropical life went by, undisturbed by outsiders, until the arrival of Captain James Cook. For the Hawaiians, life would never be the same. Cook set eyes on O'ahu from the sea on January 18, 1778, and first set foot on Hawaiian soil in Waimea on Kaua'i.

COOK'S VISITS

Captain Cook left Plymouth, England, in 1776 for what would be his third and last voyage into the Pacific. On January 18, 1778, the crews of Cook's 100-foot flagship, the HMS *Resolution,* and its 90-foot companion, HMS *Discover,* saw O'ahu from sea. Two days later they arrived on Kaua'i, their first time on Hawaiian land. Cook landed to get new supplies for his ships, and he noted in his diary that the Hawaiians looked similar to other people he had seen across the Pacific, such as in New Zealand. He traded brass medals for a mackerel and noted that the Hawaiians were quite enamored with the ships. Once ashore, sailors immediately began mixing with the women, bringing the first venereal diseases to the islands, which spread quickly. The highlights of the first meeting included mutual interest in each other, a few of the sailors' items being stolen, trades of sex and venereal disease, and that was pretty much it.

It wasn't until nearly a year later that Cook returned, and his impact would become much more significant. Cook named Hawai'i the Sandwich Islands after one of his patrons—John Montague, the Earl of Sandwich. Cook first viewed Maui from the sea on November 26, 1778, but could not find a suitable port in nearly two months of searching. So, they moved on. The *Discovery* and *Resolution* anchored in Kealakekua Bay on the Big Island's Kona Coast.

A Creation Tale

Hawaiian legends tell of the days before humans settled on Kauaʻi, when two brothers and their sister traveled to Kauaʻi in the form of rocks. It's said they stopped at islands along the way but, having not found a suitable home, continued on until they reached Kauaʻi. They decided they would like to make a home on the island. The eldest brother said, "Not under the water. I want to feel the rain on my face, the sun on my body, and the breeze at night." So they all traveled onto land looking for a place to rest. As they emerged from the water the sister saw the reef, and it called to her. "Brothers, I want to rest on the reef until my energy comes back. I want to be with the waves and spend time with the fish, birds, and crabs," she said. The brothers tried to stop her, but she resisted and lay to rest on the reef. It's said that this is how Oʻo Aʻa the sister came to Haʻena.

As the two brothers walked over the beach and through the dunes, they came to a hala tree forest. The youngest brother said, "Brother, I am tired and this looks like a comfortable place to rest. The breeze is nice and the earth is strong." The older brother warned him, "Vines will grow over you and leaves will scratch you; come with me to the mountains." But his younger brother lay down and slept. This is how Pohaku Loa came to Haʻena.

The eldest sibling continued on and began the intense climb up the mountain. Many times he grew exhausted and tried new routes to reach the top. After falling down to the bottom many times, the great god Kane saw the eldest, still in the form of a rock, and asked him why he didn't give up and rest with his siblings. "I can see the birds and clouds and feel the winds from the top of the peak. I can see the trees grow and the sea life in the ocean from up there," he explained. The brother said he wouldn't sleep like his siblings, but would stay awake and watch. So the god picked up the rock and, before setting him down on the peak of the mountain, said, "When I see you again you must tell me what you have seen. When you are ready to move on, the island will sink beneath the ocean, the water will be upon you, and you and your brother and sister can travel again." Far below the eldest brother, Oʻo Aʻa slept on the reef, and Pohaku Loa slept in the hala forest. This is how Pohaku o Kane came to Haʻena.

Coincidentally, when Cook landed on the Big Island it was the time of the *makahiki,* a celebration dedicated to the beloved god Lono. For a few days, as Cook circled the island, the Hawaiians circled it too, parading a structure held overhead of a crossbeam with two flowing white sheets of tapa (it resembled a ship's mast). On January 16, 1779, as the Hawaiians reached Kealakekua Bay, Lono's sacred harbor, Cook's ship came into the port. Because of the timing with the *makahiki,* the Hawaiians believed Cook to be a god and welcomed him to shore with respect. They brought him to Lono's sacred temple and offered him the utmost respect.

In the following weeks the Englishmen overstayed their welcome. When they left, the *Resolution* broke down at sea. Cook returned to the Big Island but was no longer welcomed. Hawaiians stole random items from the sailors, and the sailors became violent with the Hawaiians. Cook lost control after Hawaiians stole a cutter that had been moored to a buoy to protect it from the sun. Cook became furious, a change in temper that would cost him his life. He went ashore with backup, intending to take Chief Kalaniʻopuʻu hostage for ransom, but after taking the advice of his wife, the chief remained on shore. Soon, the violence escalated and Cook was eventually killed. His men sailed back to England.

At the time of Cook's visits, Hawaiʻi was in a state of political turmoil. In the 1780s, the islands were divided into three kingdoms: Kalaniʻopuʻu ruled the Big Island and the Hana District of Maui; Kahekili ruled Maui, Kahoʻolawe, Lanaʻi, and eventually Oʻahu; and Kaeo ruled Kauaʻi. Soon after, the great warrior Kamehameha conquered all the islands under one rule. This dynasty would last for a century, until the Hawaiian monarchy would fall forever.

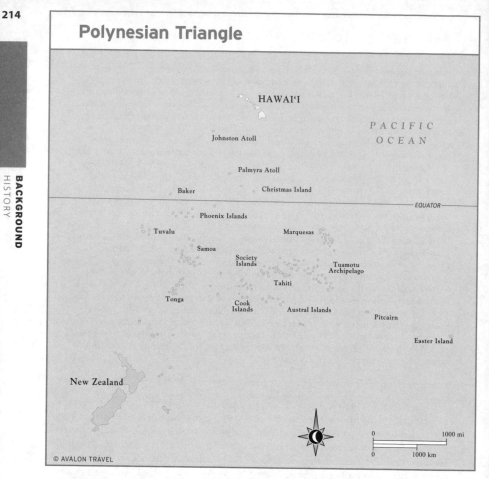

Polynesian Triangle

HAWAI'I

PACIFIC OCEAN

Johnston Atoll

Palmyra Atoll

Baker   Christmas Island

EQUATOR

Phoenix Islands

Tuvalu   Marquesas

Samoa

Society
Islands   Tuamotu
Archipelago

Tahiti

Tonga   Cook
Islands   Austral Islands

Pitcairn

Easter Island

New Zealand

0   1000 mi
0   1000 km

© AVALON TRAVEL

It soon became known that Hawai'i was a convenient stop in the route between the Pacific Northwest, Canada, and China, leading to an influx of westerners. Hawai'i was no longer a secret.

KAMEHAMEHA'S UNIFICATION OF THE ISLANDS

Kamehameha was born on the Big Island, after a prophecy that he would become a "killer of chiefs." Because of this, other chiefs ordered the child to be killed, so his mother had to sneak off to the royal birthing stones near Mo'okini Heiau. After giving birth, she gave the child to a servant, who took him down the coast to raise him in solitude. As he grew and matured, Kamehameha proved himself a fierce and hardy warrior.

In 1790, Kamehameha invaded Maui with the assistance of cannons from the *Fair American*, a ship he had gained control of. Kamehameha killed so many commoners in battle that the bodies dammed the waters. He had conquered Maui. By the time Kamehameha took over the Big Island, it was a popular stop for ships dealing in the sandalwood trade with China. The area of Kawaihae on the Big Island was covered in sandalwood trees (it is now nothing but dry grass and bare old lava). Over the next two decades, foreigners remained in Hawai'i, and whaling became popular in Hawaiian waters with the French, Russians, English, and Americans.

Kamehameha's final victories over all the islands came later. In 1794, a huge battle took place on O'ahu, between Kamehameha (and around 16,000 of his warriors) and Kalanikupule and his army, who had hold over O'ahu. The final showdown took place along the Nu'uanau Pali, giant cliffs behind where Honolulu is today. Kamehameha's men pushed Kalanikupule's warriors over the cliff to their demise. After hiding, the other chief was found and eventually put to death. Kamehameha now ruled O'ahu. In 1796, Kamehameha put down a revolt on Hawai'i, and Kaumuali'i, the king of Kaua'i, recognizing his strength, gave up the island, choosing not to suffer attack. Kamehameha now ruled all of the Hawaiian Islands.

Under Kamehameha, social order was medieval, with the *ali'i* (royalty) owing their military allegiance to the king and the serf-like *maka'ainana* paying tribute and working the lands. *Kahuna* (priests) were respected and turned to for advice.

The great king ruled until his death on May 8, 1819. Hawai'i knew a peaceful rule under Kamehameha. After years on Maui, he returned to his home in Kona on the Big Island, where he passed away. His burial place is unknown. His son, Liholiho, gained the kingdom, but Kamehameha's wife Ka'ahumanu had a strong influence and power. A truly memorable year for Hawai'i, 1819 held the great king's death and the overthrow of the *kapu* system of societal rules. Missionaries from New England arrived, dedicated to converting the natives. Eventually the islands had the first American school, printing press, and newspaper west of the Mississippi. Lahaina on the Big Island grew to be a huge whaling port, accommodating over 500 ships during its peak years.

NO MORE *KAPU*

As Ka'ahumanu used her strength to counsel Kamehameha's son and successor, Liholiho, she knew that the old ways would not carry Hawai'i into the future. In November 1819, she inspired Liholiho to eliminate the *kapu* system. Men eating with women was *kapu*, and women were forbidden to eat certain food, such as bananas and particular fish. Ka'ahumanu and Liholiho ate together in public, breaking these important taboos and marking the demise of the old ways.

MISSIONARIES

On April 4, 1820, the first missionaries landed on the Big Island and were granted a one-year trial missionary period by Liholiho. On O'ahu and the Big Island, they began to convert Hawaiians and were quite successful. Even Kamehameha's first wife and Liholiho's mother, Chieftess Keopuolani, was converted. To defy Pele, she stood in front of erupting volcano Kilauea, ate the *'ohelo* berry that was reserved for Pele, and announced that Jehovah was her god.

Keopuolani died in 1824 and had a Christian burial. Many commoners and *ali'i* followed her to the new faith, and the missionaries continued to be successful with their intention to wipe out all parts of the Hawaiian culture.

SAILORS

Generally the most dirty, uneducated, drunk, and filthy men from their own countries, the whalers took a huge toll on Hawai'i. They flaunted their drunkenness in front of Hawaiians, who tried alcohol themselves. They spread venereal diseases, along with other inflictions like measles, cold, flu, and smallpox. With no immunity, the Hawaiian population dwindled fast. Cook estimated a population of around 300,000 in 1778; by the 1850s, it was at an estimated 60,000. The whalers fathered *hapa haole* (half white) children, and they were simply very bad influences.

MISSIONARIES TAKE OVER

Kamehameha III, also known as Kauikeaouli, the brother of Kamehameha II who was the second king of the Kingdom of Hawai'i from 1819 until 1824, began to rule after his brother's death in 1824. In 1823, the first mission in Hawai'i was established in Lahaina. In 1828, Waine'e Church began construction, the first on Maui. The missionaries were motivated to stop the women from sleeping with the sailors, and also to prevent the sailors from being drunk in public. They put a curfew on sailors and prevented native women from boarding ships, which had become a common thing. Over the years there were several incidents where sailors attacked the reverend's home and shot cannons at it. The new rules didn't stop the rendezvous, but they did instill some societal control.

THE GREAT *MAHELE*

In 1840, Kamehameha III installed a constitutional monarchy, bringing about the Hawaiian Bill of Rights. The biggest change was the privatization and division *(mahele)* of land. Before this, it had all belonged to the ruling chief, who allotted pie-shaped parcels called *ahupua'a* to the people, who could utilize the resources from land to sea. Suddenly, people could own land, a hard concept for Hawaiians to understand. They believed no one could own land, just use and care for it. In 1847, Kamehameha III and his advisors divided up the land into three types: the crown land that belonged to the king, the government land for the chiefs, and the people's land, the largest allotment.

In 1848, *ali'i* entered land claims into the Mahele Book and were given ownership. Two years later commoners were given title in fee simple to land they used and lived on as tenants, and those without land could buy small farms from 50 cents an acre. In that same year, foreigners were able purchase land in fee simple. The *'aina* (land), such a part of the spirit of its people, was forever gone from the hands of its people.

SUGAR

Kaua'i stakes claim as the first island to be successful with sugar production. The Koloa Sugar Plantation successfully refined the sweet stuff in 1835. Some success was seen on Maui, and people saw promise in the business. Labor was the issue, and Hawaiians became indentured servants, with contracts lasting up to 10 years. Chinese laborers were brought in, but rather than slaving for $3 a month, they often abandoned their contracts and went on to start other businesses. Another company brought in Japanese laborers. They worked 10 hours a day, six days a week for $20 a month plus housing and medical care. Eventually, sugar was doing so well the industry seemed promising to foreigners who needed work. Boatloads of people from Japan, Portugal, Germany, and Russia came to the islands. Religions, foods, beliefs, and other cultural aspects mixed.

END OF THE MONARCHY

Kamehameha IV (Alexander Liholiho) ruled from 1855 until 1863. His only child died in 1852. He was succeeded by his older brother, Kamehameha V, who ruled until 1872. When he died, the line of Kamehameha ended. Lunalilo was elected in 1873 and left no heirs when he died in 1874. David Kalakaua ruled until 1891 and was replaced by his sister, Lydia Lili'uokalani, the last Hawaiian monarch. She began her reign in 1891, and the Hawaiian population was down to 40,000 people. When the McKinley Tariff of 1890 brought a decline in sugar profits, she didn't attempt to solve the issue and fell on the bad side of the planters, who said she was hindering their financial growth. With a mission to overthrow her, Lorrin Thurston, a Honolulu publisher, gathered about 30 men and challenged the Hawaiian monarchy. Also, U.S. president Benjamin Harrison wanted Hawai'i to be annexed, so there was motivation from different powerful people. Lili'uokalani had limited support and the coup was successful.

Lili'uokalani surrendered not to the conspirators but to the U.S. ambassador, John

Stevens, because she thought U.S. leaders would be outraged and come to her aid. They weren't entirely in favor of the coup, but when Lili'uokalani was asked about what she would do with the conspirators if she were reinstated, she said they would be hanged as traitors. Considering that the traitors were the most powerful people in Hawai'i, this didn't go over well. On January 17, 1893, the Hawaiian monarchy came to an end. In the new Hawaiian republic, the provisional government was guided by Sanford Dole.

In January 1895, a small counterrevolution by the queen did not succeed, and she was placed under house arrest in 'Iolani Palace. She was forced to abdicate her throne and swear allegiance to the new republic. She died in 1917 loyal to her people. The book *Hawaii's Story* is a wonderful read of the queen's story.

ANNEXATION

The majority of Hawaiians didn't want annexation to the United States to be successful, and a large petition was signed. However, they were prevented from voting in the new republic because they couldn't meet the property and income qualifications, which were imposed to control the majority. A big proponent of annexation was Alfred Mahon, a naval strategist who with support from Theodore Roosevelt said that the U.S. military must have Hawai'i to be a viable force in the Pacific. On July 7, 1898, President William McKinley signed the annexation agreement and that was that.

By now, as it entered the 20th century, Hawai'i was Americanized. Hawaiian language, religion, and culture were nearly gone. People dressed like westerners and practiced the Christian faith. Asians made up 75 percent of plantation workers. By 1900, almost 90 percent of all Hawaiians were literate, and everyone was encouraged to attend school. Interracial marriage was accepted, and Hawai'i was a true melting pot.

PEARL HARBOR ATTACK

On December 7, 1941, the Japanese carrier *Akagi* listened to a broadcast over its PA system of island music from Honolulu radio station KGMB. The Japanese were secretly listening for a different message of code coming from the Japanese mainland. When they heard "east wind rain," an attack on O'ahu was launched. By the end of the day, 2,325 U.S. servicemen and 57 civilians were dead, 188 planes were destroyed, 18 warships were sunk or severely damaged, and the United States was pulled into World War II. It roared on for four years through the Nagasaki and Hiroshima bombings. When it was over, Hawai'i was considered part of the United States.

STATEHOOD

During World War II, Hawai'i was placed under martial law, but no serious attempt to do anything to the Japanese population was made. There were simply way too many Japanese, many of whom gained the respect of Americans with their efforts during the war. Hawai'i's 100th Battalion became the famous 442nd Regimental Combat Team, which saved the Lost Texas Battalion during the Battle of the Bulge and went on to be the most decorated battalion in all of World War II. When they got back, they were respected and not about to be turned away from their country. When the vote happened, approximately 132,900 voted in favor of statehood, with fewer than 8,000 against.

Congress passed the Hawaii State Bill on March 12, 1959, and on August 21, 1959, President Dwight D. Eisenhower announced that Hawai'i was officially the 50th state.

Government and Economy

GOVERNMENT

The government in Hawai'i is limited to two levels, the state and county. You'll hear of state beach parks, county beach parks, and state and county land. There are no town or city governments. Hawai'i has somehow managed to keep turning out the best national voting record per capita, and the state generally supports Democrats. In the first state elections, 173,000 of 180,000 voters actually voted, a surprising 94 percent. When the election to ratify statehood occurred, 95 percent of the voters opted for statehood. The bill carried on every island except for Ni'ihau, which at the time had a population of approximately 250 who were of pure Hawaiian blood. Honolulu is the capital of Hawai'i and has been so since Hawai'i became a state.

Former governor Linda Lingle was the first Republican to be voted into the position, as well as the first woman; she broke a 40-year Democratic hold on power in 2002. Elected in 2014, Democrat David Ige is the current governor, and Hawai'i is represented in the U.S. Congress by two Democratic senators, Brian Schatz and Mazie Hirono.

Kaua'i County

Kaua'i and Ni'ihau are the two inhabited islands that belong to Kaua'i County, in addition to Lehua and Ka'ula, both uninhabited islands. The owners of Ni'ihau originally owned Lehua but turned it over to the county years ago because it served no purpose and taxes were too high. Lihu'e is the county seat and is represented by two state senators elected from the 6th district (a split district including north Kaua'i and portions of the South, Upcountry, and Hana regions for Maui) and the 7th district (which includes all of southern Kaua'i and Ni'ihau). The current mayor of Kaua'i is Bernard P. Carvalho Jr., elected in 2008 and reelected in 2010.

State Government

Each county has its own mayor. While Kaua'i County consists of Kaua'i and Ni'ihau, Maui County consists of Maui, Moloka'i, Lana'i, and Kahoolawe. O'ahu makes up Honolulu County, and the Big Island makes up the County of Hawaii. There is also a governor for the whole state, and the Hawaii State Legislature is composed of the Senate and House with senators and district representatives.

ECONOMY

Today, tourism and the military are the two prime sources of income for Hawai'i. Although the slow economy has taken a toll on the tourism industry in Hawai'i, resulting in sometimes-empty hotel rooms, the industry is still going strong. The reason may be not only the appeal of year-round warm weather and beautiful beaches, but also the increasing appeal of staying within the United States but traveling to a tropical area. Although damaging hurricanes have affected tourism on Kaua'i, it is the fourth most visited island in Hawai'i.

Around one million visitors come to the state annually. On any given day there are an estimated nearly 20,000 visitors on Kaua'i. The earliest tourists came to Kalapaki Beach in Lihu'e and soon after spread to the Coconut Coast. After that, Po'ipu was the next tourist destination to become the island's first major resort area. Princeville followed, bringing people to the north shore, and is now the second major resort area on the island. The west end is still undeveloped, but it attracts many visitors looking to go slightly off the beaten path.

The military has a strong presence on the islands too, and on Kaua'i. The Pacific Missile Range Facility (PMRF) military base has an exclusive hold on miles of beach on Kaua'i's west side, where they test missiles. There are about 125 military personnel and nearly 1,000 civilian contract workers on the island.

Land Ownership

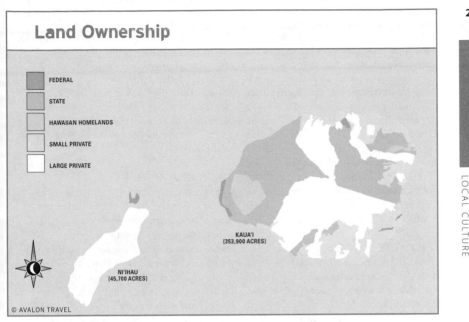

FEDERAL

STATE

HAWAIIAN HOMELANDS

SMALL PRIVATE

LARGE PRIVATE

KAUA'I
(353,900 ACRES)

NI'IHAU
(45,700 ACRES)

© AVALON TRAVEL

A tracking facility associated with PMRF is on the Makaha Ridge overlooking the south end of the Na Pali Coast.

Both tourism and the military bring over $4 billion a year to Hawai'i. Agriculture is the third-largest industry in the state.

Local Culture

POPULATION

Hawai'i is a true ethnic melting pot. More than 50 ethnic groups are represented throughout the islands, and it's the only state where Caucasians are not the majority. It's estimated that around 56 percent of people in Hawai'i were born here, while around 25 percent are from the U.S. mainland and around 18 percent are foreign born. The influx of workers during the plantation days is one of the reasons for the varied ethnic groups. Currently, social strife such as unsuitable living conditions in Micronesia has caused Hawai'i to see an influx of Micronesians.

The population of Kaua'i is currently around 67,000 people, including the very small population on Ni'ihau. The population of Kaua'i County accounts for around 5

percent of the total population of Hawai'i, and it is the least-populated county in the state. The largest town on the island is Kapa'a with 7,600 people; next is Lihu'e with 5,200 people. Around 18,500 people live along Kaua'i's east coast, 12,000 in Lihu'e and the suburban area, 5,400 people in the Koloa/Po'ipu region, 16,000 along the south coast, and 6,400 on the north shore.

PEOPLE
Hawaiians

In 1778, Captain Cook estimated a Hawaiian population of around 300,000 living on the islands. A short 100 years later, only 50,000 Hawaiians remained, having been demoralized and disrespected, their culture torn away from them. Although nearly 250,000 people claim to have some amount of Hawaiian blood, it's estimated that at maximum only 1,000 have pure Hawaiian blood, and the number is dwindling.

Hawaiians are part of a larger ethnic group called Polynesians of the Pacific. They are from certain islands located inside the Polynesian Triangle, including New Zealand, Rapa Nui, Tahiti, Fiji, Tonga, Pitcairn, the Tuamotu Archipelago, Marquesas, the Tokelau Islands, Samoa, Niue, Tuvalu, and Hawaii. The islands and people within the Polynesian Triangle are considered Polynesian. The islands outside of it are home to Micronesians and Melanesians.

THE CASTE SYSTEM

Traditional Hawaiian society was divided into rankings by a strict caste system determined by birth and from which no one could escape. The *ali'i* ranked highest, including chiefs and royalty. Both the mother's and father's ranks were passed on, and it was a set rule that the first mating of an *ali'i* be with a person of equal status.

Kahuna were highly talented people whom others would go to for advice for serious moves like offering a prayer or building a home. They were very powerful and respected. There were also *kahuna* of the commoners. The healers were called *kahuna lapa'au*, and the dark magicians were *kahuna 'ana'ana*; it was said they could pray a person to death. The healers used plants for extraordinary medicinal purposes and could cure over 250 ailments. The magicians could cast love spells or curses.

Commoners were known as *maka'ainana*, meaning the people of the land, and that they were. They were farmers, crafters, and fishermen. They lived on *ahupua'a* land owned by *ali'i*, but were not enslaved. If the situation wasn't good they were able to move on to another area. Commoners who could be called on in time of battle were called *kanaka no lua kaua*, meaning men for the heat of battle. Families, or *'ohana*, were the immediate circle of people. Farmers inland would trade their goods with those down by the sea, and this way everyone could get what they needed.

The lowest caste was the *kauwa*, a landless caste of people who were put on reservation-like land. If anyone went onto the *kauwa* lands they would be killed. If the community needed someone for a human sacrifice, the *kauwa* lands were the go-to spots. Calling someone *kauwa* is still a huge insult today.

THE *KAPU* SYSTEM

The functioning of everyday life was based on the rigid *kapu* system of rules. Men and women were assigned to certain duties, which were absolutely forbidden to the opposite sex. Men were the only ones allowed to work with taro, and this food was so sacred that there were more *kapu* concerning taro than concerning people. Men would work the taro into poi and serve it to the women. They also fished and built canoes, homes, and walls. Women worked the gardens, fished along the shoreline, and made tapa cloth. The whole *'ohana* (family) lived together in a common house called the *hale noa*.

Men and women could not eat together, and women couldn't enter the men's eating house. Pork, coconut, red fish, and bananas were *kapu* for women. Men were not allowed to partake in sex before fishing, going to battle, or going to a religious ceremony. A settlement area was made up of a men's eating hut, a communal sleeping hut, a women's menstruation hut, a prayer hut, and a women's eating hut.

Some *kapu* were only temporary. Fishing areas or certain lands would be temporarily deemed *kapu* so the wildlife or plants could replenish, a traditional sustainable method found throughout the Pacific. Commoners had to lie on the ground when a high-ranking *ali'i* came into their presence, and lesser *ali'i* required that commoners at least sit or kneel when they were around. Commoners were also not allowed to let their shadows fall on an *ali'i*. Breaking a *kapu* meant immediate death.

Local Custom: No Shoes in the House

One of the local customs that visitors often find a bit shocking is the removal of shoes before entering a house. Unless you're directly told otherwise, no shoes in the house is a definite rule. There are a few theories as to where this custom originates. Some say it's simply common sense to not trek added dirt and germs into a home, while others say it's a Japanese custom relating to not following in other people's shoes (or paths or footsteps). Whatever the origins may be, make sure to follow it if you visit a local's home, and it's usually requested by the management of vacation rentals. The rule doesn't extend to hotels or businesses, but if you happen to notice a pile of shoes at the door of a small business, it's probably a sign that the owner prefers the no-shoes rule. If you are a fan of the custom or already practice it at home, locally made "please remove shoes" signs and tiles can be purchased around the island.

TODAY'S HAWAIIANS

Hawaiians make up only approximately 13 percent of Hawai'i's population, with very few being pure-blooded. Ni'ihau has the highest concentration of pure-blooded Hawaiians today, numbering around 125. Moloka'i has the second-largest population of pure-blooded Hawaiians, along with nearly 3,000 Hawaiians living on a 40-acre piece of Hawaiian Home Lands, property that is dedicated to housing Hawaiians. O'ahu has the highest population of Hawaiians total, with around 240,000.

Chinese

The Chinese are a dominant ethnic group in Hawai'i and are the oldest immigrants next to Caucasians from New England. It's estimated there are nearly 60,000 in the islands, with the largest concentration on O'ahu. As a group they have done well and have succeeded in starting businesses lasting generations. The first Chinese were brought to Hawai'i to work on sugar plantations and arrived in 1852. They were contracted to work for $3 a month plus room and board. Working 12 hours a day, six days a week, the Chinese nearly always moved on when their contracts were done and started their own businesses or shops.

Japanese

The first official Japanese to come to Hawai'i were ambassadors sent by the Japanese shogun that stopped in Honolulu on their way to Washington in 1860. A small group came eight years later to work on the plantations, and a large influx came in 1885. After an emigration of Japanese farmers who were of a very low caste and were sent over because of the famine, from 1897 to 1908 there was a steady influx. By 1900 there were over 60,000 Japanese in the islands.

Caucasians

White people are lumped under the blanket term *haole*. It can be used with the strongest intent of insult behind it, or it can simply mean a white person with no offense at all. Tone and the situation really determine how it's used in each situation. Types of Caucasians don't matter here. *Haole* is the name for Germans, Irish, Greeks, whoever. It also doesn't matter if it's someone straight off the plane in Hawai'i for the first time or someone born and raised in the islands; you're still a *haole*. White people are the longest-standing ethnic group in the islands besides Hawaiians. They have been around since the 1820s, with the first missionaries. They became a dominant group, acquiring an extensive amount of land, power, and cultural influence. They owned huge plantations and businesses and eventually gained places in political power. Historically the white population that came to the island tried to wipe out Hawaiian cultural practices. And there is a certain level of racial tension between Hawaiians and *haole* to this day because of the racism of *haole* ancestors.

Portuguese

Between 1878 and 1887, around 12,000 Portuguese came to Hawai'i. Later on, between 1906 and 1913, 6,000 more came. They were put to work on plantations and gained a reputation as good workers. Although they were European, for some reason they weren't seen as *haole*, just somewhere in between. Nearly 27,000 Portuguese made up 11 percent of Hawai'i's population by 1920. They intermarried, and Portuguese remain an ethnic group in Hawai'i today. One item they brought that would influence local culture was the *cavaquinho*, a stringed instrument that would become the ukulele.

Filipinos

Hawai'i saw a large influx of Filipinos because they had been American nationals ever since the Spanish-American war of 1898 and therefore weren't subject to immigration laws that other immigrants were affected by. In 1906, 15 Filipino families came, with many more following in 1924. They were looked down upon by the other ethnic groups in the islands, especially the Japanese. They were the last hired for jobs. Women didn't come with the male immigrants, so by 1930 there were 30,000 men and only 360 Filipino women. The men took part in prostitution, homosexuality, and drunkenness, and hung out at cockfights.

Today there is a large Filipino population in Hawai'i of around 170,000 people, with most living on O'ahu. Today they are seen as equals with the other ethnic groups. Although they're illegal, the cockfights still happen, mostly on O'ahu. They take place secretly in neighborhoods, but have huge turnouts with thousands of Filipinos and other people. They're known to be like fairs, with treats for kids, food, and socializing. Winning roosters can win up to $30,000, sometimes more.

FOOD

Although modern Hawaiian food is extremely meat based, traditionally Hawaiians were nearly vegetarian, reserving meats for celebrations rather than daily meals. With ancient Hawaiians, the ocean was a great source for food. Yet they also cultivated successful crops of taro, sweet potatoes, breadfruit, and sugarcane on land. This took a lot of time, more so than fishing. They raised pigs for celebratory meals, as well as chicken, but didn't eat the eggs. The *'o'o* (a digging stick) was their only farming tool.

The taro root was their staple crop, and it was the first thing they got going when settling the islands. They believed the taro root was where people came from. They would pound it into poi, another meal staple that was eaten with other foods. Taro is nutritious and starchy, and women avoided the starch while pregnant in hopes of avoiding growing a large baby. Kaua'i has its very own brand of poi, Hanalei Poi. It is really good if you like poi. It can be found in nearly all supermarkets.

Another wonderful Hawaiian thing to eat is *haupia*, a wonderful sweet treat. It's a custard-like substance made from coconut that is usually found at *lu'au* or other social gatherings as a dessert. *Laulau* is another *lu'au* food and is a small package of meat, fish, or vegetables wrapped in ti leaves and baked or steamed. A dish made with fresh fish, usually ahi, is *poke*. Available at most delis and other stores, the fish is mixed with soy sauce, onions, seaweed, and other flavors and enjoyed as a snack, appetizer, or side dish.

FESTIVALS AND EVENTS

While in Hawai'i, you'll notice respect paid to all the usual American national holidays, in addition to the state's own festivals, ethnic and cultural fairs and celebrations, and other events that are Kaua'i specific. Kaua'i is home to a number of fun events, many based on the Hawaiian culture, while others pay respect to music, and even a Native American powwow happens on the island. A wonderful source for festivals and events on Kaua'i is **www.kauaifestivals.com.** The site offers a thorough listing of one-time and annual events up to a year in advance.

January

Kauaian Days is dedicated to He Inoa no Kaumuali'i, Kauai's king in 1794-1810. A parade, food, workshops, games, and other cultural festivities take place at various locations. Call 808/338-0111 for more information.

February

Each February the **Waimea Town Celebration** is organized by the West Kauai Business and Professional Association. For two days the community comes together in Waimea to enjoy food, entertainment, games, canoe races, a rodeo, and live music. The event has been held for over three decades. Find out more at www.wkbpa.org.

March

Located at Prince Kuhio Park in Po'ipu, the **Prince Kuhio Celebration of the Arts** provides cultural festivities relative to the time of the prince himself. Education on the Hawaiian culture, a *lu'au*, and live dance and music are all offered at the park, most free of charge. Other entertainment takes place at nearby resorts. Visit www.princekuhio.wetpaint.com for more details.

The **Kaua'i Orchid and Art Festival** takes place in Hanapepe. Various music events and other performances happen here in honor of the flowers and local artwork. Visit www hanapepe.org for more information.

April

Buddha Day, traditionally known as Wesak, happens on the Sunday closest to April 8 and celebrates the birth of the Buddha. Many flower festivals, dances, and other programs take place at temples across the islands, such as the **Kapaa Hongwanji Dharma School** (4-1170 Kuhio Hwy., 808/822-4667, www. kapaahongwanji.org) on the east side.

May

The **Banana Poka Festival** takes place yearly at the **Koke'e Natural History Museum** (3600 Kokee Rd., 808/335-9975, www.kokee.org). In the cooler upland air

this outdoors educational festival offers basket making, crafts, face painting, and other games and races for entertainment.

In Hawai'i, May 1 is known as **Lei Day,** or May Day in other places. Various celebrations take place around the island, including ones at the **Kaua'i Museum** (4428 Rice St., 808/245-6931, www.kauaimuseum.org) and **Kaua'i Community College** (3-1901 Kaumuali'i Hwy., 808/245-8311, www.kauai.hawaii.edu).

June

King Kamehameha Day on June 11 honors Kamehameha the Great with celebrations on each island. Look in the local paper, or keep your eye out for flyers announcing activities. Kaua'i has a parade, a *ho'olaule'a* (celebration), and arts and crafts fairs.

Known as the ultimate Sunday brunch, **Taste of Hawaii** (www.tasteofhawaii.com) is offered by the **Kapaa Rotary Club** (www. clubrunner.ca/kapaa). The event provides food and beverages created by chefs from throughout Hawaii, along with music, vendors, and other entertainment at **Smith's Tropical Paradise** (174 Wailua Rd., 808/821-6895, www.smithskauai.com).

July

The **Fourth of July** is celebrated in Hawai'i, and it's a popular day for beach going and barbecues for locals. Check the local paper or with your hotel concierge for fireworks shows and other festivities. This is the day when beach parks are packed with grills, chairs, and families hanging out.

Celebrating plantation life and times is **Koloa Plantation Days** (www.koloaplantationdays.com). A parade, food, crafts fair, music, dance, and more pay homage to a time that is a strong part of Kaua'i's history.

August

The **Kauai County Farm Bureau Fair** (P.O. Box 3895, Lihu'e, 808/337-9944, www. kauaifarmfair.org) offers agricultural displays, a petting zoo, carnival rides, live music, circus acts, an array of food, and much more. It's fun for the whole family and worth checking out.

Recognizing the day Hawai'i became a state, **Admission Day** is acknowledged on August 17.

September

Named after the flower that is native to Kaua'i, the annual **Mokihana Festival** (www.maliefoundation.org) is a weeklong event featuring a wonderful array of cultural crafts, hula, workshops, and entertainment.

Another weeklong event is the **Aloha Festivals** (www.alohafestivals.com), which celebrates the spirit of *aloha*. Through hula, music, arts, parades, *lu'au,* and other entertainment, everything *aloha* is celebrated.

October

In Koke'e the annual **Emalani Festival** (3600 Kokee Rd., 808/335-9975, www.kokee.org/festivals) is an authentic and powerful Hawaiian cultural experience. Hula masters and dancers from Hawai'i and other countries present the sacred dance at a festival held on the second Saturday of each October. The festival pays respect to Hawai'i's Queen Emma, the wife of Alexander Liholiho, Kamehameha IV, who reigned 1856-1863. She made a trip to Kaua'i's Koke'e State Park in 1871, which is why the festival is held there.

Polynesian- and coconut-themed entertainment, food, crafts, games, and more can be found at the **Coconut Festival.** It's in Kapa'a Beach Park each year, and you can learn cooking tips along with cultural education and just have fun.

November

Keeping up with the mainland United States, **Veterans Day** is celebrated statewide. Check the local paper for parade times, which usually take place through Kapa'a.

The annual **Hawaiian Slack Key Guitar Festival** (www.slackkeyfestival.com) gathers a lineup of some of Hawai'i's best slack-key artists for your enjoyment. Local food, island crafts, and other entertainment are provided.

December

To get the Christmas spirit while on Kaua'i, check out the **Waimea Christmas Parade** in historic Waimea town. Check the local paper for the date so you can listen to carols sung in Hawaiian and enjoy light displays and decorations.

Enjoy the **Lights on Rice Parade** and **Kaua'i Museum Craft Fair** (4428 Rice St., 808/245-6931, www.kauaimuseum.org) for a huge variety of crafts, classes, food booths, hula, and other cultural displays. The fair precedes the evening parade, and it's quite a community gathering.

Avid bird-watchers will enjoy the annual **Audubon Christmas Bird Count** held at **Koke'e Natural History Museum** (3600 Kokee Rd., 808/335-9975, www.kokee.org). Call for more information on specifics and the types of birds seen up here.

If you spend **New Year's Eve** on Kaua'i, check the local paper for fireworks displays and other events. There's usually a celebration taking place, but they can vary.

THE ARTS
Canoes

Considered a highly functional piece of art, Hawaiian canoes were built with few tools besides an adze and could carry 200 people. They lasted for generations and could travel thousands of miles. They were made with a small hut in the middle and were called double hulls with two canoes bound together.

Carvings

Wood was the most popular material with Hawaiian crafters, and they could turn it into canoes, tikis, furniture, and bowls. Koa was the favorite wood because of its strength and beauty, and is still highly prized today. Certain types of rock were carved into poi pounders, fish sinkers, and small idols.

Featherwork

Ancient Hawaiians loved bird feathers, and the chief's headpieces and cloaks were made of them. Their favorite colors were red and

Kaua'i's Best Arts and Crafts

Kaua'i is known for its inspiring scenery and beautiful surroundings, which serve as the muse for many artists. The island's galleries are loaded with locally made arts and crafts, and there are endless locations to visit with a sketchpad or easel and paints.

An art fan's trip to Kaua'i wouldn't be complete without a stop at **Art Night in Hanapepe,** which happens each Friday night. Around 16 galleries open their doors 6pm-9pm for a celebratory evening of everything art. You can browse local art and socialize with locals, meet artists, and sometimes enjoy live music.

Historic Kapa'a town has a good share of galleries, although the art focus isn't nearly as centralized as in Hanapepe. From a glass gallery to numerous shops with paintings, prints, and other items featuring the art of local artists, a stroll through the town offers art browsing or buying. Also in Kapa'a is the **Kaua'i Products Fair** (4-1613 Kuhio Hwy., 808/246-0988, www.thekauaiproductsfair.com, 9am-5pm daily) on the northern end of town. The majority of the products here aren't locally made (many are made in Indonesia or Thailand) even though they may have a Hawaiian style. Yet it's still a fun place to shop around for craft souvenirs.

For classes and instruction in making your own art, there are several choices. At the **Kilohana Plantation** in Lihu'e (3-2087 Kaumuali'i Hwy., 808/245-5608, www.kilohanakauai.com), there is a nice array of shops featuring local arts and crafts, along with a really nice pottery studio; at **Clayworks of Kilohana** (3-2087 Kaumuali'i Hwy., 808/246-2529, www.clayworksatkilohana. com, 10am-6pm Mon.-Sat., 11am-2pm Sun.) you can make your own clay piece and take it home with you or have it shipped. Local artist **Marionette** (www.kauai-artist.net) offers art classes around the island. She provides instruction with a variety of mediums, including watercolors, silk painting, acrylics, and more at various locations on the west and east sides of the island. Hanapepe's **Arius Hopman Gallery** (3840 Hanapepe Rd., 808/335-5616, www.hopmanart.com) offers digital photography classes by the artist himself. Hopman takes beautiful photos of the island's natural beauty, and looking at his work will make you want to take some pictures yourself.

yellow, which only came from certain birds. The *'o'o, 'i'iwi, mamo,* and *'apapane* were birds whose feathers were often used. Feathers were attached to woven nets and made into helmets, idols, and capes and cloaks. They were worn only by men, often during battle. Very special and limited lei were also made from feathers and reserved for high-ranking *ali'i* women.

Lei Making

The lei is a classic Hawaiian symbol. Any type of flower can be made into a lei, along with kukui nuts, shells, ferns, leaves, and the rare mokihana flower. Some of the most common flowers used in lei today are purple orchids and plumeria, which are very fragrant. There are different methods of lei making, which result in flat lei, round lei, and even head (hair wreath) lei. Today, people of varying ethnic groups receive lei in real life for various celebrations. Birthdays, graduations, weddings, and other celebratory moments are all times when a lei is given.

Tapa Cloth

A very beautiful creation, tapa cloth is made from tree bark and stamped with different meaningful designs. It's found throughout Polynesia and was also popular with Hawaiians. Women worked it, and mamaki bark was one of the best to use. The women would pound the bark to a pulp and then beat it into strips. It was dried and then painted and marked. You'll still see it today, but most comes from other places in Polynesia and isn't made with the same traditional methods. Tapa makes a lovely wall-hanging souvenir.

Tattoos

Tattoos were very popular throughout Polynesia, and cultures from different islands had their own motifs and meanings. Hawai'i was no less appreciative of skin art, and tattooed men and women were a common sight. While the meaning and motifs of traditional Hawaiian tattoo have been lost, cultural practitioners pull from other Polynesian societies to help understand traditional Hawaiian tattoo. Today, Polynesian motif tattoos have made a comeback. They are intricate and usually feature geometric shapes like triangles or weaving patterns.

Weaving

The *lau hala* (*lau* meaning leaf, and *hala* the pandanus tree) was used to make wonderfully beautiful and strong mats and baskets. The spine of the leaf was removed and the leaves stored in rolls. When it was time to use them, they were soaked in water and pounded to soften them and then woven into various items, even canoe sails. *Hala* bracelets and hats are a great find today, and you can also find women's purses made of it.

Essentials

Transportation

AIR

The **Lihu'e Airport** (3901 Mokulele Loop, 808/274-3800, http://hawaii.gov/lih), is roughly equidistant from the farthest points north and west, which is roughly 35 miles in either direction. Lihu'e is home to the large shops and supermarkets if you need any last-minute items before heading to your accommodations or first adventure. When choosing your seat on the plane, try to sit on the left side of the plane for views of the island as you fly in during the daytime. If you happen to be flying at the crack of dawn (this is usually the cheapest time to fly inter-island if you booked your ticket last minute), then sitting on the right side of the plane will treat you to a magnificent sunrise view. Check with your hotel before arrival regarding airport shuttles.

CAR

To the west from the airport, Route 50 runs from Lihu'e to the end of the road on the west side. To the north, Route 56 runs to Princeville, where it becomes Route 560, reaching to the very end of the road at the Na Pali Coast. Although the route numbers change a bit, it's basically one main highway that circles the island, with smaller roads jutting off and leading to beaches or sights. If you're under 25 years old, you will most likely be charged an extra $20 a day by major rental car companies. If you cannot afford this, you may want to consider other modes of transportation, which are limited to a moped, the bus, or hitchhiking, which is legal, but not a reliable alternative for getting around. Rental cars are by far the best way to get around the island. Make sure to book your car in advance.

Rental Car

All rental agencies are located at the Lihu'e Airport. Upon arrival, cross the street in front of baggage claim to the rental kiosks, and shuttles will take you to the main offices to pick up your car.

- **Alamo** (808/246-0645 or 800/327-9633, www.alamo.com)
- **Avis** (808/245-3512, 808/241-4384, or 800/381-8000, www.avis.com)
- **Budget** (808/245-1901, 808/245-903, or 800/527-7000, www.budget.com)
- **Dollar** (808/245-3652, 808/246-1150, or 800/800-4000, www.dollar.com)
- **Hertz** (808/246-0027 or 800/654-3131, www.hertz.com)
- **National** (808/245-5636 or 800/227-7368, www.nationalcar.com)
- **Thrifty** (808/245-7369 or 800/847-4389, www.thrifty.com)

BUS

The **Kaua'i Bus** (808/241-6410, www.kauai.gov/transportation, 5:27am-10:40pm Mon.-Fri., 6:21am-5:50pm Sat.-Sun. and holidays) runs island-wide, with stops from Hanalei to the west side. The bus is a green, convenient, and affordable way to get around. The last stop in Hanalei is the old Hanalei courthouse, so the bus doesn't go out to the end of the road, and on the west side it runs to Kekaha, not out to Polihale. Fares are $1 for children and seniors, and $2 for the general public. Monthly passes are also available.

TAXI

Most taxi services run island-wide, since it's quite small. One option is **Pono Taxi**

Lihu'e Airport

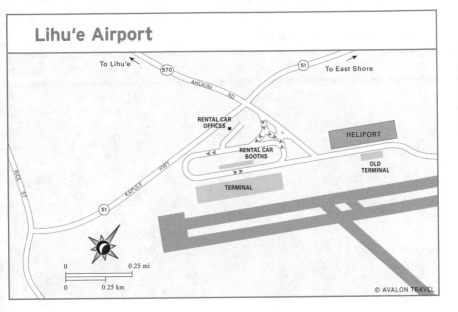

To Lihu'e
570
AHUKINI RD
51
To East Shore

RICE ST
KAPULE HWY
RENTAL CAR OFFICES
RENTAL CAR BOOTHS
HELIPORT
OLD TERMINAL
TERMINAL
51

0   0.25 mi
0   0.25 km

© AVALON TRAVEL

(808/635-3478, www.ponotaxi.com). It offers taxi, airport shuttle, and tour services island-wide and provides spacious and clean minivans.

North Shore Cab Co. (808/639-7829, www.northshorecab.com) provides island-wide rides and sightseeing tours.

For a more upscale ride, **Kaua'i North Shore Limousine** (808/828-6189, www.kauainorthshorelimo.com) offers limousine service for special dates, weddings, and corporate travel.

Island Taxi (808/639-7829) is based out of Lihu'e and provides island-wide rides. Service is prompt and friendly. **Ace Kaua'i Taxi Services** (808/639-4310) will take you wherever you need to go. Hawai'i taxi rates are $3 per mile and $0.40 per minute. Prices are per minivan, not per person.

BICYCLE

Although you *could* bike the whole island, Hanalei, Princeville, and Kapa'a are the best areas for biking. After Hanalei there are numerous one-lane bridges along the narrow, winding road to Ke'e Beach that could push bikers into the traffic. Princeville is the safest and most convenient place for a leisurely ride. To rent a beach cruiser to explore Hanalei, stop at **Pedal-N-Paddle** (Ching Young Village, 808/826-9069, www.pedalnpaddle. com, 9am-6pm daily) for hybrid road bike and cruiser rentals starting at $15 daily or $60 for the week. Biking accessories are also available, along with water-sport supplies.

On the east side, cycle the **Ke Ala Hele Makalae** bike path. The name translates to "the path that goes by the coast," and true to its name, the bike path stretches along part of the east coast while staying almost entirely level. Multiple beaches, swimming places, and picnic spots are located along the path. The path begins at the Lihi Boat Landing to the south and winds north to Kealia Beach. In Kapa'a, at **Coconut Coasters Beach Bike Rentals** (4-1586 Kuhio Hwy., 808/822-7368, www.coconutcoasters.com, 9am-6pm Tues.-Sat., 9am-4pm Sun.-Mon.), you will find a variety of bikes: classic and three-speed cruisers ($22 half day, $25 full day, $95 weekly) for adults and children, tandem bikes ($36 half day, $45 full day, $190 weekly), mountain bikes ($25 half day, $30 full day, $120 weekly), trainers that attach to adult bikes for

Pacific Crossroads

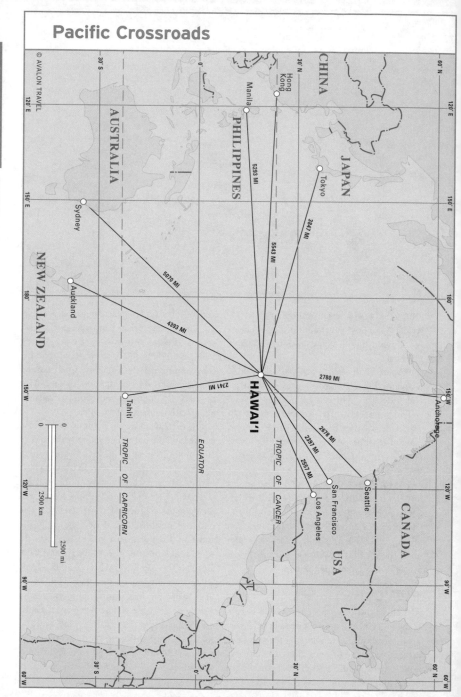

© AVALON TRAVEL

CHINA

Hong Kong
Manila
PHILIPPINES
5293 MI
JAPAN
Tokyo
3847 MI
5543 MI

AUSTRALIA
Sydney
5070 MI
NEW ZEALAND
Auckland
4393 MI

HAWAI'I
2780 MI
2678 MI
2397 MI
2557 MI
2741 MI
Tahiti

Anchorage
Seattle
San Francisco
Los Angeles
USA
CANADA

TROPIC OF CANCER
EQUATOR
TROPIC OF CAPRICORN

0   2500 km
0   2500 mi

Drive with *Aloha*

Driving is a situation where local customs specifically come into play. You'll notice that even on the highways, drivers cruise along at a generally leisurely speed. Even some of the speed limit signs are below the minimum speed on O'ahu. Off the main roads, it's essential to go very, very slow in residential neighborhoods, or on any side streets, especially when there are homes around. Going fast, even if it's not *really* speeding, can result in an angry fist shaken at your car or a call for you to slow down.

Driving customs in Hawai'i extend to the casual wave. It's highly common for two drivers who don't know each other to wave at each other as they slowly pass. This goes for slow side roads, drivers on one-lane bridges, and the like, not for each person on the highway. If you're cruising through a residential neighborhood, it's likely a person in a yard will look up and give you a casual wave, so go ahead and return it. These small efforts can go a long way, especially if you're in an area locals prefer to keep low-key.

6-9-year-olds, and covered trailers for toddlers that connect to the back of the bike. The classic beach cruiser is slightly less expensive. Rates for kids' mountain bikes and cruisers vary. Reservations are required for rentals.

Also, **Kauai Cycle** (934 Kuhio Hwy., Kapa'a, 808/821-2115, www.kauaicycle.com, 9am-6pm Mon.-Fri., 9am-4pm Sat.) offers cruisers, road bikes, and mountain bikes for rent. It also provides maps, trail information, clothing, accessories, and guidebooks. Rentals include a helmet and a lock and start at $20 per day. Multiday rates are also available, as well as car racks. It also has a full certified repair shop.

In Lihu'e, longtime bike doctor **Bicycle John** (3142 Kuhio Hwy., 808/245-7579, 10am-6pm Mon.-Fri., 10am-3pm Sat.) offers a thorough selection of road and mountain bikes to rent and own. Also available is a selection of other biking gear, including bikes, helmets, lights, repair services, and more. Bicycle John himself is known to be a straight-to-the-point kind of guy, no bells (except for bikes) or whistles, but he knows what he's doing.

SCOOTER

Hop onto a moped to zip around the east side and save on gas at **Kauai Car & Scooter Rental** (3148 Oihana St., 808/245-7177, kauaiscooter.com). They are located about a mile from the airport. Call for prices and reservations. **Kauai Mopeds** (3148 Oihana St., 808/652-7407, www.kauai-mopeds.com) rents scooters and mopeds. Mopeds are smaller and designed for a single rider at least 18 years old with a valid driver's license. Daily rates are $65 and decrease the more days you rent the vehicle. Scooters are larger and can seat two people. The driver must be at least 21 years old and have a motorcycle license. The discount scooter starts at $75 per day and the two-seater at $110 per day; prices decrease for every consecutive day. Reserve by phone or online. They will deliver the vehicle to your accommodation.

HITCHHIKING

Hitchhiking is legal on Kaua'i, as long as you stay off the paved part of the road. This is a budget option for getting around in areas like Hanalei and Kapa'a, where streets are busy and it's a short distance between a lot of beaches, sights, and shopping. If you try to thumb it all the way out to Polihale, there's a good chance of walking a very long way in the scorching sun. Remember; hitchhiking can be dangerous, so women and children should never hitchhike alone.

Visas and Officialdom

Entering Hawai'i is like entering anywhere else in the United States. Foreign nationals must have a current passport and most must have a proper visa, an ongoing or return air ticket, and sufficient funds for the proposed stay in Hawaii. A visa application can be made at any U.S. embassy or consular office outside the United States and must include a properly filled out application form, two photos, and a nonrefundable fee. Canadians do not need a visa but must have a passport. Visitors from many countries do not need a visa to enter the United States for 90 days or less. This list is amended periodically, so be sure to check in your country of origin to determine whether you need a visa for U.S. entry.

Everyone visiting Hawai'i must fill out a Plants and Animals Declaration Form and present it to an airline flight attendant or the appropriate official upon arrival in the state. Anyone carrying any of the listed items must have those items inspected by an agricultural inspection agent at the airport. These items include but are not limited to fruits, vegetables, plants, seeds, and soil, as well as live insects, seafood, snakes, and amphibians. For additional information on just what is prohibited, contact any U.S. Customs Office or check with an embassy or consulate in foreign countries.

Hawai'i has a very rigid pet quarantine policy designed to keep rabies and other diseases from reaching the state. All domestic pets are subject to a 120-day quarantine (a 30-day quarantine or a newer five-day-or-less quarantine is allowed by meeting certain pre-arrival and post-arrival requirements), and this includes substantial fees for boarding. Basically, it is not feasible to take your pet with you on your Hawaiian vacation. For complete information, contact the Department of Agriculture, Animal Quarantine Division (99-951 Halawa Valley St., Aiea, HI 96701, 808/483-7151) in Honolulu.

Travel Tips

WHAT TO PACK

Visiting Kaua'i doesn't require multiple large suitcases. You can get a lot of the basics right on Kaua'i, which can help save on airline baggage fees. Consider purchasing sunblock, toiletries, and snorkel gear on the island. However, if you're a highly experienced diver, you may not mind the cost to bring your premium gear. Nearly all beach gear can be rented on Kaua'i, and beach towels are provided at most accommodations, even long-term vacation rentals.

For almost any time of year on Kaua'i, your wardrobe can be limited to shorts and T-shirts for men, and sundresses, skirts, and shorts for women. Nearly everyone can get by wearing flip-flops, or slippers as they're called locally, unless you're going on a hike. Shoes and socks just get too hot. Casual wear is fitting for most places on Kaua'i unless you'll be spending time on a high-end golf course or going out to one of the few very formal restaurants where collared shirts and closed-toed shoes are required for men. Sunglasses and hats are a must.

Self-serve laundries can be found in Lihu'e. You can wash your clothes when needed, canceling out the need to bring two weeks' worth of attire. They're also more affordable than hotel laundry services. A light jacket or cover-up should suffice for cooler island evenings or rainy days, and you'll only want a jacket when visiting the high-elevation inland areas on the west side or on the beach at night. Generally,

Discounts

Possible discounts for shopping, accommodations, and car rentals are generally limited to four different options. *Kama'aina* (Hawai'i residents), military personnel, seniors, and college students are sometimes offered discounts at various locations. Businesses that offer discounts like these vary widely, and there's no list of each one, so check wherever you are or glance around the checkout counter for signs stating which ones, if any, they offer. *Kama'aina* discounts count for all islands, not just the one you live on, as long as you have a Hawai'i driver's license or state ID. Student and senior discounts are usually offered on a certain day of the week and require ID or a student ID. Military discounts also require proper identification.

one pair of jeans should work for a one- or two-week trip, if you're planning on doing laundry. Kaua'i is usually very warm, and those used to cold weather usually feel warmer in Hawai'i than the locals, who may find anything less than 75 degrees reason for a jacket.

Visitors in search of long, intense hikes will need good shoes or hiking boots and other hiking gear. Mosquito repellent is also good to have. If it is rainy, a small fold-up umbrella comes in handy. Covered shoes and protective pants are necessary for adventure sports like riding an ATV. Again, all of this can be found on Kaua'i, so weigh the options with your luggage fees. Make sure to bring your camera and binoculars for overlooks and whale-watching.

TRAVELING WITH CHILDREN

Kaua'i is a wonderful place to travel with children and babies, and they can visit most places on the island with you. While strollers serve their usual purposes, consider a baby carrier for newborns up to about age three. A carrier enables you to go many places your stroller can't, or where it may be too tough or long for your toddler to walk. They're great for short and long hikes, beach walks, and even shopping around town.

Playgrounds are all over the island, and there are many beaches with calm waters for the little ones. The nice thing about Kaua'i and children is that on an island so small, you're never in the car for too long to get anywhere.

To save energy and money on airline baggage fees, contact **Ready Rentals**

(800/599-8008, www.readyrentals.com) to rent various baby supplies. Cribs, tents, strollers, high chairs, and more are available to rent during your stay.

ACCESS FOR TRAVELERS WITH DISABILITIES

Travelers with a disability won't be missing out on Kaua'i. A little pre-planning will help, though. For a smooth trip, make as many arrangements ahead of time as possible to suit your needs. Let transportation and tour companies, as well as hotels, know about the nature of your disability so they can arrange to accommodate you. If you might be needing medical attention while on the island, bring medical records. Traveling with friends or family will make it easier, or arrange for an aide before arriving. Some airlines will board those in a wheelchair with a lift if they know you're coming, as some carriers board passengers via steps. Many of the island's hotels and restaurants can accommodate persons with disabilities, but you may want to call in advance to make sure. Overall, there are many accessible sites on Kaua'i for those with disabilities, and even many beaches that are easily accessible.

Commission on Persons with Disabilities

Created with the purpose of aiding those with disabilities, the commission is a source of valuable information and distributes self-help booklets that are published by the

Disability and Communication Access Board (808/586-8121) and the Hawaii Centers for Independent Living. A person with a disability would only benefit by writing or visiting the offices once on the island. Pick up the *Aloha Guide to Accessibility* (the first part is free; there's a charge for the second and third parts) from the **Hawaii Centers for Independent Living** (4340 Nawiliwili Rd., Lihu'e, HI 96766, 808/345-4034).

Kaua'i Services

Handicapped parking is available at Lihu'e Airport across from the main terminal building. Car rental companies can install hand controls on their cars if they're given enough notice, around 48 to 72 hours. If you need a special parking permit, visit the **Drivers License Division** (4444 Rice St., Lihu'e, 808/241-4242) and use your own state placard while parking here. **Gammie Homecare** (808/632-2333, www.gammie.com) provides various medical equipment rentals.

Some travel service companies make special efforts to provide services for those with special needs. Contact Greg Winston at **Watersports Adventures** (808/821-1599, www.watersportsadventures.ws), Chuck Blay of **Kauai Nature Tours** (888/233-8365, www. kauainaturetours.com), and Debra Hookano at **Liko Kauai Cruises** (808/338-0333).

LGBT TRAVELERS

Gay and lesbian travelers are welcome throughout Hawai'i and on Kaua'i. While acceptance is part of the general state of mind, Kaua'i has a smaller gay and lesbian community in the way of nightclubs, bars, or other gathering places for members of the LGBT community than on O'ahu. In early 2011, Hawai'i became the seventh state to legalize civil unions for same-sex couples.

The only accommodations option specifically geared to same-sex couples is the beautiful **Mahina Kai Ocean Villa** (4933 Aliomanu Rd., 800/337-1134 or 808/822-9451, www.mahinakai.com) in Anahola. Five rooms are offered in the style of a Japanese home, and the grounds are complete with a saltwater swimming pool and a hot tub.

To tap into the LGBT community on Kaua'i, visit www.lambdaaloha.com, the website for Lambda Aloha, a gateway for almost everything gay or lesbian on Kaua'i. Another option is to consult the **International Gay and Lesbian Travel Association** (954/630-1637, www.iglta.org). It can connect you with gay-friendly organizations and tour help.

Recreation

SNORKELING

If you're a water lover, it's a great idea to keep a complete snorkel set in the car no matter where you go on Kaua'i. That way you're always prepared to jump in the water if the conditions are right. Some people prefer to use their own gear, and a snorkel set—fins, mask, and snorkel—is easy to fit in luggage. However, renting a snorkel set is cheap, easy, and can be done in all the major visitor areas and towns. Like most water sports, the optimal conditions for snorkeling are calm, smooth waters and a rocky or reef-covered ocean bottom close to shore where fish have plenty to eat. You'll find these setups most abundant on the north and south shores. Like diving, the best conditions will be along the south shore in the winter, from October to April, and then on the north shore from May to September. Look for outfitters who offer snorkel tours along the Na Pali Coast and to Ni'ihau for extraordinary snorkeling. Remember to never step on the reef or touch the marine life.

SCUBA DIVING

The clear waters around Kaua'i are perfect for scuba diving, and there are outfitters all

Snorkeling

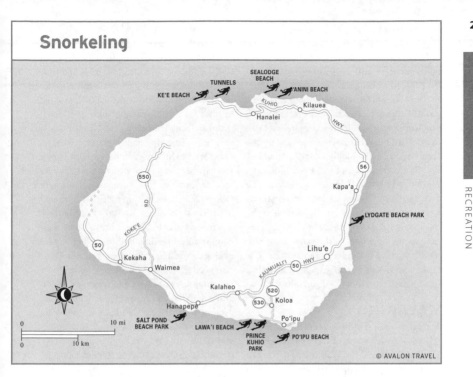

around the island offering many types of dives and offering dive equipment as part of the charter fee. Scuba diving is contingent on ocean conditions. The best diving will be along the south shore in the winter, from October to April, and then on the north shore from May to September. Look for outfitters who dive the Na Pali Coast for amazing underwater sights.

SURFING

Unlike most other water sports that rely on calm ocean conditions, surfing requires waves. There are many surf breaks all around the island suited to all levels of surfers. The most important thing for traveling surfers to remember is to respect the locals and the locales, and to know their limits. Many of the waves are far out to sea or in places where there are no lifeguards.

In Hawai'i, storms in the North Pacific bring waves to the islands from October through April. During this time, the north

shores of all islands will see waves along their beaches and reefs. The North Pacific is famous for sending huge waves to Hawai'i, so many times, it's better to watch the powerful surf than actually paddle out. Hanalei Bay is a favorite for all levels of surfers and offers several breaks and outfitters that offer lessons.

During the summer, from May to September, the South Pacific storms create waves that travel thousands of miles to Hawai'i and break along the south shores. On Kaua'i, Po'ipu is the best place to surf. You'll find waves for all levels of surfers and outfitters at Po'ipu Beach Park that offer lessons and board rentals. Generally, the surf in the summer is smaller and gentler than winter waves.

STAND-UP PADDLING (SUP)

Stand-up paddling, also known as SUP, is a relatively new sport in the surfing world. Originally practiced by O'ahu's Waikiki Beachboys, who would rest on their knees on their big longboards and use a canoe paddle to get around, today's stand-up paddleboards are high-tech, light, and very stable. Made from epoxy resin, stand-up paddleboards range 9-12 feet long, and are wide, thick, and surprisingly light. Surfers stand with their feet parallel, like a skier, in the center of the board and use a long paddle to accelerate forward. With a little practice, it's easy to pick up the technique rather quickly. Stand-up paddleboards are great for flat-water paddling (distance paddling) and for surfing. Because the boards are so big, only experienced stand-up paddlers should try surfing waves, as the boards are hard to maneuver and can be very dangerous for others in the water. Stand-up paddle surfing is a great workout, from your core to your legs and arms, and it affords a great perspective looking down over the reef.

KAYAKING

For calm-water paddling, launch your kayak on one of Kaua'i's beautiful rivers: namely the Hanalei River and the Wailua River. You can easily rent a kayak from an outfitter right on the river, go solo, or take a tour. Many of the tours of the Wailua River include a stop at a waterfall and hiking. Ocean kayaking is also popular and easily accessible at most beach parks, but you should be aware of the conditions before launching. The best ocean conditions for kayaking are calm, smooth waters with light winds. If the surf is up or if the wind is howling, head to the river to kayak. There are also many tour operators that lead groups of kayakers along the Na Pali Coast, an amazing experience with incredible views and great snorkeling.

FISHING

While rod and reel shoreline fishing can be done from the ubiquitous rocky points around the island, the best way to fish Kaua'i is with a professional sportfishing charter. You can find deep-sea fishing charters in Lihu'e, Kapa'a, and Port Allen. For freshwater fishing, there is a short trout season in Koke'e State Park at the Pu'u Lua Reservoir.

HIKING AND CAMPING

There are all manner of trails on the island. You'll find steep ascents and declines, rocky trails, ridge and forest trails, muddy and root-exposed trails, narrow cliff-side trails, amazing viewpoints, and waterfalls, as well as short, easy walks. The pinnacle of hiking on Kaua'i is the Kalalau Trail along the Na Pali Coast, an 11-mile one-way endurance test. Save for the short, flat hikes near the viewpoints where you can get away with wearing your slippers, most serious hikers will need some basic gear. Of course, proper hiking footwear is a must, but leave those thick wool socks at home if you're used to cold, alpine hiking. You'll want comfortable, breathable clothing that is quick drying, as passing showers are frequent. You'll also need the basics: sunscreen, mosquito repellent, a backpack, ample water, a poncho, and a map. Hikers planning on camping, especially along the Kalalau Trail, will also need water filtration, a tent, bedding, and food. If you arrive and find you forgot something important, there is a camping store in Lihu'e.

BIKING

Much of Kaua'i has narrow, winding roads without shoulders and therefore can be quite unsafe for biking around. However, there are a few places where renting a bicycle and hitting the road is a great way to see some sights and spend the morning or afternoon. The midday sun can be intense, so visitors planning on touring via bicycle should consider taking a break during the hottest part of the day.

Kapa'a's Ke Ala Hele Makalae bike path stretches from Lihi Boat Landing to Kealia Beach and is mostly a flat ride. It runs along the coast past several beaches, picnic areas, and scenic viewpoints. Bike shops with rentals abound in Kapa'a town, just a quick jump off the bike path and also a great place to grab lunch. Hanalei would be a second-best locale to bike around. You can rent a bike in Hanalei and bike through the neighborhoods and all along Hanalei Bay. You won't be able to see the beach or ocean, but this slow-paced mode of transportation is very fitting for Hanalei. Biking makes

Golf Courses

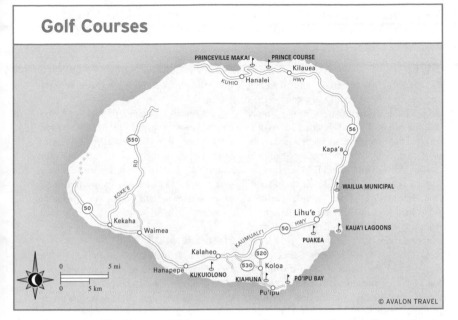

PRINCEVILLE MAKAI PRINCE COURSE
Kilauea
KUHIO Hanalei HWY
550
KOKE'E
RD
56
Kapa'a
WAILUA MUNICIPAL
50
Kekaha
Lihu'e
HWY
Waimea
KAUMUALI'I
50
KAUA'I LAGOONS
PUAKEA
Kalaheo
520
Hanapepe
KUKUIOLONO
530 Koloa
KIAHUNA
PO'IPU BAY
Po'ipu

0   5 mi
0   5 km

© AVALON TRAVEL

the most sense if you're staying in Hanalei town. Biking to the end of the road along the north shore should be avoided, as the road is very narrow and there are many one-lane bridges.

GOLF

A favorite pastime in the islands, the courses on Kaua'i offer mountain and ocean views as well as professional and challenging terrain. Most of the courses on the island have high green fees. You'll find courses in Princeville, Wailua, and Po'ipu. All the major courses have pro shops. You can rent clubs or bring your own equipment. Check with your airline carrier for any fees associated with bringing your golf bag.

Health and Safety

A report published by Health Trends said that life expectancy at birth in Hawai'i is among the longest in the nation. In 2000, people born in Hawai'i had a life expectancy of 80.8 years, more than three years longer than the U.S. average. When Hawai'i's life expectancy for 2000 was compared to that of other countries it came in fifth, behind Andorra, San Marino, Japan, and Singapore. Possibly the fresh air and somewhat relaxed lifestyle have a positive effect on health.

Hawai'i's location above the malaria belt ensures a malaria-free existence. The islands are also free of cholera and yellow fever. Although dengue fever doesn't call the islands home, several cases were confirmed a few years ago; they were brought to the islands by people who had contracted it out of the country. Animal quarantine laws are quite strict in Hawai'i, which have kept rabies out of the islands.

Due to a diet high in sugar and processed food that is different from what Pacific islanders traditionally consumed, diabetes and obesity have become rampant health problems for native Hawaiians. The great news is that the food and tap water are safe to consume, there is no need for vaccinations, and air quality on Kaua'i is top notch.

SUN

Sunburned skin is a common sight on Kaua'i, and for the sake of health and a good night's sleep, you don't want that to be you. Simply put, the sun on Kaua'i is intense. It's recommended that you put on sunblock with an SPF of at least 25 to 30 for any prolonged sun exposure. From 10am to around 3pm, the sun is at its strongest. If you do get sunburned, find some aloe fresh from the bush or an aloe gel to help with relief. Another great option is kukui nut oil, which offers great relief for sunburned skin.

Skin isn't the only body part affected by the sun, and sunglasses are a must while on Kaua'i. It's not uncommon to end up with red-tinged eyes after a day at the beach without glasses, and they enhance safety while driving. Hats are also a good idea, as well as something covering the neck while hiking. Some people prefer to hang a piece of fabric or a T-shirt over their neck or a towel over their head.

MOSQUITOES, ROACHES, AND CENTIPEDES

Insects are just as big of fans of Hawai'i as people are. They thrive in the warm weather. Luckily, there aren't many that are dangerous or bite. Mosquitoes didn't exist here until larvae were accidentally brought over in water on a ship named the *Wellington* in 1826 to Maui. Since then they have spread rapidly to all the islands. Luckily, there is no malaria in Hawai'i. However, the annoying insects are all over Kaua'i, especially in any forested area. They're usually rare on the beach, where higher winds keep them at bay. Mosquito repellent is a good idea to have on hand. Citronella is a natural option, and commercial repellents are available at supermarkets, drugstores, and the like. Health-food stores carry an array of natural options too.

The centipede is most likely Hawai'i's nastiest insect. Although they're not uncommon, they are elusive. Just step out of the way if you come across one. You can most likely let it continue on its merry way to wherever it's going, but if you see one in your car or your tent, get it out. Their bites are extremely painful.

Cockroaches are common and are found across Hawai'i, especially at night. The good news is they don't bite and they leave you alone. The worst they'll do is munch on your food if you leave it out and uncovered overnight. If you feel a small creature flutter by your shoulder at night, it's not a bird or moth, it's a cockroach.

HAOLE ROT

You may hear of or even come down with a case of *haole* rot while on the island. Its name hints that only Caucasians come down with it, but those with dark skin are no less prone to it. Although it does have a fancy scientific name if you were to go to a dermatologist, the local term refers to a type of fungus that infects only the surface of the skin. Spots that are lighter in color than the person's normal skin color appear on various parts of the body and don't tan with the rest of the skin. While some say it's caused from the sun, more evidence points to moisture, and some people are very susceptible to it while others never get it. If you're visiting for a few days or a week you probably won't get it, but those who spend months or move to the islands may pick it up after a while in the moist and humid climate.

While it's not harmful at all to your health, it is contagious. Don't share towels or unwashed clothes with a friend who has *haole* rot. To treat it, dry all towels and swimwear well. After a swim put on dry clothing. Many people use Selsun Blue shampoo to treat it, but a much less toxic and often effective alternative is dabbing tea tree oil on the spots a few times a day.

SEA URCHINS

At beaches with reefs, both exposed and underwater, sea urchins are a common sight.

They're painful if stepped on. They're called *wana* in Hawaiian, and you'll recognize them as the spiky balls usually nestled in reef crevices. Their color varies from black to pinkish. Water shoes can help, but the spikes can penetrate a lot of shoes. As a rule of thumb, you should never walk on the reef, which damages the fragile organisms. If you don't walk on the reef, you won't step on *wana*. Surfers are most prone to stepping on *wana* on shallow reefs. If you do step on one, pull out the spike. Oftentimes a little piece will get stuck, and all you can do is wait until it comes out on its own, which can be very painful.

PORTUGUESE MAN-OF-WAR

Locally called the man-o-war, this relative of the jellyfish can't swim like its cousins and simply floats, at the whim of the wind, currents, and tides. Recognizable by the blue bubble that serves as a body and by their long blue tentacles, they should be avoided at all cost. Although they're not common, they sometimes wash ashore after a heavy storm or strong winds. If you see one on the beach, there are most likely more in the water. The tentacles can be a couple feet long even when the body is the size of a nickel, which means that they can wrap around your arm and make it hard to get them off without touching them more. If you get stung, try to remove them with a gloved hand, T-shirt, stick, or whatever's around. On the sting, rub alcohol—rubbing alcohol or the kind for drinking—lemon juice, meat tenderizer, or after-shave lotion.

LEPTOSPIROSIS

Found in streams, ponds, muddy soil, and rivers, leptospirosis is a freshwater-borne bacteria found in water that infected cattle, wild boars, and other animals have urinated in. It can make you very sick. This is a very good reason not to drink river water. From two to 20 days after the bacteria enters the body, fever, chills, sweats, headaches, diarrhea, and/or vomiting suddenly strike. To prevent contracting it, do not drink river water or water from standing pools, and stay out of murky rivers if you have an open cut.

EMERGENCIES

To reach the police, fire department, and ambulance anywhere on the island, call 911 from a land line or cell phone. The **Coast Guard Search and Rescue** can be reached at 800/552-6458. In case of a natural disaster like a hurricane or tsunami, call 808/241-6336. The **Sexual Assault Crisis Line** can be reached at 808/245-4144.

MEDICAL SERVICES
Hospitals

In Lihu'e stands the island's main medical center, **Wilcox Memorial Hospital** (3-3420 Kuhio Hwy., Ste. B, 808/245-1100 or 808/245-1010 for emergencies). The smaller **West Kaua'i Medical Center** (4643 Waimea Canyon Dr., 808/338-9431) is open for emergency care and surgical needs. Both facilities are open 24 hours.

Medical Clinics

Associated with Wilcox Memorial Hospital and located at the same address is the **Kaua'i Medical Clinic** (3-3420 Kuhio Hwy., Ste. B, 808/245-1500). It has an urgent-care walk-in clinic (8am-5pm Mon.-Fri. and 8am-noon Sat.). There are other branches in 'Ele 'Ele (808/335-0499), Kapa'a (808/822-3431), and Koloa (808/742-1621).

In Hawai'i, calling 911 will connect you with emergency services 24 hours a day. This can be the fastest way to get medical attention if you are far from the hospital because various fire stations are located around the island and they, or EMTs, can respond.

Alternative Health Care

Kaua'i draws an array of people, and therefore it has a good selection of people practicing alternative healing methods. Hawaiians traditionally utilized plants from the land and sea to heal ailments and disease, and they used the traditional massage method of *lomilomi* to work on muscles and heal bones. While many massage therapists have learned and practice *lomilomi,* you can also find it at just about any independent spa or hotel spa on the island. Asian healing arts, such as acupuncture and herbal medicine, are also practiced on Kaua'i. Western massage modalities, naturopathy, reflexology, chiropractic care, and other alternative forms of medicine can be found here too.

Information and Services

TOURIST INFORMATION
Hawaii Visitors and Convention Bureau

The Hawaii Visitors and Convention Bureau, which has a **Kaua'i Visitors Bureau** (4334 Rice St., Lihu'e, 800/262-1400, www.gohawaii. com/kauai), is a great resource for travel information on Kaua'i. Dropping by the office or visiting the website offers a wealth of information and will most likely answer any question you may have. Free maps, planners, brochures, and information on accommodations, restaurants, entertainment, transportation, and more are available at the office. On the site you can explore each region visually and gain information on all aspects of the island.

Free Travel Literature

To further your knowledge of activities and places to eat, the island offers ample free magazines acting as directories and informational resources. Beginning at the airport (you can't miss the large kiosk at baggage claim loaded with publications) you'll see *This Week Kaua'i, Kaua'i Gold,* and *Kaua'i Activities and Attractions.* Other magazines include *101 Things to Do on Kaua'i, Kaua'i Menu,* and *Kaua'i Drive Guide.* In these you can find money-saving coupons, maps, information on monthly events, and more.

MONEY
Currency

U.S. currency is counted by the dollar and the cent. The drab green bills, decorated with the images of past presidents, are accompanied by coins. Bills in use these days are the $1, $2 (although rare), $5, $10, $20, $50, and $100. Coins include pennies worth one cent, nickels worth five cents, dimes valued at 10 cents, quarters worth 25 cents, and half dollars worth 50 cents, although these are uncommon. New designs have come out for the paper money since 1996 in an effort to battle counterfeiting. When you hand a salesperson a bill larger than $10, it's common to see them draw a black line on it that will disappear fast. This is a test for counterfeit bills.

ATMs (automated teller machines) are located at numerous locations around the island. You can find them in stores, at banks, gas stations, and shopping centers. Although they're convenient, keep in mind that withdrawing money from an ATM that does not belong to your bank will result in charges both from your bank as well as the bank that owns the ATM. Discuss ATM fees with your bank before traveling to see if they have affiliate ATMs that you can identify by certain logos.

Travelers Checks

Travelers checks are widely accepted at many shops, hotels, restaurants, and car rental companies, but you may want to check with them to avoid any inconvenience. Your travelers checks should be in U.S. currency, since generally only select large hotels will accept Japanese or Canadian travelers checks. Foreign travelers checks are accepted at banks, but it adds an inconvenience.

Credit Cards

Credit cards are widely accepted on Kaua'i, with most shops, businesses, hotels, and restaurants accepting Visa and Mastercard. American Express is also widely accepted, but it's not uncommon to find out that certain small merchants don't accept it. If you're planning on using your card while on Kaua'i, let your credit card company know before you arrive. Banks will often put a stop on your credit card or bank-issued debit card when they notice out-of-state or -country activity to prevent fraud. Also, write down your card numbers in case they get stolen. It's always good to ask in advance if an outfitter or business takes credit cards. Some very small and local businesses don't, but they'll usually post a sign stating so. Some small businesses will also give discounts for paying in cash.

COMMUNICATIONS AND MEDIA
Telephone
Phone service is as modern and equal in quality as any mainland phone system. Calling numbers on Kaua'i is considered local, while any call to neighbor islands are considered long distance. Inter-island long distance usually has different rates than long distance to the mainland. Although public phones that charge 50 cents for local calls can be found around the island, they are slowly disappearing. You'll most likely have a phone in any hotel room or condominium, but those will cost more than other lines. A cell phone is your best bet. Make sure to check with your carrier before you leave home about changing rates and times while on Kaua'i. If your phone breaks or you need help with service while traveling, all major carriers have stores on Kaua'i, and Walmart also sells phones and accessories. The area code for the entire state is 808, 911 will reach emergency services, 411 will reach directory assistance, and 800/555-1212 will reach a directory for toll-free numbers.

Newspapers
The main local paper is *The Garden Island* (www.thegardenisland.com), which is published daily with a Sunday edition. It is available at many stores and paper dispensers around the island.

The main daily newspaper in the islands is the *Honolulu Star-Advertiser* (www.staradvertiser.com), the product of a recent consolidation of the two papers. It is published daily with a Sunday edition. National papers such as *USA Today* and the *New York Times* are available at certain shops and Starbucks Coffee.

Kaua'i Radio Stations
If you want to take a break from the iPod (rental cars have auxiliary cable connectors), you can tune into one of the local radio stations. There are some that broadcast on Kaua'i, and some stations from O'ahu can also be picked up.

- **KKCR 91.9 and 90.0 FM:** community radio
- **KONG 93.5 FM:** the hot station on the island, playing popular music and requests
- **KITH 98.9 FM:** island music
- **KSHK 103.3 FM:** classic rock and roll
- **KTOH 99.9 FM:** oldies from the '50s to the '90s
- **KUAI 720 AM:** music, news, and sports
- **KFMN 96.9 FM:** adult contemporary
- **KSRF 95.9 FM:** island music

WEIGHTS AND MEASURES
Like the rest of the United States, Hawai'i uses the "English method" of measuring weights and distances. Ounces and pounds measure dry weight; ounces, quarts, and gallons measure liquids; and inches, feet, yards, and miles measure distances.

Electricity
If you're visiting from the continental United States, you don't have to worry about bringing an adaptor for your electronics. The same electrical current is used in Hawai'i as on the mainland. Electricity here functions on 110 volts, 60 cycles of alternating current (AC). Visitors from other countries should get the right adaptor so they can charge cameras and phones while on the island.

Campgrounds

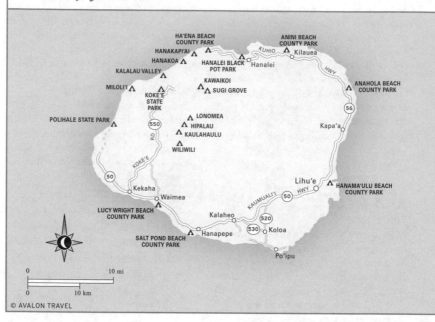

Time Zones

Daylight saving time does not apply to Hawai'i, which operates on Hawaii Standard Time (HST). When the mainland isn't on daylight saving, Hawai'i is two hours behind the West Coast, four hours behind the Midwest, and five hours behind the East Coast. Many cell phones and computers these days have apps that calculate the difference in hours between countries and states.

LOCAL RESOURCES
Weather Reports and Surfing Conditions

For a recorded weather report call 808/245-6001. For the surf conditions call 808/245-3564. It's a great resource for serious surfers who come to Kaua'i for the waves, since surf breaks and places vary with conditions. For those booking surf lessons, the schools should know about the conditions and the best places to guide you.

Camping and Hiking Permits

County park camping permits are obtained through the **Department of Parks and Recreation** (Park Permits Section, 4444 Rice St., Ste. 105, Lihu'e, 808/241-4463, www.kauai.gov, 8:15am-4pm Mon.-Fri.). Camping permits are issued for the following county beach parks:

- **Anahola Beach Park**
- **Anini Beach Park**
- **Ha'ena State Park**
- **Hanalei Black Pot Beach Park**
- **Hanama'ulu Beach Park**
- **Lucy Wright Beach Park**
- **Lydgate Park Campground**
- **Salt Pond Beach Park**

Camping permit fees are $3 per adult, per night for nonresidents and free for residents of the state of Hawai'i who can show proof of residency. Children under the age of 18 years are also free and must camp with at least one adult 18 years of age or older. Download the application form and instruction sheet from the website. Camping permit fees for Lydgate Campground are $5 per night for Hawai'i residents and $25 per night for visitors.

Permits are also available on the south shore at **Kalaheo Neighborhood Center** (4480 Papalina Rd., Kalaheo, 808/332-9770, noon-4pm Mon.-Fri.) and **Hanapepe Recreation Center** (4451 Puolo Rd., Hanapepe, 808/335-3731, 8am-noon Mon.-Fri.), on the east side at the **Kapa'a Neighborhood Center** (4491 Kou St., Kapa'a, 808/822-1931 or 808/822-0511, 10am-noon Mon., Wed., and Fri., 8am-noon Tues. and Thurs.), and on the north shore at **Kilauea Neighborhood Center** (2460 Keneke St., 808/828-1421, 10am-noon Mon., Wed., and Fri., 8am-4pm Tues. and Thurs.). Permits are available for pickup 8am-noon Monday-Friday except for holidays. Call ahead to make sure these outlets are open. These offices accept only cash as payment for camping permits.

For state beach parks such as Polihale, Koke'e Park, and state campgrounds along the Na Pali Coast, contact the **Hawaii State Parks Office** (3060 Eiwa St., Rm. 306, Lihu'e, 808/274-3444, www.hawaiistateparks.org, 8am-3:30pm Mon.-Fri.) They can be obtained in person or in advance by mail. For Hawai'i residents, it is $12 per campsite per night for up to six people and $2 per night for each additional person. The maximum fee per site is $20 a night. For nonresidents, it's $18 per campsite per night for up to six people and $3 per night for every additional person. The maximum fee per site is $30 a night. For state campgrounds along the Na Pali Coast, fees are $15 per person per night for Hawaii residents and $20 per person per night for nonresidents.

To obtain permits for the extremely far-off-the-beaten-path campsites in Waimea Canyon and Koke'e State Park, visit the **Division of Forestry and Wildlife** (3060 Eiwa St., Rm. 306, Lihu'e, 808/274-3444, www.hawaiistateparks.org, 8am-3:30pm Mon.-Fri.) for permits at no cost.

Consumer Protection

The **Kauai Chamber of Commerce** (808/245-7373, www.kauaichamber.org) is the place to contact for reporting bad service, trouble finding a place to stay, or if you get ripped off by a business. For other issues with businesses, try the **Better Business Bureau of Hawaii on O'ahu** (808/536-6956, www.hawaii.bbb.org).

Resources

Glossary

HAWAIIAN

Not long ago it was illegal to speak Hawaiian. The language was sequestered to the home, and wasn't spoken in school. However, Hawaiian culture has experienced a renaissance in recent years, beginning in the late 1970s. Today it's being taught in schools, and many more people are fluent in the language than in years past. While it's far from being the state's official language, certain words and phrases have become common in everyday conversation. Many Hawaiian words impart concepts, rather than having one simple meaning. The following words are some of the commonly used words in daily life. For a great language resource, pick up Elbert and Pukui's *Hawaiian Dictionary*. You'll see that a glottal stop, or *'okina*, represented by the upside-down apostrophe, is used in many Hawaiian words. The mark indicates a break between the separate pronunciations of two vowels that appear next to each other. Also, there is no plural form of Hawaiian words.

'a'a: gray, crumbly, old lava

'ae: yes

ahupua'a: a traditional land division running from the mountains to the ocean, in which the residents had access to all resources

aikane: buddy or friend

'aina: land

akamai: smart, clever, or wise

akua: spirit or god

ali'i: Hawaiian royalty

aloha: common greeting or word of parting; means hello, good-bye, love, or welcome

anuenue: rainbow

'a'ole: no

'aumakua: a personal or family protective animal spirit

auwe: alas

'awa: a plant found throughout Polynesia; a calming, mildly intoxicating drink is made from the root (also known as kava)

halakahiki: pineapple

halau: long house; when used with hula it means group or school

hale: house

hana: work

hanai: literally means to feed; commonly used as a term for adopted parents or children, but not in a formal or legal sense (used also to describe a close relationship)

haole: literally means no breath; used to describe Caucasians

hapa: indicates mixed ethnicities, such as part Hawaiian part Caucasian

hapai: pregnant

he'e nalu: literally means wave sliding, or surfing

heiau: a sacred rock structure used as a temple and to worship the gods

honu: sea turtle

ho'olaule'a: a celebration, usually a party or gathering

huhu: angry or irritated

hui: a group of people or a meeting

hukilau: a fishing gathering where everyone helps pull *(huki)* the fish into shore in a huge net; everyone who helped gets to enjoy the food

hula: a native Hawaiian sacred dance

huli huli: to turn over, as in *"huli* the canoe";

chicken on a rotisserie barbecue is called *huli huli* chicken

i'a: fish

imu: an earthen oven

ipo: sweetheart

kahuna: priest, sorcerer, or doctor

kai: the sea

kala: the sun

kalua: roasted underground in an *imu*

kama'aina: a child of the land or longtime resident of any ethnic group; essentially, a local

kanaka: Hawaiian (to discern from other ethnic groups)

kane: man

kapu: taboo, forbidden; do not touch

kaukau: slang for eating or food

keiki: child or baby, children

kiawe: a tree that grows along the shoreline and is covered in long, sharp thorns (Local lore says missionaries planted the tree to coerce natives into wearing shoes. It's a good wood for fuel and adds flavor to barbecue.)

kokua: help

kolohe: rascal

konane: a traditional Hawaiian game similar to checkers

Kona wind: a subtropical wind that blows from the south, hitting the leeward (dry) sides of the islands; usually brings muggy warm weather

kukui: candlenut tree, the nuts are polished and strung into lei (The oil-rich nuts were strung on the rib of a palm frond and used as candles. The oil is also wonderful for various skin treatments, from rashes to sunburns.)

kuleana: a person's right

Kumulipo: an ancient Hawaiian genealogical chant that speaks of gods, creation, and the beginning of humankind

kupuna: a grandparent or ancestor

lanai: a commonly used term for porch or veranda

lani: sky or heavens

lau hala: the leaf (*lau*) of the pandanus (*hala*) plant; used often in mat weaving

luakini heiau: human sacrifice

lei: a necklace or garland made with flowers, shells, or nuts

limu: seaweed

lo'i: area where taro is grown

lomilomi: traditional Hawaiian massage

lua: bathroom

lu'au: a celebratory party; thrown for birthdays, graduations, or other reasons to feast and enjoy dance and music

mahalo: thank you

mahele: division; the Great Mahele of 1848 broke up the traditional common lands and enabled private ownership of property

mahina: moon

mahu: traditionally referred to a third gender, similar to a transvestite; today it generally refers to a gay man; can be used in a neutral or negative light

maile: a fragrant green vine used in lei making

makai: toward the ocean, as in directions ("The house is on the *makai* side of the road.")

make: death, died

malo: a traditional loincloth

mana: a person's spirit, power, or energy

manini: small, or frugal

mauka: toward the mountains, as in directions ("The house is on the *mauka* side of the road.")

mauna: mountain

mele: a song or chant

menehune: the mystical "little people" of Hawaii; said to only come out at night (Some say they are completely made up, while others cite Hawaiian legends saying *menehune* are believed to have been Micronesians that settled the islands before Hawaiians.)

moa: chicken

moana: the ocean

moe moe: sleep

mu'umu'u: a long dress with a high neckline made from aloha print fabric

nani: beautiful

nui: big, large

'ohana: family

oli: chant

ono: delicious

'opihi: a limpet that clings strongly to rocks and is gathered to eat; often found in pupu platters or at delis

'opu: stomach

pahoehoe: black, ropy lava that is younger than *'a'a*

pakalolo: marijuana

pali: cliffs

paniolo: a Hawaiian cowboy

pau: finished, done

pilau: sticky or a bad smell

pilikia: trouble, bad news

pono: peaceful, righteous

pua: flower

puka: hole

pupule: crazy

tapa: a traditional cloth made from bark and stamped with intricate designs

ti: a plant with red or green leaves used for wrapping food and offerings

tutu: grandmother

ukulele: a small guitar-like take on the Portuguese instrument called a *cavaquinho;* very connected to the islands and used in local music

wahine: woman

wai: water

wiki: fast or speedy

USEFUL PHRASES

Aloha ahiahi. Good evening.

Aloha au ia 'oe. I love you.

Aloha kakahiaka. Good morning.

Aloha nui loa. Much love.

E komo mai. Please come in; welcome.

Hau'oli la hanau. Happy birthday.

Hau'oli makahiki hou. Happy New Year.

Mahalo nui loa. Thank you very much.

Mele kalikimaka. Merry Christmas.

PIDGIN

A blend of the original immigrant languages and English, local pidgin is English-based with an array of foreign terms and slang mixed in. Many locals speak pidgin as their primary language. It can be especially useful to decipher what a local might be saying.

an'den: and then

auntie: a respectful term for a woman of any age older than the speaker

braddah: brother, male friend

brah: used to call a male's attention

bumbye: later, after a while

da'kine: used to describe something really good, or when searching for the right word ("I went there with da'kine, you know who I mean? I forget her name.")

geev um: go for it, give them hell

grinds: food

hana hou: again, encore

hele on: let's move, let's do it

Howzit?: How are you?

kau kau: eat

li'dis an' li'dat: like this and like that

mo' bettah: good, great, better than

sista: sister, female friend

slippa: slippers, flip-flops

stink eye: a glare of dislike

talk story: chatting, catching up with someone

tanks 'ah brah: thank you

Wea ste?: Where stay? Where is he? Where is it?

Suggested Reading

From history and archaeology to can't-put-down novels, Hawai'i has a very strong regional publishing industry. Cookbooks, novels, and history books make great reads on vacation as well as wonderful souvenirs.

Those interested in natural history and Hawaiian and Pacific literature should visit the website of the **University of Hawai'i Press** (www.uhpress.hawaii.edu). Other publishers that offer Hawaiian- and Pacific-themed books include the **Bishop Museum Press** (www.bishopmuseum.org), **Kamehameha Schools Press** (www.kamehamehapublishing.org), **Bess Press** (www.besspress.com), **Mutual Publishing** (www.mutualpublishing.com), and **Petroglyph Press** (www.basicallybooks.com).

ASTRONOMY

Rhoads, Samuel. *The Sky Tonight: A Guided Tour of the Stars over Hawaii*. Honolulu: Bishop Museum, 1993. This book contains a collection of star charts for every month in Hawaii.

COOKING

Beeman, Judy, and Martin Beeman. *Joys of Hawaiian Cooking*. Hilo, Hawaii: Petroglyph Press, 1977. A nice collection of local and Hawaiian-style recipes from Big Island chefs.

Choy, Sam. *Little Hawaiian Cookbook for Big Appetites*. Honolulu: Mutual Publishing, 2003. This collection of the famous chef's favorite recipes to execute in your own home is a great take-home souvenir.

Fukuda, Sachi. *Pupus, An Island Tradition*. Honolulu: Bess Press Inc., 1995. A roundup of tasty and famous pupu, or appetizers.

Tuell, Bonnie. *Island Cooking*. Honolulu: Mutual Publishing, 1996. Inside are tasty island recipes, including pupu, dinner, and desserts.

Wong, Alan. *New Wave Luau*. Berkeley: Ten Speed Press, 1999. Hawai'i's prized chef shares wonderful recipes across the board of Hawaiian and local food.

CULTURE AND HISTORY

Cordy, Ross. *Exalted Sits the Chief*. Honolulu: Mutual Publishing, 2000. An archaeologist and professor at the University of Hawai'i West O'ahu, Cordy offers wonderful insight into the forming of the Hawaiian culture and society up until the pre-contact period. Although it focuses on the Big Island, the book integrates the history of all the islands and is a great read.

Hartwell, Jay, *Na Mamo: Hawaiian People Today*. Honolulu: Ai Pohaku Press, 1996. This book is an intriguing collection of profiles of 12 people practicing Hawaiian traditions around the world.

Kamehameha Schools Press. *Life in Early Hawaii: The Ahupua'a*, 3rd ed. Honolulu: Kamehameha Schools Press, 1994. Written to educate schoolchildren on the basic organization of old Hawaiian land use and its function, it offers an overview of Hawaiian history for those new to the subject.

Kirch, Patrick V. *Feathered Gods and Fishhooks: An Introduction to Hawaiian Archaeology and Prehistory*. Honolulu: University of Hawai'i Press, 1997. This book offers easy reading and great illustrations, sharing a wonderful insight into the pre-contact period.

Mills, Peter R. *Hawai'i's Russian Adventure: A New Look at Old History*. Honolulu: University of Hawai'i Press, 2002. A professor at the University of Hawai'i at Hilo, Mills offers a new take on the uses of Waimea's Russian Fort Elisabeth.

Moriarty, Linda Paik. *Ni'ihau Shell Leis.* Honolulu: University of Hawai'i Press, 1986. This beautiful, comprehensive book with color photos covers the social, cultural, modern, and historical aspects of the valued lei.

FAUNA

Denny, Jim. *The Birds of Kaua'i.* Honolulu: University of Hawai'i Press, 1999. An overview of the birds of Kaua'i, this is a must for any birder exploring the island.

Fielding, Ann, and Ed Robinson. *An Underwater Guide to Hawaii.* Honolulu: University of Hawai'i Press, 1987. Photos and well-written text lead you on an adventure through Hawai'i's underwater world. A great companion for those who love to snorkel and dive.

Kay, Alison, and Olive Schoenberg-Dole. *Shells of Hawaii.* Honolulu: University of Hawai'i Press, 1991. A collection of great color photos of shells of the islands, a must for ocean lovers.

Mahaney, Casey. *Hawaiian Reef Fish, the Identification Book.* University of California: Planet Ocean Publishing, 1999. This book provides photos and descriptions of common reef fish. It's the best way to identify the underwater life.

Van Riper, Charles, and Sandra van Riper. *A Field Guide to the Mammals of Hawaii.* Honolulu: Oriental Publishing. The book is a guide to the mammals introduced to Hawai'i.

FICTION AND PERSONAL NARRATIVES

Davenport, Kiana. *House of Many Gods.* New York: Ballantine Books, 2007. Davenport tells a beautiful story of love, change, and growth of a woman raised in poverty on O'ahu. It ties in to Kaua'i when the woman travels to the island during a devastating hurricane and falls in love. Like all of Davenport's books, this one is a real page-turner.

Davenport, Kiana. *Shark Dialogues.* New York: Penguin Books, 1995. The author weaves a tale of several generations of a family of women experiencing life in Hawai'i.

Hamilton, Bethany. *Soul Surfer.* New York: Pocket Books, 2004. Having lost her arm to a shark attack while surfing, the Kaua'i surfer shares her story of getting back in the water and back on the waves. It's an inspiring read.

Kaluaikoolau, Piilani, and Frances Frazier, translator. *The True Story of Kaluaikoolau: As Told by His Wife, Piilani.* Honolulu: University of Hawai'i Press, 2001. Kaluaikoolau was a Kaua'i leper. He refused to be banished to the leper colony and took his family to live deep in the Kalalau Valley. His story went down in history as a tale of resilience and resistance, and Jack London made it famous in his short story "Koolau the Leper."

Liliuokalani. *Hawaii's Story.* Honolulu: Mutual Publishing, 1990. The beloved queen tells her story, as well as the story of the fall of the Hawaiian throne. Truly a wonderful read that sheds light on Hawai'i's history and present in the form of a novel, not a textbook.

McKinney, Chris. *The Tattoo.* New York: Soho Press, 2007. Now a professor at an O'ahu community college, the author tells a tale of the darker side of Hawai'i that visitors don't see.

FLORA

Kepler, Angela. *Hawaiian Heritage Plants.* Honolulu: University of Hawai'i Press,

1998 A focus on plants used by the early Hawaiians for medicinal and cultural uses.

Miyano, Leland. *A Pocket Guide to Hawaii's Flowers*. Honolulu: Mutual Publishing, 2001. A guide that sheds light on the commonly seen flowers throughout the state.

Teho, Fortunato. *Plants of Hawaii: How to Grow Them*. Hilo, Hawaii: Petroglyph Press, 1992. A useful book for those who want instruction on successfully growing tropical plants. Some can be grown in the continental United States.

Valier, Kathy. *Ferns of Hawaii*. Honolulu: University of Hawai'i Press, 1995. This is one of the few books that focus on Hawai'i's beautiful ferns.

Wagner, Warren L., Derral R. Herbst, and H. S. Sohner. *Manual of the Flowering Plants of Hawaii*, rev. ed., vol. 2. Honolulu: University of Hawai'i Press in association with the Bishop Museum Press, 1999. The bible for Hawai'i's botanical world is a very thorough scientific and technical read.

LANGUAGE

Pukui, Mary Kawena, and Samuel H. Elbert. *Hawaiian Dictionary*. Honolulu: University of Hawai'i Press, 1986. Provides Hawaiian to English and English to Hawaiian translation. This is the best comprehensive dictionary.

Pukui, Mary Kawena, Samuel H. Elbert, and Esther T. Mookini. *Place Names of Hawaii*. Honolulu: University of Hawai'i Press, 1974. A comprehensive listing of Hawaiian and foreign place names in the state. The book

offers pronunciation, spelling, meaning, and locations.

Simonson, Douglass. *Pidgin to Da Max*. Honolulu: Bess Press, 1981. A great and humorous guide to speaking pidgin. It's fun and funny, and actually educational because it's accurate.

MYTHOLOGY AND LEGENDS

Beckwith, Martha. *The Kumulipo*. 1951 reprint. Honolulu: University of Hawai'i Press, 1972. This is the most comprehensive book of Hawai'i's folklore. It tells the creation myth.

Pukui, Mary Kawena, and Caroline Curtis. *Hawaii Island Legends*. Honolulu: Kamehameha Schools Press, 1996. The book explores Hawaiian tales and legends.

Pukui, Mary Kawena, and Caroline Curtis. *Tales of the Menehune*. Honolulu: Kamehameha Schools Press, 1960. This book is a collection of various stories about Hawai'i's mythical little people.

Wichman, Frederick B. *Kaua'i: Ancient Place Names and Their Stories*. Honolulu: University of Hawai'i Press, 1998. A compilation of stories and legends relating to places on Kaua'i, this book can add depth to an understanding of the island and accent any visit.

Wichman, Frederick B. *Kaua'i Tales*. Honolulu: Bamboo Ridge Press, 1985. A compilation of Hawaiian myths and legends related to Kaua'i, with simple yet lovely pen illustrations.

Internet Resources

GOVERNMENT

County of Hawaii
www.kauai.gov
The official website of Kaua'i offers a wealth of information, including a calendar of events and information about parks, camping, and island bus schedules.

Hawaii State Government
www.hawaii.gov
Visit this website for comprehensive information about the state of Hawai'i. You'll find information for visitors on government organizations, health, living in Hawai'i, education, and many other public topics.

TOURISM

Alternative Hawaii
www.alternative-hawaii.com
Check out this website for a guide to the path less traveled. It offers a calendar of eco-cultural events, a list of Hawai'i heritage tour guides, travel services, and a lot more.

Best Places Hawaii
www.bestplaceshawaii.com
Best Places Hawaii provides information on the best places in Hawai'i. It has very thorough information on places to see, things to do, and places to eat and stay, and even has a vacation planner.

Hawaii Ecotourism Association
www.hawaiiecotourism.com
The Hawaii Ecotourism Association website is a good source for eco-friendly information on traveling in Hawai'i, with information on individual sites and links to organizations related to ecotourism.

Hawaii Visitors and Convention Bureau
www.gohawaii.com
This website has thorough information from the state-run tourism organization about all of the major Hawaiian Islands. Information on accommodations, transportation, activities, and shopping, as well as a calendar, a travel planner, and a whole lot more can be accessed here.

Kaua'i Visitors Bureau
www.gohawaii.com/kauai
This section of the HVCB site is specifically about Kaua'i.

Index

QR

S

List of Maps

Photo Credits

Also Available

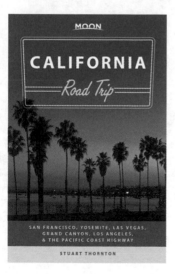

MAP SYMBOLS

≡≡≡	Expressway	○	City/Town	✈	Airport	⚲	Golf Course
——	Primary Road	⊙	State Capital	✖	Airfield	Ⓟ	Parking Area
····	Secondary Road	⊛	National Capital	▲	Mountain	▰	Archaeological Site
------	Unpaved Road	★	Point of Interest	✛	Unique Natural Feature	⌖	Church
——	Feature Trail	•	Accommodation			⌑	Gas Station
- - - -	Other Trail	▾	Restaurant/Bar	≈	Waterfall	◎	Glacier
········	Ferry			▲	Park	▨	Mangrove
≡≡≡	Pedestrian Walkway	■	Other Location	◍	Trailhead		Reef
▥▥▥	Stairs	∧	Campground	✖	Skiing Area		Swamp

CONVERSION TABLES

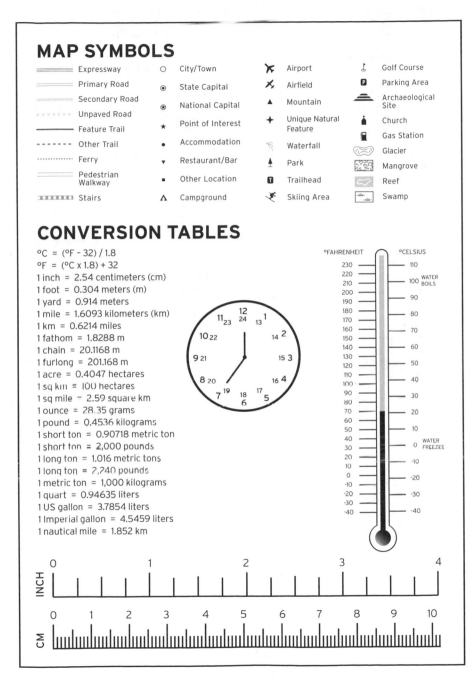

°C = (°F - 32) / 1.8
°F = (°C x 1.8) + 32
1 inch = 2.54 centimeters (cm)
1 foot = 0.304 meters (m)
1 yard = 0.914 meters
1 mile = 1.6093 kilometers (km)
1 km = 0.6214 miles
1 fathom = 1.8288 m
1 chain = 20.1168 m
1 furlong = 201.168 m
1 acre = 0.4047 hectares
1 sq km = 100 hectares
1 sq mile = 2.59 square km
1 ounce = 28.35 grams
1 pound = 0.4536 kilograms
1 short ton = 0.90718 metric ton
1 short ton = 2,000 pounds
1 long ton = 1.016 metric tons
1 long ton = 2,240 pounds
1 metric ton = 1,000 kilograms
1 quart = 0.94635 liters
1 US gallon = 3.7854 liters
1 Imperial gallon = 4.5459 liters
1 nautical mile = 1.852 km

°FAHRENHEIT   °CELSIUS
230 — 110
220 — 100 WATER BOILS
210 —
200 — 90
190 —
180 — 80
170 —
160 — 70
150 —
140 — 60
130 —
120 — 50
110 —
100 — 40
90 —
80 — 30
70 — 20
60 —
50 — 10
40 —
30 — 0 WATER FREEZES
20 —
10 — -10
0 —
-10 — -20
-20 — -30
-30 —
-40 — -40

INCH
0 1 2 3 4

CM
0 1 2 3 4 5 6 7 8 9 10

MOON KAUA'I
Avalon Travel
a member of the Perseus Books Group
1700 Fourth Street
Berkeley, CA 94710, USA
www.moon.com

Editor: Nikki Ioakimedes
Series Manager: Kathryn Ettinger
Copy Editor: Ann Seifert
Graphics Coordinator: Darren Alessi
Production Coordinator: Darren Alessi
Cover Design: Faceout Studios, Charles Brock
Moon Logo: Tim McGrath
Map Editor: Mike Morgenfeld
Cartographer: Brian Shotwell
Proofreader: Alissa Cyphers
Indexer: Rachel Kuhn

ISBN-13: 978-1-63121-256-7
ISSN: 1091-3335

Printing History
1st Edition — 1989
8th Edition — February 2016
5 4 3 2 1

Text © 2015 by Kevin Whitton & Avalon Travel.
Maps © 2015 by Avalon Travel.
All rights reserved.

Some photos and illustrations are used by permission and are the property of the original copyright owners.

Front cover photo: aerial view of the Na Pali coast
© Mint Images - Frans Lanting/Getty
Back cover photo: Wailua Falls
© Felix Lipov/123rf.com

Printed in Canada by Friesens